Control Mechanisms of Drinking

Edited by

G. Peters J. T. Fitzsimons
L. Peters-Haefeli

With 136 Figures

Springer-Verlag
New York Heidelberg Berlin 1975

This book is sponsored by the International Commission on the Physiology of Food and Fluid Intake, an agency of the International Union of Physiological Sciences

ISBN 0-387-06828-7 Springer-Verlag New York · Heidelberg · Berlin
ISBN 3-540-06828-7 Springer-Verlag Berlin · Heidelberg · New York

Preface

Practically all the chapters in this volume contain new and previously unpublished research reports and reviews on the physiological mechanisms which induce drinking of non-nutritive fluids. Though based on a Symposium on Thirst we have not called the volume by this title because thirst as such, a subjective human sensation, is not in fact discussed in these pages.

The main section headings in the list of contents give an idea of the topics dealt with and it is evident from these that a large number of contributions deal with the possible role of the renin-angiotensin system in the control of water intake. One difficulty until now in accepting the suggestion that this system could act as a mediator between the vascular system and cerebral receptors in extracellular thirst, was the fairly large doses of renin or of angiotensin which had to be injected peripherally in order to induce drinking. One contributor to this volume shows that the dose of angiotensin II required is in fact much smaller than previously reported and that this dose is within a physiologically possible range. Another difficulty arises from the fact that angiotensin and similar peptides cannot be expected to cross the blood-brain barrier. Again, observations described in this volume suggest that the receptors for angiotensin-induced drinking could be located in the walls of the ventricular system, possibly in the subfornical organ, and that angiotensin may cross the blood-CSF barrier. The question of the relationship between the cerebral and the renal renin-angiotensin systems was very much in the minds of all and there is no satisfactory resolution of this problem at present. It is possible that the cerebral system has a neurotransmitter role, especially as intracerebral angiotensin-induced drinking seems to depend on catecholaminergic, perhaps dopaminergic, systems. However, we were also reminded that there are cholinergic drinking systems in the brain, at least of the rat, and that vasopressin increases the sensitivity of drinking systems in the brain of the dog.

An 'après Cannon' role for oropharyngeal factors in the control of water intake is becoming firmly established. There is a need to take water by mouth. The self-intravenous injection experiments described here make this very clear. We are also pleased that the range of species in which thirst mechanisms are being studied has been extended. Man, the dog, the cat and the iguana, enter or re-enter the field of our investigation. Clinical aspects of the control of water and sodium intake also make a tentative entry in these pages and this is extremely welcome; we can only learn about the sensation of thirst as such in man.

The volume has been prepared by editing the proceedings of a symposium organized for the Union des Sociétés Suisses de Biologie Expérimentale (President: B. JEANRENAUD, Geneva) by G. PETERS, within the framework of the annual meeting of the Société Helvétique des Sciences Naturelles, at Lugano, Ticino, Switzerland on October 20 and 21, 1973. The symposium was sponsored by the International Commission on the Physiology of Food and Fluid Intake (ICPFFI) (Jacques LE MAGNEN, Chairman; Alan N. EPSTEIN, Secretary, Miguel R. COVIAN, James T.

FITZSIMONS, Elzbieta FONBERG, Gordon MOGENSON, Yutaka OOMURA, Georges PETERS, Mauricio RUSSEK and Kamal SHARMA), as a midterm meeting between the 1971 meeting organized for this Commission in Cambridge, U.K., by J. T. FITZSIMONS and the 1974 meeting organized in Jerusalem by Y. GUTMAN. A complementary meeting on food intake and energy balance was organized by J. LE MAGNEN at Chateau d'Ermenonville, near Paris, France on October 16 to 18, 1973. Although there have been international symposia on thirst held since 1971, only data not presented at any of these meetings were discussed at Lugano in 1973. This fact bears witness to the rapid progress in a field which had been dormant for some time prior to the 1960's.

The symposium was fully supported by the Union des Sociétés Suisses de Biologie Expérimentale; the editors express their gratitude to the Chairman of the Union, B. JEANRENAUD, Geneva and to its Treasurer, C. V. PERRIER, Geneva. Major financial worries of the organizers were alleviated by a generous gift from Interpharma, Basle, Switzerland: the editors are indebted to H. J. BEIN, Basle. Donations from the following drug manufacturers are gratefully acknowledged: C. H. Boehringer and Sohn, Ingelheim, Fed. Republic of Germany; Fresenius G.m.b.H., Hergiswil, Switzerland; Merck, Sharp & Dohme, Zurich, Switzerland; Pfizer A.G., Zurich, Switzerland; Synthelabo, Paris, France; Zyma S.A., Nyon, Switzerland.

The technical organization of the symposium was handled by Miss GRAZIA ZORZI, Mr. R. CRAUSAZ, Mrs. DOMINIQUE DE ROUGEMONT and Mrs. FRANÇOISE CHOMETY-DIEZI of the Institut de Pharmacologie de l'Université de Lausanne, whose invaluable help is gratefully acknowledged. J. T. FITZSIMONS wishes to express his appreciation to G. PETERS and his staff who were entirely responsible for the organization and the success of the meeting, and to S. KAUFMAN who helped in editing the manuscripts.

Finally the editors are indebted to W. F. ANGERMEIER of Springer-Verlag in Heidelberg for his help in preparing this volume.

Cambridge and Lausanne, April 1974
J. T. FITZSIMONS G. PETERS
L. PETERS-HAEFELI

Table of Contents

List of Contributors

ALDER, SUE
Institut für pathologische Anatomie der
Universität
4, Manessestraße
CH-8003 Zürich, Switzerland

BLACK, J.
Department of Physiology
University of Western Ontario
346 South Street, London 72,
Ontario, Canada

BROWN, J. W.
Medical Research Council
Blood Pressure Unit
Western Infirmary
Glasgow, GII 6 NT, U.K.

BUGGY, J.
Department of Psychology
University of Pittsburgh
Pittsburgh, Pa. 15260, USA

BURCKHARDT, RUTH
Institut de Pharmacologie de l'Université de
Lausanne
21, rue du Bugnon,
CH-1011 Lausanne, Switzerland

CASNER, P.
Department of Pharmacology
Basic Sciences Building
New York Medical College
Valhalla, NY 10595, USA

CHARLEBOIS, C. T.
Department of Experimental Psychology
University of Oxford

South Park Road
Oxford, OSI 3 PS, U.K.

CHINN, R. H.
Medical Research Council
Blood Pressure Unit
Western Infirmary
Glasgow, GII 6 NT, U.K.

COOLING, M. J.
Department of Pharmacy
University of Aston
Gosta Green
Birmingham B 4 7 ET, U. K.

DAY, M. D.
Department of Pharmacy
University of Aston
Gosta Green
Birmingham B 4 7 ET, U. K.

DE JONG, W.
Rudolf Magnus Institute for Pharmacology
Medical Faculty
University of Utrecht
Vondellaan 6
Utrecht, The Netherlands

EPSTEIN, A. N.
Department of Biology
Joseph Leidy Laboratory
University of Pennsylvania
Philadelphia, Pa. 19104, USA

FISHER, A. E.
Department of Psychology
459 Langley Hall
University of Pittsburgh
Pittsburgh, Pa. 15260, USA

FITZSIMONS, J. T.
Physiological Laboratory
University of Cambridge
Cambridge CB 2 3 EG, U.K.

FLUX, W. G.
Department of Physiology
The University of Tasmania
G.P.O. Box 252-C, Hobart,
Tasmania, 7001, Australia

GANTEN, D.
Pharmakologisches Institut der Universität
  Heidelberg
Hauptstraße 47–51, D-69 Heidelberg,
Fed. Rep. of Germany

GOLDMAN, M. W.
Department of Pharmacology
Basic Sciences Building
New York Medical College
Valhalla, NY 10595, USA

GROSS, F.
Pharmakologisches Institut der Universität
Heidelberg
Hauptstraße 47–51, D-69 Heidelberg,
Fed. Rep. of Germany

HAACK, DORIS
Pharmakologisches Institut der Universität
Heidelberg
Hauptstraße 47–51, D-69 Heidelberg,
Fed. Rep. of Germany

HERTTING, G.
Pharmakologisches Institut der Universität
Freiburg/i. Br.
Katharinenstr. 29, D-7800 Freiburg/i. Br.,
Fed. Rep. of Germany

HOEFER, R.
School of Allied Medical Professions
University of Pennsylvania
3901 Pine Street
Philadelphia, Pa. 19104, USA

HOMSY, E.
Pharmakologisches Institut der Universität
Heidelberg
Hauptstraße 47–51, D-69 Heidelberg,
Fed. Rep. of Germany

HSIAO, S.
Department of Psychology
University of Arizona
Tucson, Arizona, USA

HUSTON, J. P.
Pharmakologisches Institut der Universität
Zürich
Gloriastraße 32, CH-8006 Zürich,
Switzerland

HUTCHINSON, J. S.
Pharmakologisches Institut der Universität
Heidelberg
Hauptstraße 47–51, D-69 Heidelberg,
Fed. Rep. of Germany

JOHNSON, A. K.
Department of Psychology
University of Iowa
Iowa City,
Iowa 52242, USA

KAUFMAN, SUSAN
Physiological Laboratory
University of Cambridge
Cambridge, CB 2 3 EG, U.K.

KISSILEFF, H. R.
School of Allied Medical Professions
University of Pennsylvania
3901 Pine Street
Philadelphia, Pa. 19104, USA

KOHRS, GERDA
Pharmakologisches Institut der Universität
Heidelberg
Hauptstraße 47–51, D-69 Heidelberg,
Fed. Rep. of Germany

KOZLOWSKI, S.
Laboratory of Applied Physiology
Medical Research Centre, Polish Academy
of Sciences
Ul. Jazgarzewska 1,
PL-00-730 Warszawa 36, Poland

KUCHARCZYK, J.
Department of Physiology
University of Western Ontario
London,
Ontario N6A 3K7, Canada

LAZAR, J.
Pharmakologisches Institut der Universität
Heidelberg
Hauptstraße 47–51, D-69 Heidelberg,
Fed. Rep. of Germany

LEENEN, F. H.
Rudolf Magnus Institute for Pharmacology
Medical Faculty
University of Utrecht
Vondellaan 6
Utrecht, The Netherlands

LEHR, D.
Department of Pharmacology
Basic Sciences Building
New York Medical College
Valhalla, NY 10595, USA

LE MAGNEN, J.
Laboratoire de neurophysiologie
Collège de France
11, Place Marcelin Berthelot
F-75231 Paris, Cedex 05, France

LEVER, A. F.
Medical Research Council
Blood Pressure Unit
Western Infirmary
Glasgow, G 11 6 NT, U. K.

MCDONALD, R. M., JR.
Departments of Psychology and Biology

University of Pittsburgh
Pittsburgh, Pa. 15260, USA

MEYER, D. K.
Pharmakologisches Institut
der Universität Freiburg
Katherinenstraße 29
D-78 Freiburg/i. Br.,
Fed. Rep. of Germany

MISELIS, R.
Laboratoire de neurophysiologie
Collège de France
11, Place Marcelin Berthelot
F-75231 Paris, Cedex 05, France

MOGENSON, G.
Department of Physiology
University of Western Ontario
London,
Ontario N6A 3K7, Canada

MÖHRING, BÄRBEL
Pharmakologisches Institut der Universität

Heidelberg
Hauptstraße 47–51, D-69 Heidelberg,
Fed. Rep. of Germany

MÖHRING, J.
Pharmakologisches Institut der Universität
Heidelberg
Hauptstraße 47–51, D-69 Heidelberg,
Fed. Rep. of Germany

MORTON, J.
Medical Research Council
Blood Pressure Unit
Western Infirmary
Glasgow G 11 6 NT, U. K.

NICOLAÏDIS, S.
Laboratoire de neurophysiologie
Collège de France
11, Place Marcelin Berthelot
F-75231 Paris, Cedex 05, France

ORNSTEIN, K.
Pharmakologisches Institut der Universität
Zürich
Gloriastraße 32, CH-8006 Zürich,
Switzerland

OSTER, P.
Pharmakologisches Institut der Universität
Heidelberg
Hauptstraße 47–51, D-69 Heidelberg,
Fed. Rep. of Germany

PALMER, Q.
Beecham Products
Research and Development Department
Royal Forest Factory
Coleford, Glos., U. K.

PETERS, G.
Institut de Pharmacologie de l'Université de
Lausanne
21, rue du Bugnon
CH-1011 Lausanne, Switzerland

PETERS-HAEFELI, LISE
Institut de Pharmacologie de l'Université de
Lausanne
21, rue du Bugnon, CH-1011 Lausanne,
Switzerland

RAMSAY, D. J.
University Laboratory of Physiology
University of Oxford
Oxford OX 1 3 PS, U. K.

ROBERTSON, J. I. S.
Medical Research Council
Blood Pressure Unit
Western Infirmary
Glasgow, G 11 6 NT, U. K.

ROLLS, BARBARA
Department of Experimental Psychology
University of Oxford
South Parks Road
Oxford OX 1 3 PS, U. K.

ROSE, I.
Irving Clinic
Box 150
Kamloops, B. C., Canada

ROWLAND, N.
Laboratoire de neurophysiologie
Collège de France
11, Place Marcelin Berthelot
F-75231 Paris, Cedex 05, France

SCHELLING, P.
Pharmakologisches Institut der Universität
Heidelberg
Hauptstraße 47–51, D-69 Heidelberg,
Fed. Rep. of Germany

SCHÖMIG, A.
Pharmakologisches Institut der Universität
Heidelberg
Hauptstraße 47–51, D-69 Heidelberg,
Fed. Rep. of Germany

SETLER, PAULETTE
Department of Pharmacology
Smith Kline and French Laboratories
1500 Spring Garten Street,
Philadelphia, Pa. 19101, USA

SIEGFRIED, B.
Pharmakologisches Institut der Universität
Zürich
Gloriastraße 32, CH-8006 Zürich,
Switzerland

SIMPSON, J. B.
Department of Biology
Joseph Leidy Laboratory
University of Pennsylvania
Philadelphia, Pa. 19104, USA

SLANGEN, J. L.
Rudolf Magnus Institute for Pharmacology
Medical Faculty, University of Utrecht
Vondellaan 6
Utrecht, The Netherlands

STRICKER, E. M.
Department of Psychology
University of Pittsburgh
Pittsburgh, Pa. 15260, USA

SZCZEPANSKA-SADOWSKA, EVA
Laboratory of Applied Physiology
Medical Research Centre
Polish Academy of Sciences
Ul. Jazgarzewska 1,
PL-00-730 Warszawa 36, Poland

TERPSTRA, G. K.
Department of Pulmonary Diseases
University Hospital
Catharijnesingel 101
Utrecht, The Netherlands

WEIJNEN, J. A. W. M.
Psychological Laboratory
Physiological Psychological Section
University of Tilburg

Hogeschoollaan 225
Tilburg, The Netherlands

WEISINGER, R. S.
Howard Florey Institute of Experimental
Physiology and Medicine
University of Melbourne
Parkville,
Victoria 340484, Australia

ZBINDEN, G.
Institut für pathologische Anatomie der
Universität
Kantonsspital Zürich
Schmelzbergstraße 12, CH-8006 Zürich,
Switzerland

ZIGMOND, M. J.
Department of Biology
University of Pittsburgh
Pittsburgh, Pa. 15260, USA

Section 1
Introduction

Thirst and Sodium Appetite in the Regulation of the Body Fluids

J. T. FITZSIMONS

Introduction

In view of the complete dependence of the living cell on its watery environment successful colonisation of the dry land required the development of efficient mechanisms for restoring the body water to normal in dehydration as well as means for preserving the existing supplies. The earliest, at least partly terrestrial vertebrates are the amphibia. Amphibians do not drink but they show well developed behavioural responses to water, remaining in or near water and returning to it from time to time in order to rehydrate themselves after foraging on land. Most amphibians hide or even burrow away from the sun in order to reduce water losses. Some burrowing seems to be a more active search for water or at least for damp earth from which water can be absorbed through the skin. Most amphibians also return to water in order to breed and it is interesting that prolactin induces this type of "water drive" behaviour in newts (BENTLEY, 1971). We still know extremely little concerning behavioural water regulation in amphibia and further study of this primeval thirst offers the prospect of new insights into thirst mechanisms in the higher vertebrates. The fact that the animal absorbs water through the skin instead of drinking in no way lessens the relevance of such studies because the object of the behaviour is, with the probable exception of prolactin-induced water drive, the restoration of the body water.

The first truly terrestrial vertebrates are the reptiles which together with the birds and the mammals drink water when the need arises. Mechanisms of thirst have been most studied in the mammal and a certain amount is also known about the bird. However, in birds and especially in reptiles there is a paucity of data, other than the simple observational, concerning the control of water intake. The little that is known points to mechanisms similar to those in the mammal, but it is by no means clear yet whether the full repertoire of mammalian mechanisms is present in any of the other vertebrates. Their osmometric control, however, seems to be excellent, though with interesting differences from the mammal (see KAUFMAN and FITZSIMONS, this volume).

Most experimental work on the physiology of thirst has been carried out on a very restricted number of mammalian species — man, monkey, dog, goat, rat and rabbit, with the rat, and to a lesser extent the dog, attracting most attention. Even among the species examined there are notable differences. So what follows must be regarded with considerable caution.

Thirst is a motivational state in which there is a sensation of a need for water as a result of certain changes in the body fluids. It leads to the motivated behaviour of drinking. The word thirsty, however, should not be used in an operational sense as meaning the wish to drink, nor should it be inferred that an animal is experiencing thirst simply because it is drinking. For example, it is inconceivable that the excessive drinking that occurs in certain feeding schedules and which leads to gross overhydration is induced by the same drive that makes the

1

dehydrated animal drink. A willingness to drink may be aroused by causes other than thirst, as for example the craving for water after capsaicin or that produced by excessive speaking or smoking. Thirst is introspective, drinking operational and only by strict analogy with human experience is it justifiable to assume that an animal which is drinking is doing so because it is thirsty.

The occasions when animals drink water are numerous and in the analysis of mechanisms of thirst it is helpful to define two types of drinking (FITZSIMONS, 1972).

1. Primary or regulatory drinking in which there is a relative or an absolute lack of water in one or other of the fluid compartments of the body so that ingestion of water might reasonably be supposed to be initiated by, and to bear a simple relation to, the deficit.

2. Secondary or non-regulatory drinking where the immediate need for water is not obvious and where drinking does not appear to be related to the fluid economy of the animal.

Secondary or Non-Regulatory Drinking

Secondary or non-regulatory drinking is the usual way in which an animal ensures its day-to-day supplies of water when conditions are stable. The pattern of drinking and the amount of water taken are determined by circadian factors, including the feeding and activity rhythms, by the nature of the diet and by the climatic conditions. The animal appears able to predict its future requirements of fluid from oropharyngeal cues and it drinks the appropriate amount of water at mealtimes (FITZSIMONS and LE MAGNEN, 1969). Drinking is not induced by an existing need for water as is the case with primary drinking. Rhythmic, food-associated drinking is biologically advantageous because it enables the animal to anticipate its future requirements for water reasonably accurately and ensures that drinking and feeding take place within a short time of each other thereby lessening the time during which the animal is open to attack by its predators. The mechanism of normal drinking is unknown. We simply know that drinking entrained with the circadian activity cycle, has the characteristics of an autono-

mous circadian rhythm and that oropharyngeal cues are also important (FITZSIMONS, 1971).

Cellular Dehydration as a Stimulus to Drinking

Primary or regulatory drinking may be induced by cellular dehydration or by hypovolaemia. Much more is known about cellular dehydration as a stimulus to drinking and most of what we know has been derived from experiments in which drinking in response to the injection or infusion of various hypertonic solutions has been measured. By showing that hypertonic saline causes more drinking than an equiosmolar amount of urea GILMAN (1937) confirmed WETTENDORFF's (1901) suggestion that cellular dehydration is an effective stimulus to thirst. Subsequent experimentation with a variety of hypertonic solutions has shown that solutes which are excluded from the cell cause more drinking than those which penetrate into the cell, and that when due account is taken of renal osmoregulation drinking in response to cellular dehydration is precisely that needed to restore the cellular water content to normal (FITZSIMONS, 1961; 1971). The sensitivity of the system is such that a $1-2\%$ decrease in cellular water is sufficient to initiate drinking. It is therefore comparable in sensitivity to the vasopressin releasing system.

We may picture the control of cellular volume as follows. A loss of cellular water brought about by loading the animal with hypertonic solutions of substances that are excluded from the cells, or simply depriving the animal of water to drink, results in a diminution in the size of cells all over the body. Participating in this general cellular shrinkage are thirst osmoreceptors in the lateral preoptic region (BLASS and EPSTEIN, 1971; PECK and NOVIN, 1971) which initiate drinking, and osmoreceptors in the supraoptic nucleus (VERNEY, 1947) which stimulate vasopressin release thereby ensuring retention of water by the kidney. Drinking and antidiuresis restore the water content of the cells, including the osmoreceptors, to normal, the progress of the restoration being continuously monitored by the osmoreceptors. An additional component in this control is the phase advance introduced by temporary satiety mechanisms about which we know so little. Oropharyngeal and gastric metering and/or the passage of solute into the water contained in the gastrointestinal tract bring drinking to an end before significant absorption of water can take place and therefore well in advance of the restoration of cellular water content (ADOLPH, 1967). These mechanisms are surprisingly quantitative and they ensure that the amount of water drunk does not exceed the amount of water needed, drinking being a much more rapid process than absorption. The result is an economy of effort and once again a reduction in the time during which the animal is at risk from attack by its predators.

While there is still some controversy concerning the mechanisms of cellular thirst (ANDERSSON, 1973), most agree that GILMAN (1937) was essentially right when he concluded that "....*cellular* dehydration rather than an increase in cellular osmotic pressure *per se* is the stimulus of true thirst".

Extracellular Dehydration as a Stimulus to Drinking

Knowledge concerning extracellular mechanisms of thirst is much less complete though the association between thirst, and haemorrhage, severe vomiting or diarrhoea, in each of which there is loss of extracellular fluid, has been familiar for a very long time. An early report in the Lancet of 1832 by THOMAS LATTA of Leith contains a vivid description of the circulatory collapse and thirst produced by the severe diarrhoea of cholera and the dramatic relief afforded by intravenous fluids: "...the poor patient, who but a few minutes before was oppressed with sickness, vomiting, and burning thirst is suddenly relieved from every distressing symptom."

On *a priori* grounds, the existence of mechanisms to control the extracellular fluid volume is to be expected because the circulating blood volume is absolutely necessary for survival and at the same time the extracellular space in contrast to the cellular space is especially vulne-

rable owing to the huge turnover of water and solute through it. Control embraces both renal and intake mechanisms and it is now well established that an actual or a functional deficit of the extracellular fluid causes drinking (FITZSIMONS, 1972). Among the experimental procedures that cause drinking in the absence of any changes in the cellular compartment are haemorrhage, depletion of the ECF by Na depletion or hyperoncotic dialysis, mimicking the effects of a severe extracellular deficit by interfering with the circulation, and the administration of β-adrenergic drugs.

The common variable in the causes just listed is a reduction in central blood volume, either through actual loss of fluid, or because venous return has been interfered with, or in the case of isoprenaline-induced drinking because the much increased cardiac output uncovers a relative deficiency in central venous filling. In view of the vital importance of the circulation it seems entirely appropriate that a diminution in venous filling should generate thirst, and this would accord with the well known receptor role of the atria and the low pressure vessels in the thorax in the control of renal function (GAUER and HENRY, 1963).

Comparisons between renal and behavioural responses to hypovolaemia can also be made at the effector level. The importance of hormones in the control of renal function has of course been known for a considerable time, and it now seems clear that all the hormones implicated in renal control also have a direct influence on the intake of water and salts. Hormones may influence intake in a number of ways: by direct action, stimulatory or inhibitory, on mechanisms; or indirectly, through changes in the fluid and electrolyte composition of the body they produce, whether through hypersecretion or hyposecretion of the hormone. Though hormone deficiency may result in dramatic changes in thirst and Na appetite — e.g. polydipsia in diabetes insipidus, and increased Na appetite, or perhaps aversion to pure water (PETERS, 1959), after adrenalectomy, it is the direct participation of hormones in ingestive mechanisms that is especially interesting. As we shall see elsewhere in this book there is evidence that both the vasopressin and the renin-angiotensin-aldosterone systems participate directly in mechanisms of intake control.

The Satisfaction of Extracellularly Induced Thirst and Na Appetite

There is an important difference in the effects on the body fluids of drinking in response to hypovolaemia and drinking in response to cellular dehydration. A state of satiety after drinking to an osmotically effective stimulus means that cellular dehydration has been eliminated and the osmolality of the body fluids restored to normal. Drinking in response to hypovolaemia, however, results in the body fluids becoming increasingly hypotonic as water is absorbed into the body. The water drunk is distributed throughout the various fluid compartments of the body in proportion to the content of osmotic particles in each compartment with the consequence that only a small fraction of ingested water remains in the circulation. This fraction is insufficient to repair the plasma deficit, but drinking stops because further intake of water is impossible in the face of the increasing dilution of the body fluids and resulting water intoxication. The drinking that follows a number of quite different extracellular stimuli to thirst, including haemorrhage, hyperoncotic colloid, caval ligation, aortic constriction, intravenous angiotensin or subcutaneous isoprenaline, stops in each case when roughly the same amount of water has been retained in the animal. This amount of water is much less than can be retained by, for example, a nephrectomized rat given an osmotically effective hypertonic stimulus to drinking where drinking continues until isotonicity is reached.

It is only when the hypovolaemic animal is offered hypertonic saline as well as water to drink or when it is given isotonic saline in place of water that the intake of fluid matches the deficit (STRICKER and JALOWIEC, 1970). Drinking in these circumstances does not cause a progressive fall in osmolality and it can therefore continue until the extracellular deficit has been eliminated. The fact that the animal is able to make a suitable choice of what to drink and thereby restore its ECF to normal shows that

there is a second behavioural response to extracellular dehydration, namely an increased Na appetite, which does not occur in cellular dehydration.

Increased appetite for Na is manifest after a number of extracellular stimuli to drinking, notably hyperoncotic dialysis and caval ligation (FITZSIMONS, 1969; 1971), usually some hours after the animal starts to drink increased amounts of water though not, curiously enough, after renin or isoprenaline (FITZSIMONS and STRICKER, 1971). However, the intake of isotonic saline was greater after intravenous renin than it was after an osmotic stimulus (HAEFELI and PETERS, 1970). Why there should be a greater effect on Na appetite with non-hormonal extracellular stimuli to drinking than with hormonal when the latter might be expected to have the greater effect owing to increased secretion of adrenocortical hormones, which are known to stimulate Na appetite (see below) remains to be determined.

The major behavioural difference between the cellularly depleted and the extracellularly depleted animal then is that the latter shows a homeostatically appropriate interest in Na salts as well as in water. Increased Na appetite also occurs in Na deficiency, whether caused by increased Na loss as in adrenal insufficiency or by lack of Na in the diet. In the latter case mineralocorticoid secretion is increased. The preference for Na is not attributable to any possible beneficial effect that the Na deficient subject may derive from the ingested salt because the preference extends to very dilute solutions from which there can be no possible postingestional benefit. The onset of Na appetite is immediate which also indicates that no learning process is involved. Adrenalectomized rats allowed to drink saline for the first time 10 days after operation drank large quantities of saline immediately and behaved no differently in this respect from severely Na-depleted adrenalectomized rats which had had previous postoperative experience of saline (EPSTEIN and STELLAR, 1955). A rather different view on Na appetite after adrenalectomy is given by PETERS (1959) who found that adrenalectomized rats offered water and 0.9% saline did not drink more saline than normal animals, but definitely drank less pure water. The survival of the adrenalectomized rat depended less on an increase in Na appetite than on the natural preference of this species for saline.

As expected, replacement mineralocorticoid therapy reduces the Na appetite of the adrenalectomized animal to normal. Unexpectedly, however, larger-than-replacement doses of mineralocorticoids increase Na appetite (BRAUN-MENENDEZ and BRANDT, 1952; FREGLY and WATERS, 1966; WOLF and HANDAL, 1966) and this appears to be a learned response (WEISINGER and WOODS, 1971). We have the paradox that Na appetite is increased either when mineralocorticoids are absent or when they are present in excess. The explanation of this may be that increased Na preference depends on diminished concentration of salivary Na, or perhaps an altered Na: K ratio in saliva, which is detected by the Na taste receptors on the tongue. In adrenal insufficiency salivary Na is diminished at source, whereas in conditions in which there are excessive amounts of mineralocorticoids the reduction in salivary Na occurs as the saliva passes along the salivary duct and is acted upon by the duct epithelium. The importance of Na taste receptors is illustrated by the fact that lesions in the thalamic gustatory relay and midbrain tegmental region immediately caudal, result in a significant reduction in saline intake by Na-depleted rats (WOLF, 1968). Placing the burden of Na detection on a peripheral receptor is reminiscent of dry-mouth theories of thirst, and may be equally misleading.

A recent suggestion that angiotensin may have a direct stimulatory action on neurones concerned with Na appetite remains controversial (COVIAN, GENTIL and ANTUNES-RODRIGUES, 1971; FISHER, 1973, and this volume). An observation of considerable interest because of the suspected relationship between angiotensin and catecholamines is that crystalline noradrenaline introduced into the third ventricle induces rats to choose saline when they are offered both water and 1% saline to drink, whereas water is chosen after crystalline acetylcholine (CHIARAVIGLIO and TALEISNIK, 1969). Bilateral lesions in the mesencephalon where there are numerous ascending noradrenergic fibres, abolished the increased saline intake to third ventricular noradrenaline or to sodium deprivation. Stimulation of the mesencephalon by deposition of crystalline $FeCl_3$ near the periaqueductal grey induced intake of 1% saline in preference for water, but acetylcholine, noradrenaline and dopamine placed here had no effect (CHIARAVIGLIO, 1972). It is impossible at present to see how these observations fit together, but it may be that any effect of intracranial angiotensin on Na appetite is mediated through some sort of interaction with catecholaminergic circuits in the brain. Of course the possibility that angiotensin may stimulate Na appetite through aldosterone remains. There are perhaps even more problems here than with the neurology of thirst.

Conclusion

Regulation of the body fluids requires the coordination of mechanisms of intake and output. Both sets of mechanisms respond to the same deficits. Renal mechanisms slow the rate of dehydration but only intake mechanism can restore the body fluids to normal. Not only must the water content of the body be regulated, the osmotically active solutes in each fluid compartment must also be maintained. Here lies the major problem, for though renal control is clearly crucial for this, how is enough of the right solute made to enter the body for the kidneys to be able to perform their task and what is the role of the body cells in this? It is not at all clear how changes in the *absolute* content of solutes in the various compartments activate the appropriate renal and intake mechanisms. We are on somewhat safer ground with Na for we can picture Na appetite as a means of providing surplus Na for the kidneys to work upon until the extracellular content of Na is right. But up to now we have been unable to disentangle the extracellular signals for increased water intake from those for increased Na appetite, if indeed they are different. How the cellular content of osmotically active particles is maintained within normal limits is even more uncertain though we have a good understanding of cellularly induced water intake. It may be that the cellular water content is primarily regulated and that the cellular solute content is then modulated through some internal cellular concentration detector, though this of course is entirely speculative.

In many senses the kidney is the key organ in body fluid homeostasis, not simply because it is the principal effector on the excretory side, but because it is itself partly in control of the regulation. For example it forms part at least of the receptor complex for detecting changes in sodium content which it regulates through the renin-angiotensin-aldosterone system and other mechanisms. The kidney provides a link between the control of body fluids by the intake mechanism of thirst and Na appetite and the control of water and electrolyte excretion by vasopressin and aldosterone. This link is the renin-angiotensin system.

References

ADOLPH, E. F.: Regulation of water intake in relation to body water content. Handbook of Physiology. Alimentary Canal. Sect. 6, vol. 1, chapt. 12, pp. 163–171. Washington, D. C.: Am. Physiol. Soc.

ANDERSSON, B.: Osmoreceptors versus sodium receptors. In: The neuropsychology of thirst (Eds. A. N. EPSTEIN, H. KISSILEFF, and E. STELLAR) pp. 113–116, New York: Winston 1973.

BENTLEY, P. J.: Endocrines and osmoregulation. A comparative account of the regulation of water and salt in vertebrates. Berlin-Heidelberg-New York: Springer 1971.

BLASS, E. M., EPSTEIN, A. N.: A lateral preoptic osmosensitive zone for thirst in the rat. J. comp. physiol. Psychol. 76, 378–394 (1971).

BRAUN-MENENDEZ, E., BRANDT, P.: Augmentation de l'appétit spécifique pour le chlorure de sodium provoquée par la désoxycorticostérone. Caractéristiques. C. R. Soc. Biol. (Paris) 146, 1980–1982 (1952).

CHIARAVIGLIO, E.: Mesencephalic influence on the intake of sodium chloride and water in the rat. Brain Res. 44, 73–78 (1972).

CHIARAVIGLIO, E., TALEISNIK, S.: Water and salt intake induced by hypothalamic implants of cholinergic and adrenergic agents. Am J. Physiol. 216, 1418–1422 (1969).

COVIAN, M. R., GENTIL, C. G., ANTUNES-RODRIGUES, J.: Water and sodium chloride intake following microinjections of angiotensin II into the septal area of the rat brain. Physiol. Behav. 9, 373–377 (1972).

EPSTEIN, A. N., STELLAR, E.: The control of salt preference in the adrenalectomized rat. J. comp. physiol. Psychol. 48, 167–172 (1955).

FISHER, A. E.: Relationships between cholinergic and other dipsogens in the central mediation of thirst. In: The neuropsychology of thirst. (Eds. A. N. EPSTEIN, H. KISSILEFF, E. STELLAR) pp. 243–278, New York: Winston 1973.

FITZSIMONS, J. T.: Drinking by nephrectomized rats injected with various substances. J. Physiol. Lond. 155, 563–579 (1961).

— The role of a renal thirst factor in drinking induced by extracellular stimuli. J. Physiol Lond. 201, 349–368 (1969).

— The physiology of thirst: a review of the extraneural aspects of the mechanisms of drinking. Progr. Physiol. Psychol. 4, 119–201 (1971).

— Thirst. Physiol. Rev. 52, 468–561 (1972).

FITZSIMONS, J. T., LE MAGNEN, J.: Eating as a regulatory control of drinking in the rat. J. comp. physiol. Psychol. 67, 273–283 (1969).

FITZSIMONS, J. T., STRICKER, E. M.: Sodium appetite and the renin-angiotensin system. Nature New Biology 231, 58–60 (1971).

FREGLY, M. J., WATERS, I. W.: Effect of mineralocorticoids on spontaneous sodium chloride appetite of adrenalectomized rats. Physiol. Behav. 1, 65–74 (1966).

GAUER, O. H., HENRY, J. P.: Circulatory basis of fluid volume control. Physiol. Rev. 43, 423–481 (1963).

GILMAN, A.: The relation between blood osmotic pressure, fluid distribution and voluntary water intake. Am. J. Physiol. 120, 323–328 (1937).

HAEFELI, L., PETERS, G.: Rôle du système rénine-angiotensine dans le déclenchement de la soif. J. Urol. Néphrol. Paris, 76, 1011–1013 (1970).

LATTA, T.: Letter from Dr. LATTA to the Secretary of the Central Board of Health, London, affording a view of the rationale and results of his practice in the treatment of cholera by aqueous and saline injections. Lancet 2, 274–277 (1832).

PECK, J. W., NOVIN, D.: Evidence that osmoreceptors mediating drinking in rabbits are in the lateral preoptic area. J. comp. physiol. Psychol. 74, 134–147 (1971).

PETERS, G.: Aufnahme und renale Ausscheidung von Wasser und Salzen bei freiem Nahrungs- und Trinkflüssigkeitsangebot; ihre Beeinflussung durch Adrenalektomie und Behandlung mit Nebennierenrindenhormonen bei der Ratte. Naunyn-Schmiedeberg's Arch. exp. Path. Pharmakol. 235, 205–229 (1959).

STRICKER, E. M., JALOWIEC, J. E.: Restoration of intravascular fluid volume following acute hypovolemia in rats. Am. J. Physiol. 218, 191–196 (1970).

VERNEY, E. B.: The antidiuretic hormone and the factors which determine its release. Proc. R. Soc. B 135, 25–106 (1947).

WEISINGER, R. S., WOODS, S. C.: Aldosterone-elicited sodium appetite. Endocrinology 89, 538–544 (1971).

WETTENDORFF, H.: Modifications du sang sous l'influence de la privation d'eau. Contribution a l'étude de la soif. Trav. Lab. Physiol. Inst. Solvay **4,** 353–484 (1901).

WOLF, G.: Thalamic and tegmental mechanisms for sodium intake: anatomical and functional relations to lateral hypothalamus. Physiol. Behav. **3,** 997–1002 (1968).

WOLF, G., HANDAL, P. J.: Aldosterone-induced sodium appetite: dose-response and specificity. Endocrinology **78,** 1120–1124 (1966).

Section 2
Oropharyngeal and Gastric Influences in Drinking

Lingual Stimulation and Water Intake

J. A. W. M. WEIJNEN

A metering system, utilizing information obtained via the mouth, has been held responsible for the cessation of drinking behaviour in thirsty animals after ingestion of an adequate volume of water. Such a system has been postulated, because drinking stops before the time required for absorption of the water ingested. A neglected observation by Baron von MÜNCHHAUSEN, reported in the 18th century literature, does not lend support to this theory. After his horse had been cut in two parts by a falling trap door, upon entering the town of Oczakow, the thirsty animal did not stop drinking from a fountain. The water poured out of the animal at the site of the lesion just as fast

Fig. 1. Failure to stop drinking after transection of the animal (from: Avonturen van Baron von MÜNCHHAUSEN, G. B. van Goor Zn's Uitgevers Mij N. V., Den Haag)

as water intake took place (Fig. 1). No satiation in the absence of rehydration!

Evidence obtained with such a small experimental group (n = 1/2) is not very convincing. More data obtained with horses were published by BERNARD (1856). If water was allowed to escape from the animal through an oesophageal fistula, drinking continued. It is not the object of this paper to review the evidence in favour of, or against, the hypothesis that adequate water intake regulation depends on sensory stimulation of the tongue or mouth, but rather to explore to what extent such sensory stimulation modifies the amount of water ingested by thirsty rats. It will be clear that evidence in favour of an effect of oral stimulation on water intake does not imply that this information is used to meter the intake before absorption or that it is used to regulate the water balance.

Effects of gustatory stimulation on drinking behaviour are well documented in the literature. Much research has been dedicated to taste modulation of water drunk by thirsty rats and by animals that are not water deficient. The review of oropharyngeal factors in (feeding and) drinking by EPSTEIN (1967) contains a wealth of information on the subject, and much has been published since.

It seems appropriate to limit the scope of this paper to aspects of sensory input during drinking which have received less attention than gustatory stimulation of the tongue or of the mouth. An investigation of the effect of the temperature of water was an obvious choice, considering recent publications on this topic.

9

The Temperature of the Ingested Fluid

In single-stimulus tests the volume of intake is positively correlated with the temperature of the fluid up to body temperature. A 1.5- to 1.7-fold increase has been reported for water at body temperature, compared with water at 12 °C, for both tap and distilled water that was available from drinking tubes (KAPATOS and GOLD, 1972a; DEAUX and ENGSTROM, 1973a). The water was consumed in daily half hour sessions; no food was available in the test cages. In sessions of different duration (20 or 100 min), when water was presented in an open bowl, a similar effect could be demonstrated (GOLD, KAPATOS, PROWSE, QUACKENBUSH, and OX-FORD, 1973). Not only is drinking induced by water deprivation influenced by the temperature of the fluid, so also is schedule-induced drinking (CARLISLE, 1973; Fig. 2) though schedule-in-duced drinking does not result from any known physiological need. CARLISLE also stressed the influence of the ambient temperature which was varied over a wider range with a different group of animals (Fig. 2). It is not unlikely, however, that these latter results reflect effects of the temperature of water. The temperature of the drinking water in the temperature-controlled chamber may be expected to have approached the ambient temperature during the 180 min sessions.

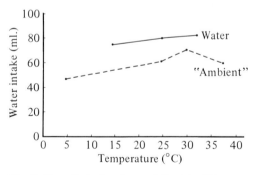

Fig. 2. The effect of water- and "ambient"-tempe-rature on schedule-induced polydipsia (adapted from CARLISLE 1973)

Can stimulation of cold receptors in the tongue or mouth account for these results? From evidence on the behavioural effects of mouth cooling *per se* it is clear that this stimulation is not aversive. On the contrary, thirsty rats will lick cold objects and an air stream persistently (HENDRY and RASCHE, 1961; MENDELSON and CHILLAG, 1970). The reinforcing properties of air licking are due to evaporative cooling of the orolingual tissues (MENDELSON, CHILLAG, and PARAMESVARAN, 1973).

These data indicate a preference for mouth cooling; but this apparently does not lead to a greater ingestion of cold than warm water.

Cool water is said to be more satiating than water of higher temperature (KAPATOS and GOLD, 1972a, b). GOLD and co-workers ob-served that even in the first few minutes of a test session the intake of cool water was suppressed, and concluded that tongue cooling during drinking acts as a short-latency satiety mecha-nism that anticipates cellular and extracellular hydration (GOLD et al., 1973). This mechanism could not account for the low intake of cool water during 100-min sessions, and other hypo-theses were needed to explain this fact.

Water intake is temporarily reduced after air licking (HENDRY and RASCHE, 1961). This observation seems to support a short-latency satiety-signal role of mouth cooling. But, as animals swallow substantial quantities of air when air drinking, resulting in distension of the gut, the feedback signal does not necessarily need to be generated in the mouth (OATLEY and DICKINSON, 1970).

It is doubtful whether assigning a short-laten-cy satiation role to mouth cooling during the first minutes of water intake is really necessary. Could not the same, yet unidentified, principle account for the overall effect of fluid tempera-ture on the volume ingested? Moreover, a lower intake of cold water for animals licking without interruption at the same frequency follows directly from the smaller volume/lick associated with drinking cool water (GOLD et al., 1973). This very condition might prevail in the first (few) minute(s) of a session. It should also be remembered that mouth cooling *per se*, during air licking, is not easily self-satiated (WILLIAMS, TREICHLER, and THOMAS, 1964).

It is not only the mouth that is being cooled when cold water is ingested. Within minutes of the start of licking cold water (12 °C) or water at room temperature (24 °C) the rat's body temperature decreases (DEAUX and ENGSTROM, 1973 a). Accordingly, mechanisms accounting for the effect of water temperature on the total volume ingested do not need to be activated via receptors in the mouth.

Is cold water more satiating (behaviourally?, physiologically?), or is it dealt with more effectively by the animal? As far as rehydration following water ingestion is concerned, cold water is relatively slow at lowering blood osmolality; warm water is sooner absorbed from the stomach (DEAUX and ENGSTROM, 1973 a, b; GOLD et al., 1973). This property would be expected to result in rapid rehydration following intake of warm water and, therefore, smaller intakes of water at higher temperatures.

Another suggestion is that ingestion of cool water might lead to a generally increased vascular tone. The animal's water need might then be reduced were the resulting decrease in vascular capacity to be interpreted by extracellular volume detectors as an increase in extracellular fluid volume (GOLD et al., 1973). However, one may wonder whether intake data obtained in the 100-min sessions, reported by the same authors support this suggestion. Recovery from the effect of cool water on vascular tone followed by a compensatory water intake later in the session would have been expected.

GOLD (1973 a) has reported that when animals had access either to cool water (6 °C) or to water at body temperature for 20 min per day on 5 successive days, there was virtually no difference in the body weights of the two groups in spite of the differences in water intake. He presumed that the animals did not retain the extra water ingested when drinking warm water. This observation suggests that intake of cold water may induce antidiuresis. Highly efficient renal reabsorption would keep renal water loss at a minimum. In this respect it is relevant that NICOLAÏDIS (1969) observed diuresis after bathing the mouth of rats with tap water, and antidiuresis after stimulating it with 5 % NaCl. These responses occured within a minute. A similar effect could be produced by gastric stimulation. Could this mechanism be sensitive to the temperature of the fluid applied to the mouth and would it influence diuresis in the way

suggested? The hypothesis is speculative, but amenable to testing.

If rats are given the choice between cold water and water at body temperature, then, initially, cold water is preferred. After a few minutes a shift to warm water occurs (KAPATOS and GOLD, 1972 b). This shift was also observed when the temperature of the testing room was raised to 30 °C, making an interpretation in terms of thermoregulation less applicable (GOLD, 1973 b). This preference shift during drinking complicates the interpretation of the results of choice tests if only the total intake over the whole session is available for each temperature (DEAUX and ENGSTROM, 1973 b). The effect of experience with water of a certain temperature, which was reported by DEAUX and ENGSTROM, appears to be another important variable in preference studies.

An initial preference for cold water could be based on the rewarding effects for thirsty animals of mouth cooling per se, and might at the same time result in lowering the demand for water by antidiuresis; the subsequent shift to a preference for warm water would facilitate water absorption and therefore rehydration. If stomach cooling were an aversive stimulus, the shift could also be easily understood.

In the regulation of water intake the temperature receptors on the tongue or in the mouth could detect water of the preferred temperature at a particular stage in the drinking process if a choice is available. Convincing evidence for a short-latency satiety mechanism based on tongue or mouth cooling is not available.

Temperature effects on water intake have only recently received attention. There is a strong need for more experimental data. It would be particularly relevant to know the water intake as a function of the temperature of the fluid under ad lib conditions. Temporarily acting mechanisms are less important for the interpretation of the results if 24 hr data are available.

Electrical Stimulation of the Tongue during Drinking

In studies requiring the recording of drinking behaviour, extensive use is made of "drinkometers". Most of these instruments pass a small electric current through the rat whenever the animal closes a circuit by making contact with the watering device. Ideally, only tongue contacts should be measured.

For a long time the possibility of behavioural consequences of the current passing through the animal has been ignored. SEGAL and ODEN (1969) recognized the problem and investigated whether the drinkometer current affected water intake during schedule-induced polydipsia. No influence could be observed. This substantiated FALK's (1964) contention that the current does not influence schedule-induced polydipsia. MARTONYI and VALENSTEIN (1971), however, did find effects produced by the current in preference studies. More of a very mildly bitter quinine solution was consumed when the drinkometer was switched on.

The current intensity in the input circuit of the drinkometers which were used in both studies did not exceed 1 μA (short circuit values, supplied by the manufacturers).

Earlier in this review the behavioural consequences of licking a stream of air or a cold object were referred to. It has been reported that electrical self-stimulation of the tongue ("current-licking") also has reinforcing properties in thirsty rats (SLANGEN and WEIJNEN, 1972; WEIJNEN, 1972). The phenomenon is illustrated in Fig. 3. Intensities of 50 to 100 μA (DC) are optimal values; licking stops at values $\leq 0.5\,\mu$A.

Persistent current licking can be obtained with rats which have had previous experience of electrical stimulation of the tongue applied during water licking. Without this experience the behaviour usually is extinguished in a few sessions. Explanations in terms of a conditioned reinforcer, however, appeared to be untenable (WEIJNEN, 1972, 1973).

What happens if electrical stimulation of the tongue with an optimal current intensity is paired with water licking in preference tests, without adding quinine as in the experiment of MARTONYI and VALENSTEIN? Fig. 4 shows the results of 10-min choice tests. No statistically significant difference was observed with 50 μA, but superimposing 100 μA on water drinking resulted in a preference for water without current. Also in other (unpublished) experiments, using different test situations, a consistent preference for water plus current has never been observed. Clear avoidance behaviour could be obtained at lower current intensities in chronic experiments. In most of these studies tap water at room temperature was used. The possibility that combining electrical stimulation of the tongue with licking cold water or water at body temperature might show different results is currently being investigated.

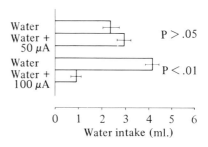

Fig. 4. Lack of preference for water plus current in 2 groups of 12 female rats that had had ample experience with current licking. The mean water intake in a 10-min session is shown with the standard error. The significance of the difference was evaluated by the Wilcoxon matched-pairs signed-ranks test

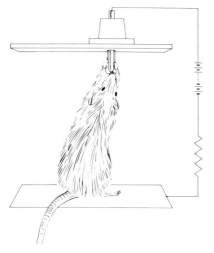

Fig. 3. Electrical self-stimulation of the tongue

References

BERNARD, C.: Leçons de physiologie expérimentale appliquée à la médecine. Vol. II, p. 51. Paris: Baillière 1856.

CARLISLE, H. J.: Schedule-induced polydipsia: Effect of water temperature, ambient temperature, and hypothalamic cooling. J. comp. physiol. Psychol. **83**, 208–220 (1973).

DEAUX, E., ENGSTROM, R.: The temperature of ingested water: Its effect on body temperature. Physiol. Psychol. **1**, 152–154 (1973a).

— The temperature of ingested water: Preference for cold water as an associative response. Physiol. Psychol., **1**, 257–260 (1973b).

EPSTEIN, A. N.: Oropharyngeal factors in feeding and drinking. In: Handbook of Physiology, Alimentary canal (ed. C. F. CODE) Vol. I, Section 6, pp. 197–218. Washington D.C.: Am. Physiol. Soc. 1967.

FALK, J. L.: Studies on schedule-induced polydipsia. In: Thirst (ed. M. J. WAYNER) pp. 95–116. New York: Pergamon Press 1964.

GOLD, R. M.: Cool water suppression of water intake: One day does not a winter make. Bull. Psychon. Soc. **1**, 385–386 (1973a).

— Water temperature as a determinant of the rewarding and satiating effects of drinking. Paper presented at the 81st annual convention of the American Psychological Association, Montreal, August 1973b.

GOLD, R. M., KAPATOS, G., PROWSE, J., QUACKENBUSH, P. M., OXFORD, T. W.: The role of water temperature in the regulation of water intake. J. comp. physiol. Psychol., **85**, 52–63 (1973).

HENDRY, D. P., RASCHE, R. H.: Analysis of a new nonnutritive positive reinforcer based on thirst. J. comp. physiol. Psychol. **54**, 477–483 (1961).

KAPATOS, G., GOLD, R. M.: Tongue cooling during drinking: A regulator of water intake in rats. Science **176**, 685–686 (1972a).

— Rats drink less cool water: a change in the taste of water? Science **178**, 1121 (1972b).

MARTONYI, B., VALENSTEIN, E. S.: On drinkometers: Problems and an inexpensive photocell solution. Physiol. Behav. **7**, 913–914 (1971).

MENDELSON, J., CHILLAG, D.: Tongue cooling: A new reward for thirsty rodents. Science **170**, 1418–1421 (1970).

MENDELSON, J., CHILLAG, D., PARAMESVARAN, M.: Effects of airstream temperature and humidity on airlicking in the rat. Behav. Biol. **8**, 357–365 (1973).

NICOLAÏDIS, S.: Early systemic responses to orogastric stimulation in the regulation of food and water balance: Functional and electrophysiological data. Ann. N.Y. Acad. Sci. **157**, 1176–1203 (1969).

OATLEY, K., DICKINSON, A.: Air drinking and the measurement of thirst. Anim. Behav. **18**, 259–265 (1970).

SEGAL, E. F., ODEN, D. L.: Effects of drinkometer current and of foot shoock on psychogenic polydipsia. Psychon. Sci. **14**, 13–15 (1969).

SLANGEN, J. L., WEIJNEN, J. A. W. M.: The reinforcing effect of electrical stimulation of the tongue in thirsty rats. Physiol. Behav. **8**, 565–568 (1972).

WEIJNEN, J. A. W. M.: Lick-contingent electrical stimulation of the tongue: Its reinforcing properties in rats under dipsogenic conditions. Utrecht: Drukkerij Elinkwijk 1972.

— The reinforcing properties of lick-contingent electrical stimulation of the tongue in thirsty rats. Paper presented at the 81st annual convention of the American Psychological Association, Montreal, August 1973.

WILLIAMS, J. L., TREICHLER, F. R., THOMAS, D. R.: Satiation and recovery of the "air-drinking" response in rats. Psychon. Sci. **1**, 49–50 (1964).

13

Systemic Versus Oral and Gastrointestinal Metering of Fluid Intake

S. NICOLAÏDIS and N. ROWLAND

More than one and a half centuries after DUPUYTREN showed that the intravenous (I.V.) injection of water into a thirsty dog prevented drinking, the respective roles of systemic and of oro-gastrointestinal factors in the control of water intake are still disputed. A number of classical studies (BELLOWS, 1939; ADOLPH, BARKER, and HOY, 1954; HOLMES and MONTGOMERY, 1960; EPSTEIN, 1960; MOOK, 1963) have led to the establishment of a logically sound scheme for dipsogenic behaviour. Simulated on a computer, this scheme performs satisfactorily (TOATES and OATLEY, 1970). The state of hydration of the extracellular and cellular spaces is monitored by receptors in these spaces, and the integrated signals yield a dipsogenic "final command". There is electrophysiological (NICOLAÏDIS, 1969; EMMERS, 1973) as well as behavioural (FITZSIMONS and OATLEY, 1968) support for this summation concept.

However, there is a large body of data which cannot be readily accommodated into such a scheme, in particular "non-homeostatic drinking" of which schedule-induced polydipsia and dry-mouth drinking are examples (KISSILEFF, 1973). It has been difficult to obtain direct evidence that even normal everyday drinking is directly related to deficit signals. It is conceivable that the role of the mouth sensors is to augment the amount ingested in response to a given systemic deficit, since in the case of non-oral drinking the rat ingests less fluid (NICOLAÏDIS and ROWLAND, 1972). The mouth could also play a more fundamental role since, when it is bypassed, the intake is not adaptable

to acute need (KISSILEFF, 1973; NICOLAÏDIS and ROWLAND, 1974). The role of the oral cavity in drinking has been investigated previously (BELLOWS, 1939; TOWBIN, 1949; MOOK, 1963) by the use of intragastric (I.G.) injections with or without concomitant oral stimulation. However, both embryologically and functionally, the gastric pouch may be likened to an invaginated oral cavity which possesses the essential attributes of the mouth itself.

Few experiments have been performed which tell us about the *long term* regulatory capabilities of organisms in the absence of external (by this we include oral, gastric and intestinal) metering, and there are only a few short term studies (HOLMES and MONTGOMERY, 1960; CLARK, SCHUSTER, and BRADY, 1961; CORBIT, 1965). We tried to dispose of some of these arguments by looking at the role of systemic receptors alone in the regulation of water and salt balance using intravenous (I.V.) fluid administration. The results show that the I.V. and I.G. routes are not equivalent to each other in the satiation of thirst. The stomach does not act as a passive transit station between the mouth and the systemic compartments. In a second series of experiments which we shall describe, we investigated the respective contribution of the oral, gastro-intestinal and systemic levels in the final integration of the ingestion of water and salt.

Presumably because of the relative difficulty of maintaining chronic I.V. preparations, few long-term I.V. experiments have been described in the literature. We developed a lightweight

14

system for infusion, attached to the skull of the rat, and permanently connected to a fluid (room temperature) reservoir. These animals were minimally stressed and remained in good health for up to several months. Food (powdered chow) was available *ad libitum* and a supply of drinking water was provided where mentioned. Adult male Wistar rats were individually housed and exposed to a 12 hr-on 12 hr-off lighting cycle. Intake of food and water and body weight were recorded at least every 24 hr. Animals were prepared with jugular, intragastric nasopharyngeal (IGNaso) (EPSTEIN, 1960) and intragastric "fistula" (IGFis) cannulae. In the IGFis preparation the tube pierced the stomach wall directly and passed subcutaneously to be attached to the skull; its use eliminates thermal and mechanical stimulation of the nasopharynx associated with the IGNaso catheter (HOLMAN, 1969).

In the first experiment to be described we explored the capability of the rat to regulate its long term water and electrolyte balance with only its systemic receptors operating. I.V. self injection of water eliminated all exteroceptive cues (NICOLAÏDIS and ROWLAND, 1972; 1974).

Intravenous "Drinking"

In the absence of oral water, rats learned to press a lever for I.V. water injections which were available *ad libitum* (standard volume 0.8 ml. every 2 minutes). After an initial period of dehydration (3 to 6 days) renal losses became minimal, and the I.V. voluntary intake matched the total losses; water and electrolyte equilibrium was maintained, thereafter, for an indefinite period, and regulation appeared to occur around a lowered set point of hydration. The daily I.V. intake was only about one half that of orally drinking rats, and in many cases appeared to be the minimum needed to cover the irreducible losses. Fig. 1 shows the cumulative lever-pressing curve for an individual rat, and serves to demonstrate several features of I.V. self injection (SII). Most SII occurred nocturnally; i.e. it paralleled reported oral drinking patterns (e.g. KISSILEFF, 1969a; FITZSIMONS and LE MAGNEN, 1969).

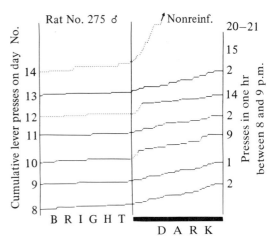

Fig. 1. Intravenous self-injection record (cumulative) for a single rat. Consecutive days (8 to 14) are marked at left. Periods of non-reinforcement for pressing are indicated by dotted lines. The number of lever presses during the first hour of darkness (20–21 hr) are indicated on the right, for each day

Usually one or two injections were taken at a time, and this was followed by prolonged periods of no responding. That the operant response is regulatory has already been shown by appropriate adaptation to experimental changes in the parameters of the I.V. reinforcement per lever-press (NICOLAÏDIS and ROWLAND, 1974). The extreme case in which lever-pressing does not provide reinforcement, is shown in Fig. 1. By day, when needs are low, the rat is insensitive to non-reinforcement but during the night when needs are high because of feeding, a typical extinction pattern of repetitive responding is evident (days 10, 12, and 14). Further, after a period of non-reinforcement, restoration of the possibility of self injection led to an inhibition of response after the first occasion at which the lever was pressed, i.e. within two minutes. Thus internal receptors alone *are* capable of metering intake, and of rapidly sensing reinforcement. The possibility of artificial external metering via salivary cues was controlled by excision of the salivary glands; surgically desalivated rats self-injected as efficiently as intact rats. A similarity between oral drinking and self-injection was the coincidence of circadian ingestion patterns. In the presence of food, SII occurred with meals, or was "periprandial" (ROWLAND and NICOLAÏ-

DIS, 1974). During food deprivation SII also persisted though it was attenuated as was the case for oral drinking (OATLEY, 1971). In these somewhat dehydrated, and therefore sensitive, preparations the temporal correlation of SII and meals may have been closer than was the case with oral drinking, whether the food was presented *ad lib* or on one- or two-meal per day schedules. There are, however, striking differences between oral drinkers and SII rats. These latter do not respond with appropriate dipsogenic behaviour to acute osmotic (hypertonic NaCl), hypovolaemic (polyethylene glycol, haemorrhage), or central dipsogenic (angiotensin II, carbachol) stimulation. In contrast, chronic osmotic stimulation by the addition of salt to the food does lead to increased I.V. intake, as does another so-called "natural stress", that of elevated ambient temperature. Not unexpectedly, restoration of oral water leads to an immediate rehydration of some 20 ml. and inhibition of SII responding.

These facts emphasise the privileged role of oral intake, and how it may amplify systemically generated need signals. Alternatively, the oral and gastric compartments may have their own intrinsic needs over and above the systemic needs. One experimental approach is to prevent the occurence of systemic deficits, and study the residual oral drinking.

Programmed Intragastric and Intravenous Injections

A pioneering approach to the problem was made by FITZSIMONS (1957, 1971) who infused rats at a steady rate of 1 ml./hr I.G., assuming that this rate approximated the systemic need. This led to only a partial reduction in oral intake, of the order of 0.4 ml. for every ml. infused. He concluded that a substantial part of normal drinking is not under homeostatic control. This reasoning was challenged by KISSILEFF (1969b; 1973) who pointed out that systemic needs are not constant, but immediately after meals of dry food they exceed the amounts of water available from such continuous infusions. This "peak need" hypothesis was tested by pairing infusions with meals. Under these conditions, oral intake

was suppressed, by 0.9 ml. per ml. infused, down to total extinction (KISSILEFF, 1973). KISSILEFF concluded that normal drinking *is* mainly under homeostatic control. However, not only did he equate I.G. with systemic, but he also used the IGNaso catheter which is known to provide satiating nasopharyngeal sensations during injections (HOLMAN, 1969). The issues are clearly not resolved. The following experiments were designed to clarify the interpretation of the above experiments, by investigating oral water intake under a variety of infusion conditions. Firstly, it is useful to propose three possible mechanisms (none exhaustive nor mutually exclusive) responsible for normal drinking:

a) The "peak need" hypothesis — that principal needs occur just after ingestion of dry food and cause drinking at that time.

b) A "modality specific" hypothesis which suggests that for each set of receptors — oral, gastric and systemic, — there exists an intrinsic and irreducible specific water requirement.

c) A "derivative hypothesis" which suggests that, in common with other physiological receptor systems, those for detecting imbalance of water and electrolytes are particularly responsive to phasic changes rather than to long-lasting deviations from the steady state.

Continuous Infusions

The first experiment extended the data of FITZSIMONS (1957) in two ways. Firstly, a wide range of rates of infusion (18 to 180 ml. per 24 hr) were studied and secondly, the effects on oral drinking of such I.G. infusions were compared

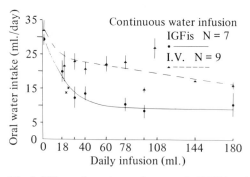

Fig. 2. Effects of continuous intragastric (IGFis) and I.V. water infusions on daily oral intake. The X's indicate data from FITZSIMONS (1971)

16

with those of I.V. infusions. The results are summarised in Fig. 2.

In the case of I.G. infusions, the oral intake fell with increasing rates of infusion, to an asymptote of about 35% of normal intake, or some 10 ml. per day. It is hard to reconcile these findings with a "peak need" interpretation, since increased rates of infusion should have led to more water infused with meals and therefore a reduction in oral drinking. For example, at 180 ml/day infusion, 1 ml. would have been infused during a "typical" 2 g meal, and would have been added to an expected small store of infusate. This amount approaches the postingestive requirement, and matches the water to food ratio observed with oral drinking.

Continuous I.V. infusions gave a rather different result (Fig. 2). The best fitting line for oral water intake shown as a function of rates of I.V. water infusion had a fairly steep slope at low infusion rates, and subsequently declined more slowly than expected. The I.V. infusions, thus, were less satiating than comparable I.G. infusions. At an infusion rate of 270 ml. per day (not on Fig. 2) the oral intake fell further to around the I. G. asymptotic level.

In an attempt to investigate the role of postingestive osmotic stimuli as determinants of satiation by I.V. "drinking", rats were infused similarly, but had 6% or 12% by weight of salt added to their diet. As seen in Fig. 3, under these conditions the I.V. infusion led to a much more dramatic decrease in oral drinking, but in all cases an asymptotic intake of about 10 ml. persisted. This apparently irreducible intake appeared to be independent of food-induced demands, and may have reflected a "modality specific" need (oral plus gastric, in the I.V. case). As confirmatory evidence, withdrawal of food for 12 hr from I.V. water infused rats (60 ml./day) did not attenuate the residual drinking.

Replacement of water by isotonic saline, as I.V. infused fluid, produced similar reductions of oral drinking, showing that the depressant effect was not due to osmotic factors alone.

Discontinuous Infusions

In order to investigate the "peak need" and "derivative" hypotheses, discontinuous infusion experiments were performed. The infused water was either paired with *ad lib* meals (ACTIVE rats), or not paired (PASSIVE rats). In this latter case, the rat was yoked to an active animal, and received injections when the active animal ate; since meal patterns of rats are similar, several chance pairings of injections with spontaneous meals occurred.

The amounts infused were varied principally by changes in the rate of infusion, although some longer-lasting injections (20 min) were tried. No systematic differences emerged, and pooled data

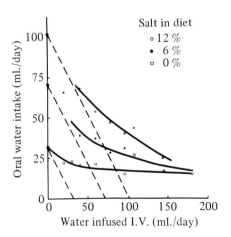

Fig. 3. Effects of continuous I.V. water infusions on daily oral water intake in rats with standard chow (0%) or chow with 6% or 12% salt added. The dashed lines represent 100% reduction

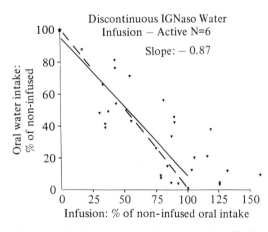

Fig. 4. Residual oral water intake, expressed as % of the *ad lib* uninfused value for each individual, as a function of the daily amount of water furnished by meal-paired injections through the IGNaso catheter. Regression sig. at $p < 0.01$

17

are presented. A comparison was made first between infusions through IGNaso and IGFis catheters.

Using the IGNaso catheter in the active, meal paired model, we replicated the results of KISSILEFF (1969, 1973). Fig. 4 shows that oral intake was reduced by 0.87 ml. per ml. infused. For passive IGNaso rats, the slope of the regression line was −0.57, which shows that the pairing did indeed enhance satiation produced by the infusions, in agreement with "peak need" predictions.

However, the result was strikingly different when similar injections were given by the IGFis route, as in Fig. 5. The reduction of oral intake was only some 0.33 ml. per ml. injected with the meal, and did not differ from the regression (−0.30) found for IGFis passive rats. Thus the nasopharyngeal sensations accompanying meals with the IGNaso catheter were in some way

satiating, and additionally provided an accurate metering of *how much* was being injected. The stomach alone (IGFis experiment) is *not* capable of such accurate metering, and as such plays only a minor role in the determination of normal drinking. It may be important that although the drinking patterns of IGNaso implanted rats were normal, the rats were generally hypodipsic when uninfused, compared with I.G. fistula rats.

For the IGNaso rats, the osmolality of the infused liquid was not the principal determinant of the metering function: meal-paired infusions of isotonic saline were as satiating as water infusions. Only volume, and mechano-thermal cues, were common to these types of injection. Incidentally, insensitivity of the gastric compartment to osmolality is well-known (BORER, 1968; KISSILEFF, 1973), since I.G. choice for water vs hypertonic fluid is difficult to demonstrate. In the IGFis case, both active and passive discontinuous infusions led to similar reductions in oral intake as did equal volumes infused continuously (c.f.: Fig. 2); the derivative hypothesis does not seem to hold for IGFis infusion.

When the experiments described above were repeated using I.V. injections of fluid they yielded the results shown in Fig. 6 and Fig. 7. In the active case, and for small infusions (Fig. 6) the reduction of oral intake was close to the theoretical but started to become insufficient (as for continuous infusions) when more than about 50% of the amount needed was infused with a meal. A residual asymptote of about 30% or 10 ml., as for continuous infusions, was clearly seen. The results for passive I.V. infusions (Fig. 7)

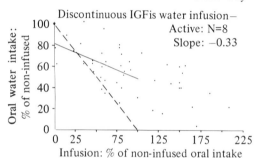

Fig. 5. Residual oral water intake, expressed as a % fraction of the water intake of the same animals in the non-infused state, as influenced by meal-paired intragastric water injections through a gastric fistula catheter

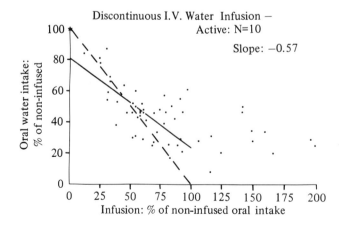

Fig. 6. Residual oral water intake, expressed as a percent fraction of the "non-infused" water intake of the same animals, as influenced by meal-paired I.V. injections of water

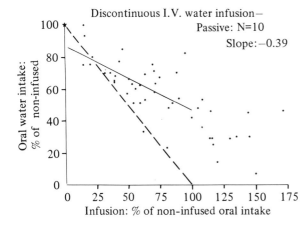

Fig. 7. Residual oral water intake, expressed as a percent fraction of the "non-infused" water intake of the same animals, as influenced by non-continuous I.V. infusion of water not directly related to eating times

were quite different; the reduction was truly linear over the whole range studied, with a suggestion that the asymptote was the same. The reduction was less than for the active, paired case. It should be noted also that the passive reduction was more pronounced than for comparable volumes infused I.V. continuously. For 30 ml. infused per day, the mean oral intake was 72% of normal for continuous infusion, and 47% for discontinuous (p < 0.01) These results support the "derivative" hypothesis. The systemic compartment does seem particularly sensitive to water infused at the times of peak need. The effect is principally osmotic, since replacement of water by isotonic saline leads to a much more modest reduction of oral intake. Thus I.G. and I.V. results differ qualitatively in most respects.

One final test of the hypotheses may be mentioned. According to a "peak need" view, infusion of water at mealtimes should *selectively* suppress postprandial drinking; in contrast, a continuous infusion would be expected to depress non-prandial and pre-prandial intake. The simultaneous recording of drinking patterns and the I.V. "active" meals, or meals in rats continuously infused I.V. strongly support these predictions. Fig. 8 shows the mean distribution of drinking bouts under these infusion conditions for a representative rat. Upon changing infusion conditions from active discontinuous to continuous the shift in drinking pattern occurred rapidly, within 2 to 3 meals at most. The mean draft size was unchanged under all these conditions.

Discussion

The present results show that systemic receptors alone are capable of sustaining drinking behaviour (I.V. self injection experiments), but in a

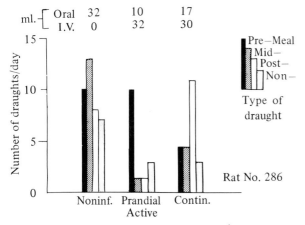

Fig. 8. Observed distribution of licking bouts in relation to spontaneous meals. Premeal bouts (black) are those occuring within 15 min of meal onset, midmeal bouts during a meal itself (considered as terminated by 15 min of no feeding), postprandial drinking in 15 min after meal end; the rest is non-prandial. Conditions are *ad lib* uninfused, active receiving I.V. meal-paired injections, and continuous I.V. infusion. Intakes in ml. shown at the top of figure

19

somewhat impoverished way compared with oral drinking. The "set point" of hydration is low, and only challenges given by the natural routes elicit corrective SII responses. Programmed injections into the systemic compartment lead to changes in oral drinking patterns. The changes are in the direction predicted by a theory advocating homeostatic functions for drinking behaviour.

But the metering capabilities of a system, inferred from observed terminations of drinking, favour the idea that oral, gastric and systemic levels can be distinguished. The total amount of oral drinking which may be eliminated by extra-oral loading is of the order of 20 ml. per day, which may in turn correspond to the systemically generated needs. It may be more than a coincidence that the daily intake of SII rats is 15–20 ml. The other 10 ml. or more of the daily intake may represent a modality specific and irreducible oral and gastric need. This is supported by the asymptotic low intakes, and may also explain the difference between I.V. and I.G. continuous infusion curves (Fig. 2). In the case of gastric infusions the irreducible oral intake represents the oral modality specific needs. Because the residual oral intake is greater when the infusions bypass the whole gastrointestinal tract; a gastric modality specific need seems to add its effect to the oral one.

The SII seems to be determined solely by osmo-volaemic imbalance, hence its periprandial distribution. Oral drinking represents *more* than correction of homeostatic imbalance, and is a "de luxe" or even antiregulatory consumption. As a matter of fact, even in the absence of food, the rats infused I.V. with 2.5 ml./hr of water still ingest 0.4 ml./hr orally. The teleological advantage of such persistent behaviour is easily conceived as a fail-safe mechanism that assures a minimal supply of water in cases of temporary failure of the regulatory system. Reappearance of such primitive ingestive reflexes in comatose patients with supramedullary traumatic damage is well known; these reflexes persist despite the extra-oral (I.V. or I.G.) supply of large amounts of both water and nutrients (S. NICOLAÏDIS: unpublished observations).

It now becomes possible to explain the IGNaso results. The nasopharyngeal sensations associated with the gastric rehydration meet not only the gastric need (and eventually the systemic need), but also the intrinisic oral requirement. Alternatively, nasopharyngeal stimulation acts to sensitize gastric receptors to repletion signals.

Systemic receptors appear to be sufficient to maintain basal consumatory behaviour; they are insufficient to initiate corrective ingestion in response to "unnatural" challenges. For response to such ecologically impossible stimuli (which bypass the sensory apparatus) external sensors are indispensable. These sensors also enhance the response to natural stimuli, and therefore increase the chance of survival. The gastrointestinal sensors complement those in the oral cavity and show some of the initiating and enhancing characteristics of the latter. In addition, it appears that both oral and gastrointestinal receptors have an intrinsic water requirement (which is somewhat independent of homeostatic needs), the "fail-safe" role of which may be important in survival.

References

ADOLPH, E. F., BARKER, J. P., HOY, P. A.: Multiple factors in thirst. Am. J. Physiol. **178,** 538–562 (1954).

BELLOWS, R. T.: Time factors in water drinking in dogs. Am. J. Physiol. **125,** 86–97 (1939).

BORER, K. T.: Disappearance of preferences and aversions for sapid solutions in rats ingesting untasted fluids. J. comp. physiol. Psychol. **65,** 213–221 (1968).

CLARK, R., SCHUSTER, C. R., BRADY, J. V.: Instrumental conditioning of jugular self infusion in the rhesus monkey. Science, **133,** 1829–1830 (1961).

CORBIT, J. D.: Effect of intravenous sodium chloride on drinking in the rat. J. comp. physiol. Psychol. **60,** 397–406 (1965).

EMMERS, R.: Interaction of neural systems which control body water. Brain Res. **49,** 323–348 (1973).

EPSTEIN, A. N.: Water intake without the act of drinking Science, **131,** 497–498 (1960).

FITZSIMONS, J. T.: Normal drinking in rats. J. Physiol. Lond. **138,** 39 (1957).

— The physiology of thirst. In: A review of the extraneural aspects of the mechanisms of drinking. Progr. physiol. Psychol. **4,** 119–201 (1971).

FITZSIMONS, J. T., LE MAGNEN, J.: Eating as a regulatory control of drinking in the rat. J. comp. physiol. Psychol. **67,** 273–283 (1969).

FITZSIMONS, J. T., OATLEY, K.: Additivity of stimuli for drinking in rats. J. comp. physiol. Psychol. **66,** 450–455 (1968).

HOLMAN, G.: Intragastric reinforcement effect. J. comp. physiol. Psychol. **69,** 432–441 (1969).

HOLMES, J. H., MONTGOMERY, V.: Relation of route of administration and types of fluid to satisfaction of thirst in the dog. Am. J. Physiol. **199,** 907–911 (1960).

KISSILEFF, H. R.: Food associated drinking in the rat. J. comp. physiol. Psychol. **67,** 284–300 (1969 a).

— Oropharyngeal control of prandial drinking. J. comp. physiol. Psychol. **67,** 309–319 (1969 b).

— Non homeostatic controls of drinking. In: Neuropsychology of thirst; new findings and advances in concepts (Eds. A. N. EPSTEIN, H. R. KISSILEFF, and E. STELLAR), p. 163–198. Washington: V. H. Winston and Sons 1973.

MOOK, D. G.: Oral and postingestional determinants of the intake of various solutions in rats with esophagal fistulas. J. comp. physiol. Psychol. **56,** 645–659 (1963).

NICOLAÏDIS, S.: Early systemic responses to orogastric stimulation in the regulation of food and water balance: functional and electrophysiological data. Ann. N.Y. Acad. Sci. **157** (2), 1176–1203 (1969).

NICOLAÏDIS, S., ROWLAND, N.: L'équilibre hydrominéral après substitution à la prise orale d'eau d'auto-injections parentérales chez le rat. C.R. Acad. Sci. (Paris), D, **275,** 991–994 (1972).

— Long term self intravenous drinking in the rat. J. comp. physiol. Psychol., **87,** 1–15 (1974).

OATLEY, K.: Dissociation of the circadian drinking pattern from eating. Nature **229,** 494–496 (1971).

ROWLAND, N., NICOLAÏDIS, S.: Periprandial self intravenous drinking in the rat. J. comp. physiol. Psychol., **87,** 16–25 (1974).

TOATES, F. M., OATLEY, K.: Computer simulation of thirst and water balance. Med. and Biol. Engng. **8,** 71–87 (1970).

TOWBIN, E. J.: Gastric distension as a factor in the satiation of thirst in esophagostomized dogs. Am. J. Physiol. **159,** 533–541 (1949).

Reduction of Saline Intake in Adrenalectomized Rats during Chronic Intragastric Infusions of Saline

H. R. KISSILEFF and R. HOEFER

Following adrenalectomy rats increase their intake of saline solutions (RICHTER, 1936). This is a direct result of increased sodium need due to loss of body sodium since its magnitude is immediately enhanced after severe depletion (EPSTEIN and STELLAR, 1955) and is decreased by hormone treatments which reduce the loss (RICHTER, 1956). The precision of this apparent regulation has never been, but could be, measured by determining the reduction in daily saline intake during intragastric saline infusion (KISSILEFF, 1972). The precision of regulation of drinking has been similarly measured by intragastric infusions (KISSILEFF, 1969, 1973) and recent work in feeding has shown that the precision of regulation in response to intragastric infusions can be greatly enhanced when injections vary with the animals' spontaneous feeding cycles (QUARTERMAIN, KISSILEFF, SHAPIRO, and MILLER, 1971). The present experiments were therefore undertaken to determine whether a similar phenomenon would apply to sodium regulation.

Adrenalectomized female rats with well demonstrated adrenal insufficiency (body weight loss of 12 to 36 gm during 4 days of sodium deprivation and subsequent 3%-saline intakes in excess of a mean of 20 ml. during 4 days) were fitted with chronic intragastric tubes (KISSILEFF, 1972) under pentobarbital anesthesia (25 mg/kg). Following recovery from surgery, which often took several weeks and required occasional feeding of palatable foods and fluids (sucrose-saline solutions, sweetened condensed milk), patterns of 3% saline intake were collected for 6 to 10 days in each of four rats, using automatic data collection and recording devices (drinkometer, print-out counter). Water, food (Purina lab chow pellets) and 3% saline were always freely available and their intakes were measured daily. After this baseline period, each rat was infused for 2 to 5 consecutive days with 3% saline solution in volumes whose total approximated the rat's daily saline intake during the baseline period. Two temporal paradigms of infusion were used at least once in each rat: 1) continuous infusion (once per minute in small aliquots); 2) in a pattern which simulated the spontaneous pattern of oral intake as determined from computerized analysis of the average amounts taken during periods of time when draft frequency was highest.

The results were as follows: 1) Intragastric infusion of saline resulted in a 60 to 70% reduction in 24-hr saline intake, but only rarely completely suppressed saline intake when the amounts infused approximated those normally drunk by the rats (i.e. infusions ranged from 97 to 108% of preinfusion intakes) (Fig. 1). Suppression efficiency (ml. reduction in intake per ml. infused, expressed as percentage) ranged from 57 to 70%. 2) Infusions of less than 100% of preinfusion intake resulted in less suppression of intake but greater suppression efficiency (Table 1). 3) Water and food intakes were not significantly affected by the infusions. 4) The suppression efficiency did not vary with the temporal paradigm of the infusions (Fig. 1).

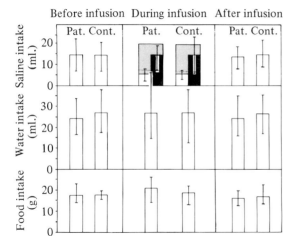

Before infusion   During infusion   After infusion

Fig. 1. Effect of saline infusions on mean daily saline, water, and food intakes of four adrenalectomized rats. The left bar of each pair shows the effect of patterned infusions and the right, the effects of continuous infusions. During saline infusion, the top line shows the amount drunk (unfilled bars), the amount infused (filled bars), and the total amount ingested (stippled bars). Lines within each bar are the ranges of the average daily intakes for each of the four rats

5) During infusions in the pattern which approximated the spontaneous saline drinking pattern, reduction in intake occurred by a reduction in both the mean size and frequency of drafts.

These results show that there is a determinant of saline intake in the adrenalectomized rat which is undeniably homeostatic, or else saline intake reduction alone would not have occurred. Second there is a non-homeostatic determinant which may require either the fulfillment of an oral urge or reflects the influence of learning, hence the failure of infusions of 100% of intake to completely suppress saline drinking. Alterna-

tively, the failure to completely eliminate saline drinking may reflect our inability to simulate and predict the animal's needs by examination of the pattern of saline ingestion alone.

Thus the efficiency of suppression of saline intake (57–71%) is less than the efficiency of suppression of food intake during patterned infusion (86%), but about the same as for food intake with continuous infusions (61%), but the variability in time of saline bouts appeared by inspection to be greater than the variability in food intakes of the previous work (QUARTERMAIN, KISSILEFF, SHAPIRO, and MILLER, 1971). The efficiency of suppression in the present experiments should also be compared with the findings of NACHMAN and VALENTINO (1966) in a short term test in which loads of 10.1 ml. intragastrically were much less effective in suppressing drinking in a test 2 1/2 hr later than was drinking of saline.

Table 1. Effect of patterned saline infusions on mean daily saline intakes with infusions at two fractions of baseline intake

Mean amount infused (ml.)	Mean daily saline intakes				Suppression efficiency (%)
	Before infusion		During infusion		
	Intake (ml.)	Number of days	Intake (ml.)	Number of days	
Infusion at 50% of baseline intake					
			intake		
11.2	22.0	8	10.3	2	104
(10.8–	(15.0–		(7.6–		
11.6)	25.8)		13.0		
Infusion at 100% of baseline intake					
16.8	16.4	8	5.1	4	67.2
(16.0–	(12.2–		(1.1–		
18.0)	21.8)		7.7)		

Note: Both sets of infusions were made into the same rat (AD-10). Approximately 2 mo. intervened between these two infusions.
Numbers in parentheses are ranges.

The suppression efficiencies calculated from their data indicate that intragastric saline is much less effective (28.4%) in a short term, than in a long term test, such as the present, in suppressing oral intake. It therefore follows that the relative suppression effectiveness of intragastric loads of saline decreases as the animal becomes more deprived, and hence deprived animals are less attentive to internal cues and more attentive to external signals than are non-deprived animals. These findings may have application to other ingestive behaviour as well.

23

Acknowledgements

The authors thank Barbara FARREN for technical assistance. Supported by NSF grant GB 33219 and a Biomedical Sciences Support Grant from the University of Pennsylvania. Some of the equipment used in these experiments was kindly loaned by Carl PFAFFMANN, Rockefeller University.

References

EPSTEIN, A. N., STELLAR, E.: The control of salt preference in the adrenalectomized rat. J. comp. physiol. Psychol. **48**, 167–172 (1955).

KISSILEFF, H. R.: Oropharyngeal control of prandial drinking. J. comp. physiol. Psychol. **67**, 309–319 (1969).

— Manipulation of oral and gastric environments. In: Methods in psychobiology (Ed. R. D. MYERS), vol. 2, pp. 125–154, New York-London: Academic Press 1972.

— Non-homeostatic controls of drinking. In: The neuropsychology of thirst: New findings and advances in concepts (Eds. A. N. EPSTEIN, H. R. KISSILEFF, and E. STELLAR) pp. 163–197. Washington D. C.: V. H. Winston and Sons 1973.

NACHMAN, M., VALENTINO, D. A.: Roles of taste and postingestional factors in the satiation of sodium appetite in rats. J. comp. physiol. Psychol. **62**, 280–283 (1966).

RICHTER, C. P.: Increased salt appetite in adrenalectomized rats. Am. J. Physiol. **115**, 155–161 (1936).

— Salt appetite in mammals — its dependence on instinct and metabolism. L'instinct (ed. M. AUTOURI), pp. 577–629. Paris: Masson et Cie 1956.

QUARTERMAIN, D., KISSILEFF, H. R. SHAPIRO, R., MILLER, N. E.: Suppression of food intake with intragastric loading: Relation to natural feeding cycle. Science **173**, 941–943 (1971).

Summary of Discussions

NICOLAÏDIS and ROWLAND to STRICKER: The efficacy of self-injection (SII) in satisfying basic water needs is not limited by rapid renal excretion of the infused water. Only water in excess of need would be excreted. The amounts additionally self-injected after dietary salt loads were rather precisely those needed to neutralise the osmotic load. The residual asymptotic oral intake was independent of the amount of salt. — To KISSILEFF: The "peak need hypothesis" would be confirmed if spontaneous oral drinking were completely abolished by meal-paired intravenous infusions. If there were no total suppression of oral intake the "modality specific hypothesis" would be supported. There is no intravenous self-injection response to an acute systemic salt load much as you have found with intragastric self-injection. — To WEIJNEN: It is unlikely that "vascular taste" affects intravenous self-injection. No taste sensations have been reported by humans in response to intravenous water or saline. — To BURCKHARDT: It would be interesting to study "orally naive" rats; the problem of innate versus learned in drinking behaviour is far from resolved. It is not technically possible at present to raise rats without allowing them to condition their water intake to sensory inputs from the oral cavity, though once on a self-intravenous injection schedule visual and tactile cues associated with lever pressing replace some oral stimuli. — To SZCZEPANSKA-SADOWSKA: We previously decribed osmosensitive cells which may be involved in drinking or in vpr. release. Nevertheless they respond to oral stimulation and occur in regions concerned with ingestive behaviour which suggests that they are involved in the integration of systemic and peripheral thirst signals. — To MOGENSON: Decreased and increased firing rates occur in response to osmotic stimili applied systemically and on the tongue. At present it is not justifiable to equate deceleration of firing rates of single neurones with inhibitory processes. Oral stimulation (e.g. saccharine) does not necessarily facilitate lateral hypothalamic discharge even though such stimulation enhances the rate of self-stimulation of the lateral hypothalamus. — FITZSIMONS: Nephrectomized rats infused intragastrically with a liquid diet continue to drink for up to 48 hr, mainly at night, and go into positive fluid balance. It is difficult to see how need for water in this case could determine the continuing nocturnal water intake.

Section 3

Vasopressin and Drinking

Mechanisms of Hypovolaemic Thirst and Interactions between Hypovolaemia, Hyperosmolality and the Antidiuretic System

S. Kozlowski and E. Szczepanska-Sadowska

The proposal that changes in plasma osmolality determine thirst was made first by Mayer (1900). It remained for Gilman (1937) to show that cellular dehydration, brought about by an increase in the effective osmotic pressure of the tissue fluid, is in fact an important stimulus to thirst.

Recently Andersson (1971) and his colleagues (Eriksson, Fernandez, and Olsson, 1971; Olsson, 1972) suggested that there are receptors situated near the 3rd cerebral vetricle which are influenced specifically by sodium concentration and which trigger both vasopressin (vpr) release and drinking to hypertonic NaCl. However, in light of this conception it is hard to explain why some hypertonic solutions such as sucrose, sorbitol (Holmes and Gregersen, 1950) or mannitol (unpublished observations) cause thirst when given intravenously whereas others like glucose (Holmes and Gregersen, 1950) and fructose (Olsson, 1972) do not. Another argument against the validity of this concept are the electrophysiological data on the existence of osmosensitive units in the vicinity of the nucleus supraopticus (NSO). Their close functional connection with neurosecretory cells of the NSO has apparently been proved (Vincent, Arnauld, and Bioulac, 1972).

We, therefore, believe that it is still justifiable to use the osmometric terms 'osmotic stimulus', 'threshold cellular dehydration' and 'osmotic reactivity' of the thirst mechanism.

The quantitative osmometric analysis of the threshold cellular dehydration, proposed by Wolf (1950), has been used in our laboratory for several years in order to assess the reactivity of the thirst mechanism of the dog to osmotic stimuli. Assuming that osmosensitive cells behave as perfect osmometers, Wolf (1950) calculated the threshold cellular dehydration both in man and dog as follows:

$$Ve' = \frac{(W + L_{H_2O})(Ve A + L_{Na})}{WA + L_{Na}} \tag{1}$$

$$Vi' = W + L_{H_2O} - Ve' \tag{2}$$

$$r(\% \text{ of } Vi) = \frac{(Vi - Vi')\,100}{Vi} \tag{3}$$

where

L_{Na} = load of salt (Na: m-equiv)
L_{H_2O} = load of water (litres)
W = initial total body water (litres)
Ve = initial extracellular fluid volume (litres)
Ve' = final extracellular fluid volume (litres)
Vi = initial intracellular fluid volume (litres)
Vi' = final intracellular fluid volume (litres)
A = initial concentration of extracellular fluid (Na: 150 m-equiv/l.)
r = threshold cellular dehydration

Wolf (1950) assumed the total body water to be 70% and the extracellular water to be 20% body weight. To obtain more precise results we performed a number of experiments in which total and extracellular body water were measured directly as volumes of distribution of tritiated water and of sodium thiocyanate respectively. Plasma sodium was also measured and the total amount of extracellular sodium calculated. Table 1 shows mean values of body fluid spaces, plasma sodium concentration, and threshold cellular dehydration in the dog. Table 2 presents the decreases in cellular water content (r in % of Vi) which theoretically occurred at the thirst threshold when the same four dogs were infused, in different experiments, with equiosmolar hypertonic solutions of either 3.6% NaCl or 20% mannitol. In this set of experiments, values of plasma osmolarity (m-osmole/l.) and osmotic load (m-osmole) were substituted for values of

Table 1. Body water spaces, plasma sodium concentration and threshold cellular dehydration producing drinking. Mean values ($\bar{x}$) with standard errors (S.E. of mean) and number of experiments (n) are shown

Body water spaces		l.	% of body weight
Total body water	$\bar{x}$	10.4	62.1
W	S.E.	0.3	0.3
	n	37	37
Extracellular water	$\bar{x}$	4.5	26.8
Ve	S.E.	0.2	0.5
	n	43	43
Intracellular water	$\bar{x}$	5.8	34.0
Vi	S.E.	0.2	0.5
	n	37	37
Plasma sodium	$\bar{x}$		150.0
concentration	S.E.		0.3
P_{Na} m-equiv/l.	n		37
Threshold cellular	$\bar{x}$		4.4
dehydration	S.E.		0.2
r % Vi	n		67

Table 2. Threshold cellular dehydration (r % Vi) producing drinking response during infusions of equiosmolar solutions of NaCl and mannitol. Mean values $\bar{x}$ with standard errors (S.E. of mean) and number of experiments (n) on four dogs are shown

Solution infused		3.6% NaCl	20% mannitol
	$\bar{x}$	2.62	2.60
r % Vi	S.E.	0.14	0.14
	n	27	24

plasma sodium concentration (Na: m-equiv/l.) and sodium load (Na: m-equiv) in WOLF's original equations. The data demonstrate that both solutions induced the dogs to drink at precisely the same threshold cellular dehydration.

In our experience, assessing the osmotic reactivity of the thirst mechanism by measuring the threshold cellular dehydration is a reliable experimental method. The results obtained from the same dogs under the same conditions were consistent and reproducible. No conditioning is observed if sham experiments are run frequently.

Using this method, we examined the reactivity of the thirst mechanism under various conditions. Student's t test for paired observations was used for statistical analysis of the results and P values under 0.05 were considered significant.

In certain circumstances, thirst and antidiuresis occur without any detectable hypertonicity of the extracellular fluid. Clinical experience seems to suggest that thirst is a symptom of reduced blood volume in man. Thirst is often present after haemorrhage and it may also be an early manifestation of cardiac failure. The latter phenomenon has been explained by assuming that the transudation of fluid to the extravascular space leads to a fall in the effective circulating blood volume and therefore to hypovolaemic thirst. The same conditions produce pronounced antidiuresis suggesting an increased release of vasopressin. Increased water intake under conditions of reduced extracellular fluid volume together with hypotonicity, have repeatedly been reported (MCCANCE, 1936; CIZEK, SEMPLE, HUANG, and GREGERSEN, 1951; and others) in man and in dogs. Increased drinking was also observed when rats were injected intraperitoneally with polyethylene glycol producing transudation of extracellular fluid into the peritoneal cavity, thus decreasing blood volume without changing its osmolality (FITZSIMONS, 1961).

On the other hand, HOLMES and MONTGOMERY (1951) did not find any relationship between the volume of blood lost and the amount of water drunk by dogs bled to the point where symptoms of shock appeared. Neither did observations on human blood donors (HOLMES, 1960) establish such a relationship. In these experiments, water intake was measured over long periods of time, so that intercompartmental water shifts in the body may have obscured the pattern of the response of the thirst mechanism to hypovolaemia.

In the present study an attempt was made to eliminate this factor by determining the changes in the osmotic thirst threshold. To determine the influence of hypovolaemia on the osmotic reactivity of the thirst mechanism, threshold cellular dehydration was compared in dogs under control conditions and immediately after loss of blood (KOZLOWSKI and SOBOCINSKA, 1966). Control measurements of the thirst threshold were made 5 to 7 times before bleeding the animals and one week after haemorrhage. Hypovolaemia was induced by rapid (10 min) bleeding from the femoral artery. The blood loss amounted to 8.2−36.0 % of the initial blood volume as measured by the Evans blue (T-1824) space.

In all animals blood loss caused a decrease in the osmotic thirst threshold, which was significantly correlated with the degree of hypovolaemia (Fig. 1). For the whole group of animals (n = 13), the threshold cellular dehydration under

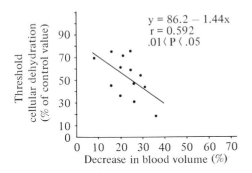

Fig. 1. Relationship between threshold cellular dehydration and decrease in blood volume

control conditions amounted to 4.6 ± 0.2 (S.E. of mean) % of the initial intracellular water and decreased to 2.4 ± 0.3% after the blood loss, the difference being statistically significant ($P < 0.01$).

In two dogs the influence of hypovolaemia on the osmotic thirst threshold was again measured after six months. A similar loss of blood resulted in an almost identical decrease in the thirst threshold each time.

It should be pointed out that on *no* occasion did hypovolaemia elicit spontaneous drinking in the dogs; the amount of water drunk within 3 hr of blood loss was the same as under control conditions. *No* difference was found in the amounts of water drunk by dogs under control conditions and after haemorrhage, in response to a threshold osmotic stimulus.

Blood loss by itself did not produce any secondary changes in the body which could be responsible for the increase in the reactivity of the thirst centre to osmotic stimuli. In control experiments ($n = 10$), the blood electrolytes and plasma osmolality were unaltered and the only change which could be correlated with the decrease in thirst threshold, was the diminished blood volume.

In order to determine whether the influence of hypovolaemia on the osmotic reactivity of the thirst mechanism is mediated by afferent nerves, the thirst threshold was measured under control conditions and after blood loss, before and after left or right cervical vagosympathectomy (SOBOCIŃSKA, 1968).

It was found that left cervical vagosympathectomy abolished the effect of hypovolaemia (loss of 10.6 to 22.4% of initial blood volume) on osmotic reactivity of the thirst mechanism (Fig. 2).

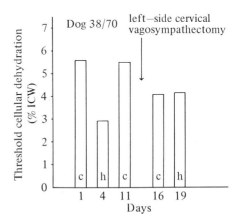

Fig. 2. Effect of hypovolaemia on the thirst threshold in the dog before and after left cervical vagosympathectomy. c-control values, h-values obtained under conditions of hypovolaemia equal to 22% of initial blood volume

The effect of hypovolaemia was also abolished in dogs in which the conductivity of the left cervical vagosympathetic trunk was temporarily blocked by cold ($n = 3$) or by procaine ($n = 3$) applied locally to the trunk previously exposed in a skin pouch (Fig. 3).

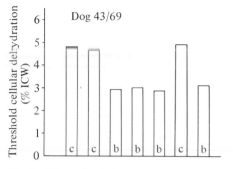

Fig. 3. Effect of cold-induced blockade of the left vagosympathetic trunk on the thirst threshold in the dog. c-control measurement, b-cold-induced blockade of the left vagosympathetic trunk

It should be emphasized that the thirst threshold was significantly lowered by left vagosympathectomy (Fig. 4) and repeated control studies showed that this effect persisted for a period of two weeks.

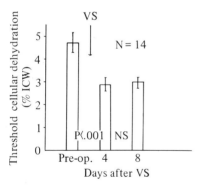

Fig. 4. Effect of left cervical vagosympathectomy on the thirst threshold in dogs. VS-vagosympathectomy

The vagosympathectomy produced no changes in the distribution of body fluids, and in particular no cellular dehydration, although there was a small but significant increase in the extracellular fluid owing to the increase in total body water and total extracellular sodium (Sobocińska, 1968). These changes, however,

cannot be held responsible for the depression of the thirst threshold. It seems more likely that cutting the vagal fibres in the vagosympathetic trunk abolished the tonic inhibitory impulses from volume receptors that are probably located in the low-pressure part of the circulatory system.

Right vagosympathectomy was ineffective in changing the thirst threshold and only infrequently diminished the influence of hypovolaemia on the thirst mechanism.

An isosmotic expansion of the extracellular space (Kozlowski, Drzewiecki, and Sobocinska, 1968) or its intravascular component (Drzewiecki, 1970) exerted an effect on the thirst mechanism opposite to that of hypovolaemia. Infusion of an isosmotic solution of macromolecular dextran which expanded the intravascular space by 10 to 20% increased the thirst threshold by 35–57% of its initial value (Fig. 5). The increase in the thirst threshold was

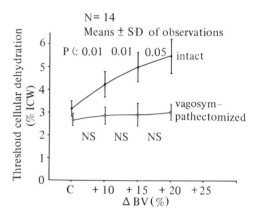

Fig. 5. Effect of an increased blood volume on threshold cellular dehydration in intact and vagosympathectomized dogs

significantly correlated with the degree of expansion of the blood volume. An increased threshold was also observed when the extravascular space was expanded by 10 to 20% by an infusion of physiological saline. Left cervical vagosympathectomy abolished the effect of expansion of the extracellular fluid or of the blood volume on the osmotic thirst threshold (Fig. 5).

The homeostatic regulation of body water depends on precise integration of the antidiuretic system controlling water output and the thirst mechanism controlling replacement of water loss. Increasing evidence indicates that the activity of the hypothalamohypophysial antidiuretic system (HHAS) is modified by isosmotic changes in blood volume. Experiments performed in our laboratory on conscious dogs (SZCZEPANSKA-SADOWSKA, 1972) established that moderate haemorrhage which decreased the blood volume by 15% produced a clear-cut and prolonged increase in the plasma vpr level (Fig. 6a). This was accompanied by a highly

significant decrease in central venous pressure (CVP) without changes in the mean blood pressure (MBP) or pulse pressure (PP) (Fig. 6b, c, d).

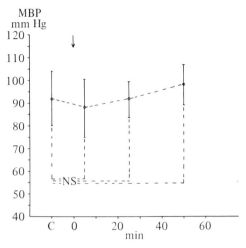

Fig. 6c. Effect of moderate hypovolaemia on mean blood pressure (MBP); ($n = 7$). C-control value; the time of bleeding is indicated by an arrow

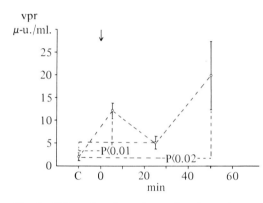

Fig. 6a. Effect of moderate hypovolaemia on plasma vasopressin (vpr) level. Data from 12 dogs (5 and 25 min) and from 13 dogs (50 min). C-control values; the time of bleeding is indicated by an arrow. In this and in subsequent figures, mean values ±S.E. of mean are given

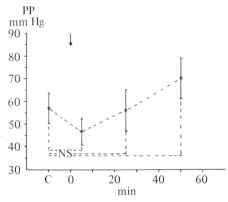

Fig. 6d. Effect of moderate hypovolaemia on pulse pressure (PP); ($n = 7$). C-control value; the time of bleeding is indicated by an arrow

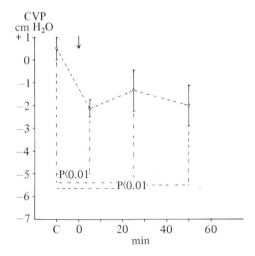

Fig. 6b. Effect of moderate hypovolaemia on central venous pressure (CVP), ($n = 8$). C-control values; the time of bleeding is indicated by an arrow

On the other hand, an increase in blood volume by the same amount depressed the plasma vpr level and suppressed the osmotic reactivity of the antidiuretic system to osmotic stimuli (Fig. 7), i.e. a standard degree of cellular dehydration (5% Vi) elicited a greater increase in plasma vpr level under control conditions than after expansion of the blood volume. The same

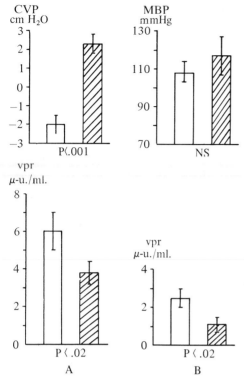

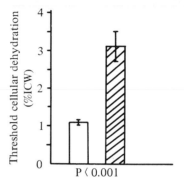

Fig. 7. Effect of a moderate expansion of blood volume on central venous pressure (CVP; $n = 9$) mean blood pressure (MBP; $n = 7$) and activity of the antidiuretic system. A-plasma vpr level found at 5% cellular dehydration ($n = 9$ before and after expansion), B-plasma vpr level before and after blood volume expansion ($n = 10$). White columns — control values, dashed columns — after blood volume expansion

DRZEWIECKI, and KOZLOWSKI, 1971) that the level of cellular dehydration which activates the antidiuretic system is lower than that which elicits drinking (Fig. 8). This means that with minor deficits of water the hypothalamo-hypophysial antidiuretic system alone may be stimulated. Only as cellular dehydration increases does this action become insufficient and the mechanism controlling water intake is activated.

Fig. 8. Extent of cellular dehydration at which the antidiuretic system (white column) and the thirst mechanism (dashed column) are activated

increase in blood volume also caused an increase of CVP without changes in MBP. Highly significant changes of CVP both in hypo- and hypervolaemia strongly support the hypothesis of GAUER and HENRY (1963) that the impulses which influence the activity of the HHAS arise in the central low-pressure part of the circulatory system and depend on changes of blood volume rather than pressure.

In the light of the data presented above it is clear that activation of both the antidiuretic system and the thirst mechanism is achieved not only through plasma hyperosmolality, but also by loss of blood. This loss elicits both vpr release and a decrease in the thirst threshold to osmotic stimuli. Increased thirst is therefore usually accompanied by an elevation of the plasma vpr level. Moreover, we found (SZCZEPANSKA,

In view of this conclusion we decided to investigate whether an increase of plasma vpr concentration may, by itself, stimulate water intake or influence the osmotic reactivity of the thirst mechanism.

Previous studies dealing with this problem yielded contradictory results, depending probably on the dose of exogenous vpr given and on the species of animals used. EPSTEIN, FITZSIMONS, and ROLLS, (1970) did not observe any stimulation of drinking in the rat when 20 m-u. of vasopressin was injected into the septal region, preoptic area, anterior hypothalamic area, lateral or medial hypothalamus. ROLLS (1971) found that the intravenous infusion of vasopressin at rates between $0.07–6.0$ m-u./kg · min did not cause drinking in the rat. When infused at rates above 2.0 m-u./kg · min, vasopressin depressed drinking caused by various thirst stimuli. On the other hand, BARKER, ADOLPH, and KELLER (1953) found that injections of Pitressin into dogs in water balance did not induce drinking. Similarly, Pitressin (0.5

u./kg) given to hydropenic dogs had no effect. However, Pitressin given in the dose of 0.1 u./kg enhanced drinking elicited by hydropenia in the dog. BARKER et al. (1953) also found that dogs lesioned in the neurohypophysial stalk overdrank while recovering from a water deficit but that no additional drinking occurred after Pitressin. In one case, a moderate dose of exogenous Pitressin even produced significantly less drinking. BARKER et al. suggested that "the dogs with neurohypophysial stalk section drank as though they already had a moderate dose of Pitressin; when Pitressin was given they drank less just as the control dogs did with a large dose of Pitressin".

We examined the effect of exogenous vasopressin (Pitressin, Parke, Davis & Co.) on the thirst threshold to osmotic stimuli. The hormone was infused intravenously over a wide range of rates so that its plasma concentration at the thirst threshold varied between 20 and 400 μ-u./ml.

In the group of experiments in which vasopressin infusion raised the plasma hormone level to 21.6–41.8 μ-u./ml. there was a statistically significant decrease in the thirst threshold ($P <$ 0.001) (Fig. 9). This decrease was proportional to the increase in plasma vpr as shown in Fig. 10. However, the thirst threshold failed to decrease at very high plasma vpr levels (Fig. 11). On the contrary, there was a distinct rise in the threshold when plasma vpr level equalled 406 ± 10

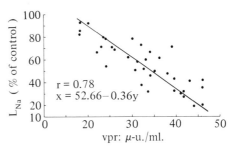

Fig. 10. The relationship between the threshold sodium load (L_{Na}-expressed as % of control value) and plasma vasopressin level

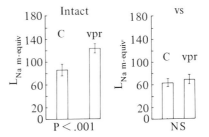

Fig. 11. The influence of a high plasma vpr level on the threshold sodium load (L_{Na}) producing drinking in intact (left side of fig.) and vagosympathectomized (right side — VS) dogs. C-control conditions, vpr — after elevation of plasma vpr to 406 ± 10 μ-u./ml.

μ-u./ml. This rise in threshold could be partially prevented by left cervical vagosympathectomy.

A high plasma vpr level also increased the central blood volume by 30–40%. No spontaneous drinking was observed in dogs infused with vasopressin in the absence of an osmotic stimulus.

Recently, we and FITZSIMONS measured the thirst threshold to osmotic stimuli when vasopressin (Pitressin, Parke, Davis & Co.) was infused into the lateral cerebral ventricle of the dog at a rate of 38 to 3750 μ-u./min (SZCZEPANSKA-SADOWSKA, FITZSIMONS, KOZLOWSKI, and SOBOCINSKA, unpublished data). The results are presented in Fig. 12 a. It appears that vasopressin given directly into the brain also influences the osmotic reactivity of the thirst mechanism. The effect appeared with an infusion rate as low as 38 μ-u./min. A slight increase of the thirst threshold was observed in some cases with the highest rate of infusion. Owing to the considerable variations in responses between different

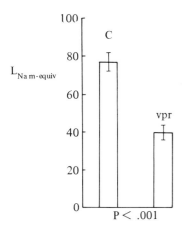

Fig. 9. Threshold sodium load (L_{Na}) producing drinking under control conditions (C) and after elevation of plasma vpr level to 42.4 ± 1.5 μ-u./ml.

dogs to the same rate of vasopressin infusion there was no consistent dose — response relationship in the whole group of animals. Nevertheless such a relationship could be demonstrated in individual dogs (Fig. 12b).

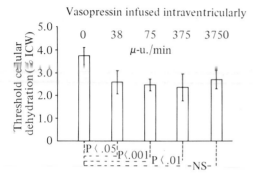

Fig. 12a. Effect of vasopressin infused into the lateral cerebral ventricle of the dog on intracellular thirst threshold. The rate of infusion is indicated

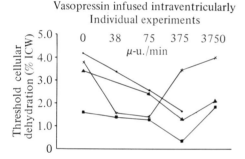

Fig. 12b. Effect of vasopressin into the lateral ventricle on thirst threshold of 4 different dogs. The rate of infusion is shown

The results suggest that vasopressin given either intravenously or into the cerebral ventricle influences the osmotic reactivity of the thirst mechanism, although it does not promote spontaneous water intake. The effect depends on the actual level of the plasma vpr. With moderate increases, of the same order of magnitude as those observed after a nonhypotensive haemorrhage (SZCZEPANSKA-SADOWSKA, 1972) vpr lowers the thirst threshold to osmotic stimuli, whereas in higher concentrations it has the opposite effect. Further studies are necessary to elucidate the mechanism, whereby the thirst threshold is lowered by a moderate concentra-

tion of vpr. If osmoreceptors of the central nervous system respond sluggishly to osmotic stimuli, vpr could facilitate the shift of water along the osmotic gradient so that the threshold cellular dehydration would be achieved faster. There may be a similar effect on the neural system controlling water intake.

The increase in thirst threshold at high vpr concentrations may result from an increase in the central blood volume and arterial blood pressure, which could inhibit thirst through a volume and/or a pressor receptor system. The observation that left cervical vagosympathectomy partially abolishes the inhibitory action of high vpr concentrations argues in favour of this suggestion (Fig. 11). On the other hand, high doses of vasopressin may depress the central neural drinking system directly, a view supported by recent results with intraventricular infusion of vpr at high rates.

The activity of the thirst mechanism is usually under the simultaneous influence of osmotic and volaemic stimuli. We examined the osmotic reactivity of the thirst mechanism in three different situations. 1) when the blood volume was increased 15% by dextran infusion, 2) when the plasma vpr level was increased to 30μ-u./ml. by exogenous vasopressin infusion, and 3) when volaemic and osmotic stimuli were applied simultaneously. The results are presented in Fig. 13. The threshold cellular dehydration was 6.04 $\pm 0.48\%$ of Vi. It increased to $8.38 \pm 1.02\%$ of

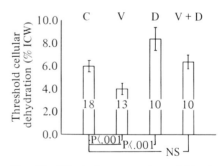

Fig. 13. Effect of vasopressin and blood volume expansion applied separately and simultaneously on threshold cellular dehydration. C-threshold cellular dehydration under control conditions ($n = 18$). V-during infusion of vasopressin ($n = 13$). D-after expansion of blood volume ($n = 10$). V + D-during simultaneous infusion of vasopressin and expansion of blood volume ($n = 10$)

Vi after expansion of blood volume ($n = 10$) and decreased to $4.03 \pm 0.52\%$ of Vi under the influence of vpr. There was no change in the thirst threshold when the expansion of blood volume and infusion of vasopressin were applied simultaneously: the threshold cellular dehydration equalled $6.36 \pm 0.63\%$ of Vi ($n = 10$). These results indicate that hypovolaemia and vasopressin exert concurrent actions on water intake. The decrease in the thirst threshold observed under conditions of hypovolaemia may be the result both of removal of inhibitory impulses from volume receptors and of stimulation of thirst neurones by an associated increase in plasma vasopressin.

We conclude that vpr increases the sensitivity of the thirst mechanism to osmotic stimuli provided that its blood concentration does not reach values at which the peptide exerts a vasoconstrictor action which induces redistribution of the blood towards the central low-pressure part of the circulatory system. The increased sensitivity of the thirst system may have particular importance in conditions of hypovolaemia, in which the increase in plasma vpr level is not accompanied by an increase in blood pressure. SZCZEPANSKA-SADOWSKA (1973a) found that, if measurements were extended over 24 hr after haemorrhage, significant changes in body water balance were then observed (Fig. 14). Water intake increased from 954 ± 54 ml. to 1305 ± 115 ml. ($n = 5$, $P < 0.05$), whereas urine volume decreased from 1146 ± 46 ml. under control conditions to 800 ± 84 ml. in hypovolaemia ($n = 5$, $P < 0.02$).

The difference between the water intake and the water eliminated during 24 hr changed from a negative value of -192 ± 58 ml. to a positive one of $+505 \pm 194$ ml. ($n = 5$, $P < 0.01$). The same degree of haemorrhage also induced prolonged activation of the antidiuretic system. In Fig. 14 the increases in plasma vpr and 24 hr water intake are given for individual experiments. It is worth noting that, in all dogs but one, there was a close relationship between these two values. These results suggest that after haemorrhage activation of thirst and the hypothalamo-hypophysial antidiuretic system restore the body water by increasing the water intake and decreasing the rate of elimination.

In summary (Fig. 15): we suggest that two interdependent systems, operating on intake and excretion, are primarily involved in the control of body fluid volume, particularly of the circulating blood volume. The systems are the thirst mechanism and the hypothalamo-hypophysial antidiuretic system. Both systems are tonically inhibited by impulses from volume

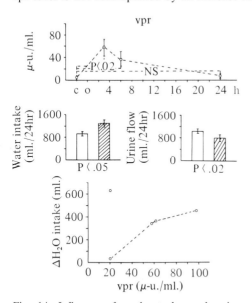

Fig. 14. Influence of moderate hypovolaemia on plasma vpr level, 24 hr water intake and urine flow. White columns — control values, dashed columns — after haemorrhage. The lowest part of the Figure presents the increase in water intake and plasma vpr level in individual dogs

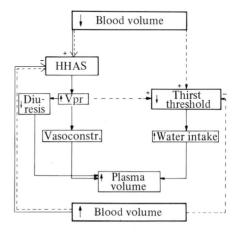

Fig. 15. Schematic representation of interactions between the blood volume and the activity of the antidiuretic system and thirst mechanism

receptors which probably lie in the left atrium and/or in the large veins.

A decrease in either extracellular or blood volume reduces this inhibitory influence. Release of the antidiuretic system from inhibition results in an increase in vpr secretion. Simultaneously the system becomes more sensitive to osmotic stimuli. Even a minor degree of cellular dehydration such as may occur in sweating is sufficient to stimulate further vpr release. The decrease in urine output defends the body against a continuing fall in body fluid volume, and against a decrease in blood flow and circulatory collapse. The vasomotor action of vpr helps to keep the central blood volume at a constant level, which is critical for maintaining normal blood pressure (SZCZEPANSKA-SADOWSKA, 1973b).

At the same time the osmotic reactivity of the thirst mechanism increases. Two factors may be responsible for the sensitization of the thirst centre to osmotic stimuli under conditions of hypovolaemia: diminished input of inhibitory impulses from circulatory volume receptors transmitted through vagal nerves and an increased vpr acting directly on neurones of the thirst centre.

From our results it appears that, under conditions of normovolaemia the "osmostat" tolerates up to 4.4% of cellular dehydration. Under conditions of hypovolaemia the tolerance to a rise in extracellular osmolality decreases which allows the retention of an additional volume of water in the body.

The mechanism is controlled by negative feed-back. The combined actions of decrease in urine output, redistribution of the blood toward the central part of the circulatory system and, eventually, water intake, restore the central blood volume to normal. Increased nervous discharge from volume receptors then inhibits the thirst mechanism and the antidiuretic system, so defending the circulatory system against the risk of a fluid overload.

References

ANDERSSON, B.: Thirst and brain control of water balance. Am. Scientist **59**, 408–415 (1971).

BARKER, J. P., ADOLPH, E. F., KELLER, A. D.: Thirst tests in dogs and modifications of thirst with experimental lesions of the neurohypophysis. Am. J. Physiol. **173**, 233–245 (1953).

CIZEK, L. J., SEMPLE, R. J., HUANG, K. C., GREGERSEN, M. I.: Effect of extracellular electrolyte depletion on water intake in dogs: Am. J. Physiol. **164**, 415–422 (1951).

DRZEWIECKI, K.: Changes in osmotic reactivity of the thirst mechanism induced by expansion of circulating blood volume. Acta Physiol. Pol. **21**, 622–626 (1970).

EPSTEIN, A. N., FITZSIMONS, J. T., ROLLS (née Simons), B. J.: Drinking induced by injection of angiotensin into the brain of rat. J. Physiol. Lond. **210**, 457–474 (1970).

ERIKSSON, L., FERNANDEZ, O., OLSSON, K.: Differences in the antidiuretic response to intracarotid infusions of various hypertonic solutions in the conscious goat. Acta Physiol. Scand. **83**, 554–562 (1971).

FITZSIMONS, J. T.: Drinking by rats depleted of body fluid without increase in osmotic pressure. J. Physiol. Lond. **167**, 344–354 (1961).

GAUER, O. H., HENRY, J. P.: Circulatory basis of fluid volume control. Physiol. Rev. **43**, 423–481 (1963).

GILMAN, A.: The relation between osmotic pressure, fluid distribution and voluntary water intake. Am. J. Physiol. **120**, 323–328 (1937).

HOLMES, J. H.: The thirst mechanism and its relation to edema. In: Edema, Mechanisms and Management. A. Hahnemann Symposium on Salt and Water Retention (Eds. MAYER, J., FUCHS, M.) Philadelphia, Saunders Co. 1960.

HOLMES, J. H., GREGERSEN, M.: Observations on drinking induced by hypertonic solutions. Am. J. Physiol. **162**, 326–337 (1950).

HOLMES, J. H., MONTGOMERY, A. V.: Observations on relation of hemorrhage to thirst. Am. J. Physiol. **167**, 796 (1951).

KOZLOWSKI, S., DRZEWIECKI, K., SOBOCINSKA, J.: The influence of expansion of extracellular fluid volume on thirst mechanism in dogs. Bull. Acad. Pol. Sci., Ser. Biol. Sci., **16**, 47–51 (1968).

KOZLOWSKI, S., SOBOCINSKA, J.: Wpływ hypowolemii na pragnienie. Proc. 10th Congr. Polish Physiol. Soc. in Lublin. (1966).

KOZLOWSKI, S. SZCZEPANSKA, E., DRZEWIECKI, H.: Hormonal influences on osmotic reactivity of the thirst mechanism in dogs. Reg. congr. Int. Union Physiol. Sci., Abstracts of papers, Brasov, Abstr. 491 (1970).

MAYER, A.: Variations de la tension osmotique du sang chez les animaux privés de liquides. C. R. Soc. Biol. **52**, 153–155 (1900).

McCANCE, R. A.: Experimental sodium chloride defficiency in man. Proc. R. Soc. B. **119**, 245–268 (1936).

OLSSON, K.: Dipsogenic effects of intracarotid infusions of various hyperosmolal solutions. Acta Physiol. Scand. **85,** 517–522 (1972).

— Further evidence for the importance of CSF Na^+ concentration in central control of fluid balance. Acta Physiol. Scand. **88,** 183–188 (1973).

ROLLS, B. J.: The effect of intravenous infusion of antidiuretic hormone on water intake in the rat. J. Physiol. Lond. **219,** 331–339 (1971).

SOBOCINSKA, J.: O wpływie zmian objętości krwi krążącej na mechanizm pragnienia. Warsaw: Ph. D. Thesis 1968.

SZCZEPANSKA-SADOWSKA, E.: The activity of the hypothalamo-hypophysial antidiuretic system in conscious dogs. I. The influence of isoosmotic blood volume changes. Pflügers Arch. ges. Physiol. **335,** 139–146 (1972).

— Plasma ADH level and body water balance in dogs after a moderate hemorrhage. Bull. Acad. Pol. Sci. Ser. Biol. Sci. **21,** 89–92 (1973a).

— Hemodynamic effects of a moderate increase of the plasma vasopressin level in conscious dogs. Pflügers Arch. ges. Physiol. **338,** 313–322 (1973b).

SZCZEPANSKA, E., DRZEWIECKI, K., KOZLOWSKI, S.: The osmotic reactivity of the hypothalamo — hypophyseal antidiuretic system and of the thirst mechanism. Experientia **27,** 1083–1084 (1971).

VINCENT, J. D., ARNAULD, E., BIOULAC, B.: Activity of osmosensitive single cells in the hypothalamus of the behaving monkey during drinking. Brain Res. **44,** 371–384 (1972).

WOLF, A. V.: Osmometric analysis of thirst in man and dog. Am. J. Physiol. **161,** 75–86 (1950).

A Radioimmunoassay for Plasma Antidiuretic Hormone and Its Application in a Case of Hypopituitarism Associated with a Loss of Thirst

J. J. Morton, J. J. Brown, R. H. Chinn, A. F. Lever, and J. I. S. Robertson

Introduction

A sensitive and specific radioimmunoassay for the estimation of plasma antidiuretic hormone and its use in a case of hypopituitarism with diabetes insipidus associated with a loss of thirst, is described in this chapter.

Radioimmunoassay of Vasopressin

Antisera to synthetic arginine vasopressin (AVP) were raised in New Zealand white rabbits. AVP was conjugated to rabbit serum albumin, emulsified with Freunds complete adjuvant, and injected into foot pads. Booster injections were given subcutaneously at fortnightly intervals. After 20 weeks the rabbits were bled and the sera checked for antibodies to AVP.

^{125}I-AVP was prepared by a slight modification of the chloramine T method of Greenwood, Hunter, and Glover (1963). The reaction mixture was purified on a DEAE sephadex column.

Vasopressin (vpr) was extracted from plasma using a modification of the method of Beardwell (1971). 20 ml. venous blood was immediately mixed with no more than 100 u. heparin. The sample was immediately centrifuged at $+4\,^{\circ}$C, the plasma acidified with 1 ml. N-HCl and stored at $-20\,^{\circ}$C until extracted. Plasma was extracted by adsorption onto florisil (100 mg). After washing the florisil with water, acetone and water in that order, the florisil was acidified by washing with 0.1 M-HCl. The supernatant

Table 1. The development of polyuria in rabbit 102 actively immunised with arginine vasopressin — rabbit serum albumin conjugate

Antiserum	No. of weeks after 1st injection	Water intake[*],[+] (ml./24 hr)	Urine output[+] (ml./24 hr)	Urine concn. (m-osmole/kg)	Dilution of antiserum which bound 50% ^{125}I labelled AVP
102/1	11	1048	—	—	1:30000
2	13	1282	—	—	1:25000
3	15	1552	1418	121	1:20000
4	17	1610	1459	117	1:16000
5	19	1814	1542	133	1:26000

[*] Average water intake before immunization was 202 ml./24 hr.
[+] Taken as the average/24 hr for the 14 days.

was discarded and the vpr eluted from the florisil by mixing with water-acetone (10:90 v/v). The eluate was collected and reduced to dryness. The dry extract was then redissolved in Tris buffer, pH 7.5 and aliquots removed for assay.

Incubations containing antiserum (1:15 000), ^{125}I-AVP (5 pg) and either standard AVP or unknown plasma extracts were set up in Tris buffer at pH 7.5. Incubations were performed for 2 days at +5 °C after which time separation of antibody-bound ^{125}I-AVP from free ^{125}I-AVP was carried out by the addition of plasma coated charcoal (HERBERT, LAW, GOTTLIEB, and BLEICHER, 1965).

Results

The formation of antibodies in three of the four rabbits immunized was inferred from the onset of thirst and polyuria of varying severity. The rabbit with the most severe symptoms (102) drank up to 15 times the normal daily intake of water (Table 1). This rabbit also produced the antiserum with the highest titre (1:26,000) and also the highest equilibrium constant (3.5 × 10^{10} l.·mole^{-1}) (Fig. 1). The cross reaction

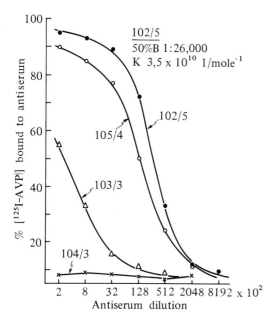

Fig. 1. Percentage 125-I-AVP bound to antisera from 4 different rabbits immunized with synthetic AVP

properties of antiserum 102/5 are shown in Fig. 2. Oxytocin cross-reacted less than 0.03% while lysine vasopressin cross-reacted only 8%. This antiserum was chosen as the most suitable for use in the assay.

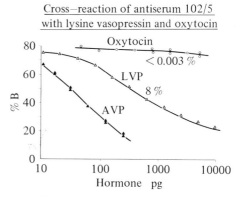

Fig. 2. Cross-reaction of lysine vasopressin and oxytocin with antiserum 102/5 and in the assay

Suitably pure ^{125}I-AVP was produced using the method described. After fractionation on DEAE sephadex, the label was shown to be greater than 97% pure. The cross-reaction properties of the labelled AVP with antiserum 102/5 were checked by comparing the ability of known and increasing amounts of ^{125}I-AVP to displace a constant amount (5 pg) of label from

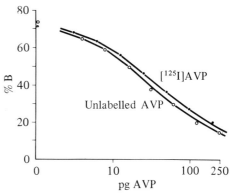

Fig. 3. Comparison of the standard curves obtained using un-iodinated AVP (X) and iodinated AVP (o) as the standard. The incubation contained standard un-iodinated AVP from 4 to 250 pg and standard iodinated AVP from 3.1 to 200 pg. Each contained antibody 102/5 at a dilution of 1:16,000 and 5 pg label, and was incubated for 2 days at +5 °C

the antiserum, with that of known and increasing amounts of standard unlabelled AVP. Fig. 3 shows such a comparison in which both ^{125}I-AVP and standard AVP demonstrate similar binding characteristics.

One of the major problems involved in the development of any method for the measurement of vpr is the extremely low levels of this hormone in plasma. This applies equally to radioimmunoassay and to bioassay. Fig. 4 shows the mean of twelve separate standard curves which were prepared on different occasions. Defining the threshold of the assay as the smallest amount of hormone which will produce a fall in the percentage bound greater than three

times the standard deviation for that point, then 4 pg AVP/tube is the smallest amount which can be detected with any accuracy. This is equivalent to 2 pg/ml plasma.

The performance of the method with regard to its replicate variation and recovery from blood is shown in Table 2.

As a means of checking the immunoassay with the corresponding bioassay, plasma samples obtained during controlled haemorrhage experiments in the dog were each assayed by radioimmunoassay, and by bioassay in water loaded alcohol anaesthetised rats (FORSLING, JONES, and LEE, 1968). Fig. 5 shows the correlation between these two assays ($r = 0.87, p < 0.001$).

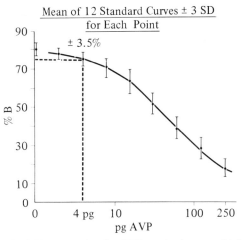

Fig. 4. The mean of twelve AVP standard curves with 3 times S.D. for each point. The incubates contained standard AVP (2–250 pg), antibody 102/5 (1:16,000) and iodinated AVP (5 pg) and were incubated for 2 days at +5°C

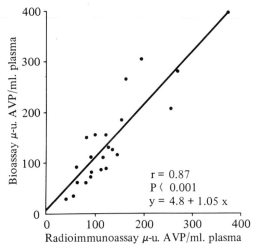

Fig. 5. Correlation obtained between the radioimmunoassay and the bioassay of AVP in 24 plasma samples obtained from dogs during three separate haemorrhage experiments

Table 2. Radioimmunoassay of arginine vasopressin. The coefficient of variation and recovery for the method

Experiment	n	Mean	Standard deviation	Range	Coefficient of variation
Between-Incubation	15	14.2	±1.1	13 −16.8	8
Between-Batch 1	9	8.4	±0.96	8.4−10.3	12
Extraction 2	12	4.5	±0.62	3.8− 5.1	13
Within-Batch Extraction	12	4.8	±0.45	4.3− 5.3	9

Mean recovery of AVP added to blood; 60 ± 6.9 (S.D.)%, n = 24.

Range of Values of Vasopressin in Normal State, after Water Deprivation and after Water Loading

A range of 4 to 8 pg vpr/ml. plasma was found in 17 normal subjects in varying states of hydration. Determinations were carried out using venous blood, all sampling being carried out between 9.00 and 10.00 and after 5 – 10 minutes recumbency.

The range found in 6 normal subjects following a period of between 12 and 18 hours fluid deprivation was 6 to 13.5 pg vpr/ml. plasma. Prior to dehydration the range was 5.1 to 7.3 pg/ml. The difference observed was significant ($t = 2.4, p < 0.05$).

Following a water load of 20 ml./kg body weight the mean plasma vpr concentration in 7 normal subjects fell from 5.6 pg/ml. to 4.1 pg/ml. Again this change was significant ($t = 2.8, p < 0.02$).

Use of the Method in a Case of Hypopituitarism with Diabetes Insipidus Associated with a Loss of Thirst

A 20 year old man was admitted to hospital in October 1970 complaining of nocturia and thirst together with a mild frontal headache. His serum electrolytes were found to be; Na 154, K 5.5 and Cl 119 m-mole/l. After several days he lapsed into coma. His serum electrolytes were now Na 162 and Cl 116 m-mole/l. During this time he was passing up to 8 litres of dilute urine per day. Rehydration and administration of Pitressin corrected the electrolyte abnormalities and he became conscious. However withdrawal of vpr caused a return of thirst and polyuria (5.7 l./day).

Other tests of the hypothalamo-pituitary function indicated considerable pituitary abnormalities including deficient corticotrophin, growth hormone and gonadotrophin secretion, as well as deficient vpr secretion. However, detailed neurological investigation failed to reveal any definite abnormality.

Further procedures, including intravenous infusion of Val[5] angiotensin II-amide and a low sodium intake of 10 m-mole Na/day, were both shown to have an antidiuretic effect. The latter procedure was accompanied by a rise in the plasma level of angiotensin II, and when the plasma angiotensin II concentration was plotted against urine flow for both procedures a significant inverse correlation was found. (Fig. 6)

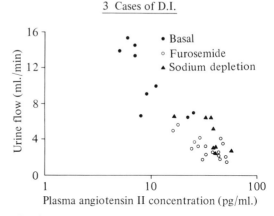

Fig. 6. The effect on urine flow of increasing the circulating angiotensin II concentration in 3 cases of diabetes insipidus

The patient was discharged on drug therapy to control his thirst and polyuria.

On August 1972 he was readmitted to hospital grossly dehydrated, and the results of various biochemical investigations carried out are shown in Table 3. His serum Na, Cl and osmolality were markedly elevated. Also his thirst had completely disappeared and he was oliguric. At this time we were able to determine his plasma vpr concentration by the method previously described. The value of 4.5 pg/ml. is just within the lower part of the normal range providing further evidence to support the previous diagnosis of diabetes insipidus. Plasma angiotensin II concentration was, however, elevated to six times the upper limit of normal. Rehydration resulted in the angiotensin II returning to normal while it was observed that there was no worthwhile change in his plasma vpr, although there was a return to a high flow of low osmolality urine. It was at this time that further neurological and clinical investigations suggested the presence of a lesion of the longitudinal bundle.

Two further episodes of severe dehydration, resulting from temporary discharge from the ward occurred; the biochemical details are given in Table 3. These episodes were similar to the previous one with very high serum electrolyte, osmolality and angiotensin II levels while the plasma vpr levels were again unaltered. Again partial rehydration resulted in some correction of these abnormalities but there was still no alteration in the plasma vasopressin.

In the last episode shown there was some increase in the level of vpr but in the light of preliminary dehydration studies in normal subjects this was still considered to be inappropriately low in relation to the state of the water balance. Though accurate measurement of urine output at this stage was very difficult it was apparent that, as before, dehydration was accompanied by oliguria despite the low plasma vpr and that polyuria returned on rehydration.

In conclusion this patient was diagnosed as having, at the outset, hypopituitarism associated with diabetes insipidus (NABARRO and DALY, 1973). Diabetes insipidus was later confirmed by radioimmunoassay of plasma vpr. However, as the disease progressed and the lesion expanded, there was a loss of thirst. Under these conditions, with a low plasma vpr dehydration occurred which led to oliguria. It is suggested that this reduction in urine flow may have been the result of the antidiuretic effect of the very high levels of angiotensin II.

References

BEARDWELL, C. J.: Radioimmunoassay of arginine vasopressin in human plasma. J. clin. Endocrin. Metabol. 33, 254–260 (1971).
FORSLING, M. L., JONES, J. J., LEE, J.: Factors influencing the sensitivity of the rat to vasopressin. J. Physiol. Lond. 196, 495–505 (1968).
GREENWOOD, F. C., HUNTER, W. M., GLOVER, J. S.: The preparation of 131-I labelled human growth hormone of high specific radioactivity. Biochem. J. 89, 114–123 (1963).
HERBERT, V., LAW, K. S., GOTTLIEB, C. W., BLEICHER, S. J.: Coated charcoal immunoassay of insulin. J. clin. Endocrin. Metabol. 25, 1375–1381 (1965).
NABARRO, J. D. M., DALY, J. J.: A case of anorexia. Brit. med. J. 2, 158–163 (1973).

Table 3. Results of some biochemical investigations carried out over a 4 month period in a case of hypopituitarism with diabetes insipidus

	23rd Aug. 1972. Admission	25th Aug. Part.hydrated	26th Aug.	1st Sept. Rehydrated	21st Dec. Dehydrated	23rd Dec. Part. Rehydrated	28th Dec. Dehydrated
Na m-mole/l.	171	159	164	135	184	153	170
K m-mole/l.	3.1	2.8	2.1	2.8	4.3	2.4	4.1
Cl m-mole/l.	120	111	118	99	132	112	130
Osmolality (m-osmole/kg)	338	324	332	279	384	298	393
Vasopressin (pg/ml., normal 4–8, dehydrated 6–13.5)	—	4.5	6.3	4.7	4.5	5.1	8.0
Angiotensin II (pg/ml., normal 5–35)	—	207	177	14	510	85	357
Fluid intake ml.	1800	3400	1706	—	1305	4800	980
Fluid output ml.	490	3395	1700	—	190 (+)	297 (+++)	270
Urine osmolality m-osmole/kg	640	96	80	—	438	300	658

Studies on Drinking-Feeding Interactions in Rats with Hereditary Hypothalamic Diabetes Insipidus

D. Haack, E. Homsy, G. Kohrs, B. Möhring, P. Oster, and J. Möhring

Rats with hereditary hypothalamic diabetes insipidus (DI) do not produce vasopressin (Miller and Moses, 1971; Valtin, 1967; Valtin, Sawyer and Sokol, 1965). Daily water intake of these animals varies between 0.5 and 1.5 l./kg body weight (Friedman and Friedman, 1965; Miller and Moses, 1971; Valtin, 1967), and is thought to reflect variations in the severity of diabetes insipidus. Since in normal rats water intake is closely related to food intake, we tested the hypothesis that in DI rats variations in water intake are also related to variations in food intake.

Owing to dehydration and/or the obligatory consumption of large amounts of water, the drive to eat might be suppressed in DI rats, so that DI rats would show the effects of mild starvation. This could explain why growth is retarded in DI rats (Valtin. 1967). If this were the case, food intake and the gain in body weight should become normal during vasopressin treatment as a consequence of normalization of water turnover. This assumption was tested in the present study.

It has been demonstrated that the intracellular fluid volume of DI rats may be high despite hyperosmolality (Friedman, Sreter, Nakashima, and Friedman, 1962). Extracellular fluid volume is reduced, and the renin-angiotensin system is stimulated. Therefore, DI rats may suffer primarily from extracellular thirst. This hypothesis was tested by studying the effects of long-term vasopressin treatment on plasma volume, plasma angiotensin II, and serum osmolality.

Materials and Methods

All studies were performed in rats with hereditary hypothalamic diabetes insipidus (DI) originally derived from the Brattleboro strain of Long-Evans rats (Valtin, 1967). Control animals were heterozygous or normal Long-Evans rats (LE). The rats were fed a commercial diet (Ssniff), and were given fresh demineralized water every day. The experiments were performed in a room with constant temperature (24 ± 1 °C) and humidity (60 ± 3%) which was lighted automatically from 6 a.m. to 6 p.m.

Experiment 1. Seventeen male DI rats and 8 normal male Long-Evans rats (LE) of similar body weights were placed in individual cages. Body weights and food and water intake were measured daily at 3 p.m. on 5 consecutive days. Then the experiment was terminated.

Experiment 2. Groups of 8 male DI and 8 male LE rats were treated similarly, as described above. After 4 control days, food was withdrawn for 3 days. Then, food was again given for 4 additional days.

Experiment 3. Eighteen male DI rats and 7 male heterozygous rats from the same 4 litters, each 6 weeks old, were treated as described above. After 8 control days daily doses of 500 m-u./kg vasopressin tannate in 0.2 ml. oil (Parke Davis & Co.) were administered subcutaneously at 3 p.m.

41

to 9 DI rats. The other animals received 0.2 ml. of the vehicle. The dose of vasopressin tannate was increased to 750 m-u./kg during the second experimental week, and to 1,000 m-u./kg during the following weeks. After 6 weeks of treatment, the experiment was terminated. The rats were anaesthetized with ether and blood was collected from the tail artery for determination of haematocrit, serum sodium and urea concentrations, serum osmolality, and plasma angiotensin II concentration (ÖSTER, HACKENTHAL, and HEPP, 1973). Hearts and kidneys were excised, cleaned from adherent tissue, and weighed.

Statistics. All values in the text, the table, and the figures are means ±S.E. of means. Linear regression equations were fitted by the method of least squares.

Results

Relationship between Water and Food Intake. As in normal LE rats, water intake of DI rats was

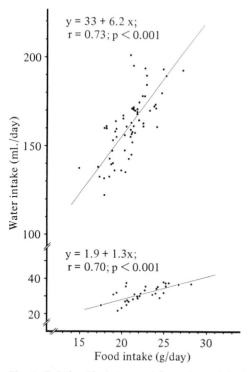

Fig. 1. Relationship between daily water and food intake in normal rats (lower regression line) and in rats with hereditary hypothalamic diabetes insipidus (upper regression line)

closely related to food intake (Fig. 1). During 3 days of food deprivation, water intake decreased in LE rats from 32 ± 2 ml. to 15 ± 2 ml. and in the DI rats from 175 ± 8 ml. to 75 ± 8 ml. When food was offered again, water intake and daily gain in weight returned to control levels within 2–3 days.

Long-Term Treatment of DI Rats with Vasopressin Tannate. At the age of 6 weeks, heterozygous rats weighed more than their homozygous litter mates (Fig. 2). Mean daily water intake during the 8 control days was 85 ± 5 ml. in the DI rats and 25 ± 2 ml. in the heterozygous animals. Mean daily food intake was 12.8 ± 0.5 g and 17.6 ± 1.2 g, respectively. After the first injection of vasopressin tannate, daily food intake increased by 2–3 g in the DI rats; no changes were observed in oil-treated DI rats and heterozygous animals. During the last week of the experiment, the water intake of substituted DI rats was similar to that of heterozygous animals (Table 1). Food intake of treated DI rats was higher than in the unsubstituted DI animals, but lower than in the heterozygous rats. With the beginning of vasopressin treatment, the body weight curve of DI rats paralleled that of heterozygous rats. The increase in body weight was similar in both groups (Fig. 2), while in unsubstituted DI rats it was always reduced. The weights of the kidney and heart were reduced in DI rats in comparison with heterozygous animals. In vasopressin-treated DI rats, kidney and heart weights increased in parallel to body weight (Table 1), indicating that the improvement in gain of body weight in DI rats after vasopressin was not due to fat deposition only.

Haematocrit, serum sodium concentration, plasma angiotensin II concentration, and serum osmolality were elevated in DI rats compared with heterozygous rats. After 6 weeks of vasopressin treatment, these values became almost normal except for serum osmolality which remained high (Table 1). Serum urea concentration increased slightly in the treated DI rats.

Discussion

As has been observed in normal rats (STROMINGER, 1946/47), water intake of DI rats is closely related to food intake (see Fig. 1). Therefore, differences in the severity of diabetes insipidus, i.e. variations of daily water intake between 0.5 and 1.5 l./kg body weight, may, at least partially, be explained by differences in food intake.

When DI rats were treated with vasopressin tannate, water intake decreased to levels found in their heterozygous litter mates. Concomitantly, food intake increased and the daily gain in weight became normal. These findings suggest

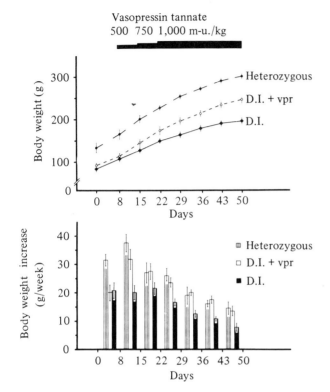

Fig. 2. Body weight gain of male rats homozygous and heterozygous for hypothalamic diabetes insipidus. Nine DI rats were treated with vasopressin tannate (vpr), while nine other DI rats and seven heterozygous rats received oil only. Values are means ±S.E. of mean

Table 1. Effects of long-term vasopressin treatment in DI rats

	Body weight (g)	Water intake (g/day)	Food intake (g/day)	Haema-tocrit (%)	Plasma A II conc. (pg/ml.)	Serum sodium conc. (m-equiv/l.)	Serum urea conc. (m-mole/l.)	Serum osmo-larity (m-osmole/l.)	Heart weight (mg)	Total renal mass (mg)
Heterozygous rats (n = 7)	303 ±8	34.5 ±1.5	22.6 ±0.5	44.0 ±0.5	97 ±17	140.4 ±0.7	7.1 ±0.3	303.1 ±1.0	761 ±22	1692 ±58
DI rats treated (n = 9)	247** ±7	35.4 ±2.2	20.4** ±0.3	44.7 ±0.6	129 ±13	143.0* ±1.0	9.4** ±0.3	317.0** ±1.7	641** ±15	1413** ±33
DI rats untreated (n = 9)	197** ±7	138** ±5	18.4** ±0.3	46.4** ±0.5	267** ±44	148.1** ±0.9	7.7 ±0.5	326.4** ±3.1	521** ±15	1120** ±66

Data from animals treated for 6 weeks with vasopression tannate in oil as described under "Methods".
Values are means ±S.E. of mean; * p < 0.05, ** p < 0.01 as compared with heterozygous rats. Values of water intake and of food intake are daily means calculated for the last experimental week.

that DI rats suffer from mild starvation. Thus, growth retardation of DI rats may be explained, at least partially, by a reduction in food intake. The reasons for the moderately suppressed drive to eat may be related to consequences of dehydration, such as hyperosmolality (KAKOLEWSKI and DEAUX, 1972), an increased activity of the renin-angiotensin system (MC FARLAND and ROLLS, 1972), and to distension of the stomach (BROBECK, 1960) from the large amounts of water consumed.

Long-term treatment of DI rats with vasopressin tannate almost restored the haematocrit, serum sodium concentration, and plasma angiotensin II concentration to normal. However, serum osmolality remained markedly elevated. This finding is striking in view of the normal water intake, and remains unexplained. It suggests that hyperosmolality may be of only minor importance in stimulating thirst in DI rats. This suggestion is in line with the observation that intracellular fluid volume of DI rats is not reduced (FRIEDMAN and FRIEDMAN, 1965; FRIEDMAN et al. 1962). Therefore, hypovolaemia and an increased activity of the renin-angiotensin system (FITZSIMONS, 1972) may be the major factors responsible for the stimulation of thirst in DI rats.

References

BROBECK, J. R.: Regulation of feeding and drinking. Handbook of Physiology, Neurophysiology II, chapter 47, pp. 1197–1206, Washington, D.C.: Am. Physiol. Soc. 1960.

FITZSIMONS, J.: Thirst. Physiol. Rev. **52**, 468–561 (1972).

FRIEDMAN, S. M., FRIEDMAN, C. L.: Salt and water distribution in hereditary and in induced hypothalamic diabetes insipidus in the rat. Canad. J. Physiol. Pharmacol. **43**, 699–705 (1965).

FRIEDMAN, S. M., SRETER, F. A., NAKASHIMA, M., FRIEDMAN, C. L.: Adrenal cortex and neurohypophyseal deficiency in salt and water homeostasis of rats. Am. J. Physiol. **203**, 697–701 (1962).

KAKOLEWSKI, J. W., DEAUX, E.: Aphagia in the presence of drinking an isosmotic NaCl solution. Physiol. Behav. **8**, 623–630 (1972).

McFARLAND, D. J., ROLLS, B.: Suppression of feeding by intracranial injections of angiotensin. Nature **236**, 172–173 (1972).

MILLER, M., MOSES, A. M.: Radioimmunoassay of antidiuretic hormone with application to study of the Brattleboro rat. Endocrinology **88**, 1389–1396 (1971).

OSTER, P., HACKENTHAL, E., HEPP, R.: Radioimmunoassay of angiotensin II in rat plasma. Experientia **29**, 353–354 (1973).

STROMINGER, J. L.: The relation between water intake and food intake in rats with hypothalamic hyperphagia and in normal rats. Yale J. Biol. Med. **19**, 279–287 (1946/47).

VALTIN, H.: Hereditary hypothalamic diabetes insipidus in rats (Brattleboro strain). Am. J. Med. **42**, 814–827 (1967).

VALTIN, H., SAWYER, W. H., SOKOL, H. W.: Neurohypophysial principles in rats homozygous and heterozygous for hypothalamic diabetes insipidus (Brattleboro strain). Endocrinology **77**, 701–706 (1965).

Summary of Discussions

KOZLOWSKI to KISSILEFF: Threshold of drinking was reached when the dog drank a single draught of more than 50 ml. water. – To EPSTEIN: Yes, threshold of cellular dehydration is the same as minimal effective dose of hyperosmolar fluid. — To RAMSAY and to MÖHRING: The plasma osmolality had increased by 3–4% when the dogs started to drink, but the stimulus to drinking was cellular dehydration, not the increased osmotic concentration by itself. — To STRICKER: Further experiments are needed to rule out the possibility that haemorrhage preceding an osmotic load may cause vasoconstriction intense enough to slow osmotic equilibration of the blood with the fluids of the body with the result that smaller osmotic loads are needed to produce an elevated blood osmolality in the region of the osmoreceptor. It is an unlikely explanation of the diminished threshold because small losses of blood not affecting the blood pressure have marked effects on the thirst threshold. — To FITZSIMONS: We think that the thirst receptors that respond to hypovolaemia are located mainly in the left atrium and other regions of distribution of the left vagal fibres. — To LE MAGNEN: It appears that in the dog hypovolaemia in the absence of an osmotic load does not induce drinking.

MORTON to FLUX: It is possible that the low plasma K and high plasma Na and osmolality were caused by increased secretion of aldosterone resulting from elevated plasma angiotensin. — To SZCZEPANSKA-SADOWSKA: Antigen was prepared by coupling synthetic arginine vasopressin to rabbit serum albumin using diethylcarbodiimide. The high angiotensin level probably did not result from the absence of vpr suppression of renin secretion, but it was the consequence of reduced plasma volume and it occurred despite the high serum Na. — To HUTCHINSON: plasma vpr was corrected for a recovery of 60%. The patient was hypotensive when dehydrated. We did not look for neurophysins.

HAACK to KISSILEFF: The suggestion that plasma hyperosmolality accounted for the decreased food intake of rats with hereditary diabetes insipidus (DI) does not explain why food intake increased after vasopressin though the plasma osmolality remained high. — To LEHR: The reasons for differences in the spontaneous food intake of DI rats are unknown. The less they eat the more severe the dehydration, although such rats also drink less. Perhaps the degree of hyperosmolality is a factor, or the variations may simply be the same as in normal rats. — To LEENEN: The time-sequence of changes in the plasma volume and angiotensin level after starting vpr therapy is unknown. — SZCZEPANSKA-SADOWSKA found that vpr (120 m-u./kg·min) caused an increase in control plasma volume after 30 min.

Section 4
Comparative Aspects of the Regulation of Water Intake

Cellular Dehydration as a Stimulus to Drinking in the Common Iguana, *Iguana Iguana*

S. KAUFMAN and J. T. FITZSIMONS

Introduction

Reptiles first appeared during the Upper Carboniferous and Permian periods about 220 million years ago. They are the first truly terrestrial vertebrates. Unlike the amphibia they have no need to return to the water in order to breed since they enclose their offspring together with necessary supplies of water within water-impermeable membranes until the young have developed sufficiently to lead an independent existence. Present-day reptiles range from the completely aquatic, for example the sea snakes and turtles, to the highly successful colonisers of the more arid regions of the world. The latter are well suited to terrestrial life by having a skin that is, relative to the skin of amphibians and aquatic reptiles, impermeable to water. In addition they reduce their urinary water losses by being uricotelic. Most important of all, however, is a new dimension in water balance, not present in the amphibia, namely the ability to drink water when the need arises.

Drinking in Reptiles

ADOLPH (1943) reported that a number of reptiles drink in response to water deprivation. He described how the desiccated Garter snake *Thamnophis sirtalis* drinks almost the amount of water by which it is dehydrated within a period of about 6 minutes. He wrote of reptiles that, "In recovery all show sudden gains of water by alimentary drinking. I recall how surprising the sudden and intermittent gains seemed, after I had first measured the smooth and gradual gains of frogs and toads". Amphibians do not drink but absorb water exclusively through the skin. It has been reported that some reptiles also absorb through the skin and in the aquatic turtle water intake by this route is appreciable (BENTLEY and SCHMIDT-NIELSEN, 1970). This is not however the case in terrestrial reptiles although the agamid lizard *Moloch horridus* was thought to do this because it does not appear to drink. However, BENTLEY and BLUMER (1962) found that in this lizard water moves by capillarity along fine channels in the skin to reach the mouth where it mixes with hygroscopic mucus and is swallowed. If the mouth is held shut the dehydrated *Moloch* is unable to restore its body water when it is immersed in water. Very little else has been published on behavioural water intake in the reptiles and in view of their pioneering evolutionary migration landwards this is indeed puzzling.

Natural History of the Common Iguana

We have undertaken a physiological study of thirst mechanisms in the common or tree iguana *Iguana iguana*. The iguana inhabits tropical forests of Central and South America (SWANSON, 1950). It generally lives on the branches of trees near rivers, but it is equally at home on the ground and it is also an excellent swimmer taking to the water in order to escape from its enemies. It can remain submerged for up to $4^1/_2$ hours (MOBERLEY, 1968 a). Iguanas probably mate on the ground in November. The eggs are laid from early February to March and are buried in the ground. The young iguana hatches after about 3 months and measures about 5 cm. It reaches sexual maturity in about 2 years but continues to grow after this. The largest specimen described by Swanson was about 1.7 metres in total length, 51 cm from snout to vent and weighed 6 kg. Very young iguanas are omnivorous but the adults feed on leaves, blossoms, buds and fruit.

Water and Electrolyte Balance in the Iguana

There are no reports on the drinking habits of the iguana but a certain amount is known about other aspects of their water and electrolyte balance (BENTLEY, 1971). The absence of loops of Henle in the kidney precludes the formation of hypertonic urine and the most that can be achieved, possibly aided by further absorption of water in the cloaca, is a urine approaching isotonicity (MURRISH and SCHMIDT-NIELSEN, 1970). However, uricotelism allows a considerable sparing of water because, as the urine becomes more concentrated, uric acid is precipitated out of solution with the result that it no longer contributes to urine osmolality. The crystals of uric acid are finally voided with the faeces.

Uricotelism results in an economy of water in the excretion of nitrogenous waste products but it does not enable the reptilian kidney to rid the body of excess salts. Many reptiles, especially those that live in an environment in which the salt intake is necessarily high, for example the Galápagos marine iguana, have an extrarenal mechanism of electrolyte excretion, the nasal salt gland. Terrestrial lizards including the common iguana also have nasal salt glands, but secretion rates are much lower than in marine birds and reptiles and K ions are usually more abundant than Na ions (SCHMIDT-NIELSEN, BONIT, LEE, and CRAWFORD, 1963; DUNSON, 1969). The K : Na ratio in the nasal fluid depends on the dietary intake of these 2 ions. TEMPLETON

(1967) found that when the false iguana *Ctenosaura pectinata* was given 0.5 ml. 1 M-NaCl by intraperitoneal injection the salt gland initially continued to excrete more potassium than sodium, but within a few days the K : Na ratio fell as the Na ions were excreted. The response of the nasal salt gland to a salt load is therefore extremely sluggish compared with the response of the mammalian kidney and, as we shall see, this has extremely important implications in the drinking responses to hypertonic solutions.

Methods

Our present report is about mechanisms of cellular thirst in the iguana. The iguanas we used came from Colombia and when we started to study them in January, were about 1 year old and weighed between 50 and 100 g. They were housed together in a cage in which they could climb and with a time-controlled heat-lamp which was on between 06.00 hr and 20.00 hr. Their diet consisted of lettuce and peas and water was also freely available though the animals rarely drank. During the experiments the iguanas were placed in individual cages to which they were well accustomed and in which water was available from an inverted graduated tube widely open at its lower end and containing nylon mesh to prevent the water escaping. The iguana is rather shy so once it had been placed in its testing cage it was disturbed as little as possible.

Response to Osmotic Stimuli

It was evident from the start that the iguana is a vigorous and efficient drinker when suitably stimulated. After a period of water deprivation if it is offered a bowl of water it puts its mouth and snout into the water, drinks for several seconds and then raises its head in chicken-like fashion (Fig. 1). It generally takes all the water that it is going to in a single draught or series of draughts and only rarely returns to drink a second time.

In order to investigate possible mechanisms of cellular thirst various amounts of hypertonic solutions (all 2 M solutions) of sodium chloride,

Fig. 1. Drinking iguanas. These animals were injected with 5 ml. 2 M-NaCl/kg body weight 4 hr prior to being photographed

sucrose, glucose or urea were injected into the peritoneal cavity. The animal was weighed, returned to its cage and allowed to drink over the next 6 hr. It was weighed at 3 hr, again at 6 hr and any water intake during the experimental period was measured.

Hypertonic saline and hypertonic sucrose were found to cause vigorous drinking but hypertonic glucose and hypertonic urea were ineffective (Fig. 2). The latency to drink was always fairly long, between 1/2 hour and 4 hours, but once drinking had started it was completed in a single short session. From the changes in body weight it was possible to estimate the amount of water retained after drinking. If the precaution were taken of emptying the cloaca at the time of injection there were trivial changes in body weight once the iguana had drunk. This small loss of weight, 1.0 g/kg body wt./hr, was attributable to evaporative water losses from the skin and lungs since urine flow remained very low and none was

voided. In view of this very low rate of insensible water loss, the amounts of water drunk were almost the same as the changes in body weight presented throughout this study.

Following injection of hypertonic saline (20 m-osmole/kg body wt.) the iguana became anuric if drinking were prevented and remained so for the next 6 hr. Injecting saline and allowing the animal to drink is roughly equivalent to injecting it with isotonic saline. When 80 ml./kg body wt. of isotonic saline (10.7 g NaCl/l.) was injected into the peritoneal cavity, urine flow rose to 1.6 ml./kg body wt./hr during the first 3 hr and fell to 1.2 ml./kg body wt./hr during the second 3 hr. These values for urine flow after salt loading are very low compared with adult mammalian figures. For example, rats injected with 23 m-osmole/kg body wt. and not allowed to drink excreted, during 6 hr, 95% of the injected load in a urine volume of 29 ml./kg body wt. In contrast, iguanas under these conditions were anuric. Similarly salt loaded rats

49

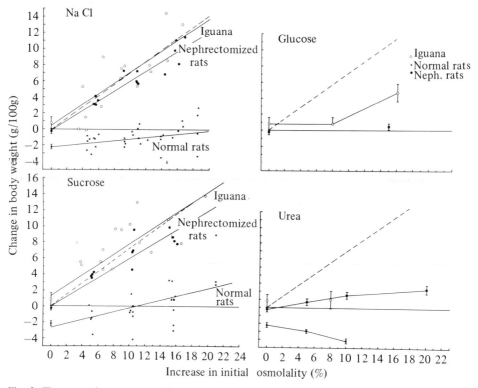

Fig. 2. The regressions or means (±S.E. of mean) of change in body wt./6 hr/100 g body wt. of iguanas, normal rats and nephrectomized rats on % increase of initial osmolality (iguanas 351 m-osmole/l., rats 290 m-osmole/l.). The dashed line shows the theoretical slope for dilution of injected solute to isotonicity. With hypertonic saline, the regressions for iguanas ($r = 0.81$, d.f. $= 28$) and for nephrectomized rats ($r = 0.96$, d.f. $= 27$) do not differ in slope ($t = 0.49$, d.f. $= 55$, $p > 0.6$) and are not displaced from each other ($t = 1.66$, d.f. $= 56$, $p > 0.1$). With hypertonic sucrose the regressions for iguanas ($r = 0.83$, d.f. $= 27$) and for nephrectomized rats ($r = 0.95$, d.f. $= 25$) do not differ in slope ($t = 0.54$, d.f. $= 52$, $p > 0.5$) but they are significantly displaced ($t = 2.75$, d.f. $= 53$, $p < 0.01$) from each other

which were allowed to drink excreted 73% of the salt in a urine volume of 34 ml./kg body wt. At best, assuming isotonic urine, the iguana could only excrete 1.5% of the salt load during the 6 hr experimental period. BENTLEY (1959) measured urine flow in the lizard *Trachysaurus rugosus* (Gray) and also found that excretion of NaCl in hypotonic or hypertonic solution was much slower than in the mammal. Hypertonic saline failed to produce an osmotic diuresis though hypertonic sucrose caused some increase in urine flow. BENTLEY also found that water loads were not excreted as efficiently as in mammals, that extrarenal loss was very small and that the lizard would tolerate extreme hypernatraemia, 230 m-equiv/l. compared with the normal 150 m-equiv/l., without ill effect.

Another indication in the present experiments of how slowly a hypertonic load of saline was excreted is the constancy of the plasma Na over the experimental period of 6 hr once the initial equilibration had taken place (Fig. 3).

It is evident from our own and BENTLEY's results that renal osmoregulation is, at best, extremely slow and the same is true for excretion by the nasal gland. In the short term the only way in which the iguana can deal with an osmotic load is by drinking, which it does with some vigour and deliberation. We were interested in seeing the precision with which the animal adjusted its intake to the osmotic load.

According to the cellular dehydration theory of thirst osmotically effective substances such as hypertonic saline and hypertonic sucrose should

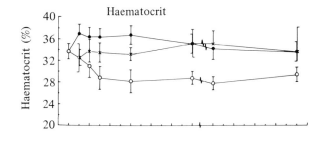

o NaCl
× Glucose
• Sucrose

Haematocrit

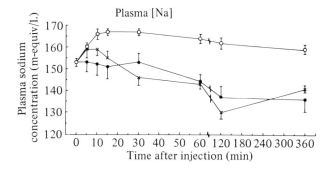

Plasma [Na]

Time after injection (min)

Fig. 3. The haematocrit (%) of iguana blood and the plasma sodium concentration (m-equiv/l.) against time after injection of hypertonic solutions (20 m-osmole/kg body wt.) of NaCl, sucrose and glucose. Vertical bars show mean ± S.E. of mean

be diluted to isotonicity by drinking if excretion of the substance is not possible (FITZSIMONS, 1961; 1971). This may be expressed quantitatively as follows.

The initial plasma osmolality, c, of the iguana was found to be 351.0 ± 9.7 m-osmole/l. (5 observations. Mean value ±S.E. of mean). The solute load, s, was the amount of substance injected expressed in μ-osmoles. and was obtained from the ideal μ-osmoles injected multiplied by the osmotic coefficient appropriate to the final approximate concentration of the body fluids after equilibration of the solute; 0.93 for NaCl, 1.05 for sucrose and 1.0 for glucose and urea. The initial body water, w, was assumed to be 70.8% body wt.; THORSON (1968) reported a mean value of 70.8 ± 0.88 in 7 iguanas. The water load, b, is the change in body wt. after injection; it does not include the volume injected.

The increase in osmolality produced by any water-soluble substance that is not stored in the body or metabolized is given by:

% increase in osmolality =

$$100 \left(\frac{cw + s}{c(w + b)} - 1 \right) \tag{1}$$

In the case of a substance excluded from the cells the cellular dehydration expressed as a percentage of the volume of the dehydrated cell is:

$$100 \cdot \frac{\Delta Vi}{Vi'} = 100 \left(\frac{cw + s}{c(w + b)} - 1 \right) \tag{2}$$

where ΔVi is the change in cellular volume, and Vi' is the dehydrated cellular volume.

By putting percentage increase in osmolality equal to 0 in equation (1), the water load required to restore the body fluids to isotonicity is obtained:

$$b_{iso} = \frac{s}{c} \tag{3}$$

It is also clear from equation (2) that when $b_{exp} = b_{iso}$ there is no residual cellular dehydration.

The responses of the iguana to various doses of the different substances injected, expressed as percentage increases in initial osmolality, are

51

plotted in Fig. 2. It is evident that there is remarkably good agreement between b_{exp} and b_{iso} in the case of the 2 osmotically effective substances, NaCl and sucrose, and no agreement at all in the case of the 2 substances known to penetrate cell walls. The drinking behaviour of the iguana to substances that dehydrate cells closely matches the behaviour of the nephrectomized rat to these substances but differs significantly from that of normal rats. The physiological situations of the iguana and the nephrectomized rat are comparable; both rely exlusively on drinking to restore the cellular water to normal, and both do this with precision. The injected solute is diluted to isotonicity and cellular dehydration thereby eliminated.

An extraordinary feature of this precise intake of fluid is that drinking is completed at a single session in a matter of minutes, presumably before any significant absorption of water into the body fluids can take place. This argues for a quantitative preabsorptive satiety mechanism though whether there is such a mechanism and how it would work are entirely unknown.

A second remarkable thing is that despite the precision of intake it does not seem to matter to the iguana when it drinks. The latencies to drink were long compared with those of the rat, varying between 1/2 hr and 4 hr. When the iguana was denied access to drinking water for 3 hr after hypertonic saline it usually drank within a few minutes of water being restored to the cage, but this was not always so. Under these conditions of delayed access the change in body weight over 6 hr was not significantly different (95 % level) from that in which the iguanas had immediate access to water. There was no obvious reason why drinking should have been so slow in onset after hypertonic saline except that it seems to be a reptilian characteristic to be able to tolerate large imbalances in the internal chemistry for lengthy periods. The fluid shifts as determined by measurement of haematocrit and plasma Na are largely completed within 15 min of injection of hypertonic saline. So the explanation does not lie here, but rather it is in the leisurely behavioural responses to these imbalances (Fig. 3). Ultimately, of course, re-equilibration takes place and is extremely precise in the case of osmoregulation.

Shifts in Body Fluids Following Injection of Hypertonic Solutions

Fluid shifts in the case of injected NaCl were rapid and simply explained. The haematocrit fell steadily and plasma sodium rose showing a rapid uptake of NaCl from the peritoneal cavity resulting in cellular dehydration (Fig. 3). Sucrose appeared to move more slowly out of the peritoneal cavity so that fluid, isotonic to extracellular fluid, was drawn into the cavity causing an initial rise in haematocrit but having no effect on plasma sodium concentration. Later, as sucrose passed into the extracellular space, cellular dehydration occurred as shown by the fall in plasma sodium concentration and the fall in haematocrit (Fig. 3). Plasma sodium concentration also fell considerably when hypertonic glucose was injected (Fig. 3). This would suggest cellular dehydration except that the animals drank very little. However, if brain cells are permeable to glucose (as in mammals) but muscle cells have much lower permeability it is conceivable that, since iguanas are 'animals of very little brain', appreciable cellular dehydration and consequent dilution of plasma sodium might occur without stimulating osmoreceptors in the brain and causing thirst. This hypothesis is supported by the findings of MOBERLEY (1968b) that bursts of activity in the iguana produce no change in the plasma glucose levels or liver glycogen stores but that glycogen reserves in the muscles are anaerobically broken down. Thus there is no need for rapid uptake of glucose into muscle cells. A second piece of supporting evidence is that injections of hypertonic sucrose and glucose have both, on occasion, caused the eyes of iguanas to collapse suggesting severe cellular dehydration. This is not unexpected with sucrose but is very surprising with glucose unless we suppose that it is excluded from cells.

Conclusion

In response to challenges with substances which dehydrate cells, the iguana was found to regulate its body osmolality precisely and efficiently provided it was able to do so by drinking. In this respect the responses of the iguana are similar to those of the nephrectomized rat since, in the short term, both rely exclusively on drinking to restore cellular water to normal.

References

ADOLPH, E. F.: Physiological Regulations. Lancaster Pa.: Jacques Cattell Press 1943.

BENTLEY, P. J.: Studies on the water and electrolyte metabolism of the lizard *Trachysaurus rugosus* (Gray). J. Physiol. Lond. **145**, 37–47 (1959).

— Endocrines and osmoregulation. A comparative account of the regulation of water and salt in vertebrates. Berlin-Heidelberg-New York: Springer 1971.

BENTLEY, P. J., BLUMER, W. F. C.: Uptake of water by the lizard *Moloch horridus*. Nature **194**, 699–700 (1962).

BENTLEY, P. J., SCHMIDT-NIELSEN, K.: Comparison of water exchange in two aquatic turtles *Trionyx spinifer* and *Pseudomys scripta*. Comp. Biochem. Physiol. **32**, 363–365 (1970).

DUNSON, W. A.: Electrolyte excretion by the salt gland of the Galápagos marine iguana. Am. J. Physiol. **216**, 995–1002 (1969).

FITZSIMONS, J. T.: Drinking by nephrectomized rats injected with various substances. J. Physiol. Lond. **155**, 563–579 (1961).

— The physiology of thirst: A review of the extraneural aspects of the mechanism of drinking. Progr. Physiol. Psychol. **4**, 119–201 (1971).

MOBERLEY, W, R.: The metabolic responses of the common iguana, *Iguana iguana*, to walking and diving. Comp. Biochem. Physiol. **27**, 21–32 (1968a).

— The metabolic responses of the common iguana, *Iguana iguana*, to walking and diving. Comp. Biochem. Physiol. **27**, 1–20 (1968b).

MURRISH, D. E., SCHMIDT-NIELSEN, K.: Water transport in the cloaca of lizards: active or passive? Science, **170**, 324–326 (1970).

SCHMIDT-NIELSEN, K., BONIT, A., LEE, P., CRAWFORD, E. C.: Nasal salt excretion and the possible function of the cloaca in water conservation. Science **142**, 1300–1301 (1963).

SWANSON, P. L.: The iguana *Iguana iguana iguana* (L). Herpetologica **6**, 187–193 (1950).

TEMPLETON, J. R.: Nasal salt gland excretion and adjustment to sodium loading in the lizard, *Ctenosaura pecturata*. Copeia 1967 (1), 136–140 (1967).

THORSON, T. B.: Body fluid partitioning in reptilia. Copeia 1968 (3), 592–601 (1968).

Summary of Discussions

KAUFMAN to EPSTEIN: We do not yet know whether the iguana drinks in response to hypovolaemia. It is certainly insensitive to isoprenaline. To PETERS: The plasma sodium rose to a plateau level within 15 min of the intraperitoneal injection of hypertonic saline and remained at this level for at least 6 hr. This is in contrast to the observation made on the desert rodent, *Merio merio Shawii* by HAEFELI and PETERS who found that plasma hyperosmolality following intravenous hypertonic saline was dispelled within 10 min of injection even though drinking was not allowed. To SIMPSON and CHARLEBOIS: It is unknown whether the iguana responds to intracranial angiotensin or whether it possesses a subfornical organ. — SIMPSON: Both the subfornical and subcommissural organs are, however, phylogenetically old circumventricular structures. — CHARLEBOIS: Marked drinking to intraventricular angiotensin has been observed in the dove, *Stretopelia risoria,* in which there is no known analogue of a subfornical organ. — FITZSIMONS: The original experiments implicating the subcommisural organ in water intake have not been confirmed. — KAUFMAN: Blood was collected into heparinized capillary tubes after cutting a claw with a razor blade. Less than 50 μl. was required for haematocrit and serum Na determinations.

Section 5

Catecholaminergic Mechanisms and Peripheral Aspects of the Renin-Angiotensin System in Drinking

Brain Catecholamines and Thirst

E. M. STRICKER and M. J. ZIGMOND

The functional significance of brain catechol-amines has been a popular subject of inquiry since their identification more than 25 years ago. While neuroanatomists and neuropharmacologists have been defining the location and regulation of central catecholamine-containing neurones during this time, other workers were discovering that these fibres were importantly involved in a wide variety of phenomena, including sleep, temperature regulation, and affective disorders. In retrospect, it is unfortunate that we who have been studying water ingestion did not initiate comparable investigations until several years ago because recent developments have indicated that many insights into the neurochemical basis of thirst can be obtained by considering the function of central catecholamine-containing neurones.

The pronounced effects on drinking that can be produced by stimulation or ablation of the ventrolateral hypothalamus has made this neural area a traditional focus in studies of central control mechanisms for drinking behaviour. Whereas initial findings were interpreted in terms of a localized "drinking centre", it has subsequently become clear that the lateral hypothalamic area includes axons of several ascending catecholamine-containing neuronal systems and that lesions there produce severe depletion of catecholamines throughout the telencephalon (UNGERSTEDT, 1971 a). The implications of these findings were clearly expressed in important reports by UNGERSTEDT (1971 c) and by OLTMANS and HARVEY (1972), who were the first to associate profound effects

on ingestive behaviour with an extensive loss of brain catecholamines in the same animals.

Some of the most dramatic and intriguing effects of brain lesions on drinking behaviour can be found after bilateral damage to the lateral hypothalamus. Characteristic features of the lateral hypothalamic syndrome are an initial adipsia (and aphagia) followed by a gradual resumption of ingestive behaviours and maintenance of body weight (TEITELBAUM and EPSTEIN, 1962). There are, however, some curious residual deficits, including prandial drinking and the loss of an immediate drinking response to acute dehydration of the intracellular (EPSTEIN and TEITELBAUM, 1964) or intravascular fluid compartments and to elevated levels of circulating angiotensin (STRICKER, 1973). The three basic questions that can be raised regarding these disturbances of drinking behaviour are first, why do animals stop drinking after brain damage; second, what is the basis for their recovery, and third, why do impairments of thirst remain after apparent recovery? In the present report we will discuss the contribution of brain catecholamines to thirst by considering their function in each of these situations. The proposed explanations also are relevant to the parallel deficits in feeding behaviour that occur after lateral hypothalamic damage.

The Initial Deficits. In accounting for the neurochemical bases of the adipsia and aphagia which follows extensive damage to the lateral hypothalamic area, UNGERSTEDT (1971 c) has emphasized the interruption of a nigrostriatal pathway which traverses the hypothalamus and includes a large dopamine-containing fibre system. He reported that comparable impairments of feeding and drinking behaviour are obtained not only with extra-hypothalamic electrothermal lesions of the nigrostriatal dopamine (DA) bundle, but also with intracerebral injections of 6-hydroxydopamine (6-HDA) along this fibre system (a procedure thought to cause relatively specific degeneration of local catecholamine-containing neurones) (UNGERSTEDT, 1971 c). In support of this hypothesis, we have found that injections of 6-HDA into the cerebral ventricles, which cause widespread depletion of brain catecholamines and considerably less nonspecific damage than any of the above intracerebral treatments, also produce adipsia and aphagia but only when there are severe losses of DA in the corpus striatum (ZIGMOND and STRICKER, 1972). These effects are perhaps most convincing when intraventricular 6-HDA is given after pretreatment with desipramine (which inhibits uptake of 6-HDA into noradrenaline-containing neurones) and pargyline (which inhibits its oxidation by MAO) (STRICKER and ZIGMOND, 1974, 1975), since striatal DA is almost totally depleted by these procedures while telencephalic noradrenaline levels are much less affected than in all other preparations (Table 1).

These results suggest that motivated ingestive behaviour depends on the activity of DA-containing neurones of the nigrostriatal bundle. In this regard, it is interesting to note that intraventricular 6-HDA treatments do not necessarily produce adipsia and aphagia even after striatal DA levels have been depleted by 90% (STRICKER and ZIGMOND, unpublished). Similarly, striatal DA depletions of 75–80% are reported to accompany the appearance of clinical symptoms in patients with Parkinson's disease, a chronic neurological disorder that is associated with degeneration of the DA-containing neurones of the nigrostriatal pathway (HORNYKIEWICZ, 1973). Collectively, these empirical findings suggest that this central catecholamine system can adjust its activity so as to maintain function even after extensive irreversible damage.

Although interruption of the nigrostriatal bundle is apparently sufficient for producing adipsia, it should be noted that drinking also can be abolished by electrolytic lateral hypothalamic lesions causing much less damage to the DA-containing fibre system (OLTMANS and HARVEY, 1972; ZIGMOND and STRICKER, 1973, 1974). There are several ways in which these findings may be interpreted. For example, the critical damage associated with functional deficits may require larger DA depletion after intraventricular 6-HDA injections than after lateral hypothalamic lesions, perhaps because it is more difficult to produce degeneration in this system by destroying all of its diffuse projections (with 6-HDA) than by severing its axons as they course through the ventral diencephalon (with electrolytic lesions). Alternatively, a specific locus of caudate damage may be more significant than the degree of damage to the entire system; thus, more extensive DA depletion after 6-HDA treatment may simply increase the possibility that this site will be damaged, while lateral hypothalamic lesions may interrupt crucial nigrostriatal projections more readily. Finally, it is

Table 1. Effects of various treatments on brain catecholamines and ingestive behaviour

Treatment	Number of Rats	Telencephalic Noradrenaline	Striatal Dopamine	Adipsia & Aphagia
Controls	18	100%	100%	No
LH lesions	5	55%	5%	Yes
6-HDA	16	7%	41%	No
P + 6-HDA	17	4%	6%	Yes
DMI + P + 6-HDA	9	96%	1%	Yes

Rats received bilateral electrolytic lesions of the lateral hypothalamus (LH) or two intraventricular injections (3 days apart) of 200 μg 6-hydroxydopamine (6-HDA) 30 min after intraperitoneal injections of 50 mg/kg pargyline (P), or pargyline plus 25 mg/kg desipramine (DMI). Data are presented as percentage of control values (0.30 μg noradrenaline and 8.60 μg dopamine per gram of fresh brain tissue)

possible that other fibre pathways which are critically involved in mediating thirst might also be damaged by lateral hypothalamic lesions. Because of these uncertainties, it would be premature to make conclusive statements about the role of damage to the nigrostriatal DA bundle in the feeding and drinking deficits after lateral hypothalamic lesions.

Recovery of Function. The lateral hypothalamic syndrome is characterized by the progressive return of ingestive behaviour after its initial disappearance (TEITELBAUM and EPSTEIN, 1962). The same sequence of recovery is observed after rats are made adipsic and aphagic by intraventricular injections of 6-HDA (STRICKER and ZIGMOND, 1974, 1975; ZIGMOND and STRICKER, 1973, 1974). That is, animals invariably eat palatable foods and fluids first, then accept dry chow, and finally drink water (Fig. 1). There also is a gradual recovery from sensorimotor impairment which closely resembles that seen in rats with bilateral electrolytic or 6-HDA-induced lesions of the lateral hypothalamus or other portions of the nigrostriatal bundle. Collectively, these findings suggest that there is a common neurochemical basis for the similar syndromes obtained in these preparations.

If destruction of the nigrostriatal DA system is held responsible for the initial adipsia and aphagia, it may seem paradoxical that ingestive behaviour returns since the catecholamine depletion appears to be permanent. However, it is possible that the resumption of feeding and drinking behaviour results from a functional recovery of the damaged system that is not reflected in the measures of amine level. Consistent with his hypothesis are the findings that rats recovered from electrolytic or biochemical lesions again become aphagic and adipsic after treatment with α-methyl-p-tyrosine (AMT), an inhibitor of catecholamine synthesis (ZIGMOND and STRICKER, 1973, 1974). These results suggest that recovery from the loss of feeding and drinking behaviour after lateral hypothalamic lesions or intraventricular 6-HDA treatment depends on compensatory processes that occur within the damaged catecholamine-containing neuronal system. Since the lesioned rats are much more sensitive to the effects of AMT than are intact control rats (Fig. 2), these findings additionally suggest that an increased catechol-

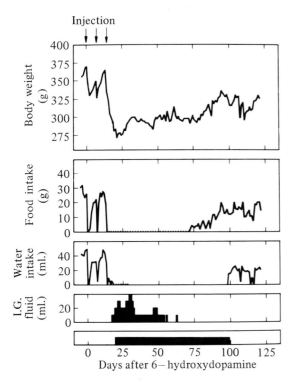

Fig. 1. Food and water intake and body weight of a rat given three intraventricular injections of 200 μg 6-hydroxydopamine each 30 min after pargyline (50 mg/kg i.p.). Intragastric (I.G.) feedings are shown. The bottom line indicates the access to special, highly palatable foods (black bar)

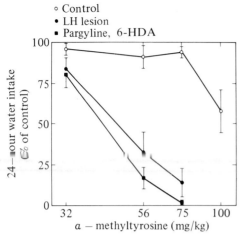

○ Control
● LH lesion
■ Pargyline, 6-HDA

24—hour water intake (% of control)

a — methyltyrosine (mg/kg)

Fig. 2. The effect of α-methyl-p-tyrosine (AMT) on 24 hour water intake in control rats (O) and rats with either bilateral electrolytic lesions of the far lateral aspects of the lateral hypothalamus (LH) (●) or two intraventricular injections of 200 μg 6-hydroxydopamine (6-HDA) given after pretreatments with 50 mg/kg pargyline (■). AMT was given (i.p.) at 8 am, 4 pm and 12 midnight, and water intakes were measured during the 24 hours following the first injection. Each point represents the mean ± the standard deviation of the mean for 4–8 rats (32, 56 and 100 mg/kg doses) or 8–12 rats (75 mg/kg)

amine turnover in the terminals of remaining fibres makes a significant contribution to the recovery of function.

Another compensatory adjustment which apparently occurs within the damaged system is an increase in sensitivity of postsynaptic receptors (UNGERSTEDT, 1971b). To the extent that the recovery of function depends on increased catecholamine turnover and receptor sensitivity, any pretreatment that would facilitate these

processes should hasten recovery. In fact, prior food deprivation (POWLEY and KEESEY, 1970), which should have increased catecholamine synthesis rate and turnover, or pretreatment with AMT (GLICK, GREENSTEIN, and ZIMMERBERG, 1972), which should have increased receptor sensitivity, have both been shown to reduce the time needed for recovery after lateral hypothalamic damage.

The Residual Deficits. Some of the permanent disruptions in thirst and drinking behaviour that are observed in rats, which have apparently recovered from lateral hypothalamic damage also can be obtained following extensive depletion of striatal DA by intraventricular injections of 6-HDA (STRICKER and ZIGMOND, 1974, 1975). For example, after injections of isoprenaline, rats with 90–98% DA depletion drank considerably less water than control rats (Table 2). Isoprenaline produces hypotension and increases renin secretion. The DA depleted rats also drank less water during the first 6 hr after treatment with a hyperoncotic solution of polyethylene glycol (PG) (Table 2). PG produces a progressive loss of plasma fluid from the circulation and thereby stimulates renin secretion. However, as with rats that have apparently recovered from hypothalamic damage, (STRICKER, 1973), extended observations indicated that thirst during hypovolaemia was delayed rather than permanently depressed. These effects could reflect the disruption of central sympathetic pathways that are involved in renin secretion, since long delays in the drinking response following hypertonic saline solution (which would not stimulate renin secretion) are observed only occasionally in the same animals

Table 2. Mean water intake (in ml.) by rats after various treatments

Treatment	Number of Rats	1M NaCl	Isoprenaline	20% PG
Controls	5–18	15.8	15.9	7.6
LH lesions	5	0.1*	0.1*	0.3*
6-HDA	5–16	15.0	12.4	6.5
P + 6-HDA	10–17	16.7	10.5	2.9*
DMI + P + 6-HDA	9	14.3	5.3*	4.8*

Treatments as in Table 1. Data refer to water intake during the first 3 hr after injections of 5 ml. 1 M NaCl (I.P.) or 0.33 mg/kg isoprenaline (s.c.), or during the first 6 hr after injection of 5 ml. 20% polyethylene glycol (PG) solution (s.c.). * = $p < 0.001$ in comparison with control animals

(Table 2). On the other hand, it is also possible that the differential effects reflect the inability of rats to withstand the more severe stress of hypovolaemia and hypotension after central sympathectomy. A sensitivity to stress could also explain the failure to increase food intake following acute cellular glucopenia that is observed in rats following lateral hypothalamic lesions (EPSTEIN and TEITELBAUM, 1967) or intraventricular 6-HDA (ZIGMOND and STRICKER, 1972).

If the recovery process depends on changes within catecholamine-containing neurones remaining in the damaged system (ZIGMOND and STRICKER, 1973, 1974), the residual deficits seen in the recovered animal may be a consequence of the inability of this repaired system to respond adequately to stimuli for ingestive behaviour. For example, such stimuli might increase activity in the remaining neurones so that catecholamine synthesis could not increase rapidly enough to keep up with turnover. The resultant decrease in receptor stimulation might then re-establish the severe deficits in feeding and drinking behaviour which characterized earlier stages of recovery. This decreased receptor stimulation would persist until rates of synthesis could increase sufficiently to support the catecholamine turnover necessary for ingestive behaviour to reappear (or until the initiating excitatory stimulus was removed). In other words, damage to catecholamine-containing neurones may not disrupt specific regulatory systems in the animals but may instead affect their general ability to behave appropriately after the abrupt onset of large nutritional needs (much like the sensitivity to stress of animals after peripheral sympathectomy).

In contrast to the rat that has apparently recovered from lateral hypothalamic damage or to the desalivate rat, rats given intraventricular injections of 6-HDA, which result in extensive depletion of striatal DA, feed efficiently (i.e. do not waste unusual amounts of food, as crumbs) when maintained on dry food pellets and drink considerable amounts of water during food deprivation (STRICKER and ZIGMOND, 1974, 1975). These results indicate that disruption of the nigrostriatal pathway does not disturb reflex salivary secretion during feeding nor does it interfere with the ability of rats to ingest dry food. Furthermore, rats treated with 6-HDA show normal thermoregulation by salivary evaporative cooling during heat stress (STRICKER and ZIGMOND, 1974, 1975). Thus, the impaired reflex salivary secretions to food or thermal stimuli after lateral hypothalamic lesions may be due to an interruption of descending fibres (not containing catecholamines) from more rostral structures to the salivary motor nuclei in the lower brain stem.

Summary and Discussion

As with lateral hypothalamic lesions, aphagia and adipsia can be produced in rats by intraventricular injections of 6-HDA or extrahypothalamic lesions of the nigrostriatal bundle. In each of these preparations there are severe losses of DA in the corpus striatum. These results suggest that the dramatic disappearance of all ingestive behaviour after lateral hypothalamic lesions may be due, in part, to transection of the ascending DA-containing neurones of the nigrostriatal bundle as they course through the diencephalon, as UNGERSTEDT (1971c) first suggested.

Recovery of function after electrolytic or biochemical lesions often occurs despite permanent depletion of brain catecholamines. In each preparation, the resumption of ingestive behaviour may represent a recovery from the broad impairment that caused the initial aphagia and adipsia. For example, the gradual reappearance of water drinking may reflect an increasing capability and willingness on the part of the lesioned rats to take water from a drinking tube as they re-acquire the sensory and motor skills necessary to locate and lap it accurately at its source. Increased synaptic transmission in remaining DA-containing neurones within the damaged system, due (in part) to increased DA synthesis and turnover plus supersensitivity of the postsynaptic receptor to DA, appears to provide the basis for this recovery of function.

The behavioural syndromes produced by lateral hypothalamic lesions and intraventricular 6-HDA treatments are similar, but not identical, and differences between the two preparations can provide some clarification of the relationship between the initial events of aphagia and adipsia following lateral hypothalamic damage, the immutable recovery sequence, and the permanent deficits of recovered animals. It seems unlikely that the gradual recovery of feeding on dry food pellets is a consequence of the disturbed salivary reflexes of rats with lateral hypothalamic damage, since rats with severe depletion of striatal DA after intraventricular 6-HDA injections show the same gradual recovery of feeding behaviour, yet do not show inefficient feeding, impaired thermoregulation during heat stress, or other disruptions of salivary secretion. It also seems unlikely that the delayed reappearance of water drinking after prolonged adipsia is a consequence of the permanent deficits in thirst of the recovered lateral hypothalamic lesioned rat, since many rats with severe depletion of striatal DA after intraventricular 6-HDA show the same gradual recovery of drinking behaviour yet drink normally to the three primary dipsogenic stimuli.

The residual deficits seen in both groups of rats following apparent recovery may reflect the fact that the repaired system is no longer able to respond adequately to abrupt large stimuli for ingestive behaviour. As such, the observed deficits in drinking (and feeding) may not be specific to a particular regulatory system but simply reflect the general inability of rats to withstand severe stress following central sympathectomy. From this perspective, it is no longer paradoxical that their ingestive behaviour is appropriate during *ad libitum* access to food and water, when the development of nutritional needs is more gradual and limited.

A direct involvement of brain catecholamines in specific drinking behaviour has been proposed recently by Fitzsimons and Setler (1971), on the basis of their finding that drinking elicited by angiotensin administered into the preoptic region is abolished by prior injection of 6-HDA or haloperidol (a drug which appears to block dopamine receptors) through the same cannula. However, it should be noted that the dipsogenic effects of angiotensin administered intraventricularly also have been markedly reduced by prior intraventricular injections of atropine, a peripheral cholinergic receptor blocking agent (Se-

vers, Summy-Long, Taylor, and Connor, 1970), or phentolamine (Severs, Summy-Long, Daniels-Severs and Connor, 1971). Thus the specific involvement of central dopamine neurones in angiotensin-induced thirst may be questioned. Furthermore, since a single intraventricular injection of 200 μg 6-HDA in rats does not alter the drinking induced by isoprenaline or PG solutions but abolishes the drinking induced by angiotensin administered intraventricularly (Table 3), one wonders whether the stimulation of thirst by intracranial angiotensin involves activation of the same neural systems that mediate thirst during hypovolaemia or systemic hypotension.

Table 3. Effects of intraventricular 6-hydroxydopamine on water intake (ml.) elicited by various treatments

Treatment	Controls (n = 5)	6-HDA (n = 5)
angiotensin	8.9	0.7*
10% PG	4.8	4.2
isoprenaline	9.5	8.3

Rats received a single intraventricular injection of 200 μg 6-hydroxydopamine (6-HDA) or the vehicle solution (controls). In subsequent weeks they were given separate injections of 0.5 μg angiotensin (intraventricularly, 1 hr drinking test), 5 ml. 10% polyethylene glycol (PG) solution (s.c., 6 hr drinking test), and 0.11 mg/kg isoprenaline (s.c., 3 hr drinking test). * = $p < 0.001$ in comparison with control animals

Finally, it should be recognized that extensive damage to the DA-containing neurones of the nigrostriatal bundle disrupts a much wider range of activities than ingestive behaviour (e.g. mating and maternal behaviour, avoidance of punishment). It is, therefore, probable that in addition to its extrapyramidal motor functions, this neural system is not merely involved in hunger and thirst but participates in motivation more generally, perhaps by mediating a central component of the "arousal" that is common to all motivated behaviour. To the extent that this is true, other neural systems must be sought to explain the mechanisms by which specific drives are expressed.

Acknowledgement. Research described in this report was supported, in part, by NIH grant MH-20620 and NSF grant GB-28830.

References

EPSTEIN, A. N., TEITELBAUM, P.: Severe and persistent deficits in thirst produced by lateral hypothalamic damage. In: Thirst in the regulation of body water (ed. M. J. WAYNER), pp. 395–406. Oxford: Pergamon Press 1964.
— Specific loss of the hypoglycemic control of feeding in recovered lateral rats. Am. J. Physiol. **213**, 1159–1167 (1967).

FITZSIMONS, J. T., SETLER, P.: Catecholaminergic mechanisms in angiotensin-induced drinking. J. Physiol. Lond. **218**, 43 P–44 P (1971).

GLICK, S. D., GREENSTEIN, S., ZIMMERBERG, B.: Facilitation of recovery by α-methyl-p-tyrosine after lateral hypothalamic damage. Science **177**, 534–535 (1972).

HORNYKIEWICZ, O.: Parkinson's disease: from brain homogenate to treatment. Fed. Proc. **32**, 183–190 (1973).

OLTMANS, G. A., HARVEY, J. A.: LH syndrome and brain catecholamine levels after lesions of the nigrostriatal bundle. Physiol. Behav. **8**, 69–78 (1972).

POWLEY, T. L., KEESEY, R. E.: Relationship of body weight to the lateral hypothalamic feeding syndrome. J. comp. physiol. Psychol. **70**, 25–36 (1970).

SEVERS, W. B., SUMMY-LONG, J., TAYLOR, J. S., CONNOR, J. D.: A central effect of angiotensin: release of pituitary pressor material. J. Pharm. exp. Ther. **174**, 27–33 (1970).

SEVERS, W. B., SUMMY-LONG, J., DANIELS-SEVERS, A., CONNOR, J. D.: Influence of adrenergic blocking drugs on central angiotensin effects. Pharmacol. **5**, 205–214 (1971).

STRICKER, E. M.: Thirst, sodium appetite, and complementary physiological contributions to the regulation of intravascular fluid volume. In: The neuropsychology of thirst (Eds. A. N. EPSTEIN, H. R. KISSILEFF, E. STELLAR), pp. 73–98. Washington, D.C.: V. H. Winston and Sons, Inc. 1973.

STRICKER, E. M., ZIGMOND, M. J.: Effects on homeostasis of intraventricular injection of 6-hydroxydopamine in rats. J. comp. physiol. Psychol. **86**, 973–994 (1974).
— Recovery of function following damage to central catecholamine-containing neurons: A neurochemical model for the lateral hypothalamic syndrome. In: Progress in psychobiology and physiological psychology, vol. 6 (Eds. J. M. SPRAGUE, A. N. EPSTEIN). New York: Academic Press, 1975.

TEITELBAUM, P., EPSTEIN, A. N.: The lateral hypothalamic syndrome: Recovery of feeding and drinking after lateral hypothalamic lesions. Psychol. Rev. **69**, 74–90 (1962).

UNGERSTEDT, U.: Stereotaxic mapping of the monoamine pathways in the rat brain. Acta Physiol. Scand. **Suppl. 367**, 1–48 (1971a).
— Postsynaptic supersensitivity after 6-hydroxydopamine induced degeneration of the nigro-striatal dopamine system. Acta Physiol. Scand. **Suppl. 367**, 69–93 (1971b).
— Adipsia and aphagia after 6-hydroxydopamine induced degeneration of the nigro-striatal dopamine system. Acta Physiol. Scand. **Suppl. 367**, 95–122 (1971c).

ZIGMOND, M. J., STRICKER, E. M.: Deficits in feeding behavior after intraventricular injection of 6-hydroxydopamine in rats. Science **177**, 1211–1214 (1972).
— Recovery of feeding and drinking by rats after intraventricular 6-hydroxydopamine or lateral hypothalamic lesions. Science **182**, 717–720 (1973).
— Ingestive behavior following damage to central dopamine neurons: Implications for homeostasis and recovery of function. In: Neuropsychopharmacology of monoamines and their regulatory enzymes (Ed. E. USDIN), pp. 385–402. New York: Raven Press, 1974.

Noradrenergic and Dopaminergic Influences on Thirst

P. E. SETLER

Two opposing roles have been proposed for central adrenergic neurones in the control of drinking, facilitatory and inhibitory. Although neither role has been established firmly, experimental evidence exists in support of each. Various pharmacological alterations of adrenergic function and different experimental conditions tend to differentially emphasize one or the other role.

An inhibitory control of drinking by noradrenergic neurones was proposed by GROSSMAN (1962) based on the observation that implantation of crystals of noradrenaline into the perifornical area of the hypothalamus of rats suppressed drinking in response to overnight deprivation of water. When implanted in the brains of satiated rats noradrenaline caused eating.

Similar effects may be obtained by injection of noradrenaline into the preoptic area anterior to the hypothalamus. At this site the antidipsogenic effect appears to be specifically noradrenergic; the effects of noradrenaline are not mimicked by either dopamine or isoprenaline.

Following overnight deprivation of water during which food was freely available, rats were placed in individual metabolism cages. Through a cannula stereotaxically placed in the preoptic area at least one week earlier each rat was injected with 1 μl. of a solution of noradrenaline bitartrate, dopamine hydrochloride or isoprenaline hydrochloride in 0.9% NaCl containing 1 μg/μl. of ascorbic acid. Five min later, access to water was permitted and water intake recorded hourly for 3 hr. Drug treatments were randomly

assigned and each animal also served as an uninjected control. The effects of the three catecholamines on water intake during the first hr are shown in Fig. 1. Significant attenuation of drinking was produced by doses of 32.5 and 65.0 n-moles of noradrenaline. Inhibition was observed within the first 15 min although the latency of drinking was unchanged. The maximal effect was seen in the first hr after injection. Equimolar doses of dopamine and of isopren-

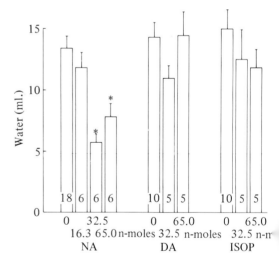

Fig. 1. The effects of noradrenaline (NA), dopamine (DA) and isoprenaline (ISOP), given into the preoptic area of rats on drinking in response to overnight deprivation of water. The test period was 1 hr. Numbers within bars indicate the numbers of rats tested; vertical lines above bars represent the standard error of the mean. * = $p < 0.05$; significantly different from control

62

aline had no effect on the amount of water drunk in this experiment.

The antidipsogenic effect of noradrenaline was attenuated by injection into the preoptic area, prior to noradrenaline, of 5 to 10 μg of the α-adrenergic antagonist phentolamine or of the β-adrenergic antagonist sotalol. Phentolamine was the more effective of the two antagonists in this regard.

When given without noradrenaline, phentolamine or sotalol each produced a slight reduction of water intake, never an increase.

Inhibition of the antidipsogenic effect of exogenous noradrenaline by specific adrenergic antagonists suggests that this effect may be mediated by a direct action of noradrenaline on adrenergic receptors within diffusion distance of the preoptic area; although the nature (α or β) of the receptor is inadequately defined by this experiment.

If the antidipsogenic effect of noradrenaline is a direct effect on adrenergic receptors, the effectiveness of noradrenaline as an inhibitor of drinking should be increased after the induction of receptor supersensitivity by denervation. It is possible to produce selective denervation of catecholamine receptors by means of 6-hydroxydopamine-induced lesions of catecholamine-containing neurones. Following active uptake into catecholamine neurones, 6-hydroxydopamine causes intraneuronal destruction and degeneration (THOENEN and TRANZER, 1968; BLOOM, ALGERI, GROPPETTI, REVUELTA, and COSTA, 1969; URETSKY and IVERSEN, 1970).

UNGERSTEDT (1971a) has demonstrated supersensitivity of dopamine receptors in the corpus striatum to dopamine-receptor stimulants after 6-hydroxydopamine-induced destruction of catecholamine-containing nigro-striatal neurones.

We attempted to demonstrate supersensitivity of noradrenergic receptors following partial depletion of brain catecholamines by 6-hydroxydopamine given intraventricularly to rats. Prior to the administration of 6-hydroxydopamine the effects of intraventricular injection of noradrenaline on ingestive behaviour were tested in two experimental situations. The antidipsogenic effect of noradrenaline was studied after water deprivation as described above except that

noradrenaline was given into the lateral ventricle in a volume of 5 μl. The stimulatory effect of noradrenaline on food and water intake was studied in the same rats after they had continuous access to food and water for at least 36 hr and were considered to be satiated at the time of testing. After injection of noradrenaline through the ventricular cannula each rat was permitted access to water and powdered rat food. At the end of 1 hr food and water intake were recorded.

After the effects of noradrenaline were established each rat was given two injections of 6-hydroxydopamine, 2 days apart. The dose of 6-hydroxydopamine given each time was 250 μg in 20 μl. of ascorbic acid-saline. During the following week the rats were observed but not tested. Except for very slight seizures immediately following the injection of 6-hydroxydopamine there was no overt change in the behaviour of the treated rats. Although complete aphagia and adipsia did not occur, all animals lost weight (mean loss = 12.5 g) after 6-hydroxydopamine but returned to control weight (mean body weight = 310 g) within 3 days after the second injection of 6-hydroxydopamine.

Seven days after the second dose of 6-hydroxydopamine the effects of noradrenaline on

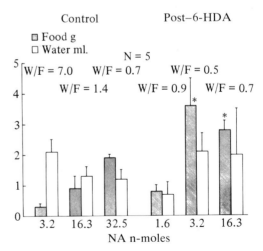

Fig. 2. The effects of noradrenaline (NA) given into the lateral ventricle on the food and water intake of satiated rats. The test period was 1 hr. The rats were tested before and seven or more days after treatment with 500 μg (2 × 250 μg intraventricularly) of 6-hydroxydopamine (6-HDA). W/F = mean water intake – mean food intake * = $p < 0.05$

food and water intake were tested once again. The experiments were performed in random order.

Fig. 2 shows the effects of noradrenaline on food and water intake in satiated rats before and after 6-hydroxydopamine. In the control experiments the amount of food eaten varied directly with the dose of noradrenaline, but there was no correlation between the dose of noradrenaline and the amount of water drunk. The ratio of mean water intake to mean food intake (W/F) varied inversely with dose.

Following 6-hydroxydopamine treatment the amount of food eaten in response to 3.2 and 16.3 n-moles of noradrenaline was significantly increased. The amount of water drunk after these doses was not significantly altered and thus the water to food ratio decreased. In the control experiments 3 out of 5 rats ate after 3.2 n-moles of noradrenaline and 4 out of 5 rats ate after 16.3 n-moles. After 6-hydroxydopamine all rats ate in response to 1.6 n-moles of noradrenaline, indicating that the absolute threshold of the response had decreased as the effectiveness of suprathreshold doses increased.

We may conclude that 6-hydroxydopamine-treated rats developed supersensitivity to the facilitatory effects of exogenous noradrenaline on eating. No such conclusions may be drawn in regard to the facilitatory effect of noradrenaline on drinking. In intact as well as treated rats, the interpretation of the effects of noradrenaline on water intake under these experimental conditions is complicated by the fact that the rats were eating varying amounts of dry food. Before 6-hydroxydopamine treatment there was no simple relationship between the dose of noradrenaline and the amount of water drunk, also, the threshold for the drinking responses to noradrenaline was not determined. These factors preclude interpretation of the dipsogenic effect of noradrenaline after 6-hydroxydopamine.

The effect of 6-hydroxydopamine-induced depletion of catecholamines on the antidipsogenic effect of noradrenaline is shown in Fig. 3. After 6-hydroxydopamine 3 out of 5 rats drank more water in response to deprivation than they had in previous deprivation experiments, but the mean control value was not significantly differ-

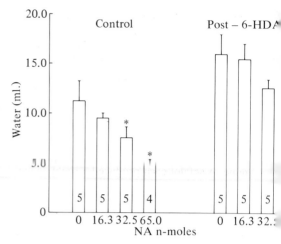

Fig. 3. The effects of noradrenaline (NA) given into the lateral ventricle on drinking in response to overnight deprivation of water. The test period was 1 hr. The rats were tested before and seven or more days after treatment with 500 μg (2 $\times$ 250 μg intraventricularly) of 6-hydroxydopamine (6-HDA) * = $p < 0.05$

ent before and after 6-hydroxydopamine. It is important to recognize that the rat's ability to respond to the dipsogenic challenge of water deprivation was not impaired after 6-hydroxydopamine. Prior to treatment with 6-hydroxydopamine, the drinking response of these rats to overnight deprivation of water was significantly reduced by injection into the lateral ventricle of 32.5 and 65.0 n-moles of noradrenaline; 16.3 n-moles produced a slight, but not significant, reduction. There was no increase in the antidipsogenic effectiveness of noradrenaline after 6-hydroxydopamine nor was there a decrease in the threshold of the effect. After 6-hydroxydopamine neither 16.3 nor 32.5 n-moles of noradrenaline effectively reduced water intake but the percent reduction in water intake produced by 32.5 n-moles of noradrenaline was not significantly different from that produced by the same dose before 6-hydroxydopamine.

In spite of the development of receptor supersensitivity to noradrenaline as demonstrated by potentiation of the eating response to noradrenaline after 6-hydroxydopamine, there was no evidence of supersensitivity to the antidipsogenic effect of noradrenaline. Therefore these two effects of noradrenaline, inhibition of drinking and facilitation of eating do not appear to be mediated by the same receptors. Failure to demonstrate denervation supersensitivity to the antidipsogenic effect of noradrenaline suggests, in fact, that this effect may not be due to a direct effect of exogenous noradrenaline on adrenergic receptors. Biochemical assay of the brains of the 6-hydroxydopamine-treated rats (method of COSTA, SPANO, GROPPETTI, ALGERI, and NEFF, 1968) showed that whole brain noradrenaline was depleted by 68.4% as compared to operated sham-injected controls, and dopamine was depleted by 37.3%.

Depletion of catecholamines probably was not uniform throughout the brain, and the possibility exists that the remaining noradrenaline neurones included a sufficient innervation of the receptors which mediate the antidipsogenic effect of noradrenaline to prevent development of supersensitivity of these receptors. This is unlikely to be the sole explanation because both noradrenaline and 6-hydroxydopamine were given via the same cannulae, at similar concentrations and 6-hydroxydopamine was given in a larger volume. Under these circumstances it might be hoped that 6-hydroxydopamine would diffuse to all areas reached by injected noradrenaline.

In a slightly different experimental approach to the same problem, the effects of acute reduction of noradrenaline levels in the brain on drinking in response to deprivation of water and eating in response to deprivation of food was studied using a dopamine β-hydroxylase inhibitor.

The major biosynthetic pathway for brain catecholamines is shown in Fig. 4. The conversion of dopamine to noradrenaline is catalyzed by the enzyme dopamine β-hydroxylase; this enzyme is selectively inhibited and noradrenaline synthesis reduced by FLA-63 [bis-(4-methyl-1-homopiperazinylthiocarbonyl)-disulfide] (SVENSSON and WALDECK, 1969; CORRODI, FUXE, HAMBERGER, and LJUNGDAHL, 1970). From two to eight hr after intraperitoneal administration of 25 mg/kg of FLA-63 whole brain noradrenaline content was markedly reduced while the dopamine content remained unchanged (CORRODI et al., 1970).

In our experiments, FLA-63 was used to acutely reduce the brain noradrenaline content of hungry or thirsty rats prior to allowing the animals access to food and/or water. The rats were deprived of food or water overnight then placed in individual cages provided with water and also, in the case of food-deprived rats, with powdered food. The animals were permitted to remain in these cages for 10 min to become familiar with the location of the drinking spout and food cup. During this period the water deprived rats drank an average of 3.5 ml.; the food deprived rats did not drink and ate an average of 0.9 g. Following this brief period of

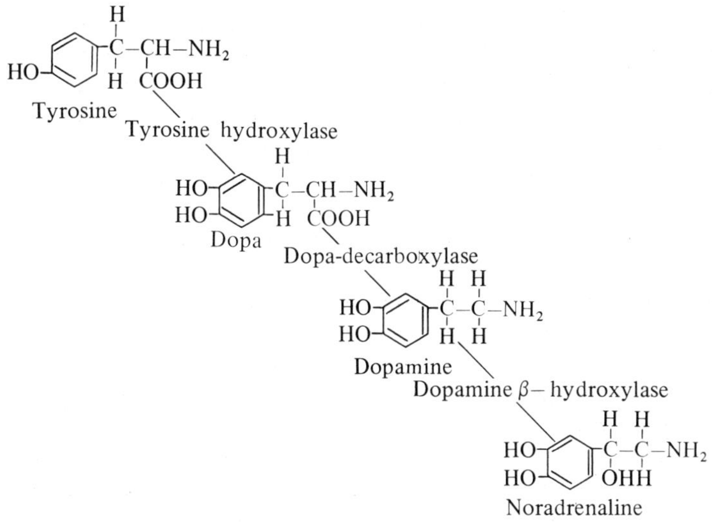

Fig. 4. The biosynthetic pathway for catecholamines

orientation the rats were randomly assigned to drug groups, and given either 25 mg/kg of FLA-63 I.P. or an equal volume of 0.9% saline I.P., the animals were then returned to their cages where they remained without food or water for $4^{1}/_{2}$ hr. At the end of this period, i.e. $4^{1}/_{2}$ hr after FLA-63, the rats were given either 100 mg/kg of levodopa I.P. or an equal volume of saline. 30 min later (5 hr after FLA-63) the rats were permitted access, for 1 hr, to food and water if deprived of food overnight or only to water if deprived of water overnight. The results of this experiment are illustrated in Fig. 5.

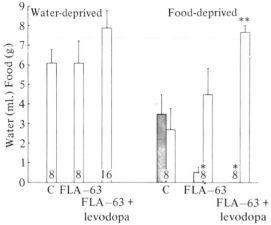

Fig. 5. The effects of FLA-63 (an inhibitor of dopamine β-hydroxylase) and the combination of FLA-63 plus levodopa on drinking in response to overnight deprivation of water and on eating and drinking in response to overnight deprivation of food. FLA-63 (25 mg/kg) was given I.P. 5 hr prior to testing; levodopa (100 mg/kg) was given I.P. 1/2 hr prior to testing. The test period was 1 hr. * = significantly different from control $p < 0.05$; ** = significantly different from control $p < 0.05$ and significantly different from FLA-63 $p < 0.05$. White columns: water intake. Black columns: food

FLA-63 had no effect on the drinking response to water deprivation; the combination of FLA-63 and levodopa caused a slight, but not statistically significant increase in drinking. In contrast, FLA-63 produced a marked decrease in food intake and an insignificant increase in water intake with a consequent increase in the water to food ratio (W/F). The effect of FLA-63 + levodopa was qualitatively the same but greater in magnitude and the amount of water

drunk by rats given this combination was significantly greater than the amount drunk by control rats or the rats given FLA-63 alone.

Brains from four rats from each group were assayed for catecholamine levels. Whole brain noradrenaline was reduced by 80% and dopamine increased by 8% in FLA-63 treated rats; in the rats which received FLA-63 + levodopa brain noradrenaline was reduced by 86% from control levels and dopamine was increased by 55%.

Partial depletion of brain noradrenaline neither inhibited nor facilitated drinking in response to water deprivation. Rats with an elevation of brain dopamine as well as a reduction in brain noradrenaline drank slightly in excess of the controls. Rats with a partial depletion of brain noradrenaline with or without elevation of brain dopamine failed to respond to the challenge of food deprivation. The volume of water drunk by these rats was inappropriate in view of the very small amount of food eaten and must be viewed as the result of a direct stimulatory effect of catecholamines on drinking in this experiment.

Recent evidence suggests that FLA-63 not only inhibits conversion of dopamine to noradrenaline with a subsequent decrease in the release of noradrenaline but that FLA-63 also increases the release of dopamine (ANDEN, ATACK, and SVENSSON, 1973). Injection of levodopa favours an even greater release of dopamine in FLA-63 treated rats. Therefore the increases in water intake in our experiment occurred under conditions of decreased noradrenaline release and increased release of dopamine; the greater the expected release of dopamine the more water was drunk.

These two series of experiments have failed to provide any evidence to support an inhibitory role of central noradrenergic neurones in the control of drinking. This is consistent with several other lines of evidence — electrolytic or biochemical lesions of the brain which produce marked regional or whole brain depletions of noradrenaline (and dopamine), usually decrease water intake in response to most dipsogenic stimuli and may cause adipsia (and aphagia) (FITZSIMONS and SETLER, 1971; SMITH, STROHMAYER, and REIS, 1972; UNGERSTEDT, 1971 b).

66

Injection of adrenergic antagonists into the brain has no significant effect on drinking in response to various dipsogenic stimuli. The bulk of the experimental evidence supports a purely facilitatory role for catecholamines in the control of drinking. The only evidence which supports an antidipsogenic role for noradrenaline is the inhibition of drinking caused by direct injection of noradrenaline into the brain or cerebral ventricle of thirsty rats. This may be a pharmacological artifact caused by interference with cholinergic neurotransmission in the brain by high concentrations of noradrenaline.

Injection of noradrenaline into the preoptic area inhibits drinking in response to some, but not all, dipsogenic stimuli. Drinking in response to water deprivation is inhibited, as discussed above, and also drinking in response to intraperitoneal injection of hypertonic saline, a stimulant of cellular thirst mechanisms. This is illustrated in Fig. 6. Administration of 32.5 n-moles of noradrenaline into the preoptic area immediately before intraperitoneal injection of 2 ml. of 2 M-NaCl, significantly inhibited drinking. The drinking response to intraperitoneal injection of 2 ml. of polyethylene glycol (50% W/W) or subcutaneous injection of isoprenaline (50 μg/kg) both of which activate extracellular thirst mechanisms (FITZSIMONS, 1961; HOUPT and EPSTEIN, 1971) were unaffected. Angiotensin-induced drinking is also related to extracellular thirst (FITZSIMONS, 1969) and is not inhibited by noradrenaline, as shown in Fig. 6. Drinking in response to extracellular thirst is thought not to involve cholinergic pathways (FITZSIMONS and SETLER, 1971; SETLER, 1973) whereas cellular thirst is probably mediated by cholinergic mechanisms (GIARDINA and FISHER, 1971). Noradrenaline thus appears to inhibit drinking only in response to dipsogenic stimuli (including water deprivation, a complex thirst stimulus) which depend at least in part on cholinergic systems. This may be due to interference by noradrenaline at cholinergic receptor sites as shown by the fact that noradrenaline effectively reduces drinking in response to direct injection of carbachol into the preoptic area (Fig. 6).

The inability of rats with acute noradrenaline depletion induced by FLA-63 to respond appropriately to food deprivation is a contribution to

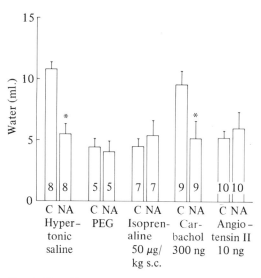

Fig. 6. The effect of 32.5 n-moles of noradrenaline given into the preoptic area on drinking in response to a variety of dipsogens: hypertonic saline (2 ml. 2 M NaCl I.P.), PEG (polyethylene glycol, 50% w/w, 2 ml. I.P.), isoprenaline (50 μg/kg, s.c.), carbachol (300 ng given into the preoptic area), angiotensin II (10 ng, given into the preoptic area). The test period was 1 hr * = p<0.05

the long list of experimental proofs of the importance of central noradrenergic neuronal mechanisms in the control of eating. These results do not suggest any facilitatory role of dopamine in the control of eating since dopamine levels were normal (or elevated) and dopamine release was increased during the period when eating was suppressed. In the animals with an increase in release of endogenous dopamine, water intake was also increased, a very significant phenomenon in view of the theory that dopamine may mediate drinking in response to extracellular thirst or, at least, in response to angiotensin (FITZSIMONS and SETLER, 1971; SETLER, 1973).

The results of the experiments discussed in this chapter emphasize the facilitatory role of catecholamines in the control of the ingestive behaviours of eating and drinking. The results do not, however, suggest a common involvement of catecholamines in the control of the two behaviours; not only does the principal catecholamine stimulating each behaviour appear to be different, but the functions of the catecholaminergic synapses within the neural network controlling each behaviour are apparently different as well.

As recently proposed by Smith (1973) the noradrenergic synapses participating in the control of eating may be "command" synapses whereas catecholaminergic (dopaminergic?) neurones participating with cholinergic neurones and angiotensin of peripheral and/or central origin in the control of drinking must have a qualitatively different, perhaps more subtle, function.

Acknowledgements. This work was partially supported by a grant from the Medical Research Council to J. T. Fitzsimons. The author wishes to thank Dr. J. T. Fitzsimons for advice and assistance and A. Cattell, P. Silimperi, and P. Thomas for assistance in the eating and drinking experiments. Brain catecholamine assays were performed by V. Hackney and W. Stack.

References

Anden, N. E., Atack. C. V., Svensson, T. H.: Release of dopamine from central noradrenaline and dopamine nerves induced by a dopamine-β-hydroxylase inhibitor. J. neural Tr. **34**, 93–100 (1973).

Bloom, F. E., Algeri, S., Groppetti, A., Revuelta, A., Costa, E.: Lesions of central norepinephrine terminals with 6-OH-dopamine: biochemistry and fine structure. Science **166**, 1284–1286 (1969).

Corrodi, H., Fuxe, K., Hamberger, B., Ljungdahl, A.: Studies on central and peripheral noradrenaline neurons using a new dopamine-β-hydroxylase inhibitor. Europ. J. Pharmacol. **12**, 145–155 (1970).

Costa, E., Spano, P.F., Groppetti, A., Algeri, S. Neff, N.: Simultaneous determination of tryptophan, tyrosine, catecholamine and serotonin specific activity in rat brain. Atti. Accad. Med. Lombarda **23**, 1100–1104 (1968).

Fitzsimons, J. T.: Drinking by rats depleted of body fluid without increase in osmotic pressure. J. Physiol. Lond. **159**, 297–309 (1961).

— The role of a renal thirst factor in drinking induced by extracellular stimuli. J. Physiol. Lond. **201**, 349–368 (1969).

Fitzsimons, J. T., Setler, P. E.: Catecholaminergic mechanisms in angiotensin-induced drinking. J. Physiol. Lond. **218**, 43P–44P (1971).

Giardina, A. R., Fisher, A. E.: Effects of atropine on drinking induced by carbachol, angiotensin and isoproterenol. Physiol, Behav. **7**, 653–655 (1971).

Grossman, S. P.: Direct adrenergic and cholinergic stimulation of hypothalamic mechanisms. Am. J. Physiol. **202**, 872–882 (1962).

Houpt, K. A., Epstein, A. N.: The complete dependence of beta-adrenergic drinking on the renal dipsogen. Physiol. Behav. **7**, 897–902 (1971).

Setler, P. E.: The role of catecholamines in thirst. In: Neuropsychology of thirst (Eds. A. N. Epstein, H. R. Kissileff, E. Stellar), pp. 279–291. Washington, D.C.: Winston and Sons 1973.

Smith, G. P.: Introduction to neuropharmacology of thirst. In: Neuropsychology of thirst (Eds. A. N. Epstein, H. R. Kissileff, and E. Stellar), pp. 231–241. Washington, D.C.: V. H. Winston and Sons 1973.

Smith, G. P., Strohmayer, A. J., Reis, D. J.: Effect of lateral hypothalamic injections of 6-hydroxydopamine on food and water intake in rats. Nature New Biology **235**, 27–29 (1972).

Svensson, H., Waldeck, B.: On the significance of central noradrenaline for motor acitivity: Experiments with a new dopamine-β-hydroxylase inhibitor. Europ. J. Pharmacol. **7**, 278–282 (1969).

Thoenen, H., Tranzer, J. P.: Chemical sympathectomy by selective destruction of adrenergic nerve endings with 6-hydroxydopamine. Naunyn-Schmiedeberg's Arch. exp. Path. Pharmak. **261**, 271–288 (1968).

Ungerstedt, U.: Postsynaptic supersensitivity after 6-hydroxydopamine induced degeneration of the nigro-striatal dopamine system. Acta physiol. Scand. **Suppl. 367**, 69–95 (1971a).

— Adipsia and aphagia after 6-hydroxydopamine induced degeneration of the nigro-striatal dopamine system. Acta physiol. Scand. **Suppl. 367**, 95–122 (1971b).

Uretsky, N. J., Iversen, L. L.: Effects of 6-hydroxydopamine on catecholamine containing neurons in the rat brain. J. Neurochem. **17**, 269–278 (1970).

The Effects of Angiotensin II, Renin and Isoprenaline on Drinking in the Dog

E. Szczepanska-Sadowska and J. T. Fitzsimons

Isoprenaline has been found to be a potent dipsogenic agent in the rat (Zamboni and Siro-Brigiani, 1966; Lehr, Mallow, and Krukowski, 1967). This effect appears to result from β-receptor stimulation, because it is entirely abolished by the β-adrenergic antagonist propranolol (Lehr, Mallow, and Krukowski, 1967; Peskar, Leodolter, and Hertting, 1970). It would appear that, in the rat, the dipsogenic action of isoprenaline is mediated by the renin-angiotensin system because firstly, the response is abolished by bilateral nephrectomy but not by ureteric ligation (Houpt and Epstein, 1971), and secondly, isoprenaline causes an increase in plasma renin level also abolished by propranolol (Meyer, Rauscher, Peskar, and Hertting, 1973).

The rat is known to drink to renin and to angiotensin (Fitzsimons, 1966; Fitzsimons and Simons, 1969) but angiotensin is relatively less effective as a dipsogenic agent in the dog although it does cause a decrease in the thirst threshold to an osmotic stimulus (Kozlowski, Drzewiecki, and Zurawski, 1972; Kozlowski, Szczepanska-Sadowska, Sobocinska, and Fitzsimons, unpublished). We therefore decided that it would be interesting to see whether isoprenaline causes drinking in this species.

Methods

Animals. The experiments were carried out on 7 animals: 3 females and 4 males. The dogs were fed twice daily (Laboratory Diet A, Cooper's Nutritional). The second meal was suppressed on the day preceding an experiment and no food was given on the day of an experiment. Water was continuously available. The animals were accustomed to the experimental situation in which partial restraint on a Pavlovian stand was required.

Experimental Procedure. Before an experiment proper and after preliminary surgical procedures the dog was allowed access to water while standing quietly on a Pavlovian stand. Then the drug was injected or an infusion was started and a detailed record of the dog's water consumption over the next 2 hr was kept, including the latency to drink and the incidence and the size of the individual draughts of water. In some experiments a continuous recording of water consumption was made on a polygraph using a strain gauge to weigh the water container.

Minor Surgical Procedures. The saphenous or cephalic vein was cannulated by passing a fine polyethylene tube (O.D. 0.8 mm) into the vein through an intravenous syringe needle. Catheters to the right atrium and to the femoral artery were introduced according to the method of Seldinger (1953). With the dog lying on its side, as small incision was made over the femoral artery under local anaesthesia and the artery was punctured through the incision with a needle (O.D. 1 mm). A nylon guide (D 0.9 mm) was introduced through the needle into the artery. The needle was then removed and a polyethylene intra-arterial catheter (O.D. 1.5) was

69

slid over the guide. When the catheter reached the thoracic aorta the guide was withdrawn.

Central venous and arterial catheters were connected to pressure transducers. Pressures together with an electrocardiograph, were recorded using a Devices 4-channel pen recorder, and the pulse rate was taken with a Neilson instantaneous ratemeter (Devices Type 2751). *Nephrectomy.* Bilateral nephrectomy was performed on 3 dogs. Anaesthesia was induced in 2 animals with chloroethane and ether and was continued with halothane. The third animal was anaesthetized with etorphine and levomepromazine (Immobilon, Reckitt and Colman) and awakened at the end of the operation with diprenorphine (Revivon, Reckitt and Colman).

The kidneys were removed through a midline abdominal incision after a double tie had been placed on each renal pedicle. The abdominal wall was closed in layers and a perforated vinyl tube was placed underneath the skin along the line of incision so that a local anaesthetic could be injected. The operation was carried out in the morning and the behavioural part of the experiment in the afternoon. At the end of the experiments a lethal dose of pentobarbital was injected intravenously.

Renin Assay. Plasma renin activity was measured by the method of SCHAECHTELIN, BAECHTOLD, HAEFELI, REGOLI, GAUDRY-PAREDES, and PETERS (1968) slightly modified.

Solutions for Injection or Infusion. Isoprenaline hydrochloride (Isuprel, Winthrop) was injected subcutaneously as the undiluted sterile solution containing 200 μg/ml. or infused intravenously diluted with 0.9% NaCl to make a solution of 100 μg/ml.

Val[5] angiotensin II-amide (Hypertensin Ciba) and lyophilized hog renin (Nutritional Biochemicals Corporation) were dissolved in 0.9% NaCl to give final concentrations of 0.5 μg/ml. and 2.0 u./ml. respectively.

Results

Single Subcutaneous Injections of Isoprenaline. Isoprenaline injected subcutaneously caused dose-dependent drinking by water-replete animals (Fig. 1). A highly significant drinking

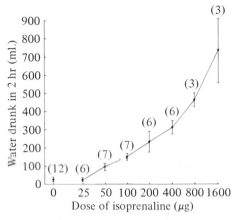

Fig. 1. Drinking in response to isoprenaline given subcutaneously. In this and subsequent figures mean values ±S.E. of the mean and numbers of observations are shown

response was observed after 50 μg/dog, a dose corresponding to 4.6 μg/kg, and some dogs drank in response to a dose of 25 μg.

This suggests that the threshold dose probably lies between 25 and 50 μg/dog. In most cases drinking was completed within 1 hr.

The Effect of an Intravenous Infusion of Angiotensin II on Drinking. Alternating intravenous infusions of angiotensin II (0.01–0.2 μg/min) and 0.9% NaCl solution were given to 4 dogs. The lowest rate of infusion of angiotensin II (0.01 μg/min) produced increases in blood pressure at the end of the infusion in 2 out of 3 dogs, but no drinking was observed. The peptide did sometimes cause water intake when infused at higher rates. One of the dogs drank a total volume of 142 ml. after successive infusions of angiotensin at rates of 0.02, 0.03 and 0.06 μg/min each lasting 25–30 min over a period of 2 hr. Each of these infusions caused a rise in mean arterial pressure. The most consistent drinking response to angiotensin II is presented in Fig. 2. In this case the dog drank a total volume of 188 ml. during or immediately after 2 infusions of angiotensin at a rate of 0.2 μg/min. Two other dogs failed to drink in response to angiotensin infused at rates of 0.01 and 0.2 μg/min for 20–30 min each.

The mean intake of these 4 dogs at the end of 2 to 2 $^{1}/_{2}$ hr of alternating angiotensin and saline infusion was 90.2 ± 44.6 ml. compared with 65.1 ± 14.7 ml. for the same 4 dogs infused over a similar period of time with isotonic saline alone.

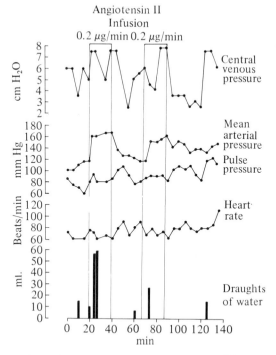

Fig. 2. Central venous pressure, mean arterial pressure, pulse pressure, heart rate and individual draughts of water drunk during infusion of angiotensin II at the rate of 0.2 μg/min

The results indicate that angiotensin II infused intravenously both in subpressor and pressor doses is relatively ineffective at causing the water-replete dog to drink.

The Effect of Intravenous Infusions of Isoprenaline and Renin on Drinking. Renin appeared to be more effective than angiotensin II at causing drinking in the dog. In Fig. 3 the mean amounts of water taken during each of the four 1/2 hr periods are plotted for the following infusion schedules: 1) isotonic saline; 2) renin at 0.05 Goldblatt u./min for the first hr, followed by 0.1 Goldblatt u./min for 1/2 hr and ending with 0.5 Goldblatt u./min for the last 1/2 hr; 3) isoprenaline at 1.5 μg/min for the first hr, followed by 3.0 μg/min for 1/2 hr and ending with 4.5 μg/min for the last 1/2 hr.

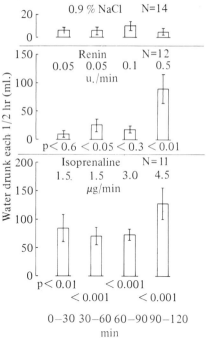

Fig. 3. Amounts of water drunk every 1/2 hr during infusion of isotonic saline, renin and isoprenaline. The rates of infusion are given above the columns

The amounts drunk during the second 1/2 hr of infusion of renin at 0.05 Goldblatt u./min and during the final 1/2 hr when the infusion rate was 0.5 Goldblatt u./min were significantly greater than the corresponding control values, whereas the intakes during the first and the third 1/2 hr were not. In a separate series of experiments renin, infused at a rate of 0.5 Goldblatt u./min, was found to cause a distinct rise in blood pressure. Increases in the mean blood pressure were also observed with a rate of 0.1 Goldblatt u./min, and sometimes even with the lowest rate of 0.05 Goldblatt u./min.

Isoprenaline produced a highly significant increase in water intake at all three rates of infusion and, at the infusions rates used, was more effective than renin (Fig. 4).

These results suggest that in the dog isoprenaline-induced drinking may not be exclusively due to activation of the renin-angiotensin system. This was confirmed by experiments performed on bilaterally nephrectomized dogs. *Isoprenaline-Induced Drinking in Bilaterally*

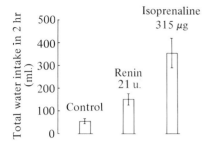

Fig. 4. Cumulative totals drunk in 2 hr after infusion of isotonic saline, renin (21 Goldblatt u.) and isoprenaline (315 μg)

Nephrectomized Dogs. Three animals were given alternating infusions of isoprenaline and saline before and after bilateral nephrectomy. The results obtained in one of these experiments are presented in Fig. 5. There was a close temporal correspondence between drinking and the periods of intravenous infusion of isoprenaline both before and after nephrectomy. The dog from Fig. 5 was anaesthetized with halothane and salivated profusely during the recovery period. The loss of fluid probably accounts for the relatively high basal water intake. Despite this, the infusion of isoprenaline caused a con-

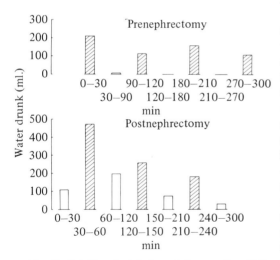

Fig. 5. Drinking to infusion of isoprenaline (4.5 μg/min) before and immediately after bilateral nephrectomy. Isotonic saline was infused at the same rate during the control periods. The white columns represent the total amount drunk during the control period and the dashed columns during infusion of isoprenaline

siderable increase in drinking each time. Similar results were obtained in two other dogs.

Discussion

Isoprenaline was found to be an effective dipsogenic stimulus in the dog. However it is clear that its mechanism of action differs, at least in degree, from that in the rat. In the rat there is good evidence for a causal relationship between activation of the renin-angiotensin system and drinking after isoprenaline. This mechanism does not appear to operate to the same extent in the dog. We confirmed the relative ineffectiveness of angiotensin II as a dipsogenic stimulus (KOZLOWSKI, DRZEWIECKI, and ZURAWSKI, 1972) and we found that renin is a more effective stimulus to drinking in the dog, but that relatively large doses are needed to produce a clear-cut response.

There is conflicting evidence whether isoprenaline releases renin in the dog. BUNAG, PAGE, and MCCUBBIN (1966) concluded that isoprenaline infused into the renal artery does not cause renin release. On the other hand, ASSAYKEEN and GANONG (1971) and GUTMANN, TAGAWA, HABER, and BARGER (1973) found a clear-cut increase in plasma renin activity after infusion of isoprenaline. In the present study, an increase of plasma renin activity was found during intravenous infusion of isoprenaline, so that it is possible that endogenous renin released by isoprenaline may play some role in the dipsogenic effect of isoprenaline in this species. However, the fact that the dipsogenic response to isoprenaline is not abolished by bilateral nephrectomy indicates that drinking after isoprenaline may occur without any involvement of the renal renin-angiotensin system and suggests that some other mechanism accounts for part, at least, of the response. What these non-hormonal mechanisms are needs further study. It seems possible that the much increased cardiac output caused by isoprenaline uncovers a deficiency in central venous filling which may be the elusive hypovolaemic stimulus in extracellularly induced thirst. Isoprenaline is also known to constrict veins, particularly in the dog. It is therefore possible that the great veins entering the heart are underfilled and that this arouses thirst.

Acknowledgement. These experiments were carried out at the Physiological Laboratory, Cambridge, during EWA SZCZEPANSKA-SADOWSKA's tenure of a British Council Scholarship.

References

ASSAYKEEN, T. A., GANONG, W. F.: The sympathetic nervous system and renin secretion. In: Frontiers in Neuroendocrinology (Eds. L. MARTINI, W. F. GANONG), pp. 67–102. New York: Oxford University Press 1971.

BUNAG, R. D., PAGE, I. H., McCUBBIN, J. W.: Neural stimulation of release of renin. Circulation Res. **19,** 851–858 (1966).

FITZSIMONS, J. T.: Hypovolaemic drinking and renin. J. Physiol. Lond. **186,** 130–131 P (1966).

FITZSIMONS, J. T., SIMONS, B. J.: The effect on drinking in the rat of intravenous infusion of angiotensin, given alone or in combination with other stimuli of thirst. J. Physiol. Lond. **203,** 43–57 (1969).

GUTMANN, F. D., TAGAWA, H., HABER, E., BARGER, G. C.: Renal arterial pressure, renin secretion, and blood pressure control in trained dogs. Am. J. Physiol. **224,** 66–72 (1973).

HOUPT, K. A., EPSTEIN, A. N.: The complete dependence of beta-adrenergic drinking on the renal dipsogen. Physiol. Behav. **7,** 897–902 (1971).

KOZLOWSKI, S., DRZEWIECKI, K., ZURAWSKI, W.: Zależność reaktywności osmotycznej mechanizmu pragnienia od poziomu angiotensyny i aldosteronu we krwi u psów. Acta Physiol. Pol. XXIII (3) (1972).

KOZLOWSKI, S., SZCZEPANSKA, E., DRZEWIECKI, K.: Hormonal influences on osmotic reactivity of the thirst mechanism in dogs. Regional Congress of The International Union of Physiological Sciences. Braşov, Rumania, Abstract No 491 (1970).

LEHR, D., MALLOW, J., KRUKOWSKI, M.: Copious drinking and simultaneous inhibition of urine flow elicited by beta-adrenergic stimulation. J. Pharmac. Exp. Ther. **158,** 150–163 (1967).

MEYER, D. K., RAUSCHER, W., PESKAR, B., HERTTING, G.: The mechanism of the drinking response to some hypotensive drugs: activation of the renin-angiotensin system by direct or reflex-mediated stimulation of β-receptors. Naunyn-Schmiedeberg's Arch. Pharmacol. **276,** 13–24 (1973).

PESKAR, B., LEODOLTER, S., HERTTING, G.: Die Wirkung verschiedener blutdrucksenkender Pharmaca auf Wasseraufnahme und -abgabe bei Ratten. Naunyn-Schmiedeberg's Arch. Pharmak. **265,** 335–346 (1970).

SCHAECHTELIN, G., BAECHTOLD, N., HAEFELI, L., REGOLI, D., GAUDRY-PAREDES, A., PETERS, G.: A renin inactivating system in rat plasma. Am. J. Physiol. **215,** 632–636 (1968).

SELDINGER, S. I.: Catheter replacement of the needle in percutaneous arteriography. Acta Radiol. **39,** 368–376 (1953).

ZAMBONI, P., SIRO-BRIGIANI, G.: Effetto delle catecholamine sulla sete e la diuresi nel ratto. Bol. Soc. Ital. Biol. Sper. **42,** 1657–1659 (1966).

The Elevation of Endogenous Angiotensin and Thirst in the Dog

B. J. Rolls and D. J. Ramsay

The work of Fitzsimons (1969) led to the suggestion that increased drinking following a reduction in blood volume may be mediated via the renin-angiotensin system. For example, nephrectomy reduces the drinking which usually follows caval ligation in the rat (Fitzsimons, 1964). In the rat intravenous infusions of angiotensin (Fitzsimons and Simons, 1969) or injections of small quantities of angiotensin directly into the brain (Epstein, Fitzsimons, and Rolls, 1970) increase water intake. Subsequently species other than the rat have been shown to drink after the administration of angiotensin.

In the dog, depletion of the extracellular fluid compartment, for example, by sodium depletion (Holmes and Cizek, 1951) or by haemorrhage (Szczepanska-Sadowska, 1973), increases drinking, but it is not clear whether the renin-angiotensin system is important in this response. The dog does not appear to be as sensitive as the rat to the intravenous administration of angiotensin. Kozlowski, Drzewiecki, and Zurawski (1972) found that intravenous angiotensin did not elicit drinking in the dog, although it did lower the threshold to an osmotic thirst stimulus.

Preliminary experiments in collaboration with M. Erskine have demonstrated that the dog will drink after the injection of angiotensin (Hypertensin, Ciba) into the third ventricle. Two dogs drank a mean of 880 ml. of water in the half hour following 8 μg angiotensin dissolved in isotonic saline, 290 ml. following 4 μg and 69 ml. following control injections of isotonic saline. A third dog did not drink consistently following angiotensin. At post-mortem the cannula of this animal was found to be in the corpus callosum and not in communication with the third ventricle. This is a preliminary study; the doses of angiotensin used were large, but it is clear that exogenous angiotensin will stimulate drinking in the dog. It was decided that before attempting to define the minimum dose of angiotensin that would stimulate drinking in the dog, it would be appropriate to look at the effect of increasing endogenous angiotensin on water intake. In the experiments described here the effects on water intake of thoracic inferior vena caval constriction, subcutaneous injection of isoprenaline, and renal hypertension following renal artery constriction were investigated. All three procedures have been shown to increase circulating levels of angiotensin.

General Methods

Preliminary experiments showed that it was necessary to keep the dogs to a strict routine. Therefore in any one experiment the dogs were always fed and exercised at the same time of day. The amount of food given was the same each day and was based on the animal's body weight. Synthetic food was given because chemical analysis showed that its composition varied less than that of meat. Most of the experiments were conducted in the animal's home kennel where a float and kymograph made continuous 24 hour records of water intake. Student's t tests were carried out using the method of paired comparisons.

Isoprenaline

Subcutaneous injection of the beta-adrenergic agonist isoprenaline elicits drinking in the rat (LEHR, MALLOW, and KRUKOWSKI, 1967). Isoprenaline usually lowers blood pressure in dogs and rats, and stimulates the release of renin (PESKAR, MEYER, TAUCHMANN, and HERTTING, 1970). The drinking which follows isoprenaline in the rat is probably due to the formation of angiotensin since nephrectomy prevents the response (HOUPT and EPSTEIN, 1971).

Isoprenaline increases water intake in the dog (RAMSAY, ROLLS, and WOOD, 1973; FITZSIMONS and SZCZEPANSKA-SADOWSKA, 1973), but it is not clear whether this response is mediated by the renin-angiotensin system. To clarify this point we measured the drinking response to isoprenaline in dogs in which the main source of angiotensin was removed by bilateral nephrectomy and in dogs in which the activity of angiotensin was blocked by the competitive angiotensin inhibitor saralasin acetate (P-113, Norwich Pharmacal Company).

In the first experiment the water intake of four dogs (15 to 30 kg) was measured for 90 minutes after a subcutaneous injection of 6 $\mu g \cdot kg^{-1}$ isoprenaline hydrochloride (Suscardia, Pharmax). The dogs were tested in their kennels where they always had free access to water. The

dogs were then bilaterally nephrectomized through a midline abdominal incision under pentobarbital anaesthesia. The dogs were injected again with isoprenaline 36 hours after the nephrectomy, by which time they had regained their usual friskiness and were eating and drinking. It can be seen in Table 1 that nephrectomy completely abolished the response to isoprenaline in three of the four dogs and that the fourth dog drank very little. A t test on the data expressed as ml. kg^{-1} showed the difference to be highly significant (p < 0.001). Two of the dogs (3 and 4) were injected with isoprenaline again 60 hours after the nephrectomy and still did not drink.

In the second experiment, the effect of infusing saralasin acetate at 2 $\mu g \cdot kg^{-1} \cdot min^{-1}$ on the drinking following isoprenaline injection was investigated in four dogs (13–17 kg). The dogs were trained to sit quietly on a table while being infused into a cannulated hind limb vein with either saralasin acetate in isotonic saline, or isotonic saline alone, at a rate of 0.15 ml. $\cdot$ min^{-1}. Just after the infusion began the dogs were injected subcutaneously with 6 $\mu g \cdot kg^{-1}$ isoprenaline. The infusion continued for an hour during which time the water intake from a bowl was measured. The dogs drank 9.0 ± 1.5 ml. $\cdot$ kg^{-1} while being infused with saline compared with 1.6 ± 0.5 ml. $\cdot kg^{-1}$ while being infused with the angiotensin inhibitor (P < 0.01). The results of this and the previous experiment indicate that in the dog the drinking response to isoprenaline is probably largely mediated by the renin-angiotensin system.[1]

Renal Hypertension

The original observation that interference with the circulation to a kidney led to a permanent increase in blood pressure was made by GOLDBLATT, LYNCH, HANZAL, and SUMMERVILLE in 1934. It is now well established that acutely reducing the renal arterial pressure leads to an increase in the renin activity in the renal venous blood and thus to an elevated plasma angioten-

Table 1

Dog	kg	Control time (min)			Nephr-ectomized time (min)		
		30	60	90	30	60	90
		Wt. in. (ml.)					
1	15	230	250	250	0	0	0
2	17	150	270	320	55	65	70
3	30	450	525	590	0	0	0
4	29	435	470	480	0	0	0

The water intake (Wt. in., ml.) of four dogs following a subcutaneous injection of isoprenaline (6 μg kg^{-1}) before (control) and 36 hours after bilateral nephrectomy. The cumulative total intake for each dog is shown for 30, 60, and 90 minutes after the injection.

[1] For a contrary view see chapter by E. SZCZEPANSKA-SADOWSKA and J. T. FITZSIMONS.

sin II level in the systemic circulation. In the dog, as in some other species, in order to obtain a constant and long-lasting increase of blood pressure following renal artery clipping, the opposite kidney must be removed (PICKERING, 1968). Experiments were therefore designed to investigate the effect on drinking of raising the plasma angiotensin level in this way.

In six dogs, records of daily drinking were obtained before operation. The dogs were lightly anaesthetised with pentobarbital, the femoral artery cannulated and the arterial pressure measured. The abdomen was then opened through a midline incision, and the left renal artery constricted to about one half its original size with a silk ligature. The right kidney was then removed, the abdomen closed in layers, and the animal returned to its kennel. The water intake of the dogs following renal artery constriction is shown in Fig. 1. A marked increase in water intake occurred even on the first post-operative day. In the one dog where this did not occur, there was no increase in measured blood pressure and, therefore, presumably, the ligature had not been applied tightly enough. All the other dogs showed signs of a rapidly developing acute renal failure on the 2nd or 3rd post-operative day and were destroyed. In three dogs it was possible to measure the arterial blood pressure which increased from 115 ± 0.2 to 149 ± 11 mm Hg ($n = 3$; mean $\pm$S.E.). Daily water intake increased from 378 ± 69.2 ml. to 1366 ± 200.6 ml. on the first post-operative day ($P < 0.01$, $n = 5$) and was 1030 ± 119.0 ml. ($P < 0.02$, $n = 4$) on the second.

Not only did the dogs show an increased 24 hour intake of water, they also exhibited a change in the pattern of drinking (Fig. 2). There was marked nocturnal drinking which does not usually occur under normal conditions. Thus renal hypertension in the dog as in the rat (FITZSIMONS, 1969) is accompanied by a marked increase in water intake.

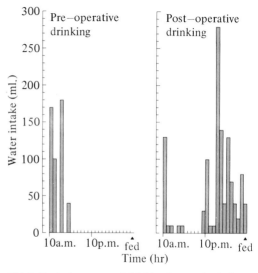

Fig. 2. Typical patterns of drinking by one dog before and after the experimental production of renal hypertension

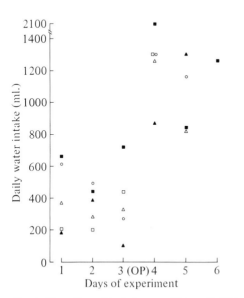

Fig. 1. The effect of inducing one-kidney Goldblatt hypertension on the water intake of five dogs. Each symbol represents a different animal. OP shows the day of operation

Thoracic Caval Constriction

An elevated plasma level of renin is associated with congestive heart failure (DAVIS, 1967). The method most often used to produce experimental low-output failure in the dog is thoracic inferior vena caval constriction, which leads to an elevated plasma renin level (SCHNEIDER, DAVIS, ROBB, and BAUMBER, 1969). We have recently reported that there is a marked elevation in water intake following constriction of the thoracic inferior vena cava to approximately one half of its original diameter (RAMSAY et al., 1973). As shown in Fig. 3 water intake rose significantly after the first post-operative day (P < 0.001) and remained elevated for at least a week. During this period, the dogs gained about a kilogram in weight and the extracellular fluid volume increased by 22% (p < 0.001).

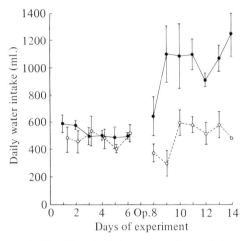

Fig. 3. The effect of inferior vena caval constriction on water intake in dogs. Points represent values of mean daily water intake, for the experimental group (●) with thoracic caval constriction ($n = 5$), and the control group (O) with abdominal caval constriction ($n = 5$). Vertical bars indicate the standard errors of the means. OP shows the day of operation (from RAMSAY et al., 1973)

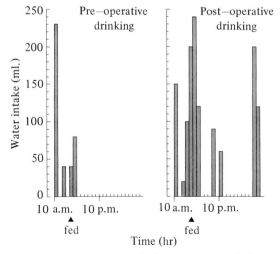

Fig. 4. Typical patterns of drinking by one dog before and after thoracic inferior vena caval constriction

In Fig. 4 the drinking pattern of a dog before and after thoracic caval constriction is shown. There was an increase in drinking during the day but not at night.

Conclusions

These experiments demonstrate that an increase of water intake in dogs follows procedures known to be associated with elevated plasma angiotensin II levels. The important question is whether angiotensin II may be considered as a causative factor. The rlationship between hypovolaemia and thirst has been reviewed by FITZSIMONS (1969). The experimental approach either involves a reduction in extracellular fluid and/or intravascular volume or a reduction in venous return to the heart by thoracic caval ligation or constriction. There are two ways in which a reduction in venous return might lead to an increase in water intake. First, a low venous return will lead to a reduction in the rate of stimulation of both cardiac distension receptors and arterial baroreceptors. Secondly, a reduction in venous return may stimulate renin release by causing arterial hypotension, a mechanism which is sensitised by cardiovascular reflexes acting via the renal sympathetic nerves (HODGE, LOWE, and VANE, 1966). Thus, following thoracic inferior vena caval constriction, both mechanisms might operate to stimulate thirst.

Following renal artery constriction, however, the situation is different. Angiotensin II levels are elevated, drinking occurs, but there is an increased cardiac and baroreceptor input. The fact that drinking still occurs is surely indicative of an important role of angiotensin as a dipsogen in the dog. The argument is reinforced by our experiments in which the dipsogenic effect of isoprenaline in the dog was markedly reduced by nephrectomy and by administration of the competitive angiotensin inhibitor, saralasin acetate.

Acknowledgement. This work was supported by the Medical Research Council. Parts of this work were done in collaboration with R. WOOD and M. ERSKINE.

We wish to thank A. W. CASTELLION of Norwich Pharmacal for supplying the saralasin acetate and Pharmax Limited for supplying the isoprenaline hydrochloride.

References

DAVIS, J. O.: In: The Adrenal Cortex, (Ed. A. B. Eisenstein), pp. 203–247, Boston, Massachusetts: Little, Brown and Company 1967.

EPSTEIN, A. N., FITZSIMONS, J. T., ROLLS, B. J.: Drinking induced by injection of angiotensin into the brain of the rat. J. Physiol. Lond. **210**, 457–474 (1970).

FITZSIMONS, J. T.: Drinking caused by constriction of the inferior vena cava in the rat. Nature **204**, 479–480 (1964).

— The role of a renal thirst factor in drinking induced by extracellular stimuli. J. Physiol. Lond. **201**, 349–368 (1969).

FITZSIMONS, J. T., SIMONS, B. J.: The effect on drinking in the rat of intravenous infusion of angiotensin, given alone or in combination with other stimuli of thirst. J. Physiol. Lond. **203**, 45–57 (1969).

FITZSIMONS, J. T., SZCZEPANSKA-SADOWSKA, E. K.: Drinking elicited by isoprenaline in the dog. J. Physiol. Lond. **233**, 19–20 P (1973).

GOLDBLATT, H., LYNCH, J., HANZAL, R. F., SUMMERVILLE, W. W.: Studies on experimental hypertension I. The production of persistent elevation of systolic blood pressure by means of renal ischemia J. exp. Med. **59**, 347–361 (1934).

HODGE, R. L., LOWE, R. D., VANE, J. R.: The effects of alteration of blood volume on the concentration of circulating angiotensin in anaesthetised dogs. J. Physiol. Lond. **185**, 613–626 (1966).

HOLMES, J. H., CIZEK, L. J.: Observations on sodium chloride depletion in the dog. Am. J. Physiol. **164**, 407–414 (1951).

HOUPT, K. A., EPSTEIN, A. N.: The complete dependence of beta-adrenergic drinking on the renal dipsogen. Physiol. Behav. **7**, 897–902 (1971).

KOZLOWSKI, S., DRZEWIECKI, K., ZURAWSKI, W.: Relationship between osmotic reactivity of the thirst mechanism and the angiotensin and aldosterone level in the blood of dogs. Acta physiol. pol. **23**, 417–425 (1972).

LEHR, D., MALLOW, J., KRUKOWSKI, M.: Copious drinking and simultaneous inhibition of urine flow elicited by beta-adrenergic stimulation and contrary effect of alpha-adrenergic stimulation. J. Pharmac. exp. Ther. **158**, 150–163 (1967).

PESKAR, B., MEYER, D. K., TAUCHMANN, U., HERTTING, G.: Influence of isoproterenol, hydralazine and phentolamine on the renin activity of plasma and renal cortex of rats. Europ. J. Pharmacol. **9**, 394–396 (1970).

PICKERING, G. W.: High Blood Pressure, 2nd Ed. London: Churchill 1968.

RAMSAY, D. J., ROLLS, B. J., WOOD, R. J.: Increased drinking in dogs during congestive heart failure. J. Physiol. Lond. **234**, 48P–50P (1973).

SCHNEIDER, E. G., DAVIS, J. O., ROBB, C. A., BAUMBER, J. S.: Hepatic clearance of renin in canine experimental models for low- and high-output heart failure. Circulation Res. **24**, 213–219 (1969).

SZCZEPANSKA-SADOWSKA, E.: Plasma ADH level and body water balance in dogs after a moderate haemorrhage. Bull. acad. Pol. Sci. **21**, 89–92 (1973).

Evidence against the Postulated Role of the Renin-Angiotensin System in Putative Renin-Dependent Drinking Responses

D. Lehr, H. W. Goldman, and P. Casner

Fitzsimons' original concept that the renal renin-angiotensin system contributes importantly to certain forms of extracellular thirst (Fitzsimons, 1969) was subsequently extended by others to encompass drinking elicited by isoprenaline and other drugs which induce preferential β-adrenergic activation (Houpt and Epstein, 1969; Meyer, Peskar, and Hertting, 1971). The concept is based in part on the persuasive, albeit circumstantial, evidence that bilateral nephrectomy, which obviates the rise in plasma-renin activity, also inhibits or abolishes these drinking responses (Fitzsimons, 1969; Houpt and Epstein, 1969).

The availability of the nonapeptide SQ 20,881, an angiotensin converting enzyme (ACE) inhibitor provided the opportunity to test the role of the renin-angiotensin system in several thirst mechanisms in a more physiological manner, that is, without the radical disturbance and inexorably progressive deterioration of homeostasis which follows bilateral nephrectomy.

It was reasoned that abolition or significant reduction of thirst in animals prevented from forming peripheral angiotensin II (A II) would strongly support the dependency of a drinking response upon systemic formation of this octapeptide, whereas undiminished thirst would seriously challenge such contention.

In the studies to be reported, it was found, unexpectedly, that pretreatment with peripheral SQ 20,881 caused a highly significant *enhancement* of the dipsogenic effect of both so-called renin-dependent as well as renin-independent thirst stimuli, but *not* of exogenous renin itself. It was found, moreover, that prior renin depletion did not significantly affect putative renin-dependent drinking. Specifically, the copious water intake following activation of β-adrenergic receptors by isoprenaline (Lehr, Krukowski, and Colon, 1966; Lehr, Mallow, and Krukowski, 1967) as well as that resulting from inferior vena cava ligation (Fitzsimons, 1969) appeared to be independent of this hormonal mechanism.

Utilizing groups of intact and bilaterally nephrectomized (Nx) rats, peripheral injection of isoprenaline and ligation of the inferior vena cava were selected as putative renin-dependent drinking stimuli. They were compared with the dipsogenic potency of s.c. polyethylene glycol (PEG) and water deprivation thirst as prototypes of renin-independent drinking stimuli, since neither of these is influenced by prior removal of the kidneys.

SQ 20,881 (3.0 mg/kg, s.c.) was administered 10 min prior to the actual drinking period. (It should be noted that this dose did not noticeably alter the general behaviour or motor activity of the animals). Immediate access to the tap water source was allowed following the parenteral administration of isoprenaline (0.1 mg/kg body weight) or renin, whereas such access was delayed for 4 hours in the case of PEG injection (5 ml Carbowax 20, s.c.) as well as following caval ligation, and for 18 hours in tests of water deprivation thirst. Water intake was measured at half-hourly intervals for the subsequent 3 hr in all experiments and food was withdrawn during this period. Data were analyzed by Student's *t* test for determination of the statistical significance between groups.

The effect of peripheral ACE inhibition upon the various drinking mechanisms investigated is illustrated for intact and Nx rats in Fig. 1. It is apparent that in the presence of SQ 20,881, intact rats showed a highly significant enhance-

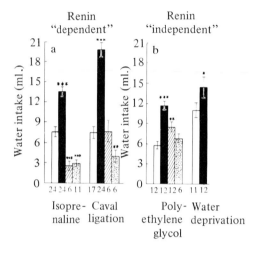

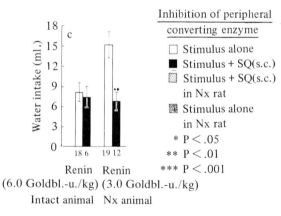

Inhibition of peripheral converting enzyme

☐ Stimulus alone
■ Stimulus + SQ(s.c.)
▨ Stimulus + SQ(s.c.) in Nx rat
▦ Stimulus alone in Nx rat

* P < .05
** P < .01
*** P < .001

Renin   Renin
(6.0 Goldbl.-u./kg) (3.0 Goldbl.-u./kg)
Intact animal Nx animal

Fig. 1. Effect of peripheral SQ 20,881 upon drinking responses elicited by renin and so-called renin-dependent and renin-independent stimuli in the intact and bilaterally nephrectomized (Nx) rat. Each bar represents the three hour water intake in ml. per rat. Figures at the base-line indicate the number of animals per group. Significance of difference in comparison with stimulus alone (blank bars) is shown by asterisks

ment of putative renin-dependent and renin-independent drinking responses, whereas renin drinking itself was not significantly affected. Since the pressor effect of renin is obviated by the dose of SQ 20,881 employed, it would seem that the dipsogenic effect of i.p. renin in the *intact* rat may be predicated upon an alternate, perhaps entirely peripheral mechanism.

It can be seen further that SQ 20,881-induced enhancement of drinking is attenuated or obviated by removal of the kidneys. Complete failure of isoprenaline to elicit drinking in Nx rats was first observed by HOUPT and EPSTEIN (1969) and MEYER et al. (1971). Nephrectomy also abolished the enhancing effect of peripheral SQ 20,881 on isoprenaline-induced drinking, and depressed, but did not abolish, the enhancing effect of SQ 20,881 on drinking induced by ligating the vena cava (Fig. 1a).

The findings with PEG thirst were similar. Although removal of the kidneys had no effect on the PEG elicited water intake itself, SQ 20,881-induced increase in drinking in Nx rats fell far short of the doubled water intake seen in intact rats (Fig. 1 b). A similar attenuation by SQ 20,881 of drinking in Nx rats was noted with renin itself, which is known to be a far more potent dipsogen in the absence of the kidneys. The copious drinking effect of 3.0 units of i.p. renin was reduced by 60% (Fig. 1c).

Since the pressor effects of i.v. as well as i.p., renin were effectively blocked by the dose of SQ 20,881 employed, the attenuation of renin-induced drinking by the ACE inhibitor appears to indicate the importance of peripheral A II formation in renin drinking. By the same token, the drinking responses produced by isoprenaline, caval ligation, PEG and water deprivation appeared to be independent of peripheral A II formation. Yet the SQ 20,881-induced *enhancement* of these four drinking stimuli was clearly renin dependent, and most likely the result of increased renin release from the kidneys and thus increased angiotensin I (A I) formation.

The findings of SEVERS, SUMMY-LONG, and DANIELS-SEVERS (1973), that the dipsogenic effect of intraventricular A I was blocked by prior injection of SQ 20,881 into the same site, but not by peripherally injected SQ 20,881, were confirmed in our laboratory. They indicate that SQ 20,881 does not cross the blood-brain barrier.

In order to determine whether the enhancement of drinking caused by peripheral SQ 20,881 was due to increased A I entry into the intracranial space, rats were stereotaxically implanted with stainless steel cannulae aimed at the lateral ventricle. SQ 20,881, in a dose of 30 μg per rat, was injected intraventricularly (ivt) with the aid of a Hamilton microdispensing syringe, 10 min prior to the 3 hr drinking period. In groups receiving both central and peripheral SQ 20,881, the inhibitor was first injected ivt., followed 5 min later by s.c. SQ 20,881 in the standard dose of 3 mg/kg. After an additional period of 5 min the drinking stimulus was applied and the water intake over 3 hr was recorded.

The results are summarized in Fig. 2. It can be seen that isoprenaline drinking was not affected by central SQ 20,881 (Fig. 2a, cross-hatched bar) whereas the enhancement of the drinking response produced by peripheral SQ 20,881 was substantially attenuated under the same circumstances (stippled bar). This is interpreted to mean that the enhancement of isoprenaline drinking by peripheral SQ 20,881 is indeed renin-dependent and the result of increased A I entry into the intracranial space, whereas the isoprenaline drinking response itself (blank bar), is not dependent upon the renin-angiotensin system. Closely similar results were obtained when the ACE inhibitor was injected ivt. in rats with inferior vena cava ligation (Fig. 2b). Again the basic drinking response was not affected (cross-hatched bar), whereas the enhancement of the response produced by peripheral SQ 20,881 (black bar) was substantially reduced in the presence of central SQ 20,881 (stippled bar).

Fig. 2c demonstrates that in the doses employed, ivt. SQ 20,881 was as effective as peripheral SQ 20,881 in blocking exogenous renin drinking in the Nx rat. The failure to obtain a complete block of peripheral renin drinking with central SQ 20,881 indicates that higher doses of the inhibitor may be required or that A I may itself possess considerable dipsogenic potency. This same reasoning could also serve to explain the incompleteness of the block, by central SQ 20,881, of the increase in isopren-

aline and caval ligation drinking in the presence of peripheral SQ 20,881.

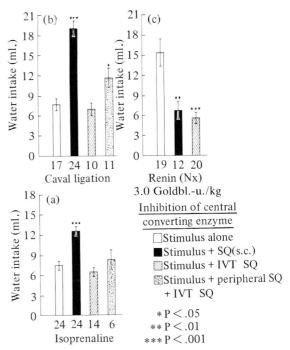

Fig. 2. Comparison of the effects of peripheral and intraventricular (ivt) SQ 20,881 and of the combined use of these routes upon drinking responses elicited by putative renin-dependent stimuli in the intact rat and renin in the bilaterally nephrectomized (Nx) rat. Each bar represents the three hour water intake per rat. Figures at the baseline indicate the number of animals per group. Significance of differences in comparison with stimulus alone (blank bars) shown by asterisks

Finally, it was found that renin-depletion produced in rats by three weeks DOCA-saline pretreatment (implantation of 25 mg DOCA pellets and 1% saline as drinking fluid, (Goodwin, Knowlton, and Laragh, 1969) had likewise no substantial influence on putative renin-dependent drinking. Such rats showed an almost undiminished drinking response to β-adrenergic stimulation and ligation of the inferior vena cava (Table 1). On the other hand, the dramatic enhancement of caval ligation drinking in the presence of peripheral SQ 20,881 was obviated by the depletion of renal renin stores, confirming the renin-dependency of this phenomenon.

Table 1. The Effect of Renin-Depletion on Thirst Induced by Either β-Adrenergic Stimulation or Inferior Vena Cava Ligation

Treatment		3-hr Water Intake (ml. ± S.E. of mean)			
		Normal Animals	n	DOCA-Saline Pretreated Animals (21 Days)	n
Control	# #	1.22 ± 0.36	23	2.81 ± 0.48	16
β-Adrenergic Stimulation	#	7.50 ± 0.90***	12	5.53 ± 0.52***	15
Caval Ligation	N.S.	7.50 ± 0.02***	17	6.42 ± 1.25*	12
Caval Ligation + SQ 20,881 (s.c.)	# # #	18.92 ± 1.19***	24	7.90 ± 1.79***	10

Statistical comparisons were made between experimental and control groups in both intact and DOCA-saline pretreated animals, respectively. $p < 0.05$ = *, $p < 0.001$ = *** and between corresponding groups of intact and DOCA-saline treated rats, $p < 0.05$ = #, $p < 0.01$ = # #, $p < 0.001$ = # # # N.S. = not significant. (Modified from LEHR, GOLDMAN, and CASNER, 1973.)

Almost undiminished thirst followed caval ligation or peripheral β-adrenergic stimulation, despite major interference with the renin-angiotensin system by depletion of renal renin stores or by peripheral and central blockade of A II formation. This puts into question a direct cause and effect relationship between the humoral system and these dipsogenic stimuli.

Summary

SQ 20,881, a competitive angiotensin converting enzyme antagonist, was utilized for the purpose of determining the quantitative contribution of the renin-angiotensin system to so-called renin-dependent drinking responses (β-adrenergic activation and ligation of the inferior vena cava).

Unexpectedly, significant enhancement, rather than reduction of "renin-dependent" as well as renin-independent drinking was observed in the presence of SQ 20,881, providing strong evidence against the importance of peripherally formed angiotensin II as a dipsogenic stimulus in these situations.

Intraventricular SQ 20,881 blocked the enhancement of drinking produced by peripheral SQ 20,881, but did not affect the thirst caused by the original stimulus itself, whereas drinking evoked by peripheral renin was inhibited. Prior renin depletion had likewise no substantial influence on so-called renin-dependent thirst.

These observations are contrary to the postulated role of the renin-angiotensin system as a primary dipsogenic mechanism in the putative renin-dependent drinking responses investigated. They suggest, on the other hand, that under conditions fovouring enhanced renin release (SQ 20,881 block of peripheral angiotensin I conversion), the decapeptide may enter the central nervous system in amounts adequate to act as a thirst stimulus by itself or to be converted in the brain to angiotensin II as the final dipsogen.

References

FITZSIMONS, J. T.: The role of a renal thirst factor in drinking induced by extracellular stimuli. J. Physiol. Lond. **201**, 349–368 (1969).

GOODWIN, F. J., KNOWLTON, A. L., LARAGH, J. H.: Absence of renin suppression by deoxycorticosterone acetate in rats. Am. J. Physiol. **216**, 1476–1480 (1969).

HOUPT, K. A., EPSTEIN, A. N.: The renin-angiotensin mediation of hypotensive drinking. Physiologist **12**, 257 (1969).

LEHR, D., GOLDMAN, W. H., CASNER, P.: Renin-angiotensin role in thirst: paradoxical enhancement of drinking by angiotensin converting enzyme inhibitor. Science **182**, 1031–1034 (1973).

LEHR, D., KRUKOWSKI, M., COLON, R.: Drinking elicited by β-adrenergic stimulation. Fed. Proc. **24,** 624 (1966).

LEHR, D., MALLOW, J., KRUKOWSKI, M.: Copious drinking and simultaneous inhibition of urine flow elicited by β-adrenergic stimulation and contrary effect of α-adrenergic stimulation. J. Pharmac. exp. Ther. **158,** 150–163 (1967).

MEYER, D. K., PESKAR, B., HERTTING, G.: Hemmung des durch blutdrucksenkende Pharmaka bei Ratten ausgelösten Trinkens durch Nephrektomie. Experientia **27,** 65–66 (1971).

SEVERS, W. B., SUMMY-LONG, J., DANIELS-SEVERS, A.: Effect of a converting enzyme inhibitor on angiotensin-induced drinking. Proc. Soc. exp. Biol. (N.Y.) **142,** 203–204 (1973).

Relationships between Increase in Plasma Renin Activity and Drinking Following Different Types of Dipsogenic Stimuli

F. H. H. LEENEN, E. M. STRICKER, R. H. McDONALD JR., and W. DE JONG

Major decreases in renal perfusion pressure are generally associated with increased renin release as well as water intake. Such acute responses can occur in the absence of increases in the effective osmolality of body fluids and of cellular dehydration, but do not occur in nephrectomized animals. These results, together with findings that drinking can be induced in the water-satiated rat by peripheral or intracerebral administration of renin, angiotensin I, or angiotensin II, suggest that angiotensin acts as a natural dipsogen as part of its role in the maintenance of circulatory homeostasis (for review, see FITZSIMONS, 1972).

In the present experiments in rats, acute and more prolonged stimuli of renin secretion have been used in order to assess the quantitative and temporal relationships between changes in plasma renin activity and in water intake.

Material and Methods

Rats weighing 150–200 g were used in the acute experiments, and rats weighing 225–275 g were used in the subacute experiments. Two-kidney Goldblatt hypertension was induced in rats of 140–160 g (LEENEN and DE JONG, 1971). Male rats were used except for the isoprenaline and methoxamine studies.

In conscious unrestrained rats with chronic cannulation of a carotid artery, blood pressure was recorded with a Statham P 23-AC transducer connected to a Grass model 5-D polygraph.

Blood pressure of hypertensive rats was measured by an indirect method at the tail (LEENEN and DE JONG, 1971).

Plasma renin activity (PRA) was measured in blood collected from the trunk following decapitation according to the method of HABER, KOERNER, PAGE, KLIMAN, and PURNODE (1969), using a radioimmunoassay for angiotensin I. PRA of renal hypertensive rats was measured according to the methods of PICKENS, BUMPUS, LLOYD, SMEBY and PAGE (1965) and LEENEN, DE JONG and DE WIED, 1973.

Results are expressed as means ± standard error of the mean (S.E.). Statistical analysis was performed using WILCOXON's two sample test.

Results

Acute Stimuli
Isoprenaline (Fig. 1). Subcutaneous administration of the β-adrenergic agent isoprenaline (Isuprel) in the dose range 1–500 μg/kg resulted in a rapid dose-related decrease in the mean blood pressure of conscious unrestrained rats. PRA increased rapidly and substantially, from a basal level of about 1×10^{-4} Goldblatt u./ml. in control rats to 25×10^{-4} Goldblatt u./ml., 15 min after 500 μg/kg. PRA returned to normal levels somewhat later than blood pressure. Despite substantial decreases in blood pressure and increases in PRA, little drinking was observed except when the higher doses were used. For example, after 500 μg/kg, 7.4 ± 1.1 ml. of

84

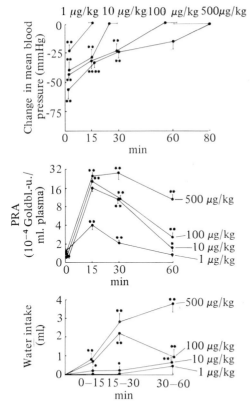

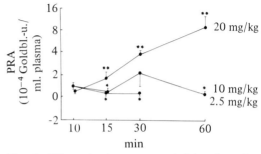

Fig. 2. Effect of subcutaneous administration of different doses of methoxamine on plasma renin activity (PRA). Results are expressed as means ±S.E. of mean ($n = 5-6$). * $p < 0.05$; ** $p < 0.01$

Fig. 1. Effect of subcutaneous administration of different doses of isoprenaline on mean blood pressure, plasma renin activity (PRA) and water intake. Results are expressed as means ±S.E. of mean ($n = 4-6$). The changes in mean blood pressure are given as the differences from the basal level. * $p < 0.05$; ** $p < 0.01$

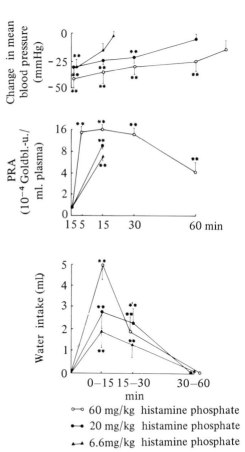

Fig. 3. Effect of subcutaneous administration of different doses of histamine phosphate on mean blood pressure, plasma renin activity (PRA) and water intake. Results are expressed as means ±S.E. of mean ($n = 4-6$). The changes in mean blood pressure are given as the differences from the basal level. ** $p < 0.01$

water was consumed in 1 hr, most of the drinking occurring between 15 and 45 min after administration of the drug.

Methoxamine (Fig. 2). The α-adrenergic agent methoxamine (Vasoxyl) was administered subcutaneously in doses of 2.5, 10 and 20 mg/kg. The smaller doses had little effect on PRA, or even decreased it. Following 20 mg/kg PRA increased slowly to 9.5×10^{-4} Goldblatt u./ml. after 60 min, but these levels are only about half of those found after the lowest dose of isoprenaline that was effective in inducing drinking. Animals treated with these doses of methoxamine did not drink water at all. Higher doses were not employed because 2 of 11 animals died after 20 mg/kg.

Histamine (Fig. 3). Subcutaneous administration of histamine phosphate resulted in a rapid decrease in the mean blood pressure of conscious, unrestrained rats. PRA increased rapidly from a basal level of about 1×10^{-4} Goldblatt u./ml. to $14-16 \times 10^{-4}$ Goldblatt u./ml. at 5, 15 and 30 min after administration of 60 mg/kg. Water intake started within $5-10$ min, but was nearly always completed by 30 min. In this period 6.9 ± 0.3 ml. was consumed by animals which received 60 mg/kg.

Subacute Stimuli

Ligation of the Inferior Vena Cava (Fig. 4). Ligation of the inferior vena cava (IVC) above the kidneys and below the liver induced a clear

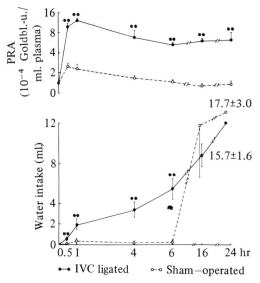

Fig. 4. Effect of ligation of the inferior vena cava (IVC) on plasma renin activity (PRA) and water intake. Results are expressed as means ±S.E. of mean ($n = 4-6$). ** $p < 0.01$

renin release. PRA reached peak values at $30-60$ min and subsequently stabilized at 6×10^{-4} Goldblatt u./ml. up to 24 h after the operation. Rats started to drink within 30 min after IVC ligation, resulting in an intake of 5.5 ± 1.0 ml. after 6 hr. During the night water intake continued, but at a slower rate and cumulative water intake was no longer significantly different from that of sham-operated rats after 16 or 24 hr (LEENEN and STRICKER 1974).

Hypovolaemia (Fig. 5). Subcutaneous administration of the hyperoncotic colloid polyethylene glycol (PEG 20-M) results in a gradual withdrawal of an isosmotic protein-free plasma fluid and fluid sequestration into the local interstitium, with plasma volume deficits (as estimated from the plasma protein concentration) proportional to the administered dose of the PEG solution (STRICKER, 1968). After 8 hr plasma volume deficits had increased to 10% and 26% for the rats given 10% PEG and 30% PEG, respectively, while PRA rose to 8×10^{-4} and 28×10^{-4} Goldblatt u./ml. Water intake also increased steadily during the 8 hr period, but to more elevated levels in rats given the more concentrated colloidal solution. After 8 hr 11.8 ± 0.6 ml. had been consumed by the 30% PEG group, 5.2 ± 0.8 ml. by the 10% PEG group and 0.8 ± 0.5 ml. by the control group (LEENEN and STRICKER 1974).

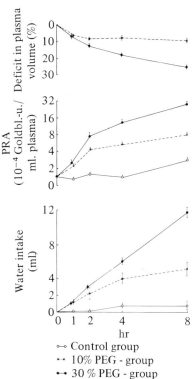

Fig. 5. Changes in plasma volume, plasma renin activity (PRA) and water intake after subcutaneous administration of 5 ml. of 10% and 30% solution of polyethylene glycol (PEG). Results are expressed as means ±S.E. of mean ($n = 5-7$). All differences are significant at $p < 0.01$

Chronic Stimulus

Two-Kidney Goldblatt Hypertension (Fig. 6). Blood pressure increased to 160–180 mm Hg or 200–230 mm Hg, depending on the internal diameter of the solid renal artery clip (LEENEN and DE JONG, 1971). No changes in peripheral PRA were observed after application of solid clips with I.D. 0.25 mm, when measured under basal conditions. After application of solid clips with I.D. 0.20 mm, basal peripheral PRA started to rise about one week after operation and was increased by 300–500% after 3–5 weeks (LEENEN, DE JONG, and DE WIED, 1973).

All animals showed a decrease in water intake during the first day after operation. After one week, water intake started to increase only in the

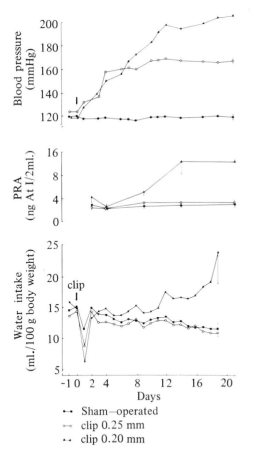

Fig. 6. Changes in systolic blood pressure, plasma renin activity (PRA) and water intake after application of solid renal arterial clips with internal diameters of 0.25 and 0.20 mm. Results are expressed as means ±S.E. of mean ($n = 6-8$)

group with the 0.20 mm clip. The increase in water intake and in basal peripheral PRA followed the same time course, and values of PRA and water intake were correlated with each other ($r = +0.77$, $p < 0.05$, $n = 8$).

Discussion

In the present experiments the quantitative and temporal relations between PRA and water intake following a number of treatments were investigated. The results clearly indicate that there is no simple relation between these variables. Water intake was absent following methoxamine despite an increase in PRA (also seen previously in man and dogs; LEENEN, REDMOND, and McDONALD, 1973; WINER, CHOKSHI, and WALKENHORST, 1969). Water intake was quantitatively the same following certain histamine and isoprenaline treatments, but the onset was more rapid following histamine despite lower levels of PRA. Following IVC ligation or administration of histamine, water intake ended despite continued high levels of PRA. Finally, PRA increased to high levels following PEG, histamine or isoprenaline treatments, yet other studies have shown that in nephrectomized animals the increase in water intake is the same after PEG but is partially diminished following histamine and is completely abolished following isoprenaline (FITZSIMONS, 1961; FITZSIMONS and STRICKER, 1971; GUTMAN and KRAUSZ, 1973).

These findings indicate that if the increase in circulating plasma renin activity is causally related to the observed water intakes, then other factors must potentiate or decrease its dipsogenic actions. For example, effective osmotic dilution might terminate drinking despite the continued presence of the dipsogenic stimulus (STRICKER, 1973).

The experiments with histamine, methoxamine and PEG appear to suggest the presence of at least one additional system involved in drinking behaviour. It is tempting to speculate that thoracic receptors in the low pressure system, comparable to those demonstrated for the control of vasopressin secretion (HENRY, GUPTA, MEEHAN, SINCLAIR, and SHARE, 1968), may influence central neural reflexes involved in thirst and drinking behaviour during hypovolaemia (FITZSIMONS, 1972; STRICKER, 1973). In this regard, activation of these receptors might be expected following PEG or histamine treatments, owing to the development of plasma deficits, but not after isoprenaline since in this case there is an increase in cardiac venous return.

Acknowledgements. The research reported in this paper was supported, in part, by training grant HLO 5467-13 (in Clinical Pharmacology) from the National Institute of Health and by Research Grant GB-28830 from the National Science Foundation (to E.M.S.)

Frans H.H. LEENEN was supported by an International Fellowship in Clinical Pharmacology from Merck, Sharp, and Dohme, during his stay at the Section of Clinical Pharmacology and Hypertension, University of Pittsburgh.

References

FITZSIMONS, J. T.: Drinking by rats depleted of body fluid without increase in osmotic pressure. J. Physiol. Lond. **159**, 297–309 (1961).

— Thirst. Physiol. Rev. **52**, 468–561 (1972).

FITZSIMONS, J. T., STRICKER, E. M.: Sodium appetite and the renin-angiotensin system. Nature New Biology **231**, 58–60 (1971).

GUTMAN, Y., KRAUSZ, M.: Drinking induced by dextran and histamine: relation to kidneys and renin. Europ. J. Pharmacol. **23**, 256–263 (1973).

HABER, E., KOERNER, T., PAGE, L. B., KLIMAN, B., PURNODE, A.: Application of a radioimmunoassay for angiotensin I to the physiological measurements of plasma renin activity in normal human subjects. J. clin. Endocr. **29**, 1349–1355 (1969).

HENRY, J. P., GUPTA, P. D., MEEHAN, J. P., SINCLAIR, R., SHARE, L.: The role of afferents from the low-pressure system in the release of antidiuretic hormone during non-hypotensive hemorrhage. Can. J. Physiol. Pharmacol. **46**, 287–295 (1968).

LEENEN, F. H. H., DE JONG, W.: A solid silver clip for induction of predictable levels of renal hypertension in the rat. J. appl. Physiol. **31**, 142–144 (1971).

LEENEN, F. H. H., DE JONG, W., DE WIED, D.: Renal venous and peripheral plasma renin activity in renal hypertension in the rat. Am. J. Physiol. **225**, 1513–1518 (1973).

LEENEN, F. H. H., REDMOND, D. P., MCDONALD, JR., R. H.: Nonspecificity of adrenergic stimulation of renin release in humans. Clin. Pharmacol. Ther. **14**, 142 (1973).

LEENEN, F. H. H., STRICKER, E. M.: Plasma renin activity and thirst following hypovolemia or caval ligation in rats. Am J. Physiol. **226**, 1238–1242 (1974).

PICKENS, P. T., BUMPUS, F. M., LLOYD, A. M., SMEBY, R. R., PAGE, I. H.: Measurement of renin activity in human plasma. Circulation Res. **17**, 438–448 (1965).

STRICKER, E. M.: Some physiological and motivational properties of the hypovolemic stimulus for thirst. Physiol. Behav. **3**, 379–385 (1968).

— Thirst, sodium appetite, and complementary physiological contributions to the regulation of intravascular fluid volume. In: The Neuropsychology of Thirst, Eds. A. EPSTEIN, H. R. KISSILEFF, E. STELLAR, Washington, D. C.: V. M. Winston and Sons, pp. 73–98, 1973.

WINER, N., CHOKSHI, D. S., WALKENHORST, W. G.: Site of action of adrenergic blocking agents on renin secretion. J. Lab. clin. Med. **74**, 1024–1025 (1969).

Drinking Induced by Direct or Indirect Stimulation of Beta-Receptors: Evidence for Involvement of the Renin-Angiotensin System

D. K. Meyer and G. Hertting

In 1966 a new phenomenon was described by Zamboni and Siro-Brigiani. They reported that the peripheral injection of isoprenaline causes drinking in rats. Up to this date drinking induced by drugs had only been observed after injections directly into the central nervous system (Grossman, 1960). Lehr, Mallow, and Krukowski (1967), confirming the results of Zamboni and Siro-Brigiani (1966), postulated that stimulation of β-receptors mediated drinking and they considered that these β-receptors were in the central nervous system.

Surprisingly, not only did β-sympathomimetic drugs such as isoprenaline produce drinking, so also did the α-sympatholytic drug phentolamine and even hydralazine, which is known to lower blood pressure by a direct action on vascular smooth muscle. The dipsogenic effect of all these drugs could be prevented by propranolol, a sympathetic β-receptor antagonist (Peskar, Leodolter, and Hertting, 1970a). Peripheral mechanisms, for example changes in haemodynamics such as hypovolaemia and/or hypotension, were postulated as the common mediator of the drinking caused by these differently acting drugs. Since Fitzsimons (1969) had demonstrated that stimulation of the renin-angiotensin system may cause drinking, it was thought possible that this endocrine system may play a role in drinking induced by these drugs.

This speculation was supported by the following findings: 1) There is an enormous increase in the plasma concentration of renin after the injection of isoprenaline, phentolamine and hydralazine (Peskar, Meyer, Tauchmann, and Hertting, 1970b; Gutman, Benzakein, and Livneh, 1971); 2) Acute nephrectomy totally abolishes drinking caused by these drugs (Meyer, Peskar, and Hertting, 1971a; Houpt and Epstein, 1971; Gutman et al., 1971); 3) Propranolol, a β-receptor blocking agent, prevents the increase in plasma renin concentration and drinking observed after the injection of isoprenaline, phentolamine and hydralazine (Meyer, Peskar, Tauchmann, and Hertting, 1971b; Gutman et al., 1971). This effect of propranolol is attributable to its blocking action on the β-receptors, since it is seen only after L-propranolol, and not after D-propranolol (D-propranolol is devoid of a β-receptor blocking effect) (Meyer, Rauscher, Peskar, and Hertting, 1973a).

It was concluded that both the enhanced water intake and the increase in plasma renin were caused by the stimulation of β-receptors. The striking correlation between plasma levels of renin and water intake suggested a role for the renin-angiotensin system in the drinking response. This assumption was confirmed by the fact, already mentioned, that removal of the renin system by acute nephrectomy totally abolishes drinking. In the following experiments the problem of how such differently acting drugs as β-sympathomimetics, α-sympatholytics and drugs such as hydralazine that lower the blood pressure by acting on vascular smooth muscle could stimulate the same type of receptor, i.e. the β-receptors.

It had been shown that phentolamine and hydralazine, in the doses used in our experiments on drinking, caused a reflexly mediated increase in the activity of the sympathetic nervous system. This increased activity of the cardiac (LEODOLTER, PESKAR, HELLMANN, and HERTTING, 1971; DAIRMAN and UDENFRIEND, 1970) and the vascular sympathetic nerves (BIGELOW, DAIRMANN, WEIL-MALHERBE, and UDENFRIEND, 1969) as well as of the adrenal medulla (DAIRMAN and UDENFRIEND, 1970) is reflected in an elevated noradrenaline turnover and an augmented catecholamine synthesis. It was thought possible that the catecholamines released in this way stimulate the β-receptors which trigger off renin release and drinking. Isoprenaline as a β-mimetic would stimulate the β-receptors directly without any assistance from catecholamine release from the sympathetic nervous system.

This assumption was tested using ganglionic blocking agents with the following results (Fig. 1): Ganglionic blockade by camphidonium or pempidine abolished the drinking and increase in the plasma concentration of renin caused by phentolamine but the responses to isoprenaline were unaffected (MEYER et al. 1973a). Since a reflexly mediated activation of the sympathetic nervous system is impossible during ganglionic blockade, phentolamine cannot release catecholamines and thus stimulate the β-receptors indirectly. The effect of isoprenaline is not attenuated, however, because this drug stimulates the β-receptors directly.

Reserpine, which depletes the catecholamine stores of the sympathetic nerves and the adrenal medulla, had the same effects as ganglionic blockade. Drinking and plasma renin elevation following phentolamine were abolished but this was not the case after isoprenaline (MEYER et al., 1973a).

The correlation between plasma renin concentrations and drinking, observed in these experiments, indicated a possible role for the renin system in this type of drinking. The fact that ganglionic blockade by camphidonium, a drug which does not penetrate the blood-brain barrier, totally abolished phentolamine-induced drinking clearly indicated that peripheral mechanisms, i.e. the sympathetic nervous sys-

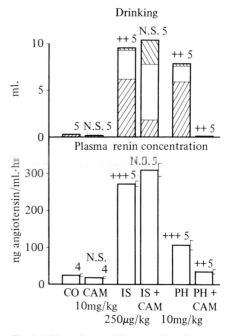

Fig. 1. Effect of camphidonium (CAM) on the water intake and the increase in plasma renin concentration induced by isoprenaline (IS) and phentolamine (PH). Water intake is expressed as ml. water drunk per animal during the first ▨, second ▭, and third ▨ hour. Plasma renin concentration is expressed as ng angiotensin II equivalents of angiotensin I produced by 1 ml. rat plasma during one hour under our incubation conditions. Bioassay was used to determine the angiotensin I generated. Results are expressed as means ±S.E. of means Numbers of animals used are shown above each column. $+, p < 0.05, ++, P < 0.01, +++, p < 0.001$, N.S., not significant. Symbols above columns showing a group of animals treated with a drug combination indicate significant differences between the group with combination of drugs and the group treated with isoprenaline (IS) or phentolamine (PH) alone. CO = controls

tem, were involved in the drinking. Fig. 2 gives a schematical presentation of the postulated mechanisms.

In contrast, other authors postulated a central site of action for isoprenaline and phentolamine (LEHR, 1969). This hypothesis was based on experiments made with brain-cannulated rats. Extremely high intracranial doses of isoprenaline (up to 40 μg/single injection) had been found to produce drinking (LEHR, 1969; LEIBOWITZ, 1971), probably brought about by a leakage of the drug from the injection site to the

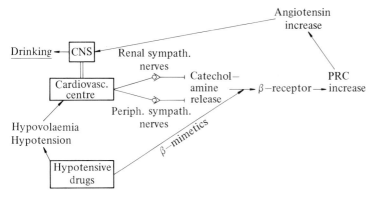

Fig. 2. The β-sympathomimetic isoprenaline acts directly on the β-receptors, which trigger renin release. Other dipsogens such as phentolamine and hydralazine cause a reflexly mediated catecholamine-release from the sympathetic nervous system. The stimuli for this release may be hypovolaemia or hypotension. These catecholamines act on the β-receptors which are responsible for renin release. The increase in plasma renin concentration induced either by β-mimetics or by catecholamine releasing agents causes an enhanced generation of angiotensin I and II. These peptides mediate drinking directly or indirectly

periphery (FISHER, 1973; LEHR, 1973). It seems likely that in these experiments too, the renin-angiotensin system may have been responsible for the drinking. The importance of the renin-angiotensin system in this type of drug-induced drinking has been further confirmed recently (MEYER and HERTTING, 1973b) and these results are now presented.

In these experiments the influence of blockers of the neuronal uptake of catecholamines on drinking, and on plasma concentrations of renin and angiotensin I after isoprenaline and phentolamine was studied. Since neuronal uptake is the main inactivation mechanism for the catecholamines released from the sympathetic nerve endings, blockade of the inactivation results in an accumulation of catecholamines, causing higher concentrations at the receptors and increased stimulation. Since drinking and increased plasma renin after phentolamine depend on a reflexly mediated catecholamine release, they should be enhanced by neuronal uptake blockers, such as amitriptyline, desipramine or cocaine. Isoprenaline-induced effects, however, should be unaffected by uptake blockers. The results of this experiment are shown in Fig. 3. Only phentolamine-induced effects were increased by amitriptyline.

The big increase in plasma angiotensin I after isoprenaline and phentolamine deserves our attention, since EPSTEIN (1972) has demonstrated

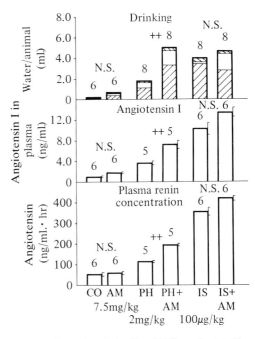

Fig. 3. Effect of amitriptyline (AM) on the drinking and the increase in plasma angiotensin I concentration and plasma renin concentration induced by isoprenaline (IS) and phentolamine (PH). Drinking is expressed as ml. water drunk per animal during the first ▨, second ▭, and third ▨ hour. Angiotensin I and renin plasma levels were determined by radioimmunoassay. Symbols above columns indicate differences between the amitriptyline-treated groups and those treated with isoprenaline, phentolamine or distilled water alone. For further explanation see Fig. 1 (MEYER and HERTTING, 1973)

that intravenously infused angiotensin I is about twice as potent a dipsogen as angiotensin II. This was corroborated by the following findings in our laboratory: 1) i.v. infusion of 72 n-mole of angiotensin I caused as much drinking in rats as 112 n-mole of angiotensin II (about 3.0 ml./animal). 2) SQ 20,881, an inhibitor of converting enzyme, potentiated the drinking caused by i.v. infusion of angiotensin I, but not that caused by angiotensin II (HERTTING and MEYER, unpublished). In Fig. 4 the plasma levels of angiotensin I observed after angiotensin I infusion or phentolamine, serotonin and isoprenaline, respectively, are compared with the amounts of water drunk by the animals.

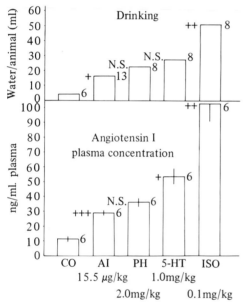

Fig. 4. Comparison of drinking and plasma levels of angiotensin I in rats after different extracellular stimuli of thirst (intravenous infusion of angiotensin I (A I) for 1 hour, phentolamine (PH), serotonin (5-HT) and isoprenaline (ISO)). Asterisks between two columns indicate significant differences between both groups. For further explanation see Fig. 1

In view of the close correlation between plasma angiotensin I and drinking it seems unlikely that the changes in activity of the renin-angiotensin system are purely coincidental and unrelated to the mechanisms regulating drinking. Of course, several other factors may well influence the drug-induced drinking.

Mechanisms which may terminate drinking are osmodilution (STRICKER, 1971) and volume expansion (JONES and ROLLS, 1971). Haemodynamic changes may also modify the drinking response. Finally, the possibility cannot be excluded that other neuro-endocrine systems operating independently or with the renin-angiotensin system may be involved in the regulation of this drinking.

The way in which the renin-angiotensin system causes drinking cannot be deduced from the results presented here. A central site of action is possible, in view of the results of EPSTEIN, FITZSIMONS, and ROLLS (1970), which showed that angiotensin II is a highly potent dipsogen, when injected into the hypothalamus.

This assumption is contested by LEHR and GOLDMAN (1973) who found that large doses of atropine given i.p. inhibited drinking caused by intracranial angiotensin II, but not that induced by isoprenaline given s.c. Since BLASS and CHAPMAN 1971 found that systemic atropine had no effect on the drinking induced by central angiotensin II this point needs further investigation.

References

BIGELOW, L. B., DAIRMAN, W., WEIL-MALHERBE, H., UDENFRIEND, S.: Increased synthesis of catecholamines and their metabolites following the administration of phenoxybenzamine. Molec. Pharmacol. **5**, 565–571 (1969).

BLASS, E. M., CHAPMAN, H. W.: An evaluation of the contribution of cholinergic mechanisms to thirst. Physiol. Behav. **7**, 679–686 (1971).

DAIRMAN, W., UDENFRIEND, S.: Effect of ganglionic blocking agents on the increased synthesis of catecholamines resulting from alpha adrenergic blockade or exposure to cold. Biochem. Pharmac. **19**, 979–984 (1970).

EPSTEIN, A. N., FITZSIMONS, J. T., SIMONS, B. J.: Drinking induced by injection of angiotensin into the brain of the rat. J. Physiol. **210**, 457–474 (1970).

EPSTEIN, A. N.: Drinking induced by low doses of intravenous angiotensin. The Physiologist **15**, 127 (1972).

FISHER, A. E.: Relationships between cholinergic and other dipsogens in the central mediation of thirst. In: Neuropsychology of thirst (Eds. A. N. EPSTEIN, H. KISSILEFF, and E. STELLAR), pp. 243–278. Washington D.C.: V. H. Winston and Sons 1973.

FITZSIMONS, J. T.: The role of a renal thirst factor in drinking induced by extracellular stimuli. J. Physiol. Lond. **201**, 349–368 (1969).

GROSSMAN, S. P.: Eating and drinking elicited by direct adrenergic or cholinergic stimulation of hypothalamus. Science **132**, 301–302 (1960).

GUTMAN, Y., BENZAKEIN, F., LIVNEH, P.: Polydipsia induced by isoprenaline and by lithium: relation to kidneys and renin. Europ. J. Pharmacol. **16**, 380–384 (1971).

HOUPT, K. A., EPSTEIN, A. N.: The complete dependence of β-adrenergic drinking on the renal dipsogen. Physiol. Behav. **7**, 897–902 (1971).

JONES, B. P., ROLLS, B. J.: Inhibition of drinking induced by intracranial angiotensin by ingestion of either isotonic saline or water. J. Physiol. Lond. **218**, 45 P–46 P (1971).

LEHR, D., MALLOW, J., KRUKOWSKI, M.: Copious drinking and simultaneous inhibition of urine flow elicited by β-adrenergic stimulation and contrary effect of α-adrenergic stimulation. J. Pharmac. exp. Ther. **158**, 150–163 (1967).

LEHR, D.: Discussion of a paper by S. P. GROSSMAN entitled: A neuropharmacologic analysis of hypothalamic and extrahypothalamic mechanisms concerned with the regulation of food and water intake. Ann. N.Y. Acad. Sci. **157**, 912 (1969).

— Invited comment. In: Neuropsychology of Thirst. (Eds. A. N. EPSTEIN, H. KISSELEFF, and E. STELLAR), pp. 307–314. Washington D.C.: V. H. Winston and Sons 1973.

LEHR, D., GOLDMAN, W.: Continued pharmacologic analysis of consumatory behavior in the albino rat. Europ. J. Pharmacol. **23**, 197–210 (1973).

LEIBOWITZ, S. F.: Hypothalamic α- and β-adrenergic systems regulate both thirst and hunger in the rat. Proc. Nat. Acad. Sci. **68**, 332–334 (1971).

LEODOLTER, S., PESKAR, B., HELLMANN, G., HERTTING, G.: The mechanism of noradrenaline depletion by hydrazinophthalazines in the rat heart. Europ. J. Pharmacol. **13**, 188–192 (1971).

MEYER, D. K., PESKAR, B., HERTTING, G.: Hemmung des durch blutdrucksenkende Pharmaka bei Ratten ausgelösten Trinkens durch Nephrektomie. Experientia **27**, 65–66 (1971 a).

MEYER, D. K., PESKAR, B., TAUCHMANN, U., HERTTING, G.: Potentiation and abolition of the increase in plasma renin activity seen after hypotensive drugs in rats. Europ. J. Pharmacol. **16**, 278–282 (1971 b).

MEYER, D. K., RAUSCHER, W., PESKAR, B., HERTTING, G.: The mechanism of the drinking response to some hypotensive drugs: Activation of the renin-angiotensin system by direct or reflex-mediated stimulation of β-receptors. Naunyn-Schmiedeberg's Arch. Pharmacol. **276**, 13–24 (1973 a).

MEYER, D. K., HERTTING, G.: Influence of neuronal uptake blocking agents on the increase in water intake and in plasma concentrations of renin and angiotensin I induced by phentolamine and iso-

prenaline. Naunyn-Schmiedeberg's Arch. Pharmacol. **280**, 191–200 (1973 b).

PESKAR, B., LEODOLTER, S., HERTTING, G.: Die Wirkung verschiedener blutdrucksenkender Pharmaka auf Wasseraufnahme und -abgabe bei Ratten. Naunyn-Schmiedeberg's Arch. Pharmakol. **265**, 335–346 (1970 a).

PESKAR, B., MEYER, D. K., TAUCHMANN, U., HERTTING, G.: Influence of isoproterenol, hydralazine and phentolamine on the renin activity of plasma and renal cortex of rats. Europ. J. Pharmacol. **9**, 394–396 (1970 b).

STRICKER, E. M.: Inhibition of thirst in rats following hypovolemia and/or caval ligation. Physiol. Behav. **6**, 293–298 (1971).

ZAMBONI, P., SIRO-BRIGIANI, G.: Effetto delle catecolamine sulla sete e la diuresi nel ratto. Boll. Soc. Ital. Biol. Sper. **42**, 1657–1659 (1966).

Summary of Discussions

NICOLAÏDIS to STRICKER: Intraventricular 6-hydroxydopamine (6-HDA) probably damaged the periventricular angiotensin-sensitive system. Therefore the response to peripherally injected angiotensin II which presumably acts through these periventricular formations was abolished. On the other hand, polyethylene glycol treatment, which is known to cause drinking in nephrectomized rats, is still 50% effective in the 6-HDA treated rats, possibly because the cerebral angiotensin-releasing mechanism being remote from the ventricles is not affected by 6-HDA. It seems that there are two angiotensin-sensitive regions for drinking; one periventricular, sensitive to peripherally-released angiotensin, and the other remote from the ventricular wall sensitive to its own endogenous angiotensin acting as a local fail-safe hypovolaemia-detecting system, and complementary to the peripheral system. I have found hypovolaemia sensitive units in the supra-chiasmatic area. — STRICKER: I am sceptical. We have found, in confirmation of work by FITZSIMONS and SETLER, that a single intraventricular injection of 6-HDA abolishes drinking by intraventricular angiotensin, but that it does not affect drinking induced by hypovolaemia or isoprenaline. It is possible that cerebral renin is somehow supporting thirst in these circumstances (particularly after isoprenaline where baroreceptors may not mediate the response), but it must be remembered that bilateral nephrectomy abolishes isoprenaline-induced drinking in the rat. — NICOLAÏDIS: Residual drinking to isoprenaline after 6-HDA may be mediated by a neural link between the kidney and brain because isoprenaline would no longer act if the link were circulating angiotensin. — SLANGEN: High intraventricular doses of 6-HDA cause presynaptic destruction of noradrenergic neurones as well as of dopaminergic neurones. Destruction of systems other than the dopaminergic nigrostriatal system may explain some of the differences between electrolytically lesioned and 6-HDA treated animals. These differences might disappear if small doses (4 μg) of 6-HDA were injected directly into the lateral hypothalamus thereby confining destruction to the nigrostriatal system. — STRICKER: Electrolytic lesions in the lateral hypothalamus damage many more fibre systems and produce a more complicated syndrome than results from intraventricular 6-HDA particularly when the noradrenergic neurones are protected by pretreatment with desipramine. — JOHNSON: The fact that the animal showed an increase in food intake in a long-term insulin test may mean that in the course of an extended test it learns that it feels better if it eats and this does not necessarily mean that its glucoprivic controls are intact. — STRICKER: Many tests used for testing specific regulatory functions have a component of stress that we tend to neglect. We should try to develop alternative tests. — NICOLAÏDIS: A lack of response to a particular ingestive challenge in a lesioned or otherwise pretreated animal may denote hypersensitivity rather than lack of sensitivity. If this were so, a near-threshold dose of a challenge such as 2-deoxy-glucose should be more effective than higher doses. — STRICKER: Perhaps, but lesioned animals may have a higher threshold so that the treatment becomes so severe that no response will occur. To ROWLAND: It is not known whether modified circadian patterns of ingestion after lateral hypothalamic lesions or after 6-HDA are due to modified circadian patterns of brain catecholamines. —

PETERS to SETLER: If the changes observed after FLA-63 are to be ascribed to increased release and production of dopamine, this could be checked by blocking dopamine (and noradrenaline) synthesis with α-methyltyrosine, an inhibitor of tyrosine-hydroxylase. — SETLER: True, however, the aim of these experiments was to compare a situation in which noradrenaline was depleted but dopamine was normal with the situation after 6-HDA where both catecholamines were depleted.

GANTEN to SZCZEPANSKA-SADOWSKA: After nephrectomy it is conceivable that isoprenaline stimulated the extrarenal isorenin-angiotensin system to release more angiotensin which overflowed into the circulation, while at the same time plasma renin remained low or immeasurable. It is therefore important to measure angiotensin levels as well as renin. — LEHR: SZCZEPANSKA-SADOWSKA's findings in the dog are in line with our concept that in the rat also, isoprenaline-induced drinking does not depend on the renin-angiotensin system. — SZCZEPANSKA-SADOWSKA: GANTEN and LEENEN's suggestion that extrarenal renin may be important in isoprenaline-induced drinking in the nephrectomized dog cannot be excluded, but in that case one must suppose that the extrarenal isorenin system plays a much more important role in the dog than it does in the rat. —

EPSTEIN to ROLLS: The fact that the angiotensin receptor blocker saralasin acetate prevented isoprenaline-induced drinking is strong evidence for a major role for the renin-angiotensin system in this response. — SZCZEPANSKA-SADOWSKA and FITZSIMONS: The difference between our results and those of ROLLS and RAMSAY may be due to the facts that we gave intravenous infusions of isoprenaline instead of single subcutaneous injections, and that we tested our dogs within 8 hr of nephrectomy instead of 36–60 hr later. — DAY: We found that in the cat isoprenaline is a more impressive dipsogen when given centrally than peripherally. Moreover the central dipsogenic effect of angiotensin II is apparently mediated by a β-adrenergic receptor mechanism. We wonder whether isoprenaline may have a dual dipsogenic effect, causing release of renin peripherally and acting directly on β-adrenergic thirst mechanisms centrally. —

MEYER to LEHR: Plasma renin levels high enough to cause drinking have been observed in rats treated with DOCA for 3 weeks and given 1% saline to drink and then stimulated with 40 μg/kg isoprenaline. — FISHER: LEHR's suggestion that his results indicate no relationship between angiotensin and hypovolaemic or hypotensive thirst must be treated cautiously. SQ 20,881 prevents the pressor effects expected to occur as a consequence of the activation of the renin-angiotensin system and extends the hypotensive or hypovolaemic effects of the thirst challenges. The drug, therefore, increases renin release and the formation of angiotensin I. Angiotensin I may therefore accumulate and enter the brain in considerably greater quantities than in the absence of SQ 20,881. This enhancement may require much more SQ 20,881 to block the action of angiotensin I in the brain. Furthermore, peripheral angiotensin I might prove to be more effective as a dipsogen because when it reaches the brain it will be converted to angiotensin II close to the site of action of angiotensin II in the brain. The paradox I am suggesting is that the data which from one reasonable point of view seem to argue against a significant role for angiotensin in hypotensive and hypovolaemic thirst may instead favour such a role. — LEHR: FISHER's remarks agree with our concept of the renin dependency and the highly significant enhancement of isoprenaline- and vena caval-induced drinking by peripheral SQ 20,881. This may be the mechanism of the enhancement because it is effectively blocked by intraventricular SQ 20,881. This fact in itself is good evidence that the large dose of SQ 20,881 used (30 μg) is effective in preventing the drinking dependent upon angiotensin II formation in the brain. This observation and the very effective block of renin-induced drinking in the nephrectomized rat by the same intraventricular dose of SQ 20,881 emphasize the failure of intraventricular SQ 20,881 to attenuate drinking to isoprenaline and caval ligation. —

LEHR to LEENEN: LEENEN's results demonstrate the lack of correlation between plasma renin levels and drinking. One week's treatment with DOCA and saline may be inadequate to cause significant renin depletion. Three weeks' treatment, however, causes more than 95% depletion of kidney renin. Yet in such renin-depleted rats we did not find any significant reduction in drinking elicited by β-adrenergic activation. — LEENEN: We also found a decrease in water intake from 6 ml. in normal rats to 2.5 ml. in DOCA-treated rats. However, not only is the total renin depletion produced by DOCA important but also the amount of releasable renin. As we showed, there is still an increase, though less than usual, in PRA following 100 μg/kg isoprenaline. — PETERS to LEENEN: Sodium depletion induced by a single injection of furosemide followed by a diet poor in sodium, in rats, induces a 10 fold increase of the plasma renin level within 10 days. Water intake, in these animals was not higher than in controls treated in the same manner but given sodium. This fact casts some doubt on the role of high plasma renin levels in increased drinking, in animals with two kidney Goldblatt hypertension. — LEENEN: These animals cannot be compared with those in the acute phase (about 3 weeks) of renal hypertension because their lower body sodium and hypovolaemia may have an anti-dipsic effect. —

EPSTEIN to MEYER: There is some merit to MEYER's speculation that the greater effectiveness of angiotensin I as a dipsogen may be due to greater amounts of it reaching the brain. Most of the conversion of angiotensin I to angiotensin II occurs in the lungs. Converting enzyme blockers injected peripherally will of course reach the pulmonary capillary bed and will permit large amounts of unconverted angiotensin I to reach the systemic circulation. The final conversion could then occur in the brain itself. Angiotensin II on the other hand will be degraded in non-pulmonary capillary beds before reaching the brain.

Section 6
Central Mechanisms in Renin-Angiotensin-Induced Drinking

Renin, Angiotensin and Drinking

J. T. FITZSIMONS

Renal Renin

Renin has been found in the outer zone of the renal cortex of every mammal investigated as well as in birds, reptiles, amphibians and some fish (CAPELLI, WESSON, and APONTE, 1970). Marine teleosts with glomerular or aglomerular kidneys have measurable quantities but the greatest amounts are found in the freshwater teleosts and the anadromous teleosts recovered from fresh water. No measurable renin was found in the kidney of the frog kept in dilute saline but significant amounts were found in animals living in fresh water. The level of renin activity in the submammalian vertebrate kidney, as in the mammalian kidney, appears to be inversely related to Na balance. It should, however, be pointed out that the tissue renin level is only an approximate guide to the rate of secretion of renin. Since aldosterone appears in significant quantities only in terrestrial vertebrates and hardly at all in fishes, the question of how, if at all, the phylogenetically older renin-angiotensin system functions in fluid and elec-trolyte homeostasis in lower vertebrates remains to be determined.

In the mammal there is a great deal of evidence that angiotensin II is the most important stimulus to aldosterone secretion, though decreased plasma Na, increased plasma K, corticotrophin and at least one other unidenti-fied humoral factor also enter into the control (PEART, 1969; COGHLAN, BLAIR-WEST, DENTON, SCOGGINS, and WRIGHT, 1971). Angiotensin has several other actions (Fig. 1), some of which may be physiological. In particular it is the most potent intracranial dipsogen known (EPSTEIN, FITZSIMONS, and ROLLS, 1970) and stimulates drinking in all mammalian species so far investigated, including monkey, dog, cat, goat, rabbit and rat, and it is also dipsogenic in the Barbary dove.

The stimuli that lead to the release of renin are a reduction in renal perfusion pressure, haemorrhage, trauma, rising from the supine to the upright posture, exercise, hypoglycaemia, low sodium diet, diuretics which cause Na depletion, and β-adrenergic agents (ASSAYKEEN and GA-

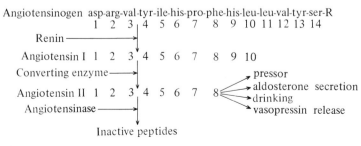

Fig. 1. The renin-angiotensin system and some of its reported functions

97

NONG, 1971; DAVIS, 1971). The three theories of how renin secretion is controlled are, (1) a renal baroreceptor responsive to changes in renal perfusion pressure, (2) the macula densa responsive to changes in distal tubular Na, and (3) receptors elsewhere in the body controlling release of renin through the sympathetic nerves to the kidney. We need not discuss these theories but simply note that most of the stimuli that cause release of renin also induce drinking in the water-replete animal and that in some cases at least drinking appears to be entirely hormonal because it is abolished by nephrectomy.

Angiotensin-Induced Drinking

The theory that the renal renin-angiotensin system plays an essential role in drinking induced by extracellular stimuli has been described elsewhere (FITZSIMONS, 1969; 1970) and is illustrated in Fig. 2. Renin, tetradecapeptide renin substrate and angiotensin I were also found to be potent intracranial dipsogens, but

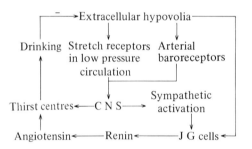

Fig. 2. The possible mechanisms for drinking caused by extracellular dehydration (from FITZSIMONS 1970)

shorter chain peptide fragments of angiotensin II were less active or totally inactive (FITZSIMONS, 1971) (Fig. 3). From Fig. 3 it is evident that the molecular requirements for the dipsogenic activity of components of the renin-angiotensin system are similar to those described (GROSS, 1971) for other physiological actions of the system except that renin substrate and angiotensin I are unexpectedly effective at causing drinking. The reasons for this must now be discussed because they re-open the question of normal involvement of renal renin in extracellularly induced drinking.

Extrarenal Renin

Renin or renin-like substances have been found in various extrarenal tissues including the submaxillary gland of the mouse, the placenta of the cat, the placenta and the pregnant and nonpregnant uterus of the rabbit, the splanchnic region of the dog, central nervous tissue in rat and dog and indeed in almost all mammalian tissues (HAYDUK, BOUCHER, and GENEST, 1970; GROSS, 1971; NAHMOD, FISCHER-FERRARO, FINKIELMAN, DIAZ, and GOLDSTEIN, 1972). The activity of extrarenal renin is extremely low compared with renal renin (except in the central nervous system) and there are sometimes differences in substrate specificities and pH optima. It is important to emphasise that tissue extracts from nephrectomized animals contained the same renin activity as extracts from normal animals so it is unlikely that extrarenal renin came from the kidney. Renin-like activity has

H.asn.arg.val.tyr.val.his.pro.phe.his.leu.leu.val.tyr.ser.OH

asp 2	3	4	ileu 6	7	8	9	10	11	12	13	14		+ + + + + +
1 2	3	4	5	6	7	8	9	10					+ + + + +
1 2	3	4	5	6	7	8							+ + + +
β asp 2	3	4	5	6	7	8							+ + + +
1 D-arg 3	4	5	6	7	8								0
2	3	4	5	6	7	8							+ +
1 2	3	4	5	6	7								0
3	4	5	6	7	8								0
4	5	6	7	8									0
5	6	7	8										0
1 2	3	4											0

Fig. 3. The relative dipsogenic activity of peptide precursors and of shorter chain peptide fragments of angiotensin II injected into the rat's brain

also been found in the plasma of anephric man many months after nephrectomy (YU, ANDERTON, SKINNER, and BEST, 1972).

The extrarenal renin of especial interest to us in view of the sensitivity of limbic structures to the dipsogenic actions of components of the renin-angiotensin system is that found in the central nervous system. Renin itself (FISCHER-FERRARO, NAHMOD, GOLDSTEIN, and FINKIELMAN, 1971; GANTEN, MARQUEZ-JULIO, GRANGER, HAYDUK, KARSUNKY, BOUCHER, and GENEST, 1971), angiotensins I and II (FISCHER-FERRARO et al. 1971; GOLDSTEIN et al. 1970; GANTEN et al. 1971), converting enzyme (YANG and NEFF, 1972), angiotensinase (GOLDSTEIN, DIAZ, FINKIELMAN, NAHMOD, and FISCHER-FERRARO, 1972) and, less certainly, renin substrate (GANTEN et al. 1971) have been demonstrated in central nervous tissue of rat and dog. All the components of an intrinsic cerebral renin-angiotension system are therefore present which immediately raises the question of what are the physiological functions of the system and what is the relationship between it and the renal system.

Peptide Specificity of Angiotensin-Sensitive Neurones

The discovery of a central nervous renin-angiotensin system has at least provided us with a possible explanation of how it is that renin, renin substrate and angiotensin I cause drinking, when it is believed that all other physiological actions of these substances are mediated through angiotensin II. The components of the cerebral system would ensure the local generation of angiotensin II when renin, renin substrate or angiotensin I is injected into the brain. It has proved possible to

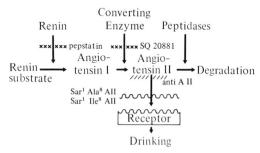

Fig. 4. The sites of action of anti-angiotensin II and of peptide antagonists of the renin-angiotensin system

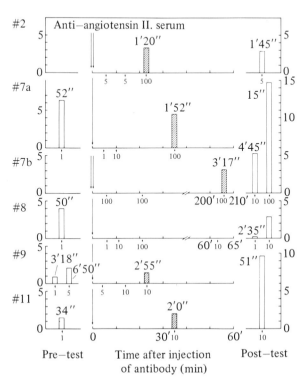

Pre-test   Time after injection   Post-test
of antibody (min)

Fig. 5. The failure to drink to intracranial angiotensin II after injection of anti-angiotensin II serum. The amounts drunk in ml. are shown before injection of antiserum (pre-test, far left) at varying intervals after antiserum (hatched columns, centre), and at least one full day after antiserum (post-test, far right). The abscissa shows minutes after injection of antiserum. The dose of angiotensin II in p-moles is given beneath each arrow and the latency to the onset of drinking is given above or next to the columns. Animal no. 7 was tested twice with an interval of 4 days between the two tests. All injections of antiserum were given unilaterally (single arrows) except for animal no. 2 and the second test in animal no. 7 where the injections were bilateral (double arrow). The volume injected through a single cannula was 10 µl. except in the second test with animal no. 7 where 12.5 µl. was given through each cannula. Angiotensin was always given unilaterally and through the same cannula as the antiserum. In control experiments (not illustrated) angiotensin-induced drinking was unaffected by prior injection of non-immune rabbit serum (from EPSTEIN, FITZSIMONS, and JOHNSON, 1973)

test this explanation by using specific antibodies and peptide antagonists of the renin-angiotensin system. These experiments were carried out in collaboration with A. N. EPSTEIN and A. K. JOHNSON, and were made possible by generous gifts of antibody from P. MEYER and Mary OSBORNE of Paris, and peptides from F. GROSS of Heidelberg, F. M. BUMPUS of Cleveland, A. CASTELLION of the Norwich Pharmacal Company and F. F. GIARRUSSO of Squibb and Son.

We examined the specificity of the angiotensin-sensitive drinking receptor by comparing the amounts of water drunk in response to the various intracranial dipsogens, given immediately after the particular antagonist, with the amounts drunk after control injections of isotonic saline. The agonists and antagonists were given through the same brain cannula. The rationale of the experiment and the antagonists used are illustrated in Fig. 4. In the first series of experiments with angiotensin II-antiserum it was found that drinking induced by antigenically active angiotensin II could be prevented (Fig. 5) and drinking to angiotensin I and renin substrate attenuated, by prior injection of antiserum (EPSTEIN, FITZSIMONS, and JOHNSON, 1973). The block is reversible.

The results of the second series of experiments (EPSTEIN, FITZSIMONS, and JOHNSON, 1974) (Fig. 6) are as follows. 1) Pepstatin, a pentapeptide inhibitor of the renin-angiotensinogen reaction (GROSS, LAZAR, and ORTH, 1972), isolated from culture filtrates of streptomycetes, significantly reduced renin- and renin substrate-induced drinking but had no significant effect on angiotensin II- and carbachol-induced drinking. — 2) SQ 20,881, a nonapeptide inhibitor of converting enzyme from the venom of the South American snake *Bothrops jararaca* (ENGEL, SCHAEFFER, GOLD, and RUBIN, 1972), in high doses, caused a significant reduction in renin-, renin substrate- and angiotensin I-induced drinking but unexpectedly enhanced angiotensin II-induced drinking in some animals. Systemic SQ 20,881 has also recently been found to increase drinking in response to isoprenaline or to caval ligation (LEHR, GOLDMAN, and CASNER, this volume). There may be a common explanation, as yet unknown, of the exaggerated drinking in the two experiments. — There are conflicting reports in the literature on the effect of SQ 20,881 on angiotensin I-induced drinking. SEVERS, SUMMY-LONG, and DANIELS-SEVERS (1973), in agreement with the present experiments, report abolition of angiotensin-I-induced drinking, whereas SWANSON, MARSHALL, NEEDLEMAN and SHARPE (1973) and BURCKHARDT, PETERS-HAEFELI and PETERS (this volume) found no inhibition. The reason for these differences remains to be elucidated. — 3) Sar[1], Ala[8] angiotensin II (saralasin acetate, Norwich Pharmacal), a specific competitive antagonist of angiotensin II (PALS, MASUCCI, DENNING, SIPOS, and FESSLER, 1971), blocked renin-, renin substrate-, angiotensin I- and angiotensin II-induced drinking almost completely without affecting carbachol-induced drink-

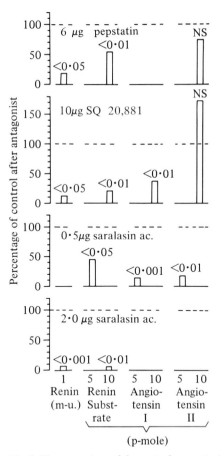

Fig. 6. The percentage of the control amounts of water drunk in 15 min when intracranial injections of various components of the renin-angiotensin system were preceded by peptide antagonists of the system

100

ing. The competitive antagonist, Sar[1], Ile[8] angiotensin II (TÜRKER, HALL, YAMAMOTO, SWEET, and BUMPUS, 1972) behaved similarly against drinking induced by angiotensin I or angiotensin II. None of the peptide antagonists caused drinking on its own.

The conclusion drawn from the two series of experiments with antagonists is that drinking in response to the components of the renin-angiotensin system injected intracranially is mainly mediated by local generation of angiotensin II, the intrinsic renin-angiotensin system providing the necessary enzymes to effect the conversion of injected substances to angiotensin II.

Conclusion

Satisfactory though it is to find that the peptide specificity of the angiotensin-sensitive thirst neurones is limited to the single substance angiotensin II, it leaves the question of what is the physiological function of the cerebral renin-angiotensin system unanswered. Is the brain's own angiotensin a neurotransmitter substance especially concerned with drinking and water retention by the kidney — for angiotensin is known to release vasopressin (MOUW, BONJOUR, MALVIN, and VANDER, 1971) as well as induce drinking? This idea might find support in view of the striking correlation between the content of angiotensin and that of noradrenaline, a proven neurotransmitter, in the rat brain (GOLDSTEIN et al. 1970). Further support for the idea is perhaps the evidence for the participation of central catecholaminergic neurones, particularly dopaminergic neurones in angiotensin-induced drinking (FITZSIMONS and SETLER, 1971; SETLER, this volume). This evidence is: 1) Angiotensin causes release of or interferes with the reuptake of noradrenaline (PALAIC and KHAIRALLAH, 1968). — 2) Angiotensin-induced drinking is markedly reduced by pretreatment with intracranial 6-hydroxydopamine which destroys catecholaminergic neurones whereas carbachol-induced drinking is unaffected. — 3) Neither angiotensin- nor carbachol-induced drinking is affected by centrally administered α- or β-adrenergic antagonists, but the dopamine

antagonist haloperidol abolishes angiotensin-induced drinking without affecting carbachol-induced drinking. — 4) Noradrenaline attenuates drinking induced by cellular dehydration and carbachol, but does not affect drinking caused by extracellular thirst stimuli or angiotensin. — 5) Intraventricular dopamine (260–520 n-moles) causes some drinking. — 6) The combination of FLA-63, an inhibitor of dopamine β-hydroxylase, and levodopa, which depletes the brain of noradrenaline and increases its dopamine content, caused decreased feeding and increased drinking in food deprived rats (SETLER, this volume).

The impression gained from these findings is of some functional relationship between angiotensin and central catecholaminergic mechanisms but how or why is unknown. Why the association should be with noradrenaline, which generally causes eating, and not with acetylcholine, a potent intracranial dipsogen in the rat, is also unclear. Angiotensin-induced drinking is quite unaffected by doses of atropine which completely block carbachol-induced drinking, nor is it affected by the nicotinic antagonist dihydro-β-erythroidine (FITZSIMONS and SETLER, 1971 and unpublished). But if the function of angiotensin is to facilitate the release and biosynthesis of a catecholamine, perhaps especially dopamine, which angiotensin does this? That locally generated, or the angiotensin formed in the plasma by renal renin? In the end the scheme illustrated in Fig. 2 may be a physiological artifact which would account for drinking in certain emergency, pathological situations, but which would have to be replaced by a scheme incorporating cerebral renin-angiotensin to explain the normal day-to-day control of primary or regulatory drinking. The crude pressor extract of kidney discovered by TIGERSTEDT and BERGMAN in 1898 and which they called renin has not yet achieved physiological quietus.

References

ASSAYKEEN, TATIANA, A., GANONG, W. F.: The sympathetic nervous system and renin secretion. In: Frontiers in Neuroendocrinology (Eds. MARTINI and W. F. GANONG). pp. 67–102 New York: Oxford University Press 1971.

CAPELLI, J. P., WESSON, L. G., APONTE, G. E.: A phylogenetic study of the renin-angiotensin system. Am. J. Physiol. **218**, 1171–1178 (1970).

COGHLAN, J. P., BLAIR-WEST, J. R., DENTON, D. A., SCOGGINS, B. A., WRIGHT, R. D.: Perspectives in aldosterone and renin control. Aust. N.Z. J. Med. **2**, 178–197 (1971).

DAVIS, J. O.: What signals the kidney to release renin. Circulation Res. **28**, 301–306 (1971).

ENGEL, S. L., SCHAEFFER, T. R., GOLD, B. I., RUBIN, B.: Inhibition of pressor effects of angiotensin I and augmentation of the depressor effects of bradykinin by synthetic peptides. Proc. Soc. Exp. Biol. Med. **140**, 240–244 (1972).

EPSTEIN, A. N., FITZSIMONS, J. T., ROLLS (née Simons), BARBARA, J.: Drinking induced by injection of angiotensin into the brain of the rat. J. Physiol. Lond. **210**, 457–474 (1970).

EPSTEIN, A. N., FITZSIMONS, J. T., JOHNSON, A. K.: Prevention by angiotensin II antiserum of drinking induced by intracranial angiotensin. J. Physiol. Lond. **230**, 42–43 P (1973).

— Peptide antagonists of the renin-angiotensin system and the elucidation of the receptors for angiotensin-induced drinking. J. Physiol. Lond., **238**, 34 P–35 P (1974).

FISCHER-FERRARO, C., NAHMOD, V. E., GOLDSTEIN, D. J.,FINKIELMAN, S.: Angiotensin and renin in rat and dog brain. J. Exp. Med. **133**, 353–361 (1971).

FITZSIMONS, J. T.: The role of a renal thirst factor in drinking induced by extracellular stimuli. J. Physiol. Lond. **201**, 349–368 (1969).

— The renin-angiotensin system in the control of drinking. In: The Hypothalamus (Eds. L. MARTINI, M. MOTTA, and F. FRASCHINI). pp. 195–212 New York: Academic Press 1970.

— The effect on drinking of peptide precursors and of shorter chain peptide fragments of angiotensin II injected into the rat's diencephalon. J. Physiol. Lond. **214**, 295–303 (1971).

FITZSIMONS, J. T., SETLER, P. E.: Catecholaminergic mechanisms in angiotensin-induced drinking. J. Physiol. Lond. **218**, 43–44 P (1971).

GANTEN, D., MARQUEZ-JULIO, A., GRANGER, P., HAYDUK, K., KARSUNKY, K. P., BOUCHER, R., GENEST, J.: Renin in dog brain. Am. J. Physiol. **221**, 1733–1737 (1971).

GOLDSTEIN, D. J., FISCHER-FERRARO, C., NAHMOD, V. E., FINKIELMAN, S.: Angiotensin I in renal and extral-renal tissues. Medicina **30**, 81–83 (1970).

GOLDSTEIN, D.J., DIAZ, A., FINKIELMAN, S., NAHMOD, V. E., FISCHER-FERRARO, C.: Angiotensinase activity in rat and dog brain. J. Neurochem. **19**, 2451–2452 (1972).

GROSS, F.: Angiotensin. In: Pharmacology of naturally occuring polypeptides and lipid-soluble acids (ed. J. M. WALKER). International Encyclopedia of Pharmacology and Therapeutics, Sect. 72, vol. 1, pp. 73–286 Oxford; Pergamon Press 1971.

GROSS, F., LAZAR, J., ORTH, H.: Inhibition of the renin-angiotensinogen reaction by pepstatin. Science **175**, 656 (1972).

HAYDUK, K., BOUCHER, R., GENEST, J.: Renin activity content in various tissues of dogs under different physiopathological states. Proc. Soc. Exp. Biol. Med. **134**, 252–255 (1970).

MOUW, D., BONJOUR, J.-P., MALVIN, R. L., VANDER, A.: Central action of angiotensin in stimulating ADH release. Am. J. Physiol. **220**, 239–242 (1971).

NAHMOD, V. E., FISCHER-FERRARO, C., FINKIELMAN, S., DIAZ, A., GOLDSTEIN, D. J.: Renin and angiotensin in extra-renal tissues. Medicina **32**, Suppl. 1, 43–47 (1972).

PALAIC, D., KHAIRALLAH, P. A.: Inhibition of norepinephrine reuptake by angiotensin in brain. J. Neurochem. **15**, 1195–1202 (1968).

PALS, D. T., MASUCCI, F. D., DENNING JR., G. S., SIPOS, F., FESSLER, D. C.: Role of the pressor action of angiotensin II in experimental hypertension. Circulation Res. **29**, 673–681 (1971).

PEART, W. S.: A history and review of the renin-angiotensin system Proc. R. Soc. B **173**, 317–325 (1969).

SEVERS, W. B., SUMMY-LONG, J., DANIELS-SEVERS, A.: Effect of a converting enzyme inhibitor (SQ 20,881) on angiotensin-induced drinking. Proc. Soc. Ex. Biol. a. Med. **142**, 203–204 (1973).

SWANSON, L. W., MARSHALL, G. R., NEEDLEMAN, P., SHARPE, L. G.: Characterization of central angiotensin II receptors involved in the elicitation of drinking in the rat: Brain Res. **49**, 441–446 (1973).

TIGERSTEDT, R., BERGMAN, P. G.: Niere und Kreislauf. Skand. Arch. Physiol. **8**, 223–271 (1898).

TÜRKER, R. K., HALL, M. M., YAMAMOTO, M., SWEET, C. S., BUMPUS, F. M.: A new, long-lasting competitive inhibitor of angiotensin. Science **177**, 1203–1204 (1972).

YANG, H.-Y. T., NEFF, N. H.: Distribution and properties of angiotensin converting enzyme of rat brain. J. Neurochem. **19**, 2443–2450 (1972).

YU, R., ANDERTON, J., SKINNER, S. L., BEST, J. B.: Renin in anephric man. Am. J. Med. **52**, 707–711 (1972).

The Mechanism of Thirst-Induction by Intrahypothalamic Renin

R. Burckhardt, L. Peters-Haefeli, and G. Peters

Introduction

A large number of experimental data suggest that the renin-angiotensin system plays the role of a mediator in eliciting thirst and drinking in response to some types of hypovolia ("extra-cellular thirst": Fitzsimons, 1972). Extracellular hypovolia is thought to elicit drinking partly by enhancing the secretion of renin from the kidneys. Renin thus liberated, would act on circulating angiotensinogen, and the angiotensin I evolved would be transformed into angiotensin II by circulating as well as by tissue-bound (mainly pulmonary) converting enzyme. Angiotensin II, in turn, is thought to act on cerebral receptors, which elicit drinking behaviour when stimulated. The fact that angiotensin II injected into the perifornical or lateral hypothalamic areas of the brain induces a drinking response has generally been interpreted as a confirmation of this concept (Fitzsimons, 1972). The drinking response to intracerebral injections of angiotensin II, in turn, suggests that angiotensin II-sensitive receptors are located within the brain. One difficulty in understanding how angiotensin II may act as a mediator from the periphery is the fact that penetration of angiotensin II from circulating blood into brain tissue has not been demonstrated with certainty (Contradictory data on c.s.f. in mice: Volicer and Loew, 1971, and in dogs: Ganten, Marquez-Julio, Granger, Hayduk, Karsunky, Boucher, and Genest, 1971).

Surprisingly, when investigating the effects of several substances of the renin-angiotensin system injected intrahypothalamically, Fitzsimons (1971) found that renin injected into angiotensin II-sensitive sites induced a drinking response comparable to (but longer than) that elicited by angiotensin II. Since it is extremely unlikely that renin itself could reach the hypothalamus from the blood stream and act as a mediator, the significance of this finding, which we repeatedly confirmed for both hog and rat renin preparations, appears obscure. It was the purpose of the present experiments to gain some insight into the mechanism and the possible role of the dipsogenic action of intrahypothalamic renin.

Renin injected intrahypothalamically may be assumed to elicit drinking by liberating angiotensin I, either from plasma angiotensinogen or from another renin substrate ("angiotensinogen") present in the brain (Ganten, Marquez-Julio et al. 1971; Ganten, Minnich, Granger, Hayduk, Brecht, Barbeau, Boucher, and Genest 1971; Fischer-Ferraro, Nahmod, Goldstein, and Finkielman, 1971). The brain, of course, does not contain extravascular plasma angiotensinogen. A small amount of exudate, presumably containing plasma proteins, however, often accumulates at the tip of the permanent canula through which intrahypothalamic injections are given. If intrahypothalamic renin acted by liberating angiotensin I from plasma substrate present either in this exudate, or in cerebral blood vessels, two different preparations of renin yielding similar amounts of angiotensin I from rat plasma substrate in vitro, should induce the same drinking response.

103

In order to investigate whether this is so, we prepared rat renin from renal cortical tissue homogenates as described previously (SCHAECHTELIN, CHOMETY, REGOLI, and PETERS, 1966) and standardized it by comparing its enzymatic activity to that of commercial hog renin standardized in Goldblatt units. The enzymatic effect of both preparations was assayed by measuring the amount of angiotensin I formed when renin was incubated with an excess of angiotensinogen obtained from rat plasma (SCHAECHTELIN et al., 1966; PETERS-HAEFELI, 1971). One unit of rat renin, therefore, by definition, liberated the same amount of angiotensin I from rat plasma substrate as one unit of hog renin.

When the two preparations of renin were injected intrahypothalamically into a large number of rats at three different dose levels, rat renin proved to be approximately ten times as potent as hog renin in eliciting drinking (Fig. 1).

These results suggest that renin injected into the hypothalamus of the rat elicits drinking by liberating angiotensin from a substrate different from plasma angiotensinogen. Cerebral tissue of dogs (GANTEN, MARQUEZ-JULIO et al., 1971) and of rats (FISCHER-FERRARO et al., 1971) has been shown to contain all the components of the renin-angiotensin system, i.e. a renin-like enzyme, an angiotensinogen-like substrate, as well as angiotensins I and II. Renal renin injected into the brain appears to act on a cerebral substrate differing from plasma angiotensinogen.

Effects of a Specific Inhibitor of the Angiotensin-Converting Enzyme

If, in the hypothalamus, angiotensin I had to be converted into angiotensin II before eliciting a

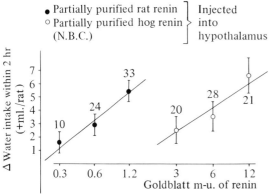

(Assayed as angiotensin evolved after incubation with rat plasma substrate)

Fig. 1. Drinking responses to intrahypothalamic rat or hog renin in rats. The figure shows calculated log dose – response regression lines and mean responses to three doses of the two renin preparations ± standard errors of the means (S.E.). The responses are expressed as "Δ water intake" within two hours of the intrahypothalamic injection. For each rat "Δ water intake" was the difference in the amounts of water drunk within two hours after intrahypothalamic renin and after intrahypothalamic saline (0.5 μl). Experiments were performed at 3–7 days intervals. Points ± S.E. refer to groups of 10–20 rats. The renin preparations used were commercial purified hog renin (NBC, Philadelphia, Pa. USA) and partially purified rat renin (SCHAECHTELIN, BAECHTHOLD, HAEFELI, REGOLI, GAUDRY-PARADES, PETERS, 1968)

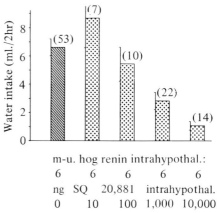

Fig. 2. Inhibition of drinking response to intrahypothalamic renin by the converting enzyme inhibitor SQ 20, 881. Columns are means ± S.E. Drinking responses are expressed as water intake in two hours after the intrahypothalamic injection of 6 mu. of hog renin (NBC, Philadelphia, Pa. USA) preceded either by saline (control) or by intrahypothalamic SQ 20,881 (Squibb, New Brunswick, N.J. USA). In each experiment, an equal number of animals were injected with renin preceded either by saline or by SQ 20,881. Each experiment was followed by a cross-over experiment using the same animals and the same doses of inhibitor and of renin. The drinking responses to renin without inhibitor in the different experiments did not differ significantly from each other and are, therefore, presented together in the 1st column. Number of experimental animals for each group shown in brackets above columns

drinking response, the dipsogenic action of intrahypothalamic renin should be blocked by inhibiting the converting enzyme.

SQ 20,881 (Squibb, New Brunswick, N.J. USA) is a nonapeptide known to specifically inhibit the angiotensin converting enzyme present in blood and in the lungs (CUSHMAN and CHEUNG, 1972; KEIM, KIRPAN, PETERSON, MURPHY, HASSERT, and POUTSIAKA, 1972; ENGEL, SCHAEFFER, GOLD, and RUBIN, 1972). When injected intrahypothalamically two minutes before a standard dose of renin, SQ 20,881 caused a dose dependent depression of the drinking response to intrahypothalamic hog renin (Fig. 2). SQ 20,881 did not induce significant drinking by itself and, as expected, did not influence the water intake after intrahypothalamic angiotensin II (Fig. 3).

SQ 20,881 should, of course, block drinking responses to angiotensin I as well as to renin. Intracerebral injections of doses of SQ 20,881 capable of blocking the dipsogenic effect of renin and approximately equal to 10 times as many n-mol of the inhibitor than of angiotensin I, however, did not result in any depression of the drinking response to the decapeptide (Fig. 4). Similarly, SWANSON, MARSHALL, NEEDLEMAN, and SHARPE (1973), did not find any inhibition of drinking induced by intrahypothalamic angiotensin I, when the decapeptide was preceded by 5–19 times as many n-moles of SQ 20,881. Neither raising the molar inhibitor: agent ratio to 80 or to 240 by giving a smaller dipsogenic dose of angiotensin I, after a larger dose of SQ 20,881, nor increasing the time interval between inhibitor and angiotensin I resulted in any depression of the drinking response (Fig. 5). (An incomplete inhibition of

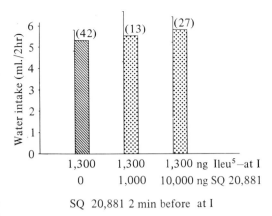

Fig. 4. Effect of intrahypothalamic SQ 20,881 on drinking responses to intrahypothalamic Ileu^5-angiotensin I. (Ileu^5-at I) Explanations as in Fig. 2

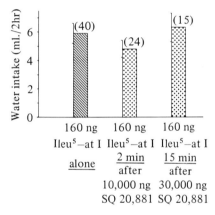

Fig. 5. Effect of intrahypothalamic SQ 20,881 on drinking responses to intrahypothalamic angiotensin I: use of a very large dose of SQ 20,881, a small dose of angiotensin I and extension of the interval between injecting the inhibitor and angiotensin I to 15 minutes (as used by other investigators: SEVERS et al., 1973). Explanations as in Fig. 2

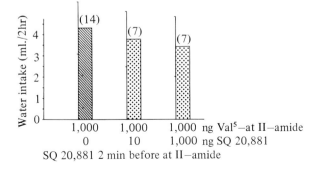

Fig. 3. Effect of intrahypothalamic SQ 20,881 on the drinking response elicited by intrahypothalamic Val^5-angiotensin II-amide. Explanations as for Fig. 2

intrahypothalamic angiotensin I-induced drinking has, however, been observed by FITZSIMONS — this volume — who used a molar inhibitor: agent ratio of 710. Using the same inhibitor: agent ratio and the same doses as FITZSIMONS we failed to reproduce these results: in our experiments drinking induced by angiotensin I was not influenced by SQ 20,881, while drinking to renin was practically suppressed. The reasons of this contradiction are not understood.

Two different conclusions may be drawn from these results: either SQ 20,881 does not inhibit the converting enzyme present in the brain, or angiotensin I, in the hypothalamus, is capable of eliciting a drinking response without prior transformation into angiotensin II.

In contrast to these findings, other investigators (SEVERS, SUMMY-LONG, DANIELS-SEVERS, 1973) recently found that SQ 20,881, injected into the third ventricle of rats between two doses of angiotensin I, inhibited the drinking response to the second dose, but had no influence on the drinking response to angiotensin II. With the protocol used in the present experiments, i.e. injections of angiotensin preceded by the potential inhibitor or by saline given on different days, we failed to detect any inhibition of drinking to angiotensin I injected into the third ventricle by SQ 20,881 (720 : 1) applied to the same site. This contradiction may be due to differences of the experimental protocol or of the rats used.

The dipsogenic effect of angiotensin I, injected either into the hypothalamus or the third ventricle, thus, appears to be insensitive to SQ 20,881. This fact suggests that either converting enzyme contained in cerebral tissue, as opposed to extracerebral converting enzyme, is quite insensitive to SQ 20,881, or alternatively, angiotensin I elicits drinking without a prior transformation into angiotensin II.

Since SQ 20,881 does not inhibit drinking after intrahypothalamic or intraventricular angiotensin I but does inhibit drinking elicited by intrahypothalamic renin, its action in the brain cannot bear on converting enzyme activity. When injected into the hypothalamus or the 3rd ventricle, SQ 20,881 appears to inhibit the reaction between injected renin (of renal origin) and the brain renin substrate.

Though known to be a converting enzyme inhibitor in peripheral tissue SQ 20,881 appears to have different actions in the brain. Thus, in the cat, SQ 20,881 has been demonstrated to inhibit the stimulation of receptors responsible for a pressor response to both intraventricular angiotensin II and angiotensin I (SOLOMON and BUCKLEY, 1972).

Summary and Conclusions

Though liberating the same amounts of angiotensin I from plasma angiotensinogen, partially purified rat renal cortical renin, injected intrahypothalamically, was approximately ten times more potent than hog renin in eliciting a drinking response in rats. It was concluded that renin injected intrahypothalamically, acts on a substrate present in brain and different from plasma angiotensinogen.

Intrahypothalamic injection of the converting enzyme inhibitor SQ 20,881, as expected, caused a dose dependent inhibition of the drinking response to intrahypothalamic renin and had no influence on the drinking response to intrahypothalamic angiotensin II. Unexpectedly, intrahypothalamic or intraventricular SQ 20,881 did not abolish the drinking response to angiotensin I injected at the same sites. It was concluded that either the converting enzyme activity present in the brain is insensitive to SQ 20,881 or that angiotensin I may elicit drinking without prior conversion to angiotensin II, *and* that SQ 20,881 inhibits the renin-angiotensinogen reaction in the brain.

Acknowledgement. This work was supported by Fonds National Suisse de la recherche scientifique, grant Nr. 3.751.72.

References

CUSHMAN, D. W., CHEUNG, H. S.: Studies in vitro of angiotensin-converting enzyme of lung and other tissues. In: Hypertension 1972 (Eds. J. GENEST, E. KOIW), pp. 532–541. Springer-Verlag, Berlin-Heidelberg-New York 1972.

ENGEL, S. L., SCHAEFFER, T. R., GOLD, B. I., RUBIN, B.: Inhibition of pressor effects of angiotensin I and augmentation of depressor effects of bradykinin by synthetic peptides. Proc. Soc. exp. Biol. Med. **140**, 240–244 (1972).

FISCHER-FERRARO, C., NAHMOD, V. E., GOLDSTEIN, D. J., FINKIELMAN, S.: Angiotensin and renin in rat and dog brain. J. exp. Med. **133**, 353–361 (1971).

FITZSIMONS, J. T.: The effect on drinking of peptide precursors and of shorter chain peptide fragments of angiotensin II injected into the rats' diencephalon. J. Physiol. (Lond). **214**, 295–303 (1971).

— Thirst. Physiol. Rev. **52**, 468–561 (1972).

GANTEN, D., MARQUEZ-JULIO, A. GRANGER, P., HAYDUK, K., KARSUNSKY, K. P., BOUCHER, R., GENEST, J.: Renin in the dog brain. Am. J. Physiol. **221**, 1733–1737 (1971).

GANTEN, D., MINNICH, J. L., GRANGER, P., HAYDUK, K., BRECHT, H. M., BARBEAU, A., BOUCHER, R., GENEST, J.: Angiotensin-forming enzyme in brain tissue. Science, **173**, 64–65 (1971).

KEIM JR., G. R., KIRPAN, J., PETERSON, A. E., MURPHY, B. F., HASSERT JR., G. L., POUTSIAKA, J. W.: Inhibition of angiotensin I-initiated hemodynamic changes in anesthetized dogs by a synthetic nonappetide. Proc. Soc. exp. Biol. Med. **140**, 149–1952 (1972).

PETERS-HAEFELI, L.: Renal cortical renin activity and renin secretion at rest and in response to hemorrhage. Am. J. Physiol. **221**, 1331–1338 (1971).

SCHAECHTELIN, G., BAECHTHOLD, N., HAEFELI, L., REGOLI, D., GAUDRY-PAREDES, A., PETERS, G.: A renin-inactivating system in rat plasma. Am. J. Physiol. **215**, 632–636 (1968).

SCHAECHTELIN, G., CHOMÉTY, F., REGOLI, D., PETERS, G.: Dosage de l'activité réninique d'extraits tissulaires par incubation avec un substrat naturel purifié. Helv. Physiol. Acta. **24**, 89–105 (1966).

SEVERS, W. B., SUMMY-LONG, J., DANIELS-SEVERS, A.: Effect of a converting enzyme inhibitor (SQ 20,881) on angiotensin-induced drinking. Proc. Soc. exp. Biol. Med. **142**, 203–204 (1973).

SOLOMON, T. A., BUCKLEY, J. P.: Inhibition of the central pressor effect of angiotensin I and II. San Francisco: 5th International Congress on Pharmacology 1972. Abstracts of Volunteer papers, 218, Abstract Nr. 1305.

SWANSON, L. W., MARSHALL, G. R., NEEDLEMAN, P., SHARPE, L. G.: Characterization of central angiotensin II receptors involved in the elicitation of drinking in the rat. Brain Research **49**, 441–446 (1973).

VOLICER, L., LOEW, C. G.: Penetration of angiotensin II into the brain. Neuropharmacology **10**, 631–636 (1971).

Angiotensin as Dipsogen

A. N. Epstein and S. Hsiao

Our understanding of the physiology of thirst has been enriched by three major advances of the past decade. First, the lateral preoptic area (LPO) has been identified as the osmosensitive zone for the thirst of cellular dehydration. As the result of the remarkably consistent work of Peck and Novin (1971) in the rabbit and of Blass and Epstein (1971) in the rat we know that the LPO must be intact for cell dehydration to induce drinking, and we know that local dehydration of the LPO arouses thirst in animals that are otherwise in water balance. Second, the work of Fitzsimons (1961) and Stricker (1966) has established extracellular volume loss or hypovolaemia as a stimulus of thirst that is coequal with cell dehydration in potency and reliability. As a consequence we are entitled to work within the context of the *double depletion hypothesis of thirst* (Epstein, Kissileff, and Stellar, 1973) which asserts that thirst is the joint outcome of depletions of both major compartments for water in animals like ourselves. Our problem is now clarified. We must work to understand how each depletion arouses drinking behaviour and to conceive how they interact in the brain to produce the complex phenomenon of thirst.

The discovery that angiotensin is a hormone of thirst is the third major finding that has enriched our understanding of drinking behaviour. It is the most novel of recent advances because there were no precedents for it in our thinking before Fitzsimons' work (1969) and because angiotensin is the first hormone for which there is sound evidence for a direct role in the control of ingestive behaviour.

The evidence for angiotensin as a natural dipsogen is impressive. First, plasma renin levels, and therefore angiotensin levels, rise in man (Maebashi and Yoshinaga, 1967) and other animals (Gross, Brunner, and Ziegler, 1965) during water deprivation. Second, all known experimental manipulations that arouse thirst by production of hypovolaemia or hypotension release renal renin (Page and McCubbin, 1968). These include hyperoncotic colloid dialysis, ligation of the inferior vena cava, haemorrhage, reduction of renal blood flow, sodium depletion, and beta-adrenergic activation (Peskar, Meyer, Tauchmann, and Hertting, 1970). Third, the thirst of several of these manipulations is attenuated by prior removal of the kidneys (Fitzsimons, 1969; Houpt and Epstein, 1971). Fourth, intravenous angiotensin and intravenous or intraperitoneal renin are dipsogenic (Fitzsimons and Simons, 1969; Fitzsimons, 1973). Fifth, the dipsogenic effect of angiotensin adds quantitatively to that of cell dehydration as is expected of cooperative natural dipsogens (Fitzsimons and Oatley, 1968). Sixth, all components of the renin-angiotensin system (renin itself, renin substrate, angiotensin I and angiotensin II) are highly dipsogenic when injected directly into the forebrain (Epstein, Fitzsimons, and Rolls, 1970; Fitzsimons, 1971). By the intracranial route angiotensin II is the most potent dipsogen known, arousing thirst reliably at doses of 100–200 picogram/rat (Simpson and Routtenberg, 1973). Seventh, there is wide species generality to the dipsogenic effect of angiotensin. All animals tested, drink to angiotensin while in water balance. This includes rat, rabbit, guinea pig, cat, dog, monkey and ring-dove (FITZSIMONS, 1972). Eighth, thirst and excessive water intake are associated in man with the high plasma renin levels of malignant hypertension and the symptoms are relieved by bilateral nephrectomy (BROWN, CURTIS, LEVER, ROBERTSON, deWARDENER, and WING, 1969; ROGERS and KURTZMAN, 1973).

We will add to the evidence for angiotensin as a natural dipsogen by describing the arousal of drinking in water replete rats by infusion of physiological doses of the hormone, and we will discuss the *hypothesis of ventricular access* which proposes that angiotensin reaches sensitive tissue in the brain through the cerebral ventricles.

Stimulation of Thirst by Physiological Doses of Angiotensin. The original report of the stimulation of thirst by intravenous angiotensin (FITZSIMONS and SIMONS, 1969) was disappointing in one major respect. Embarassingly high doses of approximately 10 μg/rat were necessary for reliable effects. The inappropriateness of these doses is appreciated if it is recalled that angiotensin circulates in the unstimulated rat at concentrations of 30 pg/ml of plasma (GOODWIN, KIRSHMAN, SEALEY, and LARAGH, 1970). At any instant in time the plasma of an adult rat (20 ml.) will, therefore, contain a total of only 0.6 ng of the hormone.

We have reduced the peripheral dipsogenic dose of the hormone by more than two orders of magnitude by combining the following improvements in technique: 1) the use of Ile[5] angiotensin II (Schwarz-Mann) which is the natural analogue in the rat (SOKABE and NAKAJIMA, 1972), 2) the use of chronic intravenous catheters that permit testing of the animal after complete recovery from the artifacts of surgery and allow us to discard the results of the animal's first experience with intravenous angiotensin. We find that the animals tend to be least sensitive during their first infusion, and 3) testing the animal in its home cage without the distractions of a novel test-chamber to which it is moved for study. Fig. 1 gives the dose-response curve for drinking stimulated by intravenous angiotensin

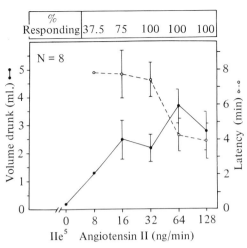

Fig. 1. Dose-response relationship between intravenous angiotensin II and elicitation of drinking in water replete rats. Volume of water intake as a function of dose is shown by the curve of filled circles connected by a solid line (ordinate to the left). Latency to the onset of drinking is shown by the curve of open circles connected by a dashed line (ordinate to the right). The percentage of animals drinking in response to each dose is given in the boxed headline (from HSIAO and EPSTEIN, 1973)

in 8 male Sprague-Dawley rats weighing 350–400 g. All 8 animals were run by counterbalance through all doses from 0 to 128 ng/min. The animals received infusions at 0.01 ml./min through right superior vena caval catheters of Asp[1], Ile[5] angiotensin II in isotonic saline for 17.5 min while resting quietly in their home cages with food pellets present and water available in chemical burettes. The curves in Fig. 1 show the volume of water drunk (to the nearest 0.1 ml.) and the latency to the onset of drinking (appearance of the first bubble raised in the burette) as a function of the dose of angiotensin II infused. *Animals that did not drink are not included in the means.* Standard errors are given for doses at which more than half the animals drank. The animals typically drank a single draught after a period of movement about the cage. The draught was frequently preceded by a brief bout of drinking (an "apéritif") and was followed by grooming. The percentages of animals drinking at each dose is given in the box above the curves. Note that threshold for drinking lies between 8 and 16 ng/min or very close to 30 ng/kg · min for a 400 g rat. The 16 ng/min

(40 ng/kg · min) and 32 ng/min (80 ng/kg · min) doses are reliable in 75% and 100% of animals respectively, and yield ingestion of volumes of water that exceed the average draught size of rats drinking spontaneously (KISSILEFF, 1969). Although latencies were still decreasing at the highest dose used, the animals drank less and were in mild distress as a result, apparently, of the pressor effect of the hormone. They were unusually immobile and held themselves close to the cage floor.

Table 1 is a summary of our findings with the improved intravenous technique. The results of five experiments are given. All were conducted with fresh groups of rats and the animals served in all cases as their own controls. First, you see that at equimolar doses Ile[5] angiotensin II is roughly twice as potent as the Val[5] angiotensin II amide which is the active material in Hypertensin (Ciba). There is no precedent for this difference in the other effects of the hormone

(PAGE and McCUBBIN, 1968). It may depend on a unique specialization of the dipsogenic receptor. Second, our work shows that prior nephrectomy (kidneys were removed under ether the afternoon before the day of testing) doubles the animal's sensitivity to the hormone. A full dose-response curve has not yet been done for the nephrectomized animal and we cannot conclude that the threshold is lowered, but note that with the single dose used the latency to drink after nephrectomy was roughly half that measured when the animals were intact. The third experiment combines minimal cell dehydration (cd) with a subthreshold dose of angiotensin II (A II, 8 ng/min). The strategy of the experiment is given in Fig. 2. Ten animals were subjected to each of three conditions in partially counterbalanced order on separate days. They were provided with water for 17.5 min either 20 min after subcutaneous injection of a small load of extracellular solute (Condition 1: cd + 0), or

Table 1. Summary of intravenous experiments

	N	N Drinkers	Latency (min, sec)	Volume ml.
32 ng/min Val[5] A II	6	2	7'14" & 13'29"	2.7 & 1.7
32 ng/min Ile[5] A II	6	6	7'16" ± 46"	3.0 ± 0.7
16 ng/min Ile[5] A II	5	5	6'27" ± 2'41"	1.4 ± 0.9
NEPHRX: 16 ng/min Ile[5] A II	5	5	3'21" ± 34"	2.0 ± 0.7
A II: 8 ng/min Ile[5] A II	10	4	>11'55" ± 2'19"	0.3 ± 0.1
cd: 0.5 ml 1M NaCl, s.c.	10	4	>12'39" ± 2'08"	0.4 ± 0.3
A II + cd	10	10	8'47" ± 1'59"	2.1 ± 0.4
32 ng/min Ile[5] A II	10	10	6'31" ± 1'	3.2 ± 0.5
285 ng/min saralasin acetate, then 285 ng/min saralasin acetate + 32 ng/min Ile[5] A II	10	2	9'02'' & 7'15''	3.0 & 0.8
40 ng/min Ile[5] A I	8	8	6'08" ± 1'44"	3.1 ± 0.7
32 ng/min Ile[5] A II	8	8	6'00" ± 1'32"	2.8 ± 0.8

	Subcutaneous injection	Intravenous infusion
Condition 1: cd + O	0.5 ml.1M NaCl ⟶	Isotonic saline
Condition 2: O + A II	Isotonic saline ⟶	Angiotensin II (8ng/min)
Condition 3: cd + A II	0.5 ml.1M NaCl ⟶	Angiotensin II (8ng/min)

Fig. 2. The strategy of the experiment combining mild cellular dehydration (cd) with a subthreshold dose of angiostensin (A II). Water was offered during the intravenous infusion (17.5 min), 20 min after subcutaneous injection. See text and Table 1 for details (from HSIAO and EPSTEIN, 1973)

during 17.5 min of intravenous infusion of angiotensin (Condition 2: O + A II), or while both treatments were combined (cd + A II). The individual data are shown in Table 2 and are summarized in Table 1. Means are of all animals including those that did not drink and therefore had latencies greater than 17.5 min. Note that approximately half the rats responded to each of the dipsogenic treatments administered by itself and that only small volumes of water were drunk. During the combined treatment all animals drank with an average latency of less than 9 min and they ingested volumes that are comparable with those produced by doses of angiotensin that are 2 to 4 times greater (see Fig. 1, 16 and 32 ng/min). The average total cumulative dose of exogenous angiotensin (at the lower right in Fig. 4) for the initiation of drinking (calculated from the average latency for the combined condition times the dose of 8 ng) is only 70 ng/rat. The fourth experiment demonstrates that a specific receptor antagonist of angiotensin II (Sar[1] Ala[8] A II, saralasin acetate of Norwich Pharmacal Co., Norwich, N. Y.) infused at 10 times the molal dose of the hormone (beginning 20 min before the hormone and accompanying it for an additional 17.5 min) blocks its dipsogenic effect. Only 2 of the 10 animals drank during the combined infusion of

antagonist and hormone and they did so with either long latency or small volume. The antagonist is equally effective intracranially in competition with intracranial angiotensin I, angiotensin II, renin substrate and renin (EPSTEIN, FITZSIMONS, and JOHNSON, 1974, and chapter by FITZSIMONS in this volume). It has no intrinsic activity as an intravenous or intracranial dipsogen. Lastly equimolal doses of angiotensin I and II are equidipsogenic provided both are the Ile[5] analogue (Table 1).

Taken together these results demonstrate that peripheral angiotensin is dipsogenic in doses that compare favourably with those for other effects of the hormone obtained by systemic infusion in intact animals. For example, the dose-response curve for the pressor response given by GROSS et al. (GROSS, BOCK, and TURRIAN, 1961) for the anaesthetized, nephrectomized rat rises from 100 ng/kg to 1.0 μg/kg. Similar pressor doses (25–100 ng/kg min) have been reported in the dog (DAY, McCUBBIN, and PAGE, 1965). Angiotensin II releases catecholamines from the adrenal medulla of the dog at doses of 50–100 ng/kg·min by intravenous infusion (PEACH, CLINE, and WATTS, 1966). Aldosterone can, however, be released at lower doses (DAVIS, 1962; GANONG, MULROW, BORYCZKA, and CERA, 1962). Moreover, our

Table 2. Individual data for 10 rats drinking to cell dehydration alone, intravenous angiotensin alone, or the combined dipsogens

Rat No.	cd + O		O + A II		cd + A II	
	Latency (min, sec)	Volume (ml.)	Latency (min, sec)	Volume (ml.)	Latency (min, sec)	Volume (ml.)
D 21	>17'30"	0	>17'30"	0	14'54"	1.0
D 22	>17'30"	0	>17'30"	0	12'38"	1.1
D 23	>17'30"	0	>17'30"	0	4'59"	3.6
D 24	4'02"	0.5	3'33"	0.2	3'22"	2.7
D 25	3'30"	0.5	6'22"	0.9	36"	1.5
D 26	2'15"	2.6	>17'30"	0	3'51"	2.2
D 27	>17'30"	0	>17'30"	0	13'39"	3.9
D 28	>17'30"	0	2'56"	1.0	2'24"	0.4
D 29	>17'30"	0	>17'30"	0	17'12"	1.5
D 30	11'46"	0.6	38"	0.4	14'14"	2.6
Mean	>12'39"	0.42	>11'55"	0.25	8'47"	2.05
S.E. of mean	>2'08"	0.25	>2'19"	0.12	1'59"	0.36
% **Response**	40		40		100	
A II dose			70.2 ng/rat			

dipsogenic doses are reasonably close to the amounts of endogenous angiotensin that can be expected in the rat's circulation during vascular depletion which releases renal renin. Circulating levels are 30 pg/ml. of plasma, making a total of 0.6 ng/rat. If we assume a 5 to 10 fold increase during hypovolaemia or hypotension, we are very close to the doses employed here, particularly in the additivity study which most closely approximates the conditions that may prevail during spontaneous drinking. Actual concentrations in the plasma at the moment when the rat begins to drink have not been measured. They will be the complex result of the amount of angiotensin infused diluted in the plasma volume, minus the amount degraded per unit of time. Exogenous angiotensin suppresses the release of renin (PAGE and McCUBBIN, 1968) and the production of endogenous angiotensin can therefore be neglected. With the very short half-life of the octapeptide during passage through capillary beds (approximately 80 sec according to OSBORNE, POOTERS, d'AURIAC, EPSTEIN, WORCEL, and MEYER, 1971) we can expect the concentration of the hormone to be only several hundred picograms per millilitre of plasma in a rat receiving approximately 10 ng/min.[1] Lastly, we have not yet studied what may be our most sensitive preparation, that is, the nephrectomized rat "primed" by mild cellular dehydration just before angiotensin infusion. *The Hypothesis of Ventricular Access.* When it was first made (FITZSIMONS, 1969; EPSTEIN, FITZSIMONS, and ROLLS, 1970) the suggestion that angiotensin is a natural hormone of thirst was immediately confronted with the objection that neither other peptides and proteins nor angiotensin could be expected to cross the blood-brain barrier. This objection was quickly confirmed by both radioassay (OSBORNE, POOTERS, d'AURIAC, EPSTEIN, WORCEL, and MEYER, 1971) and radioautography (VOLICER and LOEW, 1971). These facts confound the simple idea that angiotensin reaches the brain directly from the blood as do the steroid hormones

---

[1] To make the comparison to endogenous levels more exact, it should be noted that the commercially available angiotensins used here contain approximately 20% amyl acetate as an inactive impurity.

(McEWEN and PFAFF, 1973). An alternative route is necessary and, at least theoretically, is available. We wish to suggest that angiotensin may enter the cerebral ventricles from the blood, perhaps across the choroid plexus, and be carried in the cerebrospinal fluid to sensitive tissues that are part of the ependymal lining. The evidence for this hypothesis is given elsewhere in this volume by A. K. JOHNSON and J. B. SIMPSON in the summaries of their studies conducted separately in Philadelphia and Evanston. The essential facts are: 1) injection of angiotensin into the parenchyma of the brain is *not* more effective than injection directly into the lateral or third ventricle (see JOHNSON) . — 2) the success of an intracranial preparation is assured *if, and only if,* the cannula for hormone injection traverses a ventricle. The tissue into which the cannula opens may be irrelevant. The hormone must have access to a ventricular space either by injection directly into it, or by reflux up the sides of a cannula that passes through a ventricle (see JOHNSON). — 3) radioactivity appears rapidly and reaches a sharp peak in the cerebrospinal fluid (c.s.f.) of rats with effective (i.e., transventricular) cannulas given intraparenchymal injections of tritiated angiotensin II, but does not appear in the c.s.f. of rats with cannulas that do not cross a ventricle despite injection into the same parenchymal site (preoptic area) (see JOHNSON). — 4) destruction of the subfornical organ of the third ventricle severely attenuates or abolishes the drinking produced by angiotensin injection elsewhere into the brain (see SIMPSON). — 5) the subfornical organ is the most sensitive receptor site to the dipsogenic effect of the hormone yet reported (see SIMPSON).

With these facts before us, we have recently repeated the earlier tracer studies using a tritiated analogue of angiotensin II with high specific activity (32 Ci/m-mole) and 100% biological activity, Asp[1] Val[5] Tyr[4] angiotensin tritiated in positions 3 and 5 of the tyrosine molecule (New England Nuclear). Fig. 3 gives the results of a radioautographic study of the brain of a rat given 2 μg of the isotope intravenously. The tissue was not fixed. The brain was removed rapidly, fresh and intact (within two min of the completion of the intravenous injection of labelled hormone), was rapidly frozen, and was kept frozen throughout the entire radioautographic process to prevent displacement of the c.s.f. Grain counts were made after staining with cresyl violet. All counts were corrected for background artifact by subtracting the counts obtained from a brain injected with cold angiotensin and otherwise treated identically. The results of a radioassay

Neuroanatomical locus	Autographic grains/mm^2
Pituitary, anterior and posterior	7,528 + 692
Lateral ventricle	3,269 + 141
Choroid of lateral ventricle	3,995 + 137
Dorsal III ventricle	3,507 + 179
Ventral III ventricle	2,280 + 132
Choroid of III ventricle	3,507 + 179
Choroid of IV ventricle and IV ventricle	6,250 + 850
Median eminence	2,202 + 342
Subfornical organ	3,319 + 202
Area postrema	7,609

Neocortex	1,788 + 73
Caudate	1,782 + 66
Septum	1,510 + 85
Preoptic area	1,473 + 144
Lateral hypothalamus	1,152 + 36
Hippocampus	989 + 89
Vestibular nuclei	1,039 + 32

Fig. 3. Radioautographic grain counts from the brain of a rat given 2 µg of tritiated angiotensin II. Tissues and c.s.f.-filled ventricles within the brain but outside the blood-brain barrier are listed in the upper box, parenchymal regions of the brain are below (from JOHNSON, EPSTEIN, OSBORNE and SHRAGER, 1973)

study using the same isotope are shown in Table 3. Here the brain of a rat infused intravenously with a pulse of 200 ng of the isotope was exanguinated with saline and then dissected within two min of injection and the radioactivity of the listed regions determined by scintillation counting. Kidney and striated muscle (knee flexors) samples were also taken. The plasma sample was taken from the aorta just before exsanguination. The radioautographic and radioassay results are complementary and confirm previous findings. With the proviso that we are measuring radioactivity that may be a property of molecules other than intact angiotensin, the results show that the hormone does not reach the intrinsic tissues of the brain (lower box in Fig. 3 and lower portion of Table 3 beginning with

Table 3. Distribution of intravenous angiotensin (200 ng ^{3}H, Ile^5 A II, exsanguinated)

	c/min/g
Plasma	23,520
Kidney	28,719
Pituitary (whole)	23,254
Choroid Plexi (combined)	13,562
Striated Muscle	2,490
POA-Hypothalamus	1,896
Neocortex	1,696
Hippocampus	1,460
Floor of IV Ventricle	1,834

"POA-hypothalamus"), but has access to all those parts of the brain that are outside the blood-brain barrier (upper box in Fig. 3 and upper portion of Table 3) including the c.s.f. itself and the circumventricular structures, the subfornical organ among them. In the assay study (Table 3) the sample combining the choroid plexuses (which, since the choroids adhere to it, may have included the subfornical organ) was richer in radioactivity by almost an order of magnitude than any of the parenchymal sites sampled. Brain tissue, on the other hand, yielded fewer counts than striated muscle. Note that the preoptic area-anterior hypothalamus is included in both studies. It was, with the septum, erroneously described (EPSTEIN, FITZSIMONS, and ROLLS, 1970) as the "sensitive region" for the dipsogenic effect of angiotensin. It is now clear how we were misled. Cannulas cannot be inserted into the anterior forebrain and septum with the conventional alignment parallel to the midline without entering the lateral ventricle. Lastly, note that we continue to find an exceptionally high content of radioactive material in the pituitary, as high in the assay study as in plasma and kidney. This intriguing finding is unexplained.

The radioisotope studies are, of course, not conclusive for localization of angiotensin without evidence identifying the labelled molecule as the undegraded octapeptide, but they are congruent with the evidence of JOHNSON and SIMPSON that was obtained with three other methods (intracranial injection, c.s.f. radioassay, and surgical ablation). When considered in the context of the hypothesis of ventricular access the radioassay and radioautographic evidence that was so puzzling just a few years ago, now makes very good sense. The hormone is excluded from the brain, *per se*, while it follows a ventricular avenue that leads to an ependymal organ of unique sensitivity.

Discussion

The new results reported here strengthen the case for angiotensin as a hormone of thirst. We have shown that it acts at reasonably low doses. Its dipsogenic effect is doubled by nephrectomy, blocked by a specific peptide antagonist, and adds quantitatively to that of extracellular hyperosmolality.

We have proposed a route of access into the brain which is supported by congruent evidence based on several different experimental methods. In addition there is a precedent for it in the means by which several drugs, acetazolamide among them, reach the brain (ROTH and BARLOW, 1965). The ventricular hypothesis readily explains the means by which intracranial angiotensin reaches its target tissue and we suggest that peripheral angiotensin utilizes the same route, although a direct effect via the rich blood supply of the subfornical organ is not excluded. Once in the c.s.f. we can expect angiotensin to be degraded slowly as is the case in plasma that is not circulating through capillary beds (HODGE, NG, and VANE, 1967). This may

contribute to the unusually long duration of its dipsogenic effect (ROLLS and JONES, 1972) and is consistent with the enduring nature of thirst.

We are only at the beginning of our understanding of the dipsogenic action of angiotensin. Much remains to be learned. If the subfornical organ is the target tissue in the brain, how does the hormone act to stimulate it? The action is prompt, occurring in tenths or hundredths of a second and probably does not involve a second messenger or the production of new enzymes. There may be specific chemoreceptors on cells of the organ and the hormone may trigger nervous activity by stimulating them. Or the hormone may alter the permeability of some element in the organ for sodium (ANDERSSON, 1971) or some other solute. Even more unconventionally, the hormone may excite contractile cells in the organ or in the choroid plexus altering the dynamics or volume of the c.s.f., or the characteristics of blood flow through the choroids and the subfornical organ. Elegant radioautographic technique has recently revealed (OSBORNE, MEYER, DROZ, and MOREL, 1973) the localization of angiotensin over the mesangial (contractile) cells of the renal glomerulus. Similar cells may be present in the choroids and/or subfornical organ.

Once the target organ is aroused, how is the nervous activity that is generated by angiotensin articulated with that aroused by other thirst stimuli (cell dehydration, oropharyngeal sensations)? And what is the meaning of the fact that all of the nervous activity of thirst utilizes some tissue in the lateral hypothalamus (EPSTEIN and TEITELBAUM, 1964)? Is the lateral hypothalamus simply a funnel for tracts of similar function or does tissue there add the new and qualitatively different element of motivation to the process of thirst?

What are the other stimuli of extracellular thirst? Recall that the hypovolaemia produced by hyperoncotic colloid continues to provoke undiminished thirst in the nephrectomized animal (FITZSIMONS, 1961), and that the thirst of caval ligation is only reduced, not abolished, by nephrectomy. Afferents from the volume receptors of the great vessels of the low-pressure circulation and from the left atrium are the most likely candidate for the "other" stimulus for extracellular thirst. But we still lack direct evidence for their involvement and do not know if they can compensate completely for the absence of renal renin-angiotensin as is required by the undiminished survival of the thirst of hyperoncotic colloid dialysis in the nephrectomized animal (STRICKER, 1973).

When in the course of spontaneous drinking behaviour does the hormone act to produce thirst? Each time the animal drinks? Can we assume that the mild depletions that must occur between bouts of drinking are sufficient to stimulate the release of dipsogenic amounts of renin-angiotensin, or must the role of the hormone be reserved for prolonged deprivations or other extreme conditions such as the hypovolaemia of saliva spreading, (HAINSWORTH, STRICKER, and EPSTEIN, 1968) or upper gastrointestinal secretions after a meal (BLAIR-WEST and BROOK, 1969)?

The nature of the molecular receptors in the brain for the dipsogenic action of the hormone is discussed elsewhere in this volume by FITZSIMONS, but it can be noted here that although they are selective for angiotensin II they cannot be identical to those of vascular smooth muscle that are responsible for the pressor response; first, because the natural Ile^5 analogue is required for maximum effect, and second, because the Phe^5 Tyr^8 angiotensin II analogue blocks the pressor response but does not interfere with drinking induced by intracranial angiotensin (SWANSON, MARSHALL, NEEDLEMAN, and SHARPE, 1973).

Lastly, we must ask: what is the role of the brain's own renin-angiotensin system in thirst (GANTEN, MARQUEZ-JULIO, GRANGER, HAYDUK, KARSUNKY, BOUCHER, and GENEST, 1971)? What releases cerebral renin? Could the same stimuli (hypovolaemia, hypotension) release *both* renal and cerebral renin, yielding parallel production of angiotensin on both sides of the blood-brain barrier? And could the ventricles be the avenue by which the angiotensin from both sources reaches the target organ for its dipsogenic effect?

Acknowledgments. The original research reported here was supported by grants from the USPHS, NDS 03469 to Alan N. EPSTEIN and NIGMS 5 GM 281 to the Institute of Neurological Sciences and from the Nutrition Foundation. — We are grateful to Dr. Alan CASTELLION of the Norwich Pharmacal Company for generous supplies of the peptide analogue.

References

ANDERSSON, B.: Thirst and brain control of water balance. Amer. Scientist, **59**, 408–415 (1971).

BLAIR-WEST, J. R., BROOK, A. H.: Circulatory changes and renin secretion in sheep in response to feeding. J. Physiol. Lond. **204**, 15–30 (1969).

BLASS, E. M., EPSTEIN, A. N.: A lateral preoptic osmosensitive zone for thirst in the rat. J. comp. physiol. Psychol. **76**, 378–394 (1971).

BROWN, J. J., CURTIS, J. R., LEVER, A. F., ROBERTSON, J. I. S., DE WARDENER, H. E., WING, A. J.: Plasma renin concentration and the control of blood pressure in patients on maintenance haemodialysis. Nephron, **6**, 329–349 (1969).

DAVIS, J. O.: The control of aldosterone secretion. Physiologist, **5**, 65–86 (1962).

DAY, M. D., McCUBBIN, J. W., PAGE, I. H.: Limited hypertensive effect of infusion of angiotensin. Am. J. Physiol. **209**, 264–268 (1965).

EPSTEIN, A. N., FITZSIMONS, J. T., JOHNSON, A. K.: Peptide antagonists of the renin-angiotensin system and the elucidation of the receptors for angiotensin-induced drinking. J. Physiol. Lond. **238**, 34 P–35 P (1973).

EPSTEIN, A. N., FITZSIMONS, J. T., ROLLS, B. J.: Drinking induced by injection of angiotensin into the brain of the rat. J. Physiol. Lond. **210**, 457–474 (1970).

EPSTEIN, A. N., KISSILEFF, H. R., STELLAR, E. (Eds.): The Neuropsychology of Thirst: new findings and advances in concepts. Washington, D.C.: H. V. Winston and Sons 1973.

EPSTEIN, A. N., TEITELBAUM, P.: Severe and persistent deficits in thirst produced by lateral hypothalamic damage. In: Thirst (ed. M. J. WAYNER), pp. 395–406. Oxford: Pergamon Press 1964.

FITZSIMONS, J. T.: Drinking by rats depleted of body fluid without increase in osmotic pressure. J. Physiol. Lond. **159**, 297–309 (1961).

— The effect on drinking of peptide precursors and of shorter chain peptide fragments of angiotensin II injected into the rat's diencephalon. J. Physiol. Lond. **214**, 295–303 (1971).

— The hormonal control of water and sodium intake. In: Frontiers in Neuroendocrinology. (Eds. L. MARTINI and W. F. GANONG) pp. 103–128. New York: Oxford University Press 1971.

— The role of a renal thirst factor in drinking induced by extracellular stimuli. J. Physiol. Lond. **210**, 349–368 (1969).

— Thirst. Physiol. Rev. **52**, 468–561 (1972).

FITZSIMONS, J. T., OATLEY, K.: Additivity of stimuli for drinking in rats. J. comp. physiol. Psychol. **66**, 450–455 (1968).

FITZSIMONS, J. T., SIMONS, B. J.: The effect on drinking in the rat of intravenous infusions of angiotensin, given alone or in combination with other stimuli of thirst. J. Physiol. Lond. **203**, 45–57 (1969).

GANTEN, D., MARQUEZ-JULIO, A., GRANGER, P., HAYDUK, K., KARSUNKY, K. P., BOUCHER, R., GENEST, J.: Renin in the dog brain. Am. J. Physiol. **221**, 1733–1737 (1971).

GANONG, W. F., MULROW, P. J., BORYCZKA, A., CERA, G.: Evidence for a direct effect of angiotensin II on adrenal cortex of the dog. **109**, 381–384 (1962).

GOODWIN, F. J., KIRSHMAN, J. D., SEALEY, J. E., LARAGH, J. H.: Influence of the pituitary gland on sodium conservation, plasma renin and renin substrate concentration in the rat. Endocrinology **86**, 824–834 (1970).

GROSS, F., BOCK, K. D., TURRIAN, H.: Untersuchungen über die Blutdruckwirkung von Angiotensin. Helv. Physiol. Acta **19**, 42–57 (1961).

GROSS, F., BRUNNER, H., ZIEGLER, M.: Renin-angiotensin system, aldosterone and sodium balance. Rec. Progr. Horm. Res. **21**, 119–167 (1965).

HAINSWORTH, F. R., STRICKER, E. M., EPSTEIN, A. N.: Water metabolism of rats in the heat: dehydration and drinking. Am J. Physiol. **214**, 983–989 (1968).

HODGE, R. L., NG, K. K. F., VANE, J. R.: Disappearance of angiotensin from the circulation of the dog. Nature **215**, 138–141 (1967).

HOUPT, K. A., EPSTEIN, A. N.: The complete dependence of beta-adrenergic drinking on the renal dipsogen. Physiol. Behav. **7**, 897–902 (1971).

HSIAO, S., EPSTEIN, A. N.: The potency of peripheral angiotensin as dipsogenic agent (in preparation) 1973.

JOHNSON, A. K., EPSTEIN, A. N., OSBORNE, M. J., SHRAGER, E.: Autoradiographic analysis of rat brain following intravenous administration of angiotensin II (in preparation) 1973.

KISSILEFF, H. R.: Food-associated drinking in the rat. J. comp physiol. Psychol. **67**, 284–300 (1969).

MAEBASHI, M., YOSHINAGA, K.: Effect of dehydration on plasma renin activity. Jap. Circulation J. **31**, 609–613 (1967).

MCEWEN, B. S., PFAFF, D. W.: Chemical and physiological approaches to neuroendocrine mechanisms: attempts at integration. In: Frontiers in Neuroendocrinology (Eds. W. F. GANONG and L. MARTINI), pp. 267–335. New York: Oxford University Press 1973.

OSBORNE, M. J., MEYER, P., DROZ, B., MOREL, F.: Localisation intrarénale de l'angiotensine tritiée dans les cellules mésangiales par radioautographie. C.R. Acad. Sci. (Paris), Série D **276**, 2457–2460 (1973).

OSBORNE, M. J., POOTERS, N., ANGLES d'AURIAC, G., EPSTEIN, A. N., WORCEL, M., MEYER, P.: Metabolism of tritiated angiotensin II in anaesthetized rats. Pflügers Arch. ges. Physiol. **326**, 101–114 (1971).

PAGE, I. H., McCUBBIN, J. W.: Renal hypertension. Chicago: Yearbook Publ. 1968.

PEACH, M. J., CLINE, W. H., WATTS, D. T.: Release of catecholamines by angiotensin-II. Circulation Res. **19**, 571–575 (1966).

PECK, J. W., NOVIN, D.: Evidence that osmoreceptors mediating drinking in rabbits are in the lateral preoptic area. J. comp. physiol. Psychol. **74**, 134–147 (1971).

PESKAR, B., MEYER, D. K., TAUCHMANN, U., HERTTING, G.: Influence of isoproterenol, hydralazine and phentolamine on the renin activity of plasma and renal cortex of rats. Europ. J. Pharmacol. **9**, 394–396 (1970).

ROGERS, P. W., KURTZMAN, N. A.: Renal failure, uncontrollable thirst and hyperreninemia. J. Am. Med. Ass. **225**, 1236–1238 (1973).

ROLLS, B. J., JONES, B. P.: Cessation of drinking following intracranial injections of angiotensin in the rat. J. comp. physiol. Psychol. **80**, 26–29 (1972).

ROTH, L. J., BARLOW, C. F.: Autoradiography of drugs in the brain. In: Isotopes in Experimental Pathology (Ed. L. J. ROTH), pp. 49–62. Chicago: University of Chicago Press 1965.

SIMPSON, J. B., ROUTTENBERG, A.: Subfornical Organ: site of drinking elicitation by angiotensin II. Science, **181**, 1172–1175 (1973).

SOKABE, H., NAKAJIMA, T.: Chemical structure and role of angiotensins in the vertebrates. Gener. comp. Endocr. Suppl. **3**, 382–392 (1972).

STRICKER, E. M.: Extracellular fluid volume and thirst. Am. J. Physiol. **211**, 232–238 (1966).

— Thirst, Sodium appetite and complementary physiological contributions to the regulation of intravascular fluid volume. In: The Neuropsychology of Thirst: new findings and advances in concepts. (Eds. A. N. EPSTEIN, H. R. KISSILEFF, and E. STELLAR), pp. 73–98. H.V. Washington: Winston and Sons 1973.

SWANSON, L. W., MARSHALL, G. R., NEEDLEMAN, P., SHARPE, L. G.: Characterization of central angiotensin II receptors involved in the elicitation of drinking in the rat. Brain Res. **49**, 441–446 (1973).

VOLICER, L., LOEW, C. G.: Penetration of angiotensin II into the brain. Neuropharmacology **10**, 631–636 (1971).

The Role of the Cerebral Ventricular System in Angiotensin-Induced Thirst

A. K. JOHNSON

FITZSIMONS and his colleagues (FITZSIMONS, 1970) have implicated the renal renin-angiotensin system as being a mediator of thirst. This has been done by showing that manipulations which release renin cause drinking and that systemic infusion of angiotensin produces water intake in sated animals. The fact that drinking can be initiated by intracranial injections of very small quantities of angiotensin II relative to the size of the effective peripheral dose suggests that angiotensin II may act directly on the brain to produce its dipsogenic effect.

In an early report of the intracranial angiotensin II drinking phenomenon (EPSTEIN, FITZSIMONS, and ROLLS, 1970), an attempt was made to localize neural tissue which was sensitive to the hormone. When doses of 500 to 4000 ng were injected in volumes of 1 to 2 μl., drinking was reported to be elicited from a broad expanse of tissue which included the septal region, the anterior thalamus, the preoptic area and the anterior hypothalamic area. The following work was initially undertaken as an attempt to provide more concise localization of angiotensin sensitive tissue than was previously defined. Animals were tested with intracranial injections of angiotensin II[1] beginning several orders of magnitude below those used in the previous mapping studies. Using a remote intracranial injection

system, animals each bearing a single chronic guide cannula were injected with test solutions of 1 μl. in volume. On each test day, animals received a single injection of one dose of angiotensin II from an ascending series of 0, 1, 4, 8, 16, 32, 64, or 128 ng, until a dose was reached that reliably produced drinking in two test sessions. This dose was defined as the *lowest effective dose* for a given animal, provided that the animal did not drink to a subsequent control injection of isotonic saline.

The sensitivities of injection sites determined with this method are shown for 44 animals in Fig. 1. The number in the circle indicates the lowest effective dose for a particular animal. Those not responding to the highest angiotensin II dose (128 ng) are shown by squares. The results indicate that highly sensitive sites were apparently located in the 1) preoptic area (POA), 2) anterior hypothalamus, and 3) nucleus reuniens thalami and that relatively insensitive sites were located in 1) the caudate nucleus, 2) the septal area, 3) the hippocampal commissure, and 4) the ventral thalamus. These findings agree with those of EPSTEIN, FITZSIMONS, and ROLLS (1970) with the exception of the septal area which we have found to be consistently negative at the highest dose tested in the present work. After considering the correlation of the anatomy with the sensitivity data, we became concerned about the fact that in many cases highly sensitive animals either had cannulae with tips that ended very close to ventricles or cannulae with a shaft trajectory that passed through a ventricular

---

[1] The term "angiotensin II", throughout this paper, refers to unlabelled val[5]-angiotensin II amide (Hypertensin Ciba). The labelled (tritiated) material was ileu[5]-angiotensin II (Ed.).

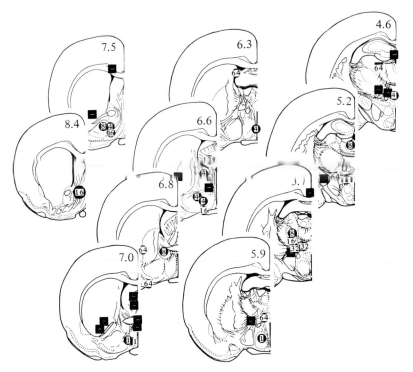

Fig. 1. Angiotensin sensitivity and location of 44 guide cannula tips. All cannulae were implanted vertically. Numbers in the circles indicate the lowest effective dose (ng) of angiotensin II amide (Hypertensin Ciba) to which a given animal responded. Squares indicate negative sites. (JOHNSON and EPSTEIN, 1975)

space. Conversely, most negative sites had cannula tips and trajectories removed from the ventricles. This observation raised the possibility that intracranially injected angiotensin II might not be exerting its effect at the tissue site at the tip of the cannula, but that the hormone may be reaching the ventricular system either by diffusion or by efflux up the outside of the guide cannula shaft.

In order to assess the likelihood of ventricular involvement we have used several techniques. First, we have made direct injections into the lateral ventricles following the testing procedure carried out in the tissue mapping study. We have found in four out of five animals with ventricular placements a reliable response to a 1 ng dose of angiotensin II (or the lowest dose employed in the tissue study). The latencies and water consumption following ventricular injection were comparable to those seen following tissue injection.

Second, as represented in Fig. 2, we have made injections into the caudate nucleus by way of a permanent guide cannula passing through the lateral ventricle. As can be seen in Fig. 1, the caudate is a relatively insensitive area. However, if the injection is made through a guide cannula which passes through a ventricular space, an

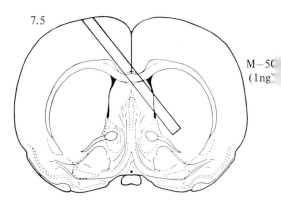

Fig. 2. Example of a caudate placement (animal M-50) with the guide cannula intentionally angled to pass through the ventricular space

118

unresponsive area can be "converted" to a responsive site.

Third, as shown in Fig. 3, cannulae were angled into the POA, which was shown to be highly sensitive with vertical cannulae with a ventricular trajectory. Animals with POA cannulae (N = 13) angled to avoid the ventricle either were unresponsive or responded only to the highest doses of angiotensin employed. The particular animal shown in Fig. 3 was negative to the 128 ng dose. Its placement can be compared with three placements from animals with cannula tips within the same region but which passed through a ventricular space. These animals were responsive to 4, 8, and 16 ng.

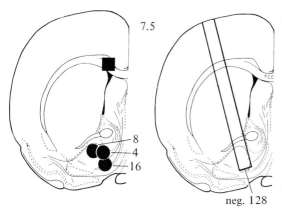

Fig. 3. *Left.* Lowest effective dose of angiotensin II amide found in four animals with vertical cannulae. In three cases the cannula tip passed through the lateral ventricle to end in the preoptic area. The cannula tip ending in the corpus callosum was negative to a 128 ng dose. *Right.* An example of a cannula in the preoptic area angled in order to avoid passing through the lateral ventricle. Note that this placement was negative to a 128 ng dose even though it was near the cannula tips shown on the left

A fourth approach was to employ labeled angiotensin II to determine whether injected material does in fact enter the cerebrospinal fluid (c.s.f.) after intracranial injection into what are supposed to be highly sensitive tissue sites. In this experiment, four animals received POA vertical cannulae with a ventricular trajectory and four animals received POA cannulae angled to miss the ventricles. All animals were screened for drinking to angiotensin. The animals with vertical cannulae reliably responded to 1 ng of

hormone and the animals with angled cannulae were unresponsive to 128 ng. A few days after the last angiotensin screening test, the animals were anaesthetized with 2.5 ml./kg Equithesin (Jenson-Salzburg laboratories), a compound solution containing 42.5 g/l. chloral hydrate, 9.7 g/l. pentobarbital and 21.3 g/l. magnesium sulphate in a water-propylene glycol-alcohol base, and mounted into a head holder with the head in severe ventroflexion with respect to the body. The atlanto-occipital membrane was exposed by excision of the skin and of the overlying neck musculature. Under a dissecting microscope, this membrane was removed to expose the dura so that the cisterna magna could be visualized. Under magnification, the tip of a beveled 30 gauge hypodermic needle was positioned in the cistern. Prior to insertion, the 30 gauge needle was attached to an 18 cm piece of PE 10 tubing and both the needle and tubing were filled with 0.9% saline. The free end of the PE tubing was lowered approximately 10 cm below the tip of the needle in the cistern. This arrangement forms a siphon and c.s.f. can be continuously collected in graduated capillary pipettes and counted in a liquid scintillation counter. After collection of control samples of c.s.f., a 1 μl. injection of 1 ng of tritiated (tyrosine-3,5-^{3}H) angiotensin II (New England Nuclear 32 c/m-mole) was made into the POA through the permanently implanted guide cannula. All of the animals in which the cannula shaft passed through the ventricle to end in the POA showed an increase of radioactivity in the cisternal c.s.f. a few minutes after the injection of labelled material, whereas none of the animals with POA cannulae angled to avoid the ventricle showed an increase of radioactivity in the c.s.f. Representative time courses of appearance of radioactivity in the c.s.f. are shown for each type of cannula orientation in Fig. 4. It can be seen that radioactivity appears in the cisternal c.s.f. within at most 4 min after the injection of labeled tracer into the POA through a vertical cannula with a ventricular trajectory. The animal with a cannula angled into the POA showed no radioactivity in the c.s.f.

From this series of studies it is clear that angiotensin injected into what was previously thought to be a highly sensitive tissue site exerts

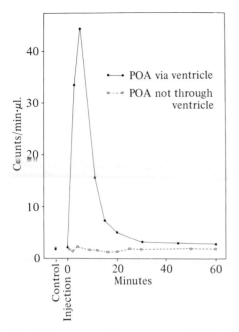

Fig. 4. Time course of the appearance of radioactivity in cerebrospinal fluid collected from animals injected intracranially with 32 nc of tritiated angiotensin II. Guide cannulae of both animals ended in the preoptic area (POA). However, the trajectory of one cannula passed through the lateral ventricle; the other one did not

its effect by gaining entrance to the ventricular system. On the basis of this work we (JOHNSON, 1972) have previously speculated that intracranially injected angiotensin II exerts its effect on some periventricular structure. Recently SIMPSON and ROUTTENBERG (1973) have provided evidence that the subfornical organ, which is such a periventricular structure, may be the target site for intracranially injected angiotensin.

At present there is virtually no evidence that angiotensin — or for that matter any peptide which is known to have a specific behavioural effect — can cross the blood-brain barrier to interact directly with central nervous tissue. MARY OSBORNE and colleagues (OSBORNE, POOTERS, ANGLES d'AURIAC, EPSTEIN, WORCEL, and MEYER, 1971), employing scintillation counting after intravenous injection of labeled angiotensin, found no selective uptake of angiotensin by any specific portion of brain. From their results, they have concluded that angioten-

sin does not readily pass the blood-brain barrier. In addition, VOLICER and LOEW (1971), using autoradiography in mice injected intravenously with labeled angiotensin, showed that there was radioactivity located in the choroid plexuses of the lateral ventricles as well as inside the lateral ventricle and inside and around the third ventricle. These results, in conjunction with our findings which implicate involvement of the ventricular system with intracranial angiotensin injections, suggest the possibility that peripherally generated angiotensin may interact with the central nervous system by first gaining entry into the ventricular system and then passing in the c.s.f. to periventricular target tissues.

As a preliminary test of this hypothesis, we have monitored c.s.f. radioactivity in rats infused systemically with labeled angiotensin through jugular catheters. The parameters used for the infusions approximate those necessary to produce drinking to peripheral angiotensin (FITZSIMONS and SIMONS, 1969; HSIAO and EPSTEIN, 1973). The results of one of these studies are shown in Fig. 5. Here we see the radioactivity of

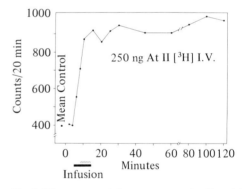

Fig. 5. Time course of the appearance of radioactivity in the cerebrospinal fluid in an animal receiving an intravenous infusion of tritiated angiotensin II (8 μc total dose)

successive c.s.f. samples collected from the cisterna magna (previously described) during and following the infusion of 250 ng of angiotensin II (New England Nuclear 32 c/m-mole). It can be seen that radioactivity is detected in the c.s.f. less than 4 min after the angiotensin infusion actually enters the rat.

In order to gain more definitive information

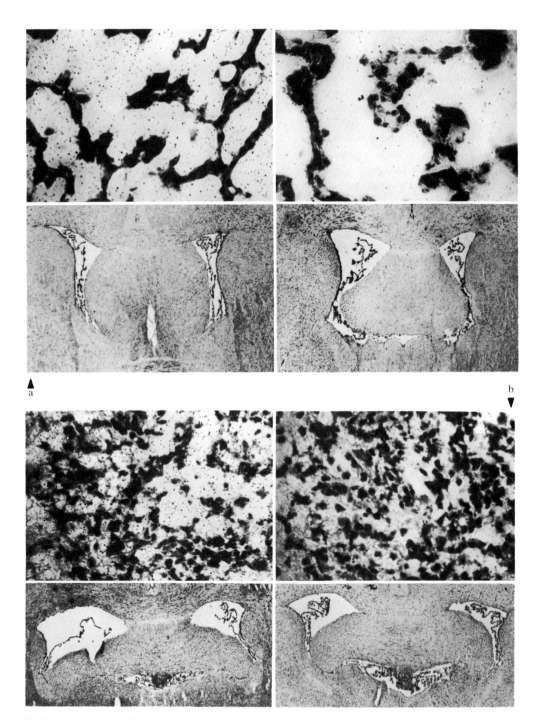

Fig. 6. Autoradiographs from animals treated intravenously with 2 μg of angiotensin II. Control animal received Hypertensin (Ciba). Experimental animal received tritiated angiotensin. (a) *Left:* High and low magnification of experimental brain showing choroid in the lateral ventricle. *Right:* High and low magnification of control brain showing choroid in the lateral ventricle. (b) *Left:* High and low magnification of experimental brain showing the subfornical organ. *Right:* High and low magnification of control brain showing the subfornical organ

regarding the possible mode of entry to the brain of systemically generated angiotensin and the site of action in the C.N.S., EPSTEIN, Mary OSBORNE, Eileen SHRAGER, and I have employed autoradiographic techniques (unpublished). In these studies, rats were injected intravenously with 2 μg of either cold or tritiated angiotensin II (New England Nuclear 32 c/m-mole). The brains were rapidly removed from the treated animals, cooled briefly with dry ice, and then quick-frozen in liquid nitrogen. Sections of brain 4 μ thick were cut in a cryostat ($-20°C$) and mounted on slides that were previously coated with Kodak NTB-3 emulsion. The slides were stored over desiccant for 4 to 6 weeks after which time they were photographically processed and stained with cresyl violet acetate.

The results of the autoradiographic experiments indicate that in animals treated with labeled angiotensin, radioactivity is high in the ventricular spaces, periventricular tissue, choroid plexuses, pituitary, pineal, subfornical organ, and the area postrema. Shown in Fig. 6 are autoradiographs of the lateral ventricle with choroid and of the subfornical organ. These results support those obtained from the scintillation analysis showing that c.s.f. contains high concentrations of radioactivity after peripheral administration of labeled angiotensin II. They are also in agreement with the autoradiographic results of VOLICER and LOEW (1971) who employed higher μg/kg doses of angiotensin in mice.

Tracer analyses of c.s.f. and autoradiography tend to implicate the ventricular system and periventricular structures as playing a significant role in the mediation of angiotensin thirst. However, at present, we must be cautious and not overinterpret these results. What we are measuring with these techniques is radioactivity and not angiotensin per se. Work is presently under way which may permit us to determine what portion of the radioactivity is undegraded hormone.

In summary, the results point to involvement of the ventricular system and periventricular structures in mediating the dipsogenic response to intracranially injected angiotensin and support the hypothesis that peripherally generated polypeptides in general and angiotensin in particular may gain access to the central nervous system by the ventricular route to exert their behavioural effects.

Acknowledgements. The work reported in this article was carried out in Dr. ALAN N. EPSTEIN's laboratory while the author was a Fellow of the Institute of Neurological Sciences at the University of Pennsylvania. Support was provided by USPHS MH 49 341-02 during this period. I wish to thank ALAN N. EPSTEIN for his warm hospitality and superb colleagueship which I enjoyed during the time I spent at Pennsylvania. In addition, I would like to thank MARY OSBORNE and EILEEN SHRAGER for their collaboration in the autoradiographic studies. I am grateful for the advice received from Dr. DONALD W. PFAFF, Dr. BRUCE S. MCEWEN, and Mr. JOHN L. GERLACH of Rockefeller University in introducing us to the techniques of autoradiography.

References

EPSTEIN, A. N., FITZSIMONS, J. T., ROLLS, B. J.: Drinking induced by injection of angiotensin into the brain of the rat. J. Physiol. Lond. **210**, 457–474 (1970).

FITZSIMONS, J. T.: The renin-angiotensin system in the control of drinking. In: The Hypothalamus (Eds. L. MARTINI, M. MOTTA, F. FRASCHINI), pp. 195–212 New York: Academic Press 1970.

FITZSIMONS, J. T., SIMONS, B. J.: The effect on drinking in the rat of intravenous infusion of angiotensin, given alone or in combination with other stimuli of thirst. J. Physiol. Lond. **203**, 45–57 (1969).

HSIAO, S., EPSTEIN, A. N.: Additivity of dipsogens: angiotensin plus cell dehydration. Fed. Proc. **32**, 384 (1973).

JOHNSON, A. K.: Localization of angiotensin sensitive areas for thirst within the rat brain. Paper read: Eastern Psychological Association Meetings. Boston 1972.

JOHNSON, A. K., EPSTEIN, A. N.: The cerebral ventricles as the avenue for the dipsogenic action of intracranial angiotensin. Brain Res. (in press) (1975).

OSBORNE, M. J., POOTERS, N., ANGLES d'AURIAC, G., EPSTEIN, A. N., WORCEL, M., MEYER, P.: Metabolism of tritiated angiotensin II in anesthetized rats. Pflügers Arch. ges. Physiol. **326**, 101–114 (1971).

SIMPSON, J. B., ROUTTENBERG, A.: Subfornical organ: site of drinking elicited by angiotensin II. Science **181**, 1172–1175 (1973).

VOLICER, L., LOEW, C. G.: Penetration of angiotensin II into the brain. Neuropharmacol. **10**, 631–636 (1971).

Subfornical Organ Involvement in Angiotensin-Induced Drinking

J. B. SIMPSON

The studies described here explore a possible central nervous dipsogenic site of action of the hormone angiotensin-II. Specifically, the involvement of the subfornical organ (SFO), an obscure telencephalic structure, in angiotensin-induced drinking was studied. The SFO has remained, until recently, a structure on which there is considerable literature dealing with morphological characteristics while its physiological role has remained enigmatic. The subfornical organ is a small, glomus-like convexity of the midline third ventricular ependyma, situated consistently, in all species investigated, near the interventricular foramen (AKERT, POTTER, and ANDERSON, 1961). An intimate relationship between elements of the organ and the ventricular cerebrospinal fluid has been postulated (AKERT, 1969). The structure is densely vascularized (SPOERRI, 1963) and pharmacological (DEMPSEY, 1968) as well as electron microscopical (ROHR, 1966) evidence indicates that the SFO neuropil is functionally located on blood side of the blood brain barrier. Additionally, physiologically uncharacterized neurosecretion from the SFO occurs both into the vasculature and into the ventricular cerebrospinal fluid (AKERT, 1969; ROHR, 1966).

It was initially demonstrated that injection of the cholinomimetic carbachol into the SFO elicited copious drinking with a short latency (ROUTTENBERG and SIMPSON, 1971). Furthermore, lesioning the structure blocked drinking induced by injection of carbachol into the third ventricle. Such lesions also produced a transient decrease in daily water intake (SIMPSON and ROUTTENBERG, 1972). These findings suggested that the SFO may also play a role in the regulation of drinking. In addition, the SFO appears to be located on the blood side of the blood-brain barrier and, therefore, accessible to angiotensin-II, which on the other hand reaches brain interstitial fluid quite slowly (VOLICER and LOEW, 1971). We first investigated the dose-response relationship and time course of drinking elicited by direct injection of angiotensin into the SFO. Each animal received a single 0.5 μl. injection of angiotensin-II solution (Val[5] angiotensin-II amide, Hypertensin Ciba) delivered to SFO via a chronically implanted cannula system (ROUTTENBERG and SIMPSON, 1971; SIMPSON and ROUTTENBERG, 1972, 1973). Water intake was measured for the subsequent 0.5 hr, and scores reflect the increment in drinking following injection relative to baseline (uninjected) water intakes (SIMPSON and ROUTTENBERG, 1972). As shown in Fig. 1 a, doses of angiotensin-II from 0.1–100 ng induced drinking behaviour following SFO injection. It is important to note that 0.1 ng, or 100 pg, of hormone elicited drinking; this dose is lower than for all other reported loci of application of the dipsogen (e.g., EPSTEIN, FITZSIMONS, and ROLLS, 1970; SWANSON, SHARPE, and GRIFFIN, 1973).

The time course of drinking also reflects the responsiveness of the SFO to angiotensin-II; short latency of drinking behaviour was consistently observed for all doses of the dipsogen, as shown in Fig. 1 b. The duration of the behavioural effect was proportional to the quantity of dipsogen administered. Injection of angiotensin into the adjacent third ventricle was consistently less effective in eliciting drinking than injection

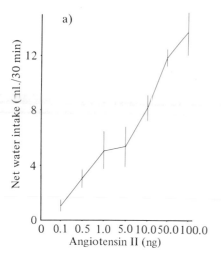

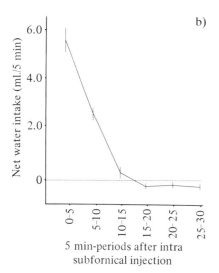

Fig. 1 a and b. (a) Net water intake during 0.5 hr testing period as a function of doses of val[5]-angiotensin-II amide injected into the subfornical organ. Each point is the mean of at least five tests ± S.E. of mean. (b) Net water intake during successive five-min time periods following injections of val[5]-angiotensin-II amide into the subfornical organ. The figure was constructed from data obtained with all doses of angiotensin-II used in the present experiment. The curve shown here is the mean of 37 animals ± S.E. of mean. The zero point on the ordinates of both 1 a and 1 b indicate the mean water intake of animals during baseline (uninjected) testing periods. From J. B. SIMPSON, A. ROUTTENBERG (1973)

directly into the SFO. In summary, then, the intracranial injection of angiotensin-II into the subfornical organ reliably produces short latency, large magnitude drinking behaviour, and the structure appears to be the most effective site of injection yet reported.

It appeared possible that the SFO could be the actual site of action of the dipsogen following application to other subcortical loci, such as the base of the telencephalon, because a) intracranially injected chemicals do diffuse widely, either via the ventricles (ROUTTENBERG, 1967; JOHNSON, this volume) or via the vasculature (GROSSMAN and STUMPF, 1969; ROUTTENBERG, 1972); and b) the threshold dose of angiotensin in the SFO was appreciably smaller than that reported for all other loci. The possibility of diffusion from the diagonal band or medial preoptic area to the SFO was therefore explored. The effect of SFO lesions on drinking induced by injection of angiotensin into the basal telencephalon was evaluated by injection of 100 or 500 ng of angiotensin-II prior to and then subsequent to an experimental lesioning procedure. It should be recalled that the preoptic regions were responsive sites of application of the dipsogen (EPSTEIN, FITZSIMONS, and ROLLS, 1970). The results of this study are given in Fig. 2: lesions of the body of the SFO reduced or blocked the effect of angiotensin-II injected into

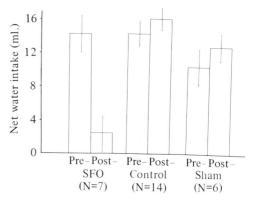

Fig. 2. Net water intake of animals after angiotensin-II has been injected into the basal telencephalon, before (pre-) and after (post-) surgical lesioning of the surbfornical organ (SFO), in control lesioned animals (Control), or in sham operated control animals (Sham). Values are means ± S.E. of mean. From J. B. SIMPSON, A. ROUTTENBERG (1973)

the preoptic area or the diagonal band: lesions into adjacent tissue (Control) or operative control procedures (Sham) were without effect on the elicited drinking. It appeared possible, then, that diffusion of dipsogen from such basal telecephalic sites of application via the vasculature or via the ventricles to the SFO would explain previous results.

A third study was performed to assess the effects of SFO lesions on drinking induced by intrajugular injection of angiotensin since delivery of hormone via the vasculature would closely mimic the route of access of the blood-borne hormone to the brain. Animals prepared with chronically indwelling intrajugular catheters were given three injections each of angiotensin-II amide (Hypertensin Ciba) solution; injections consisted of 10 µg of hormone delivered in a 0.25 ml. bolus of saline vehicle over 15 sec. Experimental brain lesions were produced in the SFO (SFO: 60–100% of the body of the structure destroyed); partially in the SFO (P-SFO: 0–45% SFO body destruction and damage in anatomically proximal tissue), or bilaterally in the dorsal preoptic areas, including the anterior commissure (POA). Sham operative control procedures (SHAM) were also used. The net water intake elicited by I.V. angiotensin-II at three days (inj = 1), 8 days (inj = 2), or 13 days (inj = 3) post-lesion are shown in Fig. 3. It is apparent that major destruction of the SFO body produced a sharp decrease in elicited water intake; partial destruction of the structure produced a less marked decrease in the elicited water intake. Bilateral lesions of the preoptic region resulted in a slight elevation of the elicited water intake. Destruction of the subfornical organ, then, reduced the magnitude of I.V. angiotensin-elicited drinking; preoptic lesions did not reduce the elicited water intake.

Taken together, these three studies provide compelling evidence for the involvement of the SFO in angiotensin-induced drinking. The effects of intracranial injection of angiotensin-II directly into SFO indicate that this structure is the most angiotensin-sensitive central nervous region described at present, and the elicitation of drinking behaviour by a 100 pg dose of hormone is approaching true physiological levels. The second and third experiments discussed here, in which SFO lesions diminished systemic or intracranial angiotensin-induced drinking, also point to SFO involvement in the dipsogenic effect of the hormone. Although these lesion effects could be due to either pharmacological or neurological characteristics of the SFO, the observed potency of intracranial injection of angiotensin at the SFO appears to favour the view that the lesion effects were due to disruption of a pharmacological site of action of the dipsogen.

If the premise that the SFO is the major dipsogenic site of action of endogenous angiotensin-II is true, then two important questions concerning this mechanism are: 1) how is endogenous hormone delivered to sensory elements within the structure; and, 2) what is the mechanism by which the SFO acts to produce drinking? Delivery of hormone to the SFO could occur via the vasculature. The SFO is densely vascularized (SPOERRI, 1963), and appears to be located on the outer side of the pharmacological blood-brain barrier (DEMPSEY, 1968; ROHR, 1966). Thus angiotensin-II, which is apparently excluded by the blood-brain barrier (VOLICER

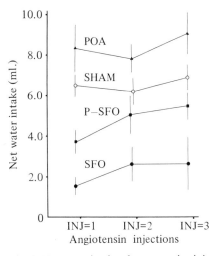

Fig. 3. Net water intake after successive injections of angiotensin-II solutions, into subfornical organ lesioned animals (SFO), partial subfornical organ lesioned animals (P-SFO), sham operated control animals (SHAM), or preoptic area lesioned animals (POA), as defined in text. Angiotensin-II solution was injected 3 (inj = 1), 8 (inj = 2), and 13 (inj = 3) days after operation. Values are means ± S.E. of mean

and LOEW, 1971), could reach the SFO interstitial fluid and then the receptive elements there.

An alternative route of access to brain dipsogenic receptors has also recently been postulated, and data suggestive of ventricular entry to the brain have been presented both by EPSTEIN and by JOHNSON (this volume). This possibility is also quite compatible with the hypothesized SFO site of action; relationships between the cerebrospinal fluid solute content and the SFO have been postulated (AKERT, 1969; FLEISCHHAUER, 1964). Angiotensin could therefore gain access to the putative SFO receptor site via the vasculature or via the ventricles, but it is not yet possible to decide which of these routes is the more important.

The interaction of the SFO with other neural systems involved in body fluid regulation is also still largely unexplored. In addition, the connections of the structure have not been identified. The presence of vascular and ventricular neurosecretion within the SFO, as well as a presumed neural efferent outflow, offer several possible ways in which the SFO could influence other central mechanisms. For example, the structure could produce immediate effects via neural outflow resulting in drinking behaviour, and it could exert a longer term influence on body fluid regulatory processes by neurosecretion into the ventricles which would then influence other neural systems via ependymal cell transport (KOBAYASHI and MATSUI, 1969; MILLHOUSE, 1971). In summary then, although a role for the SFO in the dipsogenic effects of angiotensin-II now seems likely, we are still relatively ignorant about the full physiological significance of this structure in drinking behaviour. Further experimentation with pharmacological, anatomical, and electrophysiological techniques is required to specify precisely the extent of the involvement of the subfornical organ in body fluid regulatory processes and, especially, in thirst.

Acknowledgement. The experimental work was supported by NIH grant NS HL 10768-01 to ARYEH ROUTTENBERG, Northwestern University, Chicago, Ill., USA.

References

AKERT, K.: The mammalian subfornical organ. J. Neurovisc. Relat., Suppl. IX, 78–93 (1969).

AKERT, K., POTTER, H. D., ANDERSON, J. W.: The subfornical organ in mammals. J. comp. Neurol. 116, 1–13 (1961).

DEMPSEY, E. W.: Fine structure of the rat's intercolumnar tubercle and its adjacent ependyma and choroid plexus, with especial reference to the appearance of its sinusoidal vessels in experimental argyria. Engl. J. med. 32, 568–580 (1968).

EPSTEIN, A. N., FITZSIMONS, J. T., ROLLS, B. J.: Drinking induced by injection of angiotensin into the brain of the rat. J. Physiol. Lond. 210, 457–474 (1970).

FLEISCHHAUER, K.: Fluoreszenzmikroskopische Untersuchungen über den Stofftransport zwischen Ventrikelliquor und Gehirn. Z. Zellforsch. 62, 639–654 (1964).

GROSSMAN, S. P., STUMPF, W. E.: Intracranial drug implant: an autoradiographic analysis of diffusion. Science 166, 1410–1412 (1969).

KOBAYASHI, H., MATSUI, T.: Fine structure of the median eminence and its significance. In: Frontiers in Neuroendocrinology (Eds. W. F. GANONG, L. MARTINI), pp. 1–46. Oxford University Press: New York 1969.

MILLHOUSE, O. E.: A Golgi study of third ventricle tanycytes in the adult rodent brain. Z. Zellforsch. 121, 1–13 (1971).

ROHR, V. U.: Zum Feinbau des Subfornikalorgans der Katze I. Der Gefäßapparat. Z. Zellforsch. 73, 246–271 (1966).

— Zum Feinbau des Subfornikalorgans der Katze II. Neurosekretorische Aktivität. Z. Zellforsch. 75, 11–34 (1966).

ROUTTENBERG, A.: Drinking induced by carbachol: thirst circuit or ventricular modification? Science 157, 838–839 (1967).

— Intracranial chemical injection and behavior: a critical review. Behav. Biol. 7, 601–642 (1972).

ROUTTENBERG, A., SIMPSON, J. B.: Carbachol-induced drinking at ventricular and subfornical organ sites of application. Life Sci. 10, 481–490 (1971).

SIMPSON, J. B., ROUTTENBERG, A.: The subfornical organ and carbachol-induced drinking. Brain. Res. 45, 135–157 (1972).

— Subfornical organ: site of drinking elicitation by angiotensin-II. Science 181, 1172–1175 (1973).

SPOERRI, O.: Über die Gefäßversorgung des Subfornikalorgans der Ratte. Acta. Anat. 54, 333–348 (1963).

SWANSSON, L. W., SHARPE, L. G., GRIFFIN, D.: Drinking to intracerebral angiotensin II and carbachol: dose-response relationships and ionic involvement. Physiol. Behav. 10, 595–600 (1973).

VOLICER, L., LOEW, C. G.: Penetration of angiotensin II into the brain. Neuropharmacol. 10, 631–636 (1971).

Evidence that the Lateral Hypothalamus and Midbrain Participate in the Drinking Response Elicited by Intracranial Angiotensin

G. J. Mogenson and J. Kucharczyk

Angiotensin-II has been shown to induce copious drinking in rats which are in normal water balance. The areas of the brain responsive to direct chemical stimulation by this hormone include the preoptic area, septum and anterior hypothalamus (Epstein, Fitzsimons, and Rolls, 1970) and the subfornical organ (Simpson and Routtenberg, 1973). It has been suggested that these areas may contain chemosensitive receptors for angiotensin. If this is so, where are the signals from these receptors transmitted and how are they processed? The present study was undertaken to investigate these questions.

Chronic cannulae were implanted either unilaterally or bilaterally into the preoptic region in male Wistar rats weighing 250–350 g according to the procedure described by Black, Kucharczyk, and Mogenson (1974). Following complete postoperative recovery, each animal was tested once daily for the occurrence of drinking following the injection of 100 ng of synthetic angiotensin-II-amide (Hypertensin, Ciba) dissolved in 1 μl of distilled water. In rats with bilateral cannulae, the test sites were alternated. Only those animals which drank more than 5 ml. of water during each of six consecutive 30 min tests were used in the subsequent experiments. In the first series of 23 rats with a unilateral cannula the animals were anaesthetized with urethane and the effects of angiotensin-II on the discharge rate of single neurones in the lateral hypothalamus and midbrain were investigated. In a second series of 16

animals with bilateral cannulae the effects of lesions of the lateral hypothalamus or midbrain on drinking elicited by the application of angiotensin-II to the preoptic region were examined.

Recording from Neurones of the Lateral Hypothalamus and Midbrain

Angiotensin-II was administered to sites in the preoptic region from which drinking had been

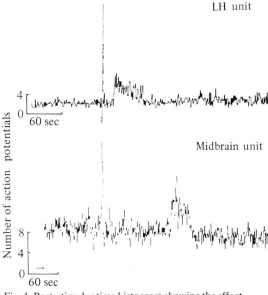

Fig. 1. Post-stimulus time histogram showing the effect of a single injection of 50 ng of angiotensin-II into the preoptic area on the unit discharge rate of a lateral hypothalamic (LH) and a midbrain neurone. The stimulus artifact indicates the time of angiotensin administration

elicited in earlier behavioural tests and the effect on the discharge rate of 75 lateral hypothalamic neurones was studied. The discharge rate of approximately one-third of these neurones was increased following the injection of angiotensin-II (Black, Mok, Cope, and Mogenson, 1973). A typical response is shown in Fig. 1. Desynchronization of cortical e.e.g. and an increase in

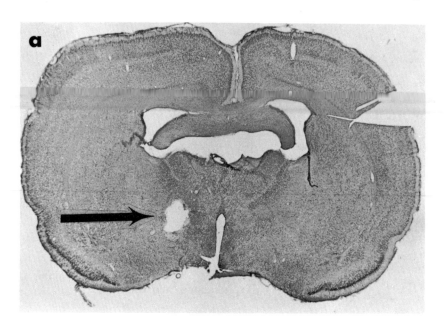

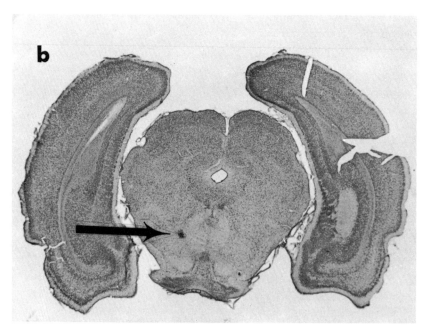

Fig. 2. Photomicrographs of brain from an animal in the first series showing the location of the unilateral cannula implant in the preoptic area (a) and the microelectrode recording site in the ventral tegmental area of the midbrain (b). Magnification 7 times

arterial pressure usually accompanied the change in the discharge rate of the hypothalamic neurone when 100 ng of angiotensin-II was administered. With lower doses of angiotensin (25 and 50 ng, also dissolved in 1 μl. of distilled water) blood pressure changes were slight or not detectable although in several cases an increased rate of discharge of lateral hypothalamic neurones was observed.

Thirty of 59 midbrain neurones increased their firing frequency following the administration of angiotensin-II. Twenty seven of the 30 neurones activated by preoptic angiotensin were either in the ventral tegmentum ($n = 18$) or in an area ventrolateral to the central grey ($n = 9$). A post-stimulus time histogram representing the response of one such neurone appears in Fig. 1 b and photomicrographs showing the recording site and the site of the cannula used for administering the angiotensin are shown in Fig. 2. At the highest dose of angiotensin-II (100 ng) an increased firing of midbrain neurones occurred concomitantly with desynchronization of cortical e.e.g. and a slight increase of mean arterial pressure (mean change = +5 mm Hg). At the lower doses of angiotensin-II (25 and 50 ng) cortical e.e.g. and blood pressure changes were not detectable (Fig. 3).

Lesions of the Lateral Hypothalamus and Midbrain

It was decided on the basis of the results obtained from the electrophysiological experiments to lesion the lateral hypothalamus and midbrain and observe what effects such lesions might have on drinking elicited by administration of angiotensin to the preoptic area.

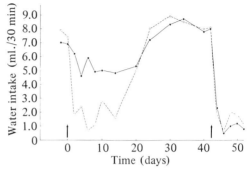

Fig. 4. Water intake (ml./30 min) in a single rat following administration of angiotensin-II to the preoptic region before and after a unilateral lesion of the lateral hypothalamus (designated by arrow). Solid line indicates drinking elicited from the side contralateral to the lesion; broken line indicates drinking elicited from the ipsilateral side. The arrow at 42 days indicates the placement of a second LH lesion contralateral to the first

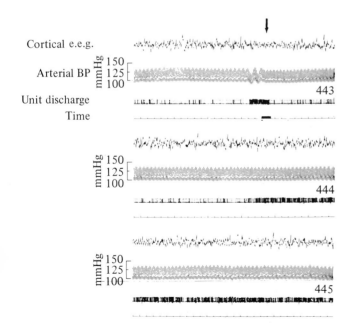

Fig. 3. Continuous polygraph tracings showing cortical e.e.g., arterial blood pressure and discharge of a neurone in the ventral tegmental area. Arrow on the top trace indicates the time of injection of 50 ng angiotensin-II into the preoptic area. Each division of the time marker denotes one second

Unilateral lesions of the lateral hypothalamus caused a severe depression of drinking in response to angiotensin administered to the preoptic region ipsilateral to the lesion (Fig. 4). A smaller reduction in water intake was observed when angiotensin was administered to the contralateral side. Recovery of the drinking response to angiotensin occurred gradually within 3–5 weeks. A second lesion, contralateral to the first, was then placed (Fig. 4) and caused a severe and prolonged deficit in drinking elicited by angiotensin administered to either side of the preoptic region.

In preliminary experiments, unilateral lesions of the midbrain tegmentum or the region ventrolateral to the central grey have resulted in an attenuation of the drinking response to preoptic angiotensin. In a single rat with bilateral lesions of the ventral tegmentum drinking to preoptic angiotensin was completely abolished.

The electrophysiological and lesion data reported in the present communication indicate that signals from angiotensin-sensitive neurones in the forebrain are transmitted through the lateral hypothalamus to the midbrain. It has been proposed that midbrain structures are concerned with integrating the motor patterns for complex behaviour such as drinking (KILMER and McCULLOCH, 1969) so that "command signals" from angiotensin receptors in the forebrain could activate appropriate mesencephalic systems. The results of anatomical studies suggest that these signals may be conducted along fibres of the medial forebrain bundle (NAUTA, 1958; NAUTA and HAYMAKER, 1969).

Although a rostro-caudally directed forebrain-hypothalamus-midbrain system mediating angiotensin-induced drinking provides an attractive working model, it has some major difficulties. For example, it is uncertain whether angiotensin-II is able to cross the blood-brain barrier from the systemic circulation and thereby gain access to the postulated receptors in the preoptic region. It is probable that if polypeptides such as angiotensin-II are able to penetrate neural tissue at all, they do so very slowly. This would be consistent with the finding of a long latency between intravenous infusion of angiotensin and the onset of drinking (FITZSIMONS and SIMONS, 1969).

SIMPSON and ROUTTENBERG (1973) have reported that very low doses of angiotensin-II administered directly to the subfornical organ are effective in eliciting drinking, and that drinking elicited by preoptic angiotensin is disrupted by lesions of this circumventricular structure. They suggest that the receptors for angiotensin are in the subfornical organ and that angiotensin administered through cannulae into the preoptic region diffuses through neural tissue into the ventricles and eventually reaches the subfornical organ. This ventricular hypothesis is an attractive one, mainly because it is known that the subfornical organ lies outside the blood-brain barrier (AKERT, 1969) and could therefore be readily acted upon by blood-borne substances. However, it is difficult to explain the long latency to drink following the infusion of angiotensin via a jugular cannula (FITZSIMONS and SIMONS, 1969) and the relatively short latency when angiotensin is injected directly into the preoptic region (EPSTEIN, FITZSIMONS, and ROLLS, 1970; KUCHARCZYK and MOGENSON, unpublished observations) if the receptors are in the subfornical organ. The hypothesis of SIMPSON and ROUTTENBERG is also inconsistent with the observation that unilateral lesions of the lateral hypothalamus have differential effects on drinking elicited by the administration of angiotensin-II to the ipsilateral and contralateral preoptic regions (Fig. 2; BLACK, KUCHARCZYK, and MOGENSON, 1974).

A definitive interpretation of the lesion data reported here will depend on knowing the locus of the receptors for angiotensin. However, whether this hormone acts on receptors in the preoptic region or at some other neural structure, it appears that the lateral hypothalamus and midbrain have an important role in the initiation of drinking by centrally administered angiotensin.

Summary

Intracranial injection of angiotensin-II through cannulae implanted in the preoptic region elicited drinking in rats and in subsequent acute experiments increased the discharge rate of neurones in the lateral hypothalamus and midbrain (ventral tegmental area and reticular formation). Lesions of the lateral hypothalamus, ventral tegmentum or the region ventrolateral to the central grey attenuated the drinking elicited by preoptic angiotensin. It is concluded that the lateral hypothalamus and midbrain participate in the drinking response initiated by the central administration of angiotensin.

References

AKERT, K.: The mammalian subfornical organ. J. Neurovisc. Relat. Suppl. IX, 78–93 (1969).

BLACK, S. L., KUCHARCZYK, J., MOGENSON, G. J.: Disruption of drinking to intracranial angiotensin by a lateral hypothalamic lesion. Pharmac. Biochem. Behav. 2, 515–522 (1974).

BLACK, S. L., MOK, A. C. S., COPE, D. L., MOGENSON, G. J.: Activation of lateral hypothalamic neurons by the injection of angiotensin into the preoptic area of the rat. Fed. Proc. 32, Abstract No. 930 (1973).

EPSTEIN, A. N., FITZSIMONS, J. T., ROLLS, B. J.: Drinking induced by angiotensin into the brain of the rat. J. Physiol. Lond. 210, 457–474 (1970).

FITZSIMONS, J. T., SIMONS, B.: The effect on drinking in the rat of intravenous infusion of angiotensin, given alone or in combination with other stimuli of thirst. J. Physiol. Lond. 203, 45–57 (1969).

KILMER, W., McCULLOCH, W. S.: The reticular formation and control system. In: Information Processing in the Nervous System (ed. K. N. LEIBOVIC), pp. 297–307. Berlin-Heidelberg-New York: Springer 1969.

NAUTA, W. J. H.: Hippocampal projections and related neural pathways to the mid-brain in the cat. Brain 81, 319–340 (1958).

NAUTA, W. J. H., HAYMAKER, W.: Hypothalamic nuclei and fiber connections. In: The Hypothalamus (Eds. W. HAYMAKER, E. ANDERSON, and W. J. H. NAUTA), pp. 136–203. Springfield-Illinois: Thomas 1969.

SIMPSON, J. B., ROUTTENBERG, A.: Subfornical organ: site of drinking elicitation by angiotensin II. Science 181, 1172–1174 (1973).

Angiotensin-Induced Drinking in the Cat

M. J. COOLING and M. D. DAY

Cats do not readily drink water when maintained on a tinned meat diet (CARVER and WATERHOUSE, 1962). Drinking has been elicited in the cat following the central administration of hypertonic saline (MILLER, 1961; GLASER and WOLF, 1963) but there are no reports in the literature of drinking initiated by central administration of drugs. Since renin and angiotensin II are potent dipsogens in the rat and several other species (FITZSIMONS, 1972), we have investigated their activity in the cat.

Cats were prepared for intraventricular administration of drugs according to the method of FELDBERG and SHERWOOD (1953) and in addition the right jugular vein was cannulated for the peripheral administration of drugs. Cats were housed in separate cages and allowed free access to water.

Drinking was induced when angiotensin II amide (0.001 to 4 μg) was infused into the cerebral ventricles in a total volume of 100 μl. at the rate of 25 μl. $\cdot$ min^{-1} dissolved in 0.9% sodium chloride. The response began 1 to 10 min after the start of the infusion and usually continued for about 30 min; the amount consumed ranged from 10 to 180 g.

The response was dose-related and reached a maximum at a dose of about 0.1 μg. The response could be elicited at hourly intervals for 4 hr but the volume consumed declined with time. In addition the maximal response also declined with repeated use of the animal and after 4–5 intraventricular doses of angiotensin II on different days the maximal response became stabilised at about 50 g.

Ile^5 angiotensin I (0.1–2.5 μg) and hog renin (0.1–0.25 Goldblatt u.) each caused drinking when administered intraventricularly. The responses to angiotensin I and angiotensin II were similar in magnitude and duration but renin produced a prolonged effect on drinking with delayed onset.

Infusions of angiotensin II (200 ng $\cdot$ Kg^{-1} $\cdot$ min^{-1}) into the jugular vein after 4 to 6 min initiated drinking behaviour which stopped before the end of the infusion at 20 min.

Sar^1 Ala^8 angiotensin II, a competitive inhibitor of the myotropic and vasoconstrictor actions of angiotensin II (PALS, MASCUCCI, DENNING, SIPOS, and FESSLER, 1971) was tested as a potential antagonist of angiotensin II-induced drinking. In a group of 5 cats drinking induced by intraventricular angiotensin II (1 μg) 30 and 150 min after an intraventricular infusion of 100 μl. of 0.9% sodium chloride solution. Three days later the same group of cats was tested 30 and 150 min after intraventricular Sar^1 Ala^8 angiotensin II (5 μg). The results are summarised in Table 1. The antagonist analogue itself caused brief drinking behaviour in one of the 5 cats used and significantly reduced angiotensin II-drinking at 30 min but not at 150 min. The drinking response to intraventricular angiotensin I was also inhibited by the angiotensin analogue whilst the response to renin was considerably delayed in onset and reduced in size.

The effects of centrally administered autonomic blocking drugs on the drinking response induced by intraventricular angiotensin II (1 μg)

132

were examined one hour before and one hour after administration of the blocker. The results are summarised in Table 2. The vehicle (0.9% sodium chloride) in which all the drugs were dissolved did not affect angiotensin II-induced drinking nor did atropine (200 µg) although this drug caused some increase in motor activity. The adrenergic neurone blocking drug betanidine (400–600 µg) caused a significant and dose-related inhibition of angiotensin II-induced drinking. The α-adrenoceptor blocking agents tolazoline (600 µg) and phenoxybenzamine (250 µg) did not affect the response but drinking was almost abolished by phentolamine (250 µg). The β-adrenoceptor blocking drug D,L-propanolol (450 µg) abolished angiotensin-II drinking and practolol (400 µg) markedly reduced it. In other experiments it was shown that L-propranolol

(250 µg) caused a marked reduction in angiotensin II-induced drinking whilst D-propranolol (250 µg) did not produce any significant change, suggesting that the action of propranolol is mediated via its β-adrenoceptor blocking action.

In an initial series of experiments it has been shown that the intraventricular administration of the β-adrenoceptor stimulant drug isoprenaline (50 µg) induced drinking in 10 of 16 cats tested.

Conclusions

The central administration of renin, angiotensin I and angiotensin II and the peripheral intravenous infusion of angiotensin II initiated water drinking in water-replete cats. This confirms the

Table 1. Effect of Sar^1 Ala^8 Angiotensin II on angiotensin-induced drinking in the cat

Intraventricular stimulus	Intraventricular pretreatment	Drinking response (gH$_2$O ± S.E.)		N
		30 min	150 min	
Angiotensin II	100 µl 0.9% NaCl	46 ± 2	44 ± 2	
(1 µg)	5 µg Sar^1 Ala^8 A II	7 ± 3*	38 ± 4	5
Angiotensin I	100 µl 0.9% NaCl	36 ± 7	29 ± 3	
(1 µg)	5 µg Sar^1 Ala^8 A II	9 ± 2*	27 ± 5	5

* Significantly different ($p < 0.01$) from values in saline pretreated animals 30 and 150 min, and from saralasin pretreated animals at 150 min.

Table 2. Effect of central administration of drugs on angiotensin II-induced drinking in the cat

Central Drug Treatment	Angiotensin II-induced drinking		No. of cats	P <
	1 hr before drug	1 hr after drug		
	(g ± S.E.)	(g ± S.E.)		
0.9% NaCl 100 µl	48 ± 2	45 ± 6	10	NS
Atropine 200 µg	33 ± 5	38 ± 4	8	NS
Betanidine 400 µg	45 ± 4	25 ± 3	5	0.01
600 µg	37 ± 3	10 ± 7	5	0.01
Phentolamine 250 µg	45 ± 4	1 ± 1	5	0.001
Phenoxybenzamine 250 µg	40 ± 5	36 ± 6	4	NS
Tolazoline 600 µg	35 ± 4	41 ± 4	4	NS
D,L-propranolol 450 µg	50 ± 4	0	6	0.001
Practolol 400 µg	48 ± 4	10 ± 4	5	0.01
L-propranolol 250 µg	41 ± 3	3 ± 3	3	0.01
D-propranolol 250 µg	40 ± 7	28 ± 4	3	NS

results of other workers in the rat (FITZSIMONS and SIMONS, 1969; EPSTEIN, FITZSIMONS, and ROLLS, 1970; FITZSIMONS, 1971). Since drinking can be elicited by doses of angiotensin II centrally which are ineffective when given peripherally angiotensin II appears to act via receptors in the brain.

We have demonstrated that Sar[1] Ala[8] angiotensin II, a competitive inhibitor of the myotropic and vasopressor actions of angiotensin II, reversibly inhibits drinking induced by central administration of either renin, angiotensin I or angiotensin II. This analogue of angiotensin was shown in our experiments to possess only very weak intrinsic dipsogenic activity. These observations conflict with results of SWANSON, MARSHALL, NEEDLEMAN, and SHARPE (1973) in the rat. These workers reported that other 8-substituted analogues of angiotensin II were themselves potent dipsogens and did not reduce angiotensin II-induced drinking. The differences in these observations could be accounted for either in terms of a species difference between the rat and the cat or it may be that substitution of angiotensin II in position 1 in addition to position 8, as in the analogue we have used, reduces agonist and increases antagonist activity of the analogues. Our finding that Sar[1] Ala[8] angiotensin II has a relatively prolonged antagonist action when given centrally suggests that this substance may be a useful tool in the elucidation of the role of the renin-angiotensin system in thirst mechanisms.

Since angiotensin II can cause release of acetylcholine from the cat brain (ELIE and PANISSET, 1970) and inhibits neuronal uptake of noradrenaline in the rat brain (PALAIC and KHAIRALLAH, 1968), it would appear possible that central cholinergic and/or adrenergic mechanisms may be involved in angiotensin II-induced drinking. The lack of effect of centrally administered atropine on angiotensin II induced drinking argues against the involvement of cholinergic mechanisms in the cat. The finding that intraventricular betanidine markedly reduced angiotensin II-induced drinking, strongly suggests the involvement of adrenergic neurones in the response thus supporting the results of FITZSIMONS and SETLER (1971) in the rat. Our results with α-adrenoceptor blocking agents

were confusing since neither tolazoline nor phenoxybenzamine given centrally affected the response to angiotensin whilst phentolamine virtually abolished it. We can only suggest that this action of phentolamine is unrelated to its α-adrenoceptor blocking action. The results with β-adrenoceptor blockers were much clearer: both propranolol and practolol inhibited the response to angiotensin. Moreover D-propranolol which has high membrane stabilising activity and low β blocking activity was virtually without effect on the response. This strongly suggests the involvement of β-adrenoceptors in the drinking response induced by angiotensin II. This view is further substantiated by the finding that centrally administered isoprenaline induced water drinking in 10 of 16 cats so far tested.

Acknowledgements. We are grateful to the Medical Research Council for financial support. M.C. would like to thank the Physiological Society and the Wellcome Trust for travel grants. We are grateful to Dr. A. W. CASTELLION of Norwich Pharmacol. Co. for a gift of Sar[1] Ala[8] angiotensin II.

References

CARVER, D. S., WATERHOUSE, H. N.: The variation in the water consumption of cats. Proc. Anim. Care Panel **12**, 267–270 (1962).

ELIE, R., PANISSET, J. C.: Effect of angiotensin and atropine on the spontaneous release of acetylcholine from the cat cerebral cortex. Brain Res. **17**, 297–305 (1970).

EPSTEIN, A. N., FITZSIMONS, J. T., ROLLS, B. J.: Drinking induced by injection of angiotensin into the brain of the rat. J. Physiol. Lond. **210**, 457–474 (1970).

FELDBERG, W. S., SHERWOOD, S. L.: A permanent cannula for intraventricular injection in cats. J. Physiol. Lond. **120**, 3–5P (1953).

FITZSIMONS, J. T.: The effect of intracranially administered renin or angiotensin and other thirst stimuli on drinking. J. Physiol. Lond. **214**, 295–303 (1971).

— Thirst. Physiol. Rev. **52**, 468–561 (1972).

FITZSIMONS, J. T., SETLER, P. E.: Catecholaminergic mechanisms in angiotensin-induced drinking. J. Physiol. Lond. **218**, 43–44P (1971).

FITZSIMONS, J. T., SIMONS, B. J.: The effect on drinking in the rat of angiotensin given alone or in combination with other thirst stimuli. J. Physiol. Lond. **203**, 45–57 (1969).

GLASER, G. H., WOLF, G.: Seizures induced by intraventricular sodium. Nature **200**, 44–46 (1963).

MILLER, N. E.: Learning and performance motivated by direct stimulation of the brain. In: Electrical Stimulation of the Brain (ed. D. E. SHEER), pp. 387–396. Austin: Univ. Texas Press 1961.

PALAIC, D., KHAIRALLAH, P. A.: Inhibition of norepinephrine re-uptake by angiotensin in brain. J. Neurochem. **15**, 1195–1202 (1968).

PALS, D. T., MASUCCI, F. D., DENNING, G. S., SIPOS, F., FESSLER, D.: Role of the pressor action of angiotensin II in experimental hypertension. Circulation Res. **29**, 673–681 (1971).

SWANSON, L. W., MARSHALL, G. R., NEEDLEMAN, P. A., SHARPE, L. G.: Characterisation of central angiotensin II receptors involved in the elicitation of drinking in the rat. Brain Res. **49**, 441–446 (1973).

Summary of Discussions

GANTEN to FITZSIMONS: We have found that pepstatin inhibits brain isorenin as it does kidney renin, which explains your results. Brain tissue levels of isorenin and angiotensin though smaller than those found in the kidney are usually higher than the plasma values. — FITZSIMONS to STRICKER: The fact that both renin and renin substrate cause drinking when injected into the brain indicates that the amounts of substrate and isorenin present in the brain are rate limiting for the generation of angiotensin II. — FITZSIMONS to PETERS: We found that the converting enzyme inhibitor SQ 20,881 attenuates drinking induced by angiotensin I but enhanced angiotensin II-induced drinking. We think therefore that the receptor is less sensitive to angiotensin I than to angiotensin II. We used a molal ratio, inhibitor: angiotensin I, of 1000 compared with your range of 3 to 180 and we agree that another enzyme inhibitor SQ 20,475 has no effect on angiotensin II-induced drinking. However the possibility that angiotensin I has some dipsogenic action remains. — EPSTEIN: Two facts suggest that the dipsogenic receptor for angiotensin II in the brain is not identical with the receptors in vascular smooth muscle. Firstly, the Phe^4–Tyr^8 analogue does not block the dipso-

genic effect of intracranial angiotensin II though it does block the pressor response to intraventricular angiotensin II, and secondly, $Ileu^5$-angiotensin II is twice as potent as an intracranial dipsogen as Val^5-angiotensin II amide (Hypertensin Ciba). — PETERS: This difference in potency may be due to the amino acid in position 5, or else to amidation of Asp^1. — FITZSIMONS: Intracerebral atropine in doses up to 10 μg does not inhibit angiotensin II-induced drinking in the rat. Larger doses may be inhibitory, possibly by spilling over into the periphery. — LEHR: Peripheral atropine has been found to abolish renin- or angiotensin-induced drinking, but not drinking in response to isoprenaline.

GANTEN to BURCKHARDT: We have been able to concentrate and partially purify angiotensin from brain tissue of the dog. Brain substrate has a higher affinity for brain isorenin than for kidney renin. Also, brain isorenin has a higher affinity for the synthetic tetradecapeptide substrate used by FITZSIMONS than it has for plasma renin substrate. — EPSTEIN: There are already conflicting results in the literature concerning the effectiveness of SQ 20,881 in blocking drinking induced by intracranial angiotensin. SEVERS et al. have reported successful blockade; SWANSON et al. have reported the opposite. SQ 20,881 is active against cerebral converting enzyme but high doses may be required to reach it in the intact brain. — BURCKHARDT: We feel that observations in which the inhibitor: substrate ratio must be raised to 1000 are not relevant with SQ 20,881 which inhibits peripheral converting enzyme at much lower concentrations. On the other hand, "cerebral converting enzyme" may not be identical with "hypothalamic converting enzyme". — FITZSIMONS: It is difficult to make a valid comparison between effective molal ratio for blocking in the periphery and in the central nervous system. The accessibility of the converting enzyme to the blocker must be very different in the two situations.

EPSTEIN to MOGENSON: It is unlikely that hyperosmolar injections cause drinking by reaching the ventricles because, 1) bilateral intracranial injections are required to evoke drinking, 2) bilateral lesions of the lateral preoptic area abolish the response to systemic hyperosmolality, and 3) BLASS has found that intraventricular injections are not as effective as tissue injections in yielding the effect. — To GANTEN: Saralasin acetate blocks drinking to intravenous angiotensin II in the rat at 10–100 times the molal dose of agonist. — KOZLOWSKI: Angiotensin II does lower the thirst threshold to osmotic stimuli in the dog.

GANTEN to JOHNSON: I am impressed by the steep rise in radioactivity in the cerebrospinal fluid. However, we find that after intravenous infusion of angiotensin II, the angiotensin levels in the cerebrospinal fluid do not run parallel with plasma levels. The question of where cerebrospinal fluid angiotensin originates from is unresolved. It appears to be independent of plasma angiotensin, and it may originate from the cerebral isorenin angiotensin system. Massive intravenous infusions of angiotensin II did not result in increased cerebrospinal angiotensin levels. — EPSTEIN: I agree that angiotensin does not cross the blood-brain barrier. The hormone is a potent dipsogen when it reaches the brain via the circulation, but it must reach brain tissue by some route other than the conventional blood to brain path. We suggest that it does so by entering the ventricular cerebrospinal fluid. The angiotensinases in the choroid plexuses are not an obstacle to our suggestion. Macerated lung is rich in angiotensin peptides but the intact lung does not degrade the hormone significantly. — EPSTEIN to STRICKER: We can easily differentiate radioactivity in brain tissue and in the choroid plexus from that still in the circulation although we use no fixative. — PETERS: The angiotensin used in these experiments was tagged (tritiated) only in respect of one amino acid. In view of the fact that the half life of angiotensin II is of the order of 50 sec, its autoradiographic distribution pattern should be compared with that of this particular amino acid.

HUTCHINSON to SIMPSON: Infusion of angiotensin I or II at rates that are subpressor systemically may cause a rise in arterial blood pressure when infused into the vertebral artery of the dog. The vascular supply of the subfornical organ suggests that smaller intra-arterial amounts of angiotensin could be used in these experiments and may have physiological actions. — SIMPSON: The anterior choroid, posterior

choroid and subfornical arteries all form portions of the dense capillary plexus located within the structure. Vascular delivery of the octapeptide to the subfornical organ is possible in view of the extra blood-brain barrier characteristics of the structure and much smaller intravenous doses should be given. — SIMPSON to FITZSIMONS: I think that angiotensin reaches the subfornical organ by the vascular route rather than through the cerebrospinal fluid. We know little about the connections between the subfornical organ and the rest of the brain. — MOGENSON: Isn't the vascular route unlikely in view of the long latency of drinking when angiotensin is administered by jugular cannula? — SIMPSON: Perhaps not, there were noticeable cardiovascular effects which occurred prior to the onset of drinking and which may have prevented a rapid onset of drinking. — MOGENSON: The "arousal drinking" that results from handling the animal in order to infuse it with angiotensin may have given an abnormally low estimate of threshold and latency. — SIMPSON: This was adequately controlled. — ROLLS: Lesions in the preoptic area do not affect the drinking that follows injection of angiotensin into the lateral hypothalamus, but lesions in the lateral hypothalamus abolish drinking that follows injections of angiotensin into the preoptic area. Therefore the lateral hypothalamus may well be in the neural circuit responsible for angiotensin induced drinking. — WEISINGER: Drinking induced by injection of angiotensin into the preoptic region is eliminated by lesions of the subfornical organ but MOGENSON has shown that this drinking is also eliminated by midbrain lesions. Why do you think that the subfornical organ is the unique site of the angiotensin-receptor? — SIMPSON: The two sets of results are not contradictory. Efferent information from the subfornical organ may well travel in the pathways described by MOGENSON. — NICOLAÏDIS: Only a portal system could account for movement of chemicals from the subfornical organ to elsewhere in the brain, if you exclude the cerebrospinal fluid as the medium of transport. — SIMPSON to HUSTON: Subfornical organ-lesioned animals appear to be neurologically normal, and the deficit in angiotensin-induced drinking does not appear to be due to any perceptual-motor disturbance. Latencies to drink were unchanged.

MOGENSON to ORNSTEIN: We have not observed any effect of angiotensin on feeding, nor do we have evidence that it is rewarding. — To ROLLS: We were able to hold some units for 2–3 hr. Some neurones respond both to angiotensin II and to carbachol. — NICOLAÏDIS: Angiotensin-sensitive units occur in the same regions where baro-sensitive responses are found. Did you test the responses of the angiotensin-sensitive units to changes in arterial pressure (not produced by angiotensin), or to intravenous or intra-arterial injections of angiotensin? — MOGENSON: We are aware that there are both local (central) and peripheral cardiovascular effects to intracranial angiotensin. OOMURA's microiontophoretic studies of unit responses to angiotensin are therefore of great interest, and we also plan to record from single neurones during intravenous infusions of angiotensin II. — To

SIMPSON: It is our impression that we normally record from the larger neurones in the lateral hypothalamus and midbrain. The number of units sampled was very small; this is always a problem with microelectrode recording experiments.

LEHR to COOLING: The results of COOLING and DAY suggest that in the cat angiotensin may be a mediator of β-adrenergic-induced drinking since angiotensin-induced water intake is effectively inhibited by β-adrenergic blocking agents. As regards α-adrenergic blocking agents, if it is any comfort to these authors, we found the opposite to be true in the rat. In confirmation of the work of FITZSIMONS and SETLER phentolamine does not affect angiotensin-induced drinking, whereas tolazoline is inhibitory. We likewise have no explanation of this discrepancy and are thinking of actions other than α-adrenergic blockade.

Section 7
Salt Appetite

Central Mediation of Water and Sodium Intake: A Dual Role for Angiotensin?

A. E. Fisher und J. Buggy

Introduction

Available data establish that angiotensin II (as well as its precursor angiotensin I, or renin) can directly or indirectly influence the neural systems mediating water ingestion in the mammal. All of these compounds elicit drinking following either intravascular infusion or injection into certain brain regions (Epstein, Fitzsimons and Simons, 1970; Fitzsimons and Simons, 1969). In fact, angiotensin is the most potent and experimentally useful dipsogen yet discovered, as indicated by threshold and latency data, reproducibility of action and effectiveness across species (Andersson and Westbye, 1970; Epstein, 1972; Fitzsimons, 1972; Setler, 1971). However, conceptual difficulties arise if one asks why this should be so, and whether the data reflect meaningful physiological mechanisms. For example, angiotensin is a pressor hormone formed from kidney-based renin in response to hypovolaemia and hypotension (Leenen and Stricker, this volume; Meyer, Peskar, Tauchmann and Hertting, 1971; Brown, Davies, Lever, Robertson, and Verniory, 1966; Peart, 1969; Pitcock, Hartroft, and Newmark, 1959; Vander, 1967) Water ingestion is not an adaptive response to such challenges, since the outcome of the behaviour will not relieve the imbalance which triggered it because most ingested water is distributed intracellularly. Consequently, several laboratories, including our own, have sought evidence to link

angiotensin to facilitation of sodium intake as well as water intake (Fitzsimons and Stricker, 1971; Radio, Summy-Long, Daniels-Severs, and Severs, 1972; Stricker, 1971). An adaptive response to hypovolaemia for hypotension would involve ingestion of water and electrolytes in isotonic proportions, since this would most rapidly and effectively restore vascular volume.

In fact, hypovolaemia has been shown to result in an immediate preference for isotonic saline over water and a delayed (6–10 hr) acceptance of unpalatable hypertonic salt solutions (Smith and Stricker, 1969; Stricker and Jalowiec, 1970; Stricker and Wolf, 1966). Nevertheless nobody has yet reported increased sodium intake, directly linked to angiotensin, which is independent of its possible role in the release of aldosterone. Moreover some evidence suggests that angiotensin may not play any significant role, immediate or delayed, in regulating sodium intake in the rat (Fitzsimons and Stricker, 1971; Stricker, 1971).

We here present a series of experiments which indicate that angiotensin does have a rapid facilitatory effect on sodium intake, as well as suggestive evidence that the hormone may indeed act centrally to facilitate selection and ingestion of a mixture of water and electrolytes best suited to overcome deficits in circulatory volume or pressure. The large number of separate experiments to be reported relates to our awareness that it is difficult to devise an entirely adequate control measure against which to assess the effects of angiotensin on fluid preference. Consequently, a variety of experimental and control conditions have been utilized in separate studies. Power or persuasiveness of our results and interpretations depend on cumulative evidence rather than on the outcome of any single study.

Experimental Procedures and Results

Experiments were conducted on adult, male, hooded rats of the Long-Evans strain, weighing between 250 and 350 g and implanted stereotaxically with 23 gauge cannulae for chemical brain stimulation. Following surgery, all animals were individually housed with free access to food, deionized water, and the saline solution with which they would be tested. All animals were allowed at least one week to recover from surgery and become adapted to the saline solutions. The positions of the drinking tubes were kept constant so that the rats would learn to associate a particular tube position with either water or a saline solution. Drugs for central injection were prepared with isotonic saline as the vehicle. Microinjections of drug solution were administered in volumes of 1 μl. through a hollow injector cannula placed in the permanently implanted guide shaft so that the tips coincided. The hollow injector cannula was connected via polethylene tubing to a syringe equipped with a micrometer drive.

Differential Effects on Sodium Intake of Angiotensin, Carbachol and Cellular Dehydration

In an initial experiment the effects of centrally administered angiotensin and carbachol on intake of water and isotonic saline were compared in a two bottle choice test. Rats were implanted with cannulae in the preoptic or septal regions and were screened with intermediate doses of each drug. Eleven animals which responded with fluid intakes in excess of 4 ml. to each drug were retained for study. These animals were then run through a test sequence involving 3 doses of angiotensin (10, 100, and 1000 ng) and 3 doses

of carbachol (0.25, 1, and 2.5 μg) given in random order with each test separated by at least three days. Because of the possibility that the long test sequence might produce or encompass marked baseline changes, results were analyzed in terms of the change in percentage of isotonic saline intake. For the 23 hr period before a given test, the spontaneous intake of each solution was measured, and the ratio of saline to total fluid ingested was used as a measure of the baseline fluid preference. This baseline preference measure was then compared to the preference measure obtained in the 1 hr test period following drug administration. Similar results were obtained for animals with either a preoptic of septal cannula, so the data were combined. Under these conditions, cholinergic stimulation by cannula resulted in a preference shift towards water (average -26%) so that over 70% of the total fluid consumed during the hour after cholinergic stimulation was from the water burette. In contrast, angiotensin (at all dose levels) shifted the animals preference strongly towards isotonic saline (average shift $+31\%$), and 74% of the total fluid consumed was from the saline burette. Table 1 gives a summary of the results at each dose level. A paired sample sign test indicated that the test period preference ratios were statistically different from *ad lib* preference ratios for each dose level of each drug.

Table 1. Percent isotonic saline drunk (relative to water) under baseline, central angiotensin, or central carbachol stimulation conditions

Stimulation	Dose	23-hr baseline, % Saline	1-hr post-drug % Saline
Angiotensin	10 ng	47	68
	100 ng	43	81
	1,000 ng	39	73
Carbachol	0.25 μg	50	26
	1 μg	56	33
	2.5 μg	57	27

Values are means from 11 rats.

The next series of experiments were designed to determine if angiotensin stimulation could result in an enhanced intake of normally non-preferred, hypertonic saline solutions. Rats implanted with cannulae in the preoptic area or nucleus accumbens were adapted to water and 1.8 % saline for at least 1 week prior to testing. In 32 rats, the saline fraction of the total intake averaged 11 % during a 24 hour *ad lib* period and 41 % during the test hour following brain stimulation with 500 ng of angiotensin. The observed shift in preference was significant at the < 0.01 level (paired sample t-test). Actual fluid intake after central injection of 500 ng of angiotensin averaged 9.6 ml. of water and 6.8 ml. of 1.8 % saline. The large intake of 1.8 % saline after angiotensin stimulation stands in marked contrast to the effects of cholinergic stimulation which resulted in virtually no intake of this hypertonic solution. Following carbachol (1 μg) stimulation, 15 animals ingested 9.5 ml. of water and only 0.5 ml. of 1.8 % saline.

As an additional control measure, 14 rats adapted to water and 1.8 % saline solution were given a subcutaneous injection of 5 ml. of 1.5 M NaCl (9.0 %) to induce thirst. Preference for 1.8 % saline fell from 19.1 % of the total intake during the 24 hr *ad lib* period, to 4 % during the test period following saline injection. Fluid intakes after cellular dehydration were 21.7 ml. of water and only 0.9 ml. of 1.8 % saline. Thus, thirst induced by cholinergic stimulation or cellular dehydration resulted in preference shifts toward water, rather than the consistent shift toward saline observed following thirst induced by angiotensin.

An additional test was conducted with rats adapted to water and 2.7 % NaCl. Normal rats do not consume appreciable quantities of this concentrated salt solution when water is also available. When a choice between water and 2.7 % saline was provided, 15 rats took only 3.7 % of their total intake from the saline burette during a 24 hr *ad lib* period. Following a 500 ng injection of angiotensin into the preoptic area or the nucleus accumbens, this measure rose to 19 % with 8.8 ml. of water and 2.1 ml. of saline being ingested during the test hour. The observed increase in preference for 2.7 % saline was significant at the < 0.05 level.

Preliminary observations suggest that enhanced saline intake induced by angiotensin is not peculiar to central administration only. When given intraperitoneal injections of renin

(20 u./kg. of body weight), 7 rats ingested an average of 5.5 ml. of water and 3.6 ml. of 1.8 % saline.

Since the results reported thus far could be due in part to a diminished taste sensitivity under angiotensin, 10 animals were injected with intracranial angiotensin (500 ng) and offered a choice between water and 0.01 % quinine solution. Although this strength of quinine solution is normally aversive to rats, it is ingested readily following 24 hours of fluid deprivation or hypovolaemia induced by polyethylene glycol if it is the only fluid available in a one bottle test situation (BURKE, MOOK, and BLASS, 1972). If taste discriminations were impaired following angiotensin stimulation and this was the cause of enhanced saline intake, then an appreciable intake of the quinine solution might be expected also. The results indicate that taste discriminations were not obviously impaired. Intake of water following angiotensin injections averaged 7.3 ml., while only 0.2 ml. of quinine solution was consumed.

Effects of Angiotensin on Fluid Intake in Water or Salt Deprived Animals

The experiments just discussed indicate that angiotensin stimulation in the sated, or non-deprived animal, results in intake of both water and saline when the animal is permitted free access to both. If a potentiation of sodium as well as water intake is characteristic of angiotensin action, this should also be evident when animals with a pre-existing appetite for water or sodium are stimulated with angiotensin.

Following periods of fluid deprivation, rats will consistently ingest small quantities of saline solutions as well as water. With increasing periods of fluid deprivation, the amount of saline consumed, or the tonicity of solution accepted, increases. After adaptation to 1.8 % saline solution for a week, 13 animals were deprived of all fluids for 24 hr (food was not removed). At the end of the deprivation period, 7 of the animals received injections of angiotensin (500 ng) into the nucleus accumbens or the preoptic area. Fluids were then returned to all animals and intakes of water and saline were recorded for a 1 hr period. Several days later, in a cross-over experiment, the animals were again deprived of fluids for 24 hr. Before presentation of fluids, the other 6 animals in the group received intracranial injections of angiotensin. Therefore all animals had a test period of 1 hr following deprivation alone and following deprivation plus central angiotensin. Results are illustrated in Fig. 1. Angiotensin stimulation significantly increased both the amount of water and 1.8 % saline consumed following 24 hr of deprivation (paired sample t-test, $p < 0.01$). Water intake following deprivation plus angiotensin was 6.8 ml. greater than for deprivation alone, while intake of 1.8 % saline following deprivation plus angiotensin was 8.7 ml. greater than for deprivation alone. Therefore under these conditions, the intake directly attributable to angiotensin action was actually slightly hypertonic.

Water versus 1.8 % NaCl

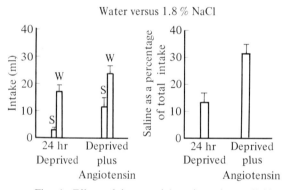

Fig. 1. Effect of intracranial angiotensin on fluid intakes following 24 hr deprivation. Values are mean ± S.E. of mean

A similar study, with cross-over deprivation alone and deprivation plus angiotensin test sessions, was carried out on 10 animals, but with a 48 hr period of fluid deprivation and a choice test between water and 2.7 % saline. Results are illustrated in Fig. 2. With angiotensin, water intake was increased (but not significantly) by 3.3 ml., while intake of 2.7 % saline was significantly increased ($p < 0.01$) by 3.9 ml. Thus, when angiotensin stimulation is superimposed on a background of fluid deprivation, potentiation of sodium intake is more apparent than potentiation of water intake.

We next assessed the extent to which angio-

Water versus 2.7 % NaCl

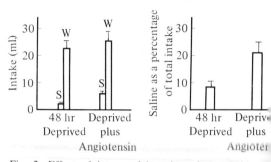

Fig. 2. Effect of intracranial angiotensin on fluid intakes following 48 hr deprivation. Values are mean ± S.E. of mean

tensin could potentiate an existing appetite for sodium, uncomplicated by an accompanying thirst for water. Animals were adapted to water and 2.7 % saline during the week following implantation of an intracranial cannula. Animals were then maintained on water and sodium-deficient chow (General Biochemicals), a regime which leads to a gradually developing sodium appetite. After seven days on this regime, half of the animals received 500 ng of angiotensin intracranially and all were then given a 1 hr two-bottle preference test with water and 2.7 % saline. After the test, the saline was removed and after another week on the sodium-deficient diet, the testing conditions for the two groups were reversed with the other half of the animals receiving intracranial angiotensin before presentation of the salt solution. Mean intakes of the animals without angiotensin were 1.6 ml. of water and 2.8 ml. of 2.7 % saline in the 1 hr test

Water versus 2.7 % NaCl
Time on sodium deficient diet

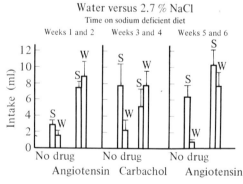

Fig. 3. Effect of intracranial angiotensin on intake of water and NaCl solution following sodium deprivation. Values are mean ± S.E. of mean

142

period. When the angiotensin injection preceded the test period the mean intakes observed were 8.5 ml. of water and 7.5 ml. of saline (Fig. 3). Under these conditions, angiotensin caused an increased water intake and also markedly potentiated the intake of the unpalatable saline solution (increases in salt and water intake were significant at the < 0.01 level on a paired sample t-test). Furthermore the 4.5 ml. increase in salt intake attributable to the action of angiotensin was much greater than the intake of 2.7 % saline previously obtained following angiotensin injection into the non-sodium deprived animal.

In order to study the effects of another central dipsogen, carbachol, under conditions of sodium deprivation, the animals were maintained for a third and fourth week on sodium-deficient chow. At the end of week 3, half of the 6 animals responsive to cholinergic stimulation were given access to 2.7 % saline for 1 hr while the other half received an intracranial injection of 1 μg. of carbachol prior to testing. At the end of week 4 the testing conditions for the two groups were reversed. Intake of water without carbachol was 2.3 ml. and with carbachol was significantly increased to 7.7 ml. However, unlike angiotensin, carbachol did not potentiate sodium intake, but decreased it slightly. Intake of 2.7 % saline fell from 7.8 ml. without carbachol to 5.2 ml. with carbachol (Fig. 3). Since the failure of carbachol to potentiate salt intake may have been due to a ceiling effect (maximum sodium appetite), tests with angiotensin were continued for a fifth and sixth week on the sodium deficient diets. These tests confirmed that angiotensin was still effective in potentiating sodium intake. Water intake rose from 0.9 ml. to 7.9 ml. with angiotensin while salt intake rose from 6.6 ml. to 10.4 ml. with angiotensin. The key point is that angiotensin, but not carbachol, markedly increased the sodium intake of rats already manifesting a sodium appetite, while both drugs enhanced water intake.

Water and Salt Intake after Prolonged Infusions of Angiotensin

The preceding experiments show that single injections of angiotensin into the brain result in ingestion of saline solutions as well as water when both are available. Enhanced intake of solutions containing sodium after single injections of angiotensin was demonstrable in the sated animal as well as in animals with a pre-existing water or sodium appetite induced by deprivation. Conditions which would lead to an increase in endogenous renin and angiotensin levels, however, often involve a prolonged enhancement of such levels. LEENEN and STRICKER (this volume) have found renin and angiotensin levels to be elevated for at least 24 hours following experimental dipsogenic manipulations such as hypovolaemia induced by polyethylene glycol or infrahepatic ligation of the inferior vena cava. Interestingly, in polyethylene glycol-induced hypovolaemia acceptance of hypertonic saline was reported to occur around the time at which plasma renin levels were showing a second steeper elevation over baseline.

In order to simulate a prolonged elevation of renin and angiotensin levels more closely, long term intraventricular infusions of val^5-angiotensin II-amide were carried out on several animals. Tubing from an infusion pump system was run into a swivel commutator mounted on top of the testing cages. Another length of tubing connected a permanently implanted ventricular cannula with the swivel commutator so that the animal could move freely during an 8 hr intraventricular infusion. Infusion rates of 500 ng/μl. $\cdot$ 8 min. were well tolerated by the animals during the entire infusion period with no signs of distress. Seven rats were offered a choice of water and 1.8 % saline during the infusion period; fluid intakes were measured and urine was collected for analysis of sodium content. Fig. 4 illustrates the mean cumulative water and electrolyte intakes and losses in urine for the 7 animals. Analysis of drinkometer records revealed that intake of saline often began as soon as water intake with the animals showing alternating bouts of drinking between the two solutions such that an isotonic mixture was selected. Sodium intake was greater than sodium loss in the urine and the animals ended the infusion period in positive sodium balance (2 m-equiv Na$^+$). Therefore, sodium intake does not appear to be secondary to sodium loss in urine. Under these

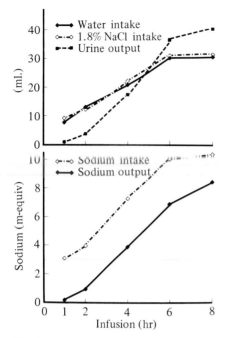

Fig. 4. Mean water and sodium intake and urine losses of 7 rats during ventricular infusion of angiotensin at a rate of 500 ng/μl./8 min. Sodium content of urine was determined by flame photometry

and the total tonicity of ingested fluid were not as great as noted with the infusion in the water vs. 1.8 % NaCl condition. This may be due to the extreme unpalatability of the 2.7 % saline, as unusual drinking postures were often noted at this burette. However, the intake of 15 ml. of 2.7 % NaCl is substantial and is comparable to the salt intake after recognized stimuli for salt appetite in the rat such as aldosterone or hypovolaemia. Analysis of drinking patterns indicated that the salt intake occurred too early in the infusion period to be easily attributable to overhydration.

Discussion

Angiotensin led to an increased acceptance of sodium solutions under all conditions investigated. However, initial intake of water following single angiotensin injections into an otherwise unchallenged animal appears to be a lower threshold response than is the enhanced intake of sodium. This seems evident because animals which were 'in balance' when given such an injection did not ingest sufficient sodium to reach isotonicity with the water ingested, even though they did drink considerably more isotonic or hypertonic saline (relative to water) than they did under control conditions of following induction of thirst by cholinergic stimulation or cellular dehydration.

However, when angiotensin was infused for several hours or when a single injection of angiotensin was superimposed on a background of increased endogenous angiotensin (the animal kept on a sodium-free diet or deprived of water for 24–48 hr) the intake of saline and water strictly attributable to the exogenous

conditions of long-term angiotensin infusion into the cerebral ventricles, intake of a normally non-preferred saline solution was rapid and substantial, being equal in magnitude to the water intake.

In a similar experiment including 8 hr infusion of angiotensin at 500 ng/μl. · 8 min. 6 rats were offered a choice of water and 2.7 % saline. The total intake (8 hr) was 44.6 ml. of water and 15.4 ml. of saline (Table 2). Urine losses did not exceed oral intake of sodium at any time during this period. However, the margin by which sodium intake was greater than sodium output

Table 2. Angiotensin infusion (500 ng/μl. · 8 min) into cerebral ventricles: mean cumulative data for 6 rats in water vs. 2.7% NaCl choice test

Hour	Water intake (ml.)	Saline intake (ml.)	Urine volume (ml.)	Na input (μ-equiv)	Na output (μ-equiv)
1	15.2	4.3	—	2059	693
2	20.8	4.9	9.5	2326	2031
4	25.4	7.1	18.2	3408	3280
6	29.0	9.3	23.7	4453	4292
8	44.6	15.4	33.1	7361	5256

angiotensin was at least isotonic (long term infusion and sodium-free diet experiments) or even hypertonic (water deprivation experiments). We take this to mean that angiotensin may play a dual central role by "facilitating" a neuronal substrate for thirst as well as a substrate monitoring sodium levels and intake. The capacity to select an isotonic mixture under certain conditions may be related to an alternating inhibition of these substrates by negative feedback. That is, water ingestion leads to overhydration of central and/or peripheral receptors monitoring tonicity, and the firing of 'thirst' neurones then subsides. Since angiotensin also facilitates a substrate for sodium, however, sodium is accepted until negative feedback leads to inhibition of this substrate. So long as angiotensin levels remain elevated, and/or the volume deficit remains — these 'systems' will be alternately facilitated and inhibited to permit the selection of the mixture most appropriate to the particular conditions.

A model encompassing these observations is illustrated in Fig. 5 (from FISHER, 1973). Cellular dehydration activates a thirst excitatory system which preferentially leads to water intake. This system appears to be mediated in part by cholinergic neurones in the rat (BLOCK and FISHER, 1970). Activation of this thirst system through cellular dehydration with hypertonic saline injections or centrally with carbachol, does not lead to appreciable saline intake. CHIARAVIGLIO and TALEISNIK (1969) have reported that activity in cholinergic systems may

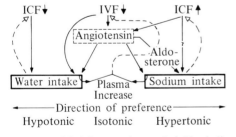

Fig. 5. Model of the central control of thirst indicating angiotensin effect on both water and sodium intake. ICF = intracellular fluid decrease (and/or Na$^+$ decrease) in monitor neurones; IVF = intravascular fluid volume (and/or pressure) decrease; solid line and arrow = facilitatory effect; dashed line and open arrow = inhibitory (negative feedback) effect

even inhibit sodium intake, while cholinergic blockade facilitates sodium intake. Intravascular fluid depletion, on the other hand, is depicted as activating neural systems which facilitate sodium intake as well as water intake, although acceptance of aversive concentrations of sodium does not occur for some time. Several separate elements may sequentially excite this system, including baroreceptor input, angiotensin, and aldosterone. It is interesting to speculate on the question whether the effects of angiotensin may interact with those of known neurotransmitters. Drinking induced by angiotensin does not appear to depend on cholinergic neurones, as anticholinergic blockade with atropine does not attenuate angiotensin-induced drinking in the rat (GIARDINA and FISHER, 1971; FITZSIMONS and SETLER, 1971; SWANSON, MARSHALL, NEEDLEMAN, and SHARPE, 1973) or the monkey (BLOCK, 1972). FITZSIMONS and SETLER (1971) have reported that dopaminergic neural systems may mediate angiotensin drinking in the rat, as pretreatment with haloperidol blocks angiotensin drinking when both drugs are injected into the preoptic area. However, SWANSON, MARSHALL, NEEDLEMAN, and SHARPE (1973) were unable to block angiotensin II induced drinking with haloperidol, when both drugs were injected into the medial septal preoptic area. In our laboratory, pretreatment with 10 µg of haloperidol failed to block angiotensin II-induced thirst (100 ng) in the monkey, when both injections were made through the same cannula into the dorsal fornix (CANFIELD and BUGGY, unpublished observations). Also, with injections into cerebral ventricles in rats, 5 µg. of haloperidol had no effect on drinking elicited by 500 ng of angiotensin II, although 5 µg. of haloperidol did attenuate drinking to 100 ng of angiotensin II by 42 %. Interestingly, drinking induced by intravascular fluid depletion appears to depend on both cholinergic and dopaminergic neural systems (BLOCK, 1972).

In the rat, aldosterone may be involved in sodium appetite. However, sodium intake may be induced by hypovolaemia in the adrenalectomized rat (WOLF and STRICKER, 1967). Thus, aldosterone is not exclusively responsible for the sodium intake observed during states such as hypovolaemia. Our data suggest that angiotensin II is one of the factors which may directly influence the animal's intake of sodium as well as water.

The amount of sodium intake, or the ratio of water to sodium intake induced by angiotensin II appears to be state dependent. If the animal is in normal water and sodium balance, angiotensin II moderately enhances sodium intake following a single injection. If there is a pre-existing intravascular volume deficit, generated by long periods of fluid deprivation or by elimination of sodium in food, then sodium intake induced by angiotensin II is larger and more dramatic.

In summary, our results imply that drinking induced by angiotensin is qualitatively different from thirst induced by carbachol or by cellular dehydration. Angiotensin II appears to facilitate intake of sodium solutions as well as water, with the total intake often being close to the isotonic mixture that is most appropriate for repairing deficits in the extracellular fluid compartment (SMITH and STRICKER, 1969; STRICKER, 1969). Cellular dehydration, on the other hand, leads to an equally appropriate preference for water. In the animal in normal water and salt balance, angiotensin does not lead to a large intake of highly unpalatable saline, the usual criterion for salt appetite, yet an increased preference for isotonic and mildly hypertonic solutions is immediately evident. Also when sodium is witheld from the diet, angiotensin II, but not carbachol, greatly potentiates salt intake. Thus, our results imply that angiotensin may play a larger role in modulating sodium intake and repairing vascular fluid deficits than is presently recognized. The extent to which the recently discovered cerebral renin-angiotensin system (GANTEN, MINNICH, GRANGER, HAYDUK, BRECHT, BARBEAU, BOUCHER, and GENEST, 1971) may be involved remains to be determined.

Acknowledgements. The technical assistance of R. GROSSMAN, P. BENYO, and J. LUCOT is greatly appreciated. We thank Ms. Claudia Kraft for help in the preparation of the manuscript. Supported by NSF Predoctoral Traineeship to J. B.; and by NIH Grant MH 1951 to A. E. F.

References

ANDERSSON, B., WESTBYE, O.: Synergistic action of sodium and angiotensin on brain mechanisms controlling water and salt balance. Nature **228,** 75 (1970).

BLOCK, M. L.: Unpublished Ph. D. dissertation, Univ. of Pittsburgh (1972).

BLOCK, M. L., FISHER, A. E.: Anticholinergic blockade of salt aroused and deprivation induced drinking. Physiol. Behav. **5,** 525–527 (1970).

BROWN, J. J., DAVIES, D. L., LEVER, A. F., ROBERTSON, J. I. S., VERNIORY, A.: The effect of acute haemorrhage in the dog and man on plasma renin concentration. J. Physiol. Lond. **182,** 649–663 (1966).

BURKE, G. H., MOOK, D. G., BLASS, E. M.: Hyperreactivity to quinine associated with osmotic thirst in the rat. J. comp. physiol. Psych. **78,** 32–39 (1972).

CHIARAVIGLIO, E., TALEISNIK, S.: Water and salt intake induced by hypothalamic implants of cholinergic and adrenergic agents. Am. J. Physiol. **216,** 1418–1422 (1969).

EPSTEIN, A. N.: Drinking induced by low doses of intravenous angiotensin. Physiologist **15,** 127(1972).

EPSTEIN, A. N., FITZSIMONS, J. T., SIMONS, B. J.: Drinking induced by injections of angiotensin into the brain of the rat. J. Physiol. Lond. **210,** 457–474 (1970).

FISHER, A. E.: Relationships between cholinergic and other dipsogens in the central mediation of thirst. In: The Neuropsychology of Thirst (Eds. A. N. EPSTEIN, H. R. KISSILEFF, and E. STELLAR), pp. 273–278. Chicago: H. V. Winston and Sons 1973.

FITZSIMONS, J. T.: Thirst. Physiol. Rev. **52,** 468–561 (1972).

FITZSIMONS, J. T., SETLER, P. E.: Catecholaminergic mechanisms in angiotensin induced thirst. J. Physiol. Lond. **218,** 43 P–44 P (1971).

FITZSIMONS, J. T., SIMONS, B. J.: The effect on drinking in the rat of intravenous angiotensin, given alone or in combination with other stimuli for thirst. J. Physiol. Lond. **203,** 45–57 (1969).

FITZSIMONS, J. T., STRICKER, E. M.: Sodium appetite and the renin-angiotensin system. Nature **231,** 58–60 (1971).

GANTEN, D., MINNICH, J., GRANGER, P., HAYDUK, K., BRECHT, H., BARBEAU, A., BOUCHER, R., GENEST, J.: Angiotensin forming enzyme in brain tissue. Science **173,** 64–65 (1971).

GIARDINA, A. R., FISHER, A. E.: Effect of atropine on drinking induced by carbachol, angiotensin, and isoproterenol. Physiol. Behav. **7,** 653–655 (1971).

MEYER, D. K., PESKAR, B., TAUCHMANN, U., HERTTING, G.: Potentiation and abolition of the increase in plasma renin activity seen after hypotensive drugs in rats. Europ. J. Pharmacol. **16,** 278–282 (1971).

PEART, W. S.: The renin-angiotensin system. Proc. R. Soc. Biol. **173**, 317–325 (1969).

PITCOCK, J. A., HARTROFT, P. M., NEWMARK, L. N.: Increased renal pressor activity (renin) in sodium-deficient rats and correlation with juxtaglomerular cell granulation. Proc. Soc. Exp. Biol. Med. **100**, 868–869 (1959).

RADIO, G. J., SUMMY-LONG, J., DANIELS-SEVERS, A., SEVERS, W. B.: Hydration changes produced by central infusion of angiotensin II. Am. J. Physiol. **223**, 1221–1226 (1972).

SETLER, P. E.: Drinking induced by injection of angiotensin II into the hypothalamus of the rhesus monkey. J. Physiol. Lond. **217**, 59P–60P (1971).

SMITH, D. F., STRICKER, E. M.: The influence of need on the rats preference for dilute NaCl solutions. Physiol. Behav. **4**, 407–410 (1969).

STRICKER, E. M.: Osmoregulation and volume regulation in rats: inhibition of hypovolemic thirst by water. Am. J. Physiol. **217**, 98–105 (1969).

— Effects of hypovolemia and/or caval ligation on water and NaCl solution drinking by rats. Physiol. Behav. **6**, 299–305 (1971).

STRICKER, E. M., JALOWIEC, E.: Restoration of intravascular fluid volume following acute hypovolmia in rats. Am. J. Physiol. **218**, 191–196 (1970).

STRICKER, E. M., WOLF, G.: Blood volume and tonicity in relation to sodium appetite. J. comp. physiol. Psychol. **62**, 275–279 (1966).

SWANSON, L. W., MARSHALL, G. R., NEEDLEMAN, P., SHARPE, L. G.: Characterization of central angiotensin II receptors involved in the elicitation of drinking in the rat. Brain Res. **49**, 441–446 (1973).

VANDER, A. J.: Control of renin release. Physiol. Rev. **47**, 359–382 (1967).

WOLF, G., STRICKER, E. M.: Sodium appetite elicited by hypovolemia in adrenalectomized rats. J. comp. physiol. Psychol. **63**, 252–257 (1967).

Conditioned and Pseudoconditioned Thirst and Sodium Appetite

R. S. Weisinger

The regulation of body fluids is essential to the maintenance of life. It involves both physiological and behavioural components, i. e., the conservation and replacement of water and salt. Research into the behavioural component has been mainly concerned with identifying the physiological stimuli which elicit the innate responses described as thirst and sodium appetite. Little attention, however, has been given to the role of learned or conditioned responses involved in the behavioural regulation of body fluids.

Two questions will be examined in this paper. First, can the innate behaviour associated with thirst and salt appetite be modified by experience? That is, can thirst and salt appetite be conditioned? Second, if conditioning is possible, what is its role in the behavioural component of body fluid regulation? Specifically can conditioning explain the paradoxical sodium appetite elicited by aldosterone?

Conditioned Thirst and Sodium Appetite

Previously neutral stimuli have been shown to elicit enhanced water intake following their repeated association with thirst inducing treatments. These treatments include hypertonic NaCl injections (MINEKA, SELIGMAN, HETRICK, and ZUELZER, 1972; SELIGMAN, MINEKA, and FILLIT, 1971), hypothalamic angiotensin injections (SELIGMAN, et al. 1971), and water deprivation (HARGRAVE, 1968, unpublished M. Sc. thesis, Sacramento State Univ.). However, not

all investigators have been able to demonstrate conditioned thirst (GREENBERG, 1954, unpublished dissertation, Univ. of Pennsylvania; ANDERSSON and LARSSON, 1956; HUSTON and BROZEK, 1972; PIEPER and MARX, 1963). These failures might be explained by the investigators' choice of neutral stimuli. In most of these cases the neutral stimulus was auditory or visual (i.e., external). It has been shown that internal stimuli (e.g., one hour deprivation period, olfactory stimuli) are more easily associated with internal consequences (e. g., cellular dehydration) (GARCIA, ERVIN, and KOELLING, 1966).

WEISINGER and WOODS (1972) conditioned both sodium appetite and thirst by repeatedly pairing the odour of menthol (conditioned stimulus, CS) with injections of formalin. Subcutaneous injections of formalin cause decreases in both plasma sodium concentration and plasma volume which result in sodium appetite and thirst (WOLF and STEINBAUM, 1965; STRICKER, 1966). In this experiment, rats were given six conditioning trials, one every third day. A conditioning trial consisted of the following procedure. The rat was removed from its cage, a blood sample was taken and an injection of formalin (Experimental group) or distilled water (Control group) was given. The rat was placed in a mentholated chamber for 3 hours, a second blood sample was taken and the rat returned to its home cage where it was allowed access to 0.33 M NaCl solution and water for 20 minutes.

Fig. 1 and 2 show the intake of saline and water, respectively, during the control period, acquisition, and extinction, for the experimental and control groups. An extinction trial consisted of the same events as a conditioning trial except that all animals received an injection of distilled water. The results show that the experimental group consumed significantly more saline and water during acquisition and during the first extinction trial. The fact that the experimental group consumed more saline and water during the first extinction trial suggests that the previously neutral conditioned stimulus (CS) has acquired the motivational properties of the unconditioned stimulus (US).

Fig. 3 shows the change in plasma sodium concentration and haematocrit for the experimental and control groups over trials. It is clear that significant decreases in both plasma sodium levels and plasma volume occurred on conditioning trials. However, no such decreases were evident on the extinction trial. This suggests that the drinking observed on the first extinction trial was not due to any conditioned physiological change, and that the drinking responses were not unconditioned responses.

A second experiment was run to ensure that the CS had acquired motivational properties and that unrecognized physiological changes were not responsible for the drinking behaviour observed during the first extinction trial of

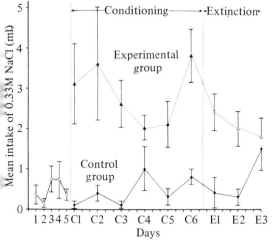

Fig. 1. Conditioning of intake of 0.33 M NaCl solution after formalin injections (US) to the odour of menthol (CS). Open circles represent all animals on the preconditioning trials; solid circles and open triangles represent animals receiving water injections on that trial; solid triangles represent animals receiving formalin injections on that trial. Bars represent ± S.E. From WEISINGER and WOODS (1972)

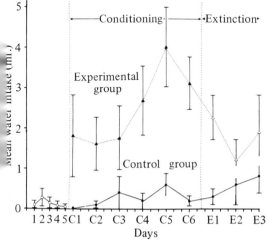

Fig. 2. Water intake (means ± S.E.) for the two groups shown in Fig. 1. The symbols are the same as in Fig. 1. From WEISINGER and WOODS (1972)

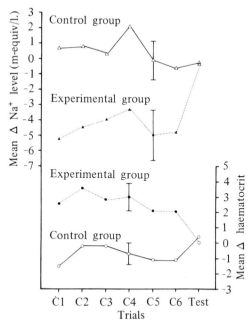

Fig. 3. Mean changes in sodium and haematocrit values for the two groups shown in figures 1 and 2 over trials. Only the mean S.E. of means have been drawn because there was homogeneity of variance. From WEISINGER and WOODS (1972)

Experiment 1. The procedure used was similar to that of Experiment 1 except that first no blood samples were taken, and secondly, half of the animals which had been given menthol-formalin training were tested in extinction without presentation of the CS, these animals remaining in their cages for the three hours prior to test.

Table 1 shows the saline and water intake on the first extinction trial for the three groups. The results show that only the experimental group tested with the CS had enhanced intake on the test trial. This rules out the possibility that some unmeasured effect of formalin was present and responsible for the conditioned appetites observed in Experiment 1. Furthermore, the results indicate that the CS had acquired drive properties due to its association with the US.

A third experiment was run to determine whether or not the temporal relationship used in Experiments 1 and 2 was essential. That is, were the conditioned appetites due to classical conditioning or to some other form of conditioning, i. e., pseudoconditioning? In order to differentiate classical from pseudoconditioning, it is essential that the CS be clearly defined such that the temporal relationship between CS and US can be investigated. To establish the CS unequivocally as the odour of menthol, other stimuli present on conditioning trials (handling, injection) have to be rendered neutral.

In this experiment, animals were given an injection every eight hours, nine injections for every one conditioning trial. The control group received nine injections of distilled water. The experimental group received eight injections of distilled water and one injection of formalin. The formalin injection always preceded placement of the rat in the mentholated chamber. The pseudoconditioned group also received eight injections of distilled water and one injection of formalin. However, the formalin injection was given in any one of the nine injection positions. The position was randomly determined. Therefore this group had experience with menthol and formalin, but the menthol did not reliably precede the US.

Fig. 4 and 5 show the saline and water intake over trials for the three groups. Both the experimental and pseudoconditioned groups showed significantly enhanced saline and water intake, compared with the control group, on the extinction trial. This indicates that the CS does not have to reliably predict the US, nor does it have to be repeatedly presented in close temporal relationship with the US for the CS to acquire motivational properties. Thus, pseudoconditioning and not classical conditioning is the simplest explanation for the conditioned appetites.

The results of these three experiments are important for several reasons. First, they show that both thirst and sodium appetite can be conditioned. Second, they show that conditioned physiological changes are not necessary for obtaining the conditioned behaviours. Finally, the results suggest that the conditioned appetites were due to pseudoconditioning. However, it is possible that the conditioned appetites were due to long-delay conditioning (REVUSKY and GARCIA, 1970). That is, formalin injections result in

Table 1. Mean intakes (in ml.) of 0.33 M saline and water on test trial for the three groups of the experiments described on pages 149–150.

| | Experimental group | | | | Control group | |
| | Injection | | No injection | | | |
	Saline (A)	Water (B)	Saline (C)	Water (D)	Saline (E)	Water (F)
Mean	3.00	2.33	0.88	0.13	1.13	0.88
S.E.	0.29	0.60	0.59	0.13	0.43	0.52

Note. — There were significant ($p < 0.05$) differences between A and C, A and E, and B and D. The difference between B and F approached significance ($p < 0.10$). From WEISINGER and WOODS (1972)

both physiological changes and pain. It is possible that these events would be associated with the olfactory stimulus even though there be a variable time interval between the two stimuli.

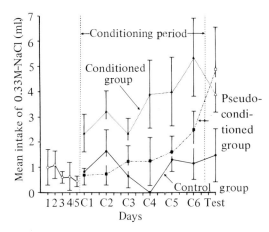

Fig. 4. Conditioning and pseudoconditioning of intake of 0.33 M NaCl solution after formalin injections (US) to the odour of menthol (CS). Open circles represent all animals on the preconditioning trials; solid circles, open squares, and open triangles represent animals receiving water injections on that trial; solid triangles represent animals receiving formalin injections on that trial; solid squares represent animals receiving no injection on that trial (although one animal per trial in this group occasionally received a formalin injection here due to the randomization procedure). From WEISINGER and WOODS (1972)

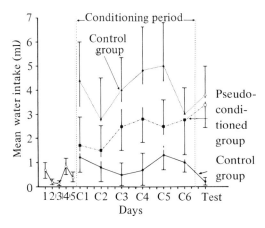

Fig. 5. Water intake (means ± S.E.) of the animals of Fig. 4. (The symbols are the same as in Fig. 4)

Conditioning: An Explanation for Aldosterone-Elicited Sodium Appetite

The role of the adrenocortical hormone aldosterone is one of the most perplexing problems in salt appetite. It has been clearly established that aldosterone is not essential for the development of salt appetite in rats (RICHTER, 1936), rabbits (DENTON and NELSON, 1970), or sheep (DENTON, ORCHARD, and WELLER, 1970). On the other hand, aldosterone injections, which increase both plasma sodium concentration and plasma volume (WEISINGER and WOODS, 1971), have been shown to cause a specific appetite for sodium in rats (WOLF, 1964; WOLF and HANDAL, 1966). Although the doses used by WOLF (1964) have been questioned (DENTON, NELSON, ORCHARD, and WELLER, 1969), the doses used by WOLF and HANDAL (1966) appear to be within the physiological range established by BOJESEN (1966). A positive role for aldosterone can also be inferred from differences between intact and adrenalectomized rats following various treatments (WOLF and STEINBAUM, 1965; JALOWIEC and STRICKER, 1973).

Two alternative hypotheses have been advanced to explain aldosterone-elicited sodium appetite in rats: (1) Aldosterone innately elicits sodium appetite. The nature of the physiological state being sensed could be either the high levels of aldosterone or the decrease in intracellular sodium of some receptor. (2) Aldosterone-elicited sodium appetite is a learned behaviour. In a classical conditioning model, high levels of aldosterone would be the CS with some aspect of low body sodium as the US. Thus, high aldosterone levels without prior association with low body sodium would not be effective in eliciting sodium appetite.

Two studies (WEISINGER and WOODS, 1971; WEISINGER, 1971) have examined these alternative explanations. The former study utilized a two bottle drinking test, while the latter utilized an operant conditioning experiment similar to that of KRIECKHAUS and WOLF (1968). The results of the latter will be discussed for two reasons. First, operant tasks are very sensitive to motivational effects. Second, postingestional effects are eliminated on the test day.

In this experiment, rats, on three successive days, were allowed to lever press for one hour. The animals were water deprived and the reinforcement was 0.33 M NaCl solution. There was no other source of water during training. The schedule of reinforcement was variable interval (VI) 15 (day 1), VI 30 (day 2), and VI 60 (day 3). Following training, the experimental group was injected with 150 μg/kg body weight aldosterone, while the control group received an equal volume of the vehicle. All animals were then allowed free access to water, but not food, for 24 hours and then tested for one hour under extinction conditions (i. e., no reinforcement given).

Table 2 shows the extinction scores for normally raised rats of the experimental and control groups. The extinction score is the ratio of the number of bar presses made during the one-hour extinction period to the number of bar presses made during the last hour of acquisition. The results show that aldosterone injected rats press at a significantly higher percentage of their acquisition rates in extinction than do control rats (32.2 % vs. 10.8 %). Using the same extinction score, formalin treated rats will press at about 30–35 % of their acquisition rates

(WEISINGER, WOODS, and SKORUPSKI, 1970; WOODS, WEISINGER, and WALD, 1971).

KRIECKHAUS and WOLF (1968) reported that the formalin effect was specific for sodium-containing solutions. Enhanced rates of lever pressing following formalin treatment were not observed in animals trained to lever press for KCl, $CaCl_2$, or water. Since the rats respond to sodium solutions only, and since the rats were trained while thirsty, it must be concluded that the association between sodium need and sodium had to be present prior to the animal's entering the experiment. Assuming laboratory animals had not experienced sodium need followed by sodium intake, the association between sodium need and sodium had to be innate.

In order to test the idea that both aldosterone- and sodium deficiency-elicited sodium appetite are innate, the latter assumption had to be established. Hence, laboratory rats were raised with access to food, water, and 1 % NaCl solution (saline-raised rats). This procedure ensured that the animals would not experience sodium deficiency since this concentration of NaCl is a preferred fluid and avidly consumed in great quantities.

Table 3 shows the extinction scores for saline-raised rats trained and tested as in the experiment of WEISINGER (1971). One additional experimental group was tested following 500 μg/kg aldosterone. Note that the enhanced rate of bar pressing shown in Table 2 was completely eliminated by raising rats with access to NaCl. Even the unphysiological dose of aldosterone did not result in enhanced responding. These results suggest that aldosterone-elicited sodium appetite is learned rather than innate. That is, raising rats with NaCl eliminates the association between high aldosterone levels and low body

Table 2. Extinction scores for normal-raised male rats. The extinction score is the percentage of bar presses made in extinction relative to the number of bar presses made in acquisition (VI-60), S.E. standard error of the mean; N number of subjects in a particular group

	Control	Aldosterone (150 μg/kg)
Mean	10.8	32.3
S.E.	3.91	5.64
N	6	6

Table 3. Extinction scores for saline-raised male and female rats

	Males		Females		
	Control	Aldosterone (150 μg/kg)	Control	Aldosterone (150 μg/kg)	Aldosterone (500 μg/kg)
Mean	9.5	4.5	14.7	13.7	14.6
S.E.	4.78	0.95	3.93	4.11	3.26
N	4	4	4	4	6

sodium, and thus eliminates the conditioned response.

In order to examine whether or not sodium deficiency-elicited sodium appetite is innate, saline-raised experimental rats were injected with formalin.

Table 4 shows the results of this experiment. Formalin-treated animals press significantly more than control animals. This result is important for several reasons: (1) it supports the view that sodium deficiency innately elicits sodium appetite, (2) it eliminates the possibility that raising rats with saline disrupts all sodium intake behaviour, and (3) the lower extinction score observed in this experimental group compared with the scores obtained in previous experiments (21.8 vs. 30–35 %) might be explained by the fact that aldosterone-elicited sodium appetite has been eliminated.

Table 4. Extinction scores of saline-raised male rats

	Control	Formalin 1.5% (2.5 ml.)
Mean	7.6	21.8
S.E.	2.56	4.47
N	5	5

The observed differences between normal and saline-raised rats, however, could be a function of body sodium level at the time of test. That is, WOLF (1964) had to use unphysiological doses of aldosterone in order to demonstrate sodium appetite. However, by maintaining rats on sodium deficient chow for one day prior to experimentation, the dose needed was markedly reduced (WOLF and HANDAL, 1966). This explanation was tested by giving normally raised rats access to NaCl for 4–6 weeks prior to experimentation. These animals had had an opportunity to learn and they had a high body sodium at the time of test.

Table 5 shows the extinction scores for these animals. The results are very similar to those shown in Table 2. Therefore the view that high body sodium at the time of the test is responsible for the results shown in Table 4 is not true.

Hence, aldosterone-elicited sodium appetite was present in animals in which there had been a chance for conditioning to occur. Although it is unlikely that normally raised rats are chronically sodium deficient, it is possible that there are fluctuations in aldosterone and body sodium levels of sufficient magnitude to allow conditioning to occur. It has been shown that aldosterone levels fluctuate with sodium intake (SINGER, 1960; BOJESEN, 1966). Furthermore, there is some evidence that the brain can sense both aldosterone levels (SWANECK, HIGHLAND, and EDELMAN, 1969) and sodium levels (ANDERSSON, 1953; ANDERSSON and MCCANN, 1955).

On the other hand, sodium deficiency-elicited sodium appetite was present regardless of raising procedure. It is, therefore, unlikely that any learning is necessary for this appetite to occur. While it is possible that there is an, as yet unexamined, explanation for the observed differences, it appears that deficiency- and aldosterone-elicited sodium appetite operated via different mechanisms.

Summary and Conclusions

1. Conditioned thirst and sodium appetite were produced by pairing the odour of menthol (CS) with injections of formalin.
2. Conditioned physiological changes were not responsible for the conditioned behaviour.
3. The conditioned appetites were due to either pseudoconditioning or long delay-conditioning.
4. Raising rats with access to 1% NaCl solution eliminated aldosterone-, but not sodium deficiency-elicited sodium appetite.
5. Elimination of aldosterone-elicited sodium appetite was not due to either 1) complete disruption of all sodium intake behaviour, or 2) high body sodium at time of test.

Table 5. Extinction scores or normal-raised female rats which had access to saline for 4–6 weeks

	Control	Aldosterone (150 μg/kg)
Mean	17.5	33.8
S.E.	3.99	3.00
N	6	5

6. Aldosterone- and sodium deficiency-elicited sodium appetite operate via different mechanisms, the former possibly a learned response.

References

ANDERSSON, B.: The effect of injections of hypertonic NaCl solutions into different parts of the hypothalamus of goats. Acta physiol. scand. **28**, 188–201 (1953).

ANDERSSON, B., LARSSON, S.: An attempt to condition hypothalamic polydipsia. Acta physiol. scand. **36**, 377–382 (1956).

ANDERSSON, B., McCANN, S.: A further study of polydipsia evoked by hypothalamic stimulation in the goat. Acta physiol. scand. **33**, 333–345 (1955).

BOJESEN, E.: Concentrations of aldosterone and corticosterone in peripheral plasma of rats. The effects of salt depletion, salt repletion, potassium loading and intravenous injections of renin and angiotensin II. Europ. J. Steroids **1**, 145–170 (1966).

DENTON, D. A., ORCHARD, E., WELLER, S.: The relation between voluntary sodium intake and body sodium balance in normal and adrenalectomized sheep. Behav. Biol. **3**, 213–221 (1969).

DENTON, D. A., NELSON, J.: Effect of deoxycorticosterone acetate and aldosterone on the salt appetite of wild rabbits. Endocrinology **87**, 970–977 (1970).

DENTON, D. A., NELSON, J., ORCHARD, E., WELLER, S.: The role of adrenocortical hormon secretion in salt appetite. In: Olfaction and Taste (ed. C. PFAFFMANN), pp. 535–547: Rockefeller Univ. Press 1969.

GARCIA, J., ERVIN, F., KOELLING, R.: Learning with prolonged delay of reinforcement. Psychon. Sci. **5**, 121–122 (1966).

HUSTON, J., BROZEK, G.: Attempt to condition eating and drinking elicited by hypothalamic stimulation in rats. Physiol. Behav. **8**, 973–975 (1972).

JALOWIEC, J., STRICKER, E. M.: Restoration of body fluid balance following acute sodium deficiency in rats. J. comp. physiol. Psychol. **70**, 94–102 (1970).

— Sodium appetite in adrenalectomized rats following dietary sodium deprivation. J. comp. physiol. Psychol. **83**, 66–77 (1973).

KRIECKHAUS, E., WOLF, G.: Acquisition of sodium by rats: Interaction of innate mechanisms and latent learning. J. comp. physiol. Psychol. **65**, 197–201 (1968).

MINEKA, S., SELIGMAN, M., HETRICK, M., ZUELZER, K.: Poisoning and conditioned drinking. J. comp. physiol. Psychol. **79**, 377–384 (1972).

PIEPER, W., MARX, M.: Conditioning of a previously neutral cue to the onset of a metabolic drive: Two instances of negative results. Psychol. Records **13**, 191–195 (1963).

REVUSKY, S., GARCIA, J.: Learned association over long delays. In: The Psychology of Learning and Motivation: Advances in Research and Theory (Eds. G. BOWER and J. T. SPENCER), pp. 1–84. New York: Academic Press 1970.

RICHTER, C.: Increased salt appetite in adrenalectomized rats. Am. J. Physiol. **115**, 155–161 (1936).

SELIGMAN, M., MINEKA, S., FILLIT, H.: Conditioned drinking produced procaine, NaCl and angiotensin. J. comp. physiol. Psychol. **77**, 110–121 (1971).

SINGER, B.: Further studies on the secretion of aldosterone by the rat adrenal gland. J. Endocr. **19**, 310–324 (1960).

STRICKER, E. M.: Extracellular fluid volume and thirst. Am. J. Physiol. **211**, 232–238 (1966).

SWANECK, G., HIGHLAND, E., EDELMAN, I.: Stereospecific nuclear and cytosol aldosterone-binding proteins in various tissues. Nephron. **6**, 297–316 (1969).

WEISINGER, R.: Mineralocorticoid administration in normal and adrenalectomized rats: Effects on sodium chlorid solution intake. Ph. D. Thesis, University of Washington (1971).

WEISINGER, R., WOODS, S.: Aldosterone-elicited sodium appetite. Endocrinology. **89**, 538–544 (1971).

— Formalin-like sodium appetite and thirst elicited by a conditioned stimulus in rats. J. comp. physiol. Psychol. **80**, 413–421 (1972).

WEISINGER, R., WOODS, S., SKORUPSKI, J.: Sodium deficiency and latent learning. Psychon. Sci. **19**, 307–308 (1970).

WOLF, G.: Sodium appetite elicited by aldosterone. Psychon. Sci. **1**, 211–212 (1964).

WOLF, G., HANDAL, P.: Aldosterone-elicited sodium appetite: Dose-response and specificity. Endocrinology, **78**, 1120–1124 (1966).

WOLF, G., STEINBAUM, E.: Sodium appetite elicited by subcutaneous formalin: Mechanism of action. J. comp. physiol. Psychol. **59**, 335–339 (1965).

WOODS, S., WEISINGER, R., WALD, B.: Conditioned aversions produced by subcutaneous injections of formalin in rats. J. comp. physiol. Psychol. **77**, 410–415 (1971).

Thirst and Salt Appetite in Experimental Renal Hypertension of Rats

J. Möhring, B. Möhring, D. Haack, J. Lazar, P. Oster, A. Schömig, and F. Gross

Partial constriction of one renal artery of the rat without touching the contralateral kidney induces sodium retention for a period of two to three weeks (Möhring, Näumann, Möhring, Philippi, and Gross, 1971). Subsequently, sodium balance is re-established. However, in those animals in which blood pressure exceeds a critical level, salt and water loss occur (Gross, Dauda, Kazda, Kyncl, Möhring, and Orth, 1972; Möhring et al. 1971); the activity of the renin-angiotensin system is further elevated, plasma aldosterone production is markedly stimulated, and malignant nephrosclerosis of the contralateral kidney may be found (Dauda, Möhring, Hofbauer, Homsy, Miksche, Orth, and Gross, 1973; Möhring et al. 1971; Möhring, Dauda, Haack, Hofbauer, Homsy, Näuman, Orth, and Gross, 1972; Vecsei and Münter, 1973).

The present paper reports on studies concerned with thirst and salt appetite during the early phase of renal hypertension in rats, i. e. during the phase of sodium retention, and on studies performed during the onset of malignant hypertension, i. e. during the phase of sodium and fluid loss.

Materials and Methods

Experiments on Thirst

Experiment 1. Twenty-one male Sprague-Dawley rats were placed into metabolism cages. Electrolyte and water balances were measured

daily as described previously (Möhring and Möhring, 1972b). When the rats reached a body weight of about 150 g, they were anaesthetized with ether and systolic blood pressure was measured by tail plethysmography. Then, in 12 rats the left renal artery was constricted by a silver clip (I. D. = 0.2 mm), and the remaining 9 rats were sham-operated. Subsequently, balance measurements were continued for 35 days. Blood pressure was measured once or twice a week.

Experiment 2. Fifty male Sprague-Dawley rats were placed in individual cages. In 20 rats, the left renal artery was clamped, while the other 30 rats were sham-operated. Body weight, and food and water intake were measured daily, and blood pressure twice a week. Ten days after clamping, the plasma volume and haematocrit were measured in 15 sham-operated control rats and in 8 renal hypertensive rats. In the remaining animals, these measurements were performed 28 days after clamping.

The rats were anaesthetized with ether and 0.2 ml. of a 0.5 % solution of Evans blue was injected into the left saphenous vein. Ten minutes after the injection, 1 ml. of blood was taken from the tail artery into heparinized collecting tubes. Glass capillaries were filled with collected blood and the haematocrit was determined. The plasma concentration of the dye was measured photometrically. From values of plasma volume and haematocrit blood volumes were calculated (Wang, 1959).

Experiment 3. Forty-six male Sprague-Dawley rats were treated as described for experiment

155

2. In 26 animals the left renal artery was clamped the remaining 20 rats were sham-operated. Ten days after clamping, blood was collected from 10 hypertensive and 10 control rats for the measurement of haematocrit, plasma angiotensin II concentrations (OSTER, HACKENTHAL, and HEPP, 1973) serum osmolality and plasma sodium and urea concentrations. In the remaining animals, the same measurements were performed 3 to 5 weeks after clamping.

Experiments on Salt Appetite (Self-Selection Studies)

Experiment 1. Groups of 8 rats were clamped and sham-operated. They were treated as described above. On the ninth day after clamping, blood pressure was measured. Subsequently, one bottle of demineralized water and one bottle containing 0.9 % NaCl were offered simultaneously for five days. On the first, third and fifth days of the self-selection study, blood pressure was measured. After five days the experiment was terminated.

Experiment 2. In groups of 13 clamped and 8 sham-operated rats a similar self-selection study was performed for a period of 10 to 20 days during the third to fifth week after clamping. Since compulsive saline drinking was observed in malignant hypertensive rats, saline intake on the first day of the self-selection study was measured 1, 5, 14, and 24 hours after start of the study.

Statistics. All values in the text, tables, and figures are means $\pm$ S. E. of mean. Linear regression equations were calculated by the method of least squares.

Results

The observations made on changes in electrolyte balances may be summarized as follows: during the first to third week after renal artery constriction, sodium balance was positive and potassium balance negative. Subsequently, sodium and potassium balances were re-established in one group of renal hypertensive rats. In those rats in

Table 1. Mean daily water intake and urine volume in rats after clamping the left renal artery without touching the contralateral kidney

Water intake	1	2	3	4	5	weeks
Controls	20.9 ± 0.7 (9)	24.2 ± 0.9 (9)	24.0 ± 0.8 (9)	22.9 ± 0.8 (9)	25.2 ± 1.0 (8)	
Hypertensives	26.1 ± 1.3** (12)	29.4 ± 1.6** (12)	28.7 ± 1.4** (8)	30.4 ± 1.8**	32.7 ± 1.4** (6)	BH §
			37.6 ± 3.6** (4)	43.0 ± 3.9** (4)	40.4 ± 4.1** (4)⁺	MH §
Urine volume	1	2	3	4	5	weeks
Controls	11.1 ± 0.7 (9)	12.9 ± 0.9 (9)	13.1 ± 0.9 (9)	13.5 ± 0.9 (9)	15.0 ± 1.2 (8)	
Hypertensives	15.2 ± 1.2** (12)	16.7 ± 1.4** (12)	15.9 ± 1.2** (8)	19.1 ± 1.6** (8)	21.1 ± 1.4** (6)	BH §
			26.6 ± 4.9** (4)	31.4 ± 4.4** (4)	32.0 ± 4.3** (4)⁺	MH §

Values are means ±S.E. of mean; * $p < 0.05$, ** $p < 0.01$ as compared with controls. § BH refers to benign hypertensive rats, MH to malignant hypertensive rats. ⁺ One MH rat died at the end of week 4, while in one MH rat blood pressure fell at the beginning of week 5 and water intake decreased to 22.1 ml; this rat is not included in the group of MH which systolic blood pressure exceeded a critical level of about 180 mmHg, sodium and potassium loss occured. The details of these observations will be reported elsewhere.

Experiments on Thirst

Water intake and urine volume were increased during the first week after clamping and remained elevated throughout the period of observation (Table 1). In those renal hypertensive rats in which salt loss occurred and which showed the syndrome of acute malignant hypertension (DAUDA et al. 1973; MÖHRING et al. 1971; MÖHRING et al. 1972) water intake and urine volume increased further.

Water intake increased within two to three days during the onset of the malignant phase of hypertension, as is shown for a typical case in Fig. 1. Concomitantly, body weight decreased slightly, although food intake was reduced for one day only. Subsequently, the animal recovered; water intake decreased, and body weight gain and food intake normalized. Then, on day 27, the beginning of a second crisis was observed. Blood was collected for the determination of plasma angiotensin II concentration, haematocrit, serum sodium and serum urea concentrations, and serum osmolality. The animal was then withdrawn from the experiment.

Mean daily water intakes, as calculated for each weekly period were significantly correlated with the mean weekly blood pressures in those animals which did not lose sodium (Fig. 2).

Plasma volume and calculated blood volume were elevated ten days after clamping (Fig. 3). At the end of the fourth week after clamping, plasma volume, haematocrit and blood volume were increased in the benign hypertensive rats

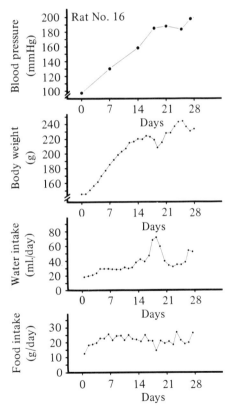

Fig. 1. Blood pressure, body weight, water intake, and food intake of a renal hypertensive rat. At day 0, the left renal artery was clamped. During the third week after clamping, signs of a malignant crisis were observed: decrease of body weight, increase of water intake, reduction of food intake. A second crisis began two days before the experiment was terminated

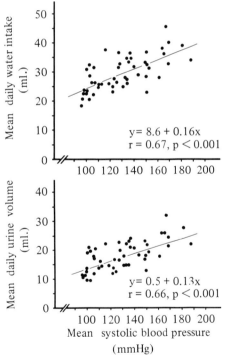

Fig. 2. Relationship between blood pressure and water intake and urine volume in renal hypertensive rats. Blood pressure values are means of two weekly measurements. Values of water intake and of urine volume are daily means calculated for weekly periods. Only rats which did not lose sodium are included

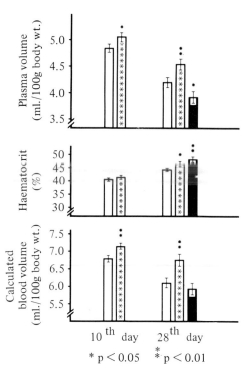

Fig. 3. Plasma volume, haematocrit, and blood volume of renal hypertensive rats 10 and 28 days after clamping. Blood volumes derived from plasma volume and haematocrit according to WANG (1959). White columns: Controls.-Columns with asterisks: all hypertensive animals on day 10, animals with the "benign" type of two kidney Goldblatt-hypertension on day 28 (see text). — Black columns: animals with the "malignant" type of renal hypertension: see text. Values are means ± S.E. of mean * $p < 0.05$, ** $p < 0.01$ as compared with control rats

(BH = rats which did not lose sodium), while in the malignant hypertensive rats (MH), plasma volume and calculated blood volume were reduced and haematocrit further elevated (Fig. 3).

Plasma sodium and urea concentrations, serum osmolality and haematocrit were unchanged in renal hypertensive rats 9 days after clamping (Table 2). However, plasma angiotensin II concentrations were increased by more than 30 %. Four weeks after clamping, haematocrit, plasma urea concentration, and plasma angiotensin II concentration were slightly elevated in BH rats, and plasma sodium concentration and serum osmolality fell within the normal range (Table 2). In MH rats, serum sodium concentration was reduced, while the other parameters measured were markedly elevated (Table 2).

Experiments on Salt Appetite (Self-Selection Studies)

During the second week after clamping, i. e. the period of positive sodium balance (MÖHRING et al. 1971), salt intake was increased while water intake was reduced in comparison with the sham-operated control animals (Fig. 4).

During the third to fifth week after clamping, saline was markedly preferred by those rats which showed signs of MH. In these animals, "compulsive saline drinking" was observed. When at 5 p.m., the saline was offered for the first time to the MH rats, the 7 animals studied all drank continuously for 34 to 48 minutes. Only short breaks of 10 to 20 seconds duration were observed during the period

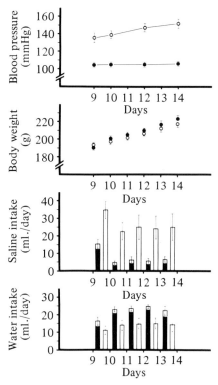

Fig. 4. Self-selection study in renal hypertensive rats during the second week after clamping (days 10 to 14). Open columns and circles refer to hypertensive rats (n = 8), black columns and dots to sham-operated controls (n = 8). Values are means ± S.E. of mean

Table 2. Haematocrit, plasma angiotensin II concentration, plasma sodium and urea concentration, and serum osmolality of rats during the early phase of renal hypertension (day 9 after clamping) and during the malignant phase of renal hypertension (days 28–34 after clamping)

DAY 9	haematocrit (%)	plasma angiotensin II concentration (pg/ml.)	plasma sodium concentration (m-equiv/l.)	plasma urea concentration (m-mole/l.)	serum osmolality (m-osmole/kg)
Controls (n = 10)	43.4 ± 0.5	149 ± 8	139.5 ± 0.4	5.6 ± 0.3	298.9 ± 1.4
Hypertensives (n = 10)	44.3 ± 0.5	199 ± 15**	138.9 ± 0.5	5.5 ± 0.3	301.5 ± 1.0
DAYS 28 to 34					
Controls (n = 10)	46.1 ± 0.3	80 ± 7	140.1 ± 0.4	5.4 ± 0.2	300.4 ± 1.6
Benign hypertensives (n = 9)	47.8 ± 0.5**	207 ± 13**	139.8 ± 0.4	6.0 ± 0.3*	302.0 ± 0.9
Malignant hypertensives (n = 7)	52.0 ± 0.8**	467 ± 94**	135.1 ± 1.0**	12.0 ± 1.8**	310.1 ± 3.1**

Values are means ±S.E. of mean; * $p < 0.05$, ** $p < 0.01$ as compared with control rats

of compulsive saline drinking. At the end of the first hour of observation, saline intake was more than 20 ml. in the MH rats and increased to values above 100 ml. during the subsequent 23 hours (Fig. 5). The phenomenon of compulsive saline drinking was not observed in any of the BH and control rats.

At the end of the first day of the self-selection study, blood pressure had fallen in all MH rats (187 ± 7 mmHg vs. 153 ± 8 mmHg; p < 0.01, paired data), while in the BH rats it increased further (162 ± 5 vs. 170 ± 7 mmHg; p < 0.01 paired data). The condition of the MH rats improved and the gain in body weight became normal (for examples see Fig. 6 and 7).

The time-course of events in the MH rats during the subsequent days was rather variable. Therefore, two typical cases are presented. In one rat (Fig. 6), the syndrome of MH was observed during the third post-operative week. Water intake rose over two days to 80 ml., while body weight decreased. Then, when food intake fell to nearly zero, water intake also declined, and a substantial loss of body weight occurred. The animal was now in very bad condition and such animals generally die. At that moment, saline was offered to the animal. Its drinking behaviour was remarkable: within 24 hours it had consumed 157 ml. of saline, i. e. 23,6 mEq of sodium. Blood pressure fell from 185 mmHg to 135 mmHg and the condition of the animal improved remarkably. Saline intake also fell during the next two days, to increase again as the blood pressure again rose. But this time the gain in body weight and food intake remained normal.

A similar time-course of events was observed in another rat (Fig. 7). In this animal, MH

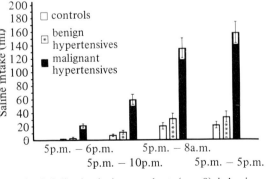

Fig. 5. Saline intake in control rats (n = 8), in benign hypertensive rats (n = 6), and in malignant hypertensive rats (n = 7) during the first day of a self-selection study. Demineralized water and 0.9% NaCl were offered simultaneously. Values are means ± S.E. of mean

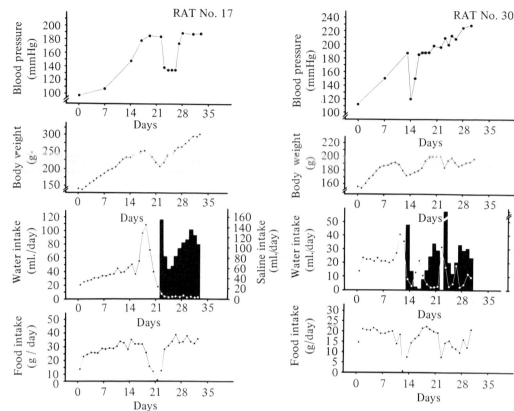

Fig. 6. Blood pressure, body weight, water and food intake in a malignant hypertensive rat before and after saline was offered in addition to water

Fig. 7. Blood pressure, body weight, water and food intake in a malignant hypertensive rat before and after saline was offered in addition to water. On day 23 of the study, saline was withdrawn

occurred towards the end of the second week after clamping. Saline had the same effect on blood pressure as in the other rat presented. Blood pressure rose again during the subsequent two days and saline intake increased again. On day 10 of this self-selection study, saline was withdrawn, and the condition of the animal worsened dramatically within 24 hours. Therefore, saline was again given and this time the rat drank 320 ml. of saline within 24 hours! However, no fall in blood pressure was observed. During the following days, saline intake declined; it increased again as the blood pressure rose further.

Similar observations were made in four other rats. In one MH rat, saline intake decreased to 2–25 ml. and remained so, although blood pressure increased again. Withdrawal of saline had no effect on the condition of the animal.

Discussion

Thirst and Salt Appetite during the Early Phase of Renal Hypertension in Rats

After clamping one renal artery in rats without touching the contralateral kidney, water turnover increased in parallel with blood pressure. These observations agree with previous studies by KRAMER and OCHWADT (1972) and micropuncture experiments in two kidney Goldblatt-hypertensive rats, in which water reabsorption in the ascending limp of Henle's loop of the contralateral kidney was reduced in proportion to the height of blood pressure (STUMPE, LOWITZ, and OCHWADT, 1970). From these studies it may be concluded that in renal hypertensive rats increasing blood pressure induces renal fluid loss, which in turn enhances water intake.

160

However, in the present study it has been demonstrated that during the early phase of renal hypertension plasma volume and blood volume were elevated, suggesting that water balance was positive. Therefore, the increase in water intake might have contributed to the elevation in blood pressure during the early phase of renal hypertension in rats. Consistent with such a conclusion is the recent observation that water restriction in two kidney Goldblatt-hypertensive rats may partially prevent the increase in blood pressure (LEENEN, DE JONG, and DE WIED, 1972).

Of the thirst-stimulating factors investigated in the present study (see Table 2 and Fig. 3), plasma angiotensin II concentration could have contributed to the increase in water intake during the early phase of renal hypertension. Despite positive sodium balance and an increase in plasma volume, plasma angiotensin II concentrations were elevated by more than 30 % during the second week after clamping. It is possible that the elevated plasma concentrations of angiotensin II induced positive water balance by stimulating both ADH secretion (MOUW, BONJOUR, MALVIN, and VANDER, 1971) and thirst (FITZSIMONS, 1972).

A similar pattern of events was found for renal salt excretion and salt appetite. During the early phase of renal hypertension, renal salt excretion was diminished resulting in a positive salt balance (MÖHRING et al. 1971) and salt appetite was enhanced as has been shown in the present studies. The combination of positive sodium balance and enhanced salt appetite has only been observed so far with DOCA or aldosterone treatment (GROSS et al., 1972; MÖHRING and MÖHRING, 1972a; WOLF, 1965; WOLF and HANDAL, 1966). Recently, we have found that aldosterone production in two kidney Goldblatt-hypertensive rats is augmented 9 days after clamping (DIETZ, MAST, GLESS, VECSEI, MÖHRING, OSTER, HACKENTHAL, and GROSS, 1973). Therefore, an elevated plasma aldosterone concentration might have induced both a positive sodium balance and an enhanced salt appetite during the early phase of renal hypertension.

Thirst and Salt Appetite during the Malignant Phase of Renal Hypertension in Rats

When blood pressure exceeded a critical level of about 180 mmHg, salt loss occurred in renal hypertensive rats (MÖHRING et al. 1971). Despite very high water intakes, fluid balance became negative as is evident from the weight loss and reduction in plasma volume. The subsequent further stimulation of thirst might have been due to high plasma angiotensin II concentrations, to hyperosmolality and to hypovolaemia.

Besides thirst, salt appetite was markedly stimulated in MH rats, and compulsive saline drinking was observed. One factor which might have contributed to compulsive saline drinking of MH rats is the further increase of the aldosterone production (DIETZ et al. 1973; VECSEI and MÜNTER, 1973).

Another striking observation in the present study was that blood pressure fell in all MH rats during the first 24 hours of high saline intake, and that the general condition of the animals improved. Although blood pressure increased again, the beneficial effect of salt during the malignant phase of renal hypertension was obvious. These findings confirm recent studies on the "vicious circle in malignant hypertension", in which we demonstrated the therapeutic and preventive effect of salt during the malignant phase of renal hypertension in rats (DAUDA et al. 1973).

These findings in rats support and suggest explanations for clinical observations of thirst in malignant hypertension (BARRACLOUGH, 1966; BROWN, CURTIS, LEVER, ROBERTSON, DE WARDENER, and WING, 1969). In addition, they indicate a therapeutic effect of salt under conditions of salt and fluid loss in malignant hypertension, when the renin-angiotensin system is markedly activated (BROWN et al. 1969; BRUNNER, LARAGH, BAER, NEWTON, GOODWIN, KRAKOFF, BARD, and BÜHLER, 1972).

Successful intervention with salt has been reported in patients with hypertensive crises (KINCAID-SMITH, personal communication 1973; ROBINSON, 1958).

References

BARRACLOUGH, M. A.: Sodium an water depletion with acute malignant hypertension. Am. J. Med. **40**, 265–272 (1966).

BROWN, J. J., CURTIS, J. R., LEVER, A. F., ROBERTSON, J. I. S., DE WARDENER, H. E., WING, A. J.: Plasma renin concentration and the control of blood pressure in patients on maintenance haemodialysis. Nephron **6**, 329–349 (1969).

BRUNNER, H. R., LARAGH, J. H., BAER, L., NEWTON, M. A., GOODWIN, F. T., KRAKOFF, L. R., BARD, R. H., BÜHLER, F. R.: Essential hypertension: renin, aldosterone, heart attack and stroke. New Engl. J. Med. **286**, 441–449 (1972).

DAUDA, G., MÖHRING, J., HOFBAUER, K. G., HOMSY, E., MIKSCHE, U., ORTH, H., GROSS, F.: The vicious circle in acute malignant hypertension of rats. Clin. Sci. **45**, 251s–255s (1973).

DIETZ, R., MAST, G. J., GLESS, K. H., VECSEI, P., MÖHRING, J., OSTER, P., HACKENTHAL, E., GROSS, F.: Aldosterone and corticosterone secretion in rats with benign and malignant hypertension. Advance abstracts, VI Meeting International Study Group for Steroid Hormones, Rome 1973.

FITZSIMONS, J.: Thirst. Physiol. Rev. **52**, 468–561 (1972).

GROSS, F., DAUDA, G., KAZDA, S., KYNCL, J., MÖHRING, J., and ORTH, H.: Increased fluid turnover and the activity of the renin-angiotensin system under various experimental conditions. Circulation Res. **31**, 173–181 (1972).

KRAMER, P., OCHWADT, B.: Wasserhaushalt und Elektrolytstoffwechsel bei Ratten mit experimentellem und spontanem Hochdruck. Pflügers Arch. ges. Physiol. **332**, 56–72 (1972).

LEENEN, F. H. H., DEJONG, W., DE WIED, D.: Water intake schedules and development of experimental renal hypertension in the rat. Abstract No. **587**, Advance abstracts, IV Int. Congr. Endocr., Excerpta Medica Int. Congr. Ser. No. 256, Amsterdam 1972.

MÖHRING, J., NÄUMANN, H. J., MÖHRING, B., PHILIPPI, A., GROSS, F.: Sodium balance and plasma renin activity in renal hypertensive rats. Europ. J. Clin. Invest. **1**, 384–389 (1971).

MÖHRING, J., DAUDA, G., HAACK, D., HOFBAUER, K. G., HOMSY, E., NÄUMANN, H. J., ORTH, H., GROSS, F.: Malignant phase of renal hypertension in rats. Europ. J. Clin. Invest. **2**, 297 (1972).

MÖHRING, J., MÖHRING, B.: Reevaluation of DOCA escape phenomenon. Am. J. Physiol. **223**, 1237–1245 (1972a).

— Evaluation of sodium and potassium balance in rats. J. appl. Physiol. **33**, 688–692 (1972b).

MOUW, D., BONJOUR, J.-P., MALVIN, R. L., VANDER, A.: Central action of angiotensin in stimulating ADH release. Am. J. Physiol. **220**, 239–242 (1971).

OSTER, P., HACKENTHAL, E., HEPP, R.: Radio-immunoassay of angiotensin II in rat plasma. Experientia **29**, 353 (1973).

ROBINSON, M.: Salt in pregnancy. Lancet **274**, 178–181 (1958).

STUMPE, K. O., LOWITZ, H. D., OCHWADT, B.: Fluid reabsorption in Henle's loop and urinary excretion of sodium and water in normal rats and rats with chronic hypertension. J. Clin. Invest. **49**, 1200–1212 (1970).

VECSEI, P., MÜNTER, R.: Conversion of precursors to aldosterone in vivo, IV Int. Endocr., Excerpta Medica Int. Congr. Ser. 790–794 (1974).

WANG, L.: Plasma volume, cell volume, total blood volume and F_{cells} factor in the normal and splenectomized Sherman rat. Am. J. Physiol. **196**, 188–192 (1959).

WOLF, G.: Effect of deoxycorticosterone on sodium appetite of intact and adrenalectomized rats. Am. J. Physiol. **208**, 1281–1285 (1965).

WOLF, G., HANDAL, P. J.: Aldosterone-induced sodium appetite: dose-response and specificity. Endocrinology **78**, 1120–1124 (1966).

Summary of Discussions

FITZSIMONS to FISHER: We have found that single intracranial injections of angiotensin II in doses of 1, 10, 100 and 1,000 ng gave the same two bottle preference functions as intracranial carbachol in doses of 3, 30, 300 and 600 ng. There was certainly no evidence from our studies that intracranial angiotensin caused drinking of a previously aversive concentration of saline, nor was the total intake of isotonic saline affected. We have tentatively concluded that any effect of angiotensin on sodium appetite is an indirect one, and that there is no direct stimulatory action on the central neuronal systems concerned with sodium appetite. Is the difference between our interpretation and yours simply a question of what we mean by sodium appetite? In our experience, any large intake of water is often followed by a period of saline drinking, perhaps because dilution of the body fluids and the resulting diuresis uncovers a relative deficiency of sodium. — FISHER: I have been aware of these data and concerned about the discrepancy. So far as interpretations are concerned, the key difference would seem to be that I see a potentiality for a biologically and functionally significant role for angiotensin in modulating the effects I have documented. FITZSIMONS seems to be suggesting that the saline intake observed is merely a non-specific result of antecedent water intake, having nothing specifically to do with the precise mode of inducing drinking. However, the reciprocal angiotensin-carbachol results, the lack of similar effects following water ingestion after water deprivation, the early emergence of enhanced saline ingestion in many of the studies, and the precision of selection of an isotonic mixture in others, appears to us to argue against the explanation suggested by FITZSIMONS and to favour angiotensin-induced facilitation of neural substrates related to both water and sodium intake. — PETERS: In agreement with FISHER's findings with intracranial angiotensin, we have found that intravenous renin increases the intake of isotonic saline as well as of water, while cellular thirst induced by hyperosmolar injection only enhances water intake and slightly depresses saline intake. *Chronically* increased or decreased plasma renin in rats does not appear to influence water intake; there are, however, no data on salt intake. — WEISINGER: Aldosterone does increase the intake of 0.15 M NaCl. Different doses of aldosterone have been shown to produce different effects. I have observed that adrenalectomized rats do increase their preference for isotonic saline. — PETERS: We have never doubted that different doses of aldosterone would produce different effects. Aldosterone, however, does not appear to increase saline intake in normal or adrenalectomized rats given a choice between water and isotonic (0.15 M) NaCl. They prefer the isotonic solution as most rats of sound minds do.

PETERS to MÖHRING: A chronically elevated plasma renin activity (PRA) was apparently correlated with water intake, in the presence of an elevated blood pressure. On the other hand, we found that a ten-fold chronic elevation of PRA induced by salt-depletion followed by a salt-free diet did not induce polydipsia within a period of one week. Can you give reasons for this difference? — MÖHRING: We made similar observations during the first ten days on a sodium-deficient diet. But after this time, i.e. if you wait long enough, water intake increases. Further-

more, 5 days after rats have been placed on a sodium-deficient diet the serum osmolality tends to fall. It is therefore possible that the initial hypo-osmolality may counterbalance the effects of a high PRA in eliciting thirst. — MÖHRING to GANTEN: 5–10 days after malignant hypertensive rats had been offered saline in addition to water, PRA and angiotensin II levels were normal or even reduced and the haematocrit, serum sodium and urea had also returned to normal. — STRICKER: Rats given furosemide and put on a sodium-deficient diet do not drink remarkably at first, but later as renal function is restored, osmotic dilution lessens and polydipsia appears. If the animals are given NaCl the hypovolaemia and polydipsia disappear. HOLMES made similar observations on sodium-deficient dogs more than 20 years ago. — MÖHRING: PRA and angiotensin II levels may increase 5 to 10 times in a malignant crisis, but generally the increase is 2-fold. — LEHR: The therapeutic effect of high salt intake in malignant hypertension may then be due to suppression of renin release, which is in agreement with Laragh's concept of the more serious nature of "high renin" hypertension. — MÖHRING: Yes, we suggested previously that the high renin plus the high blood pressure might induce malignant nephrosclerosis subsequent to salt and fluid loss. We tested this hypothesis by giving saline to the rat, and we found that in addition to restoring the PRA to normal we could prevent or "cure" acute malignant nephrosclerosis in our rats. In a discussion remark, KINCAID-SMITH reported similar observations made in patients with a malignant hypertensive crisis. These patients showed severe Na and fluid loss. — MÖHRING to HUTCHINSON: Plasma angiotensin II in the rat was about 100 pg/ml. in our studies. In man it is about 20 pg/ml. Other hormone levels are also higher in the rat than in man.

LE MAGNEN to WEISINGER: That feeding and drinking responses can be modified by conditioning is known from preference-aversion studies. In contrast to the results obtained with these studies, you observed extinction after 2–3 days. The difference is perhaps due to how closely the CS und UCS are related. Smell may be a privileged CS; but this is certainly not true of the injection procedure. — WEISINGER: First,

163

though the evidence for conditioned aversions is substantial, the evidence for conditioned preference is not. Secondly, the relation between CS and UCS is extremely important. For example, in most, if not all, of the studies dealing with conditioned thirst where negative results have been reported, an external stimulus such as a light or a tone was used. It is possible that the menthol CS is more related to the UCS than a light but not as related as some other stimulus.
— LEENEN: As WEISINGER said, aldosterone is not the only factor involved in sodium appetite. Plasma aldosterone measured by radioimmunoassay following caval ligation or polyethylene glycol (PG) administration is high, whereas sodium appetite only occurs after PG treatment.
— STRICKER: Salt intake on test trials is understandable since repeated experience of salt need and salt ingestion during conditioning results in a permanent increase in acceptability of NaCl solution, as it does in less complicated situations. The failure of similarly injected, but unconditioned, rats to respond may be because menthol functioned as a cue that salt was coming rather than as a stimulus to salt appetite. —
WEISINGER: I do not believe this to be the situation. During the test trial several things occur which arouse and provide cues for the No CS rats. First, other animals are being removed from the mentholated boxes and being placed in their cages. This would certainly awaken the No CS rats. Secondly, the placement of drinking tubes on the No CS rat cages would certainly show that saline and water are present. Lastly, the No CS rats drink some saline and water indicating that they were indeed aware of the presence of the fluid.

Section 8
Other Aspects of Thirst

Classical Conditioning of Consumatory Behaviour

J. P. HUSTON

The present report summarizes recent studies and presents new results relating to one aspect of the problem of conditioning influences on ingestive behaviour, namely, on the question of whether consumatory responses, or their motivational substrates, can be classically conditioned. This area has been traditionally treated in isolation from the alternative more generic theoretical and experimental approaches (e. g. BOOTH, 1972; LeMAGNEN, 1972) to the analysis of learning influences in the control of consumatory behavior.

The early literature on this topic was couched in terms of theoretical controversy on the "externalization of drive" (ANDERSON, 1941), of whether appetitive "drives" can be acquired or learned by the pairing of a neutral stimulus with a primary need state. For learning and personality theory (eg. MOWRER, 1960; DOLLARD and MILLER, 1950) it was important to demonstrate the conditioning of appetitive drive by analogy with the more readily demonstrable conditioned aversive drive states (MILLER, 1948), although closer inspection may reveal that this distinction between appetitive and aversive drives is an artificial one (see discussion by SELIGMAN, MINEKA, and FILLIT, 1971).

Evidence for conditioning of hunger has been sparse and controversial. The conceptual ambiguities surrounding this issue have precluded the design of experimental tests totally immune to post-hoc reinterpretation. The problem stems partly from the fact that different theoretical stances are taken with respect to the dynamics of learning processes, each with its own set of postulates and experimental requirements. Furthermore, a demonstration of classical conditioning uncontaminated by operant conditioning may be impossible, especially when dealing with the conditioning of "drive" and consumatory behaviour, which can hardly be divorced from the instrumental conditioning concepts of reward, incentive, etc..

CRAVENS and RENNER (1970) provide a comprehensive and critical review of the older literature on this problem. The most commonly used experimental design was to deprive animals of food and to expose them, usually at various "drive levels", to distinctive surroundings (CS), and at an intermediate level of deprivation observe the amount or rate of food consumption in the presence of the CS (eg. CALVIN, BICKNELL, and SPERLING, 1953; WRIGHT, 1965; WIKE, COUR, and MELLGREN, 1967; SIEGEL and MacDONNELL, 1954). The few successful demonstrations of conditioned drive are shadowed by failures of replication or by reinterpretation. At the time of CRAVENS and RENNER's review this area of research seemed to have reached an impasse.

Recently, Neal MILLER, who has stimulated much thought and work in this area, speculated that he previously might have failed to find evidence for conditioned appetitive drives analogous to learned drives based on pain (MYERS and MILLER, 1954), because hunger and thirst develop too gradually, and that new methods for inducing hunger rapidly could solve this problem (MILLER, 1973). Precise control over the onset and duration of the consumatory act (and thus, presumably the motivational substrates "hunger" and "thirst") permits the design of Pavlovian conditioning experiments with adequate control of CS-UCS and response parameters. Therefore there are now better means to answer the basic question of whether control can be established over consumatory behavior (or hunger) by classical conditioning procedures.

Two studies using electrical stimulation of the hypothalamus to induce consumatory behaviour failed to provide evidence for classical conditioning. ANDERSSON and LARSSON (1956) paired a tone with hypothalamic stimulation that induced drinking in goats. No conditioning was manifested after from 46 to 110 UCS-CS pairings. HUSTON and BROZEK (1972) elicited eating and drinking in rats with lateral hypothalamic stimulation. The tone CS failed to induce eating or drinking after between 100 and 800 pairings of the CS with 8 sec electrical UCS. These studies are limited and inconclusive, since hypothalamic stimulation can also have rewarding properties (HUSTON, 1971), the conditioning of which could interfere with the manifestation of a conditioned consumatory response.

The one rather limited experiment in which drinking was elicited with chemical injection into the hypothalamus yielded positive results. SELIGMAN et al. (1971) injected angiotensin into the hypothalamus as the UCS, and found conditioned drinking to the test-chamber CS, with rapid extinction.

An attempt by NOVIN and MILLER (1962) to condition drinking induced by the feeding of dry food to rats was unsuccessful.

Successful conditioning of insulin-induced hyperphagia was reported by BALAGURA (1968). Animals were first trained to work for food under continuous reinforcement schedules. After 12 days of conditioning, whereby insulin injection (the UCS) induced lever-pressing for food, conditioned responding with rapid extinction occurred to the saline injection alone. SIEGEL and NETTLETON (1970) were able to replicate these results using a variable interval reward schedule, but not when the rats were prevented from lever-pressing during the conditioning trials. Hence, they argued that BALAGURA's rats did not show conditioning of a motiva-

tional state, but rather a placebo-induced instrumental response previously reinforced by a reduction of insulin-induced stress. It could just as well be assumed, however, that prevention of the consumatory response during a state of hunger is an aversive state, which if conditioned could cause the CS to induce escape or other response incompatible with consumatory behaviour. Evidence that a CS paired with hunger can assume aversive "drive" properties exists (CRAVENS and RENNER, 1969), and such a consideration could explain the many failures to find conditioned feeding in the early studies in which a CS was paired with some state of deprivation during which the animals were not allowed to engage in consumatory behaviour (see CRAVENS and RENNER, 1970).

Another way of artificially inducing drinking is to inject hypertonic NaCl, usually subcutaneously. SELIGMAN, IVES, AMES, and MINEKA (1970) demonstrated conditioned drinking in rats by pairing a compound CS with an injection of hypertonic saline and procaine. Conditioning occurred irrespective of whether or not the rats were allowed to drink during conditioning trials (WAYNER and COTT, 1971). The failure of drinking to undergo extinction, however, made the interpretation suspect. SELIGMAN et al. (1970) then reported that extinction did occur, but only when a discriminative conditioning procedure was used. They subsequently (SELIGMAN et al. 1971) showed that procaine alone led to unconditioned as well as substantial conditioned drinking which did not undergo extinction, and that with hypertonic NaCl in the absence of procaine conditioned drinking was less dramatic. In a further study, MINEKA, SELIGMAN, HETRICK, and ZUELZER (1972) demonstrated that procaine and hypertonic saline paired with saccharin produced taste aversions, suggesting that these substances act as poisons, the effects of which are relieved by drinking. The conditioned drinking represents an avoidance response. Furthermore, COTT, WAYNER, and MILLNER (1972) found that the conditioning to NaCl injection is not confined to drinking, because the rats also ate more food and ran more in activity wheels during extinction. This suggests a nonspecific conditioned increase in motor excitability to the salt injection. Also relevant is the control of blood glucose changes by classical conditioning. The possibility that blood glucose level, a correlate of nutritional state and hence "hunger", is subject to classical conditioning has obvious implications for the problem of conditioned appetitive states. There are indications that classical conditioning of insulin-induced hypoglycaemia is possible in man, though these results are quite controversial (see LICHKO, 1959, and ZAKHAROV, 1960, for reviews of the Soviet literature). Successful conditioning has been reported also in the dog (ALVAREZ-BUYLLA and CARRASCO-ZANINI, 1960; SEGURA, 1962) and the rat (WOODS and SHOGREN, 1972). The results are far from conclusive however. SIEGEL (1972) for example, contests the reports of conditioned hypoglycaemia in rats because he found conditioned *hyper*glycaemia after insulin injection, suggesting the establish-'ment of a compensatory conditioned glycaemic response.

Two studies on classical conditioning are presented in the remainder of this chapter. A study done in collaboration with BERT SIEGFRIED provides evidence for classical conditioning of feeding and drinking elicited by KCl-induced single waves of spreading depression in the cortex, striatum and hippocampus of rats. Another study, done with KURT ORNSTEIN, shows that after pairing hypothalamic stimulation, which does not elicit feeding or drinking, with deprivation-induced eating, the brain stimulation comes to serve as a CS to elicit eating when the animals are satiated. This raises the possibility that classical conditioning plays a role both in the stability and "plasticity" of hypothalamically elicited stimulus-bound consumatory behaviour.

Conditioning of Consumatory Behaviour Elicited by Spreading Depression

"Spreading depression" refers to the silence in electrical activity that follows the slowly spreading (3 mm/min) wave of depolarization and steady potential change, resulting from a variety of insults to brain tissue. The technique of spreading depression (SD) has found extensive application as a "reversible ablation" (BURES,

1959). Fig. 1 illustrates the steady potential shifts that accompany single waves of spreading depression induced in one or both hemicortices of rats by iontophoretic injection of K^+ ions. It

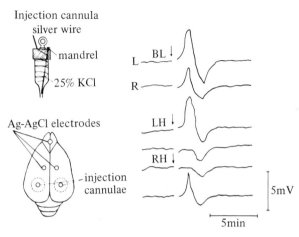

Fig. 1. Examples of steady potential changes resulting from K^+-induced single waves of spreading depression induced bilaterally, in the left and right hemispheres of a rat

was found that eating and drinking could be elicited by single waves of unilateral or bilateral potassium-induced SD in the cortex of rats (HUSTON and BUREŠ, 1970) and rabbits (HUSTON and BROZEK, 1971). We have recently found (unpublished) that in rats consumatory behaviour can be elicited also by unilateral striatal and hippocampal SD. Furthermore, SD in these structures induced a high incidence of yawning and penile erection as previously found with cortical SD (HUSTON, 1971). In summary, dorsal hippocampal SD primarily elicited eating (93 %, n = 177), whereas cortical and caudate SD induced both eating and drinking with ratios of 92:41 (n = 133) and 60:12 (n = 72), respectively. These and other differences suggest that different mechanisms may be involved, one for hippocampal eating, the other for the cortex-caudate eating and drinking (the caudate and cortex effects are probably related, since cortical SD spreads via the amygdala to the striatum, and vice versa, in most rats: FIFKOVA and SYKA, 1964; STILLE and SAYERS, 1969). These effects are robust, as hippocampal, cortical and caudate elicited behaviour occurred with

167

93 % (n = 29), 74 % (n = 49), and 92 % (n = 13) of all hemispheres tested. Frontal cortical SD (2 mm anterior from bregma) induced consumatory behaviour significantly sooner than posterior cortical SD (3 mm posterior from bregma), with onset latencies of 4.9 min (n = 27) and 5.8 min (n = 65), supporting the hypothesis advanced earlier that the frontal pole area is a focus for this effect (HUSTON and BURES 1970; HUSTON and BURES, 1973). Mean onset latencies for hippocampal and caudate SD-induced behaviour were 5.1 min (n = 164) and 5.6 min (n = 60) respectively.

It should be mentioned that during SD-elicited eating the animals consistently avoided quinine adulterated food. Furthermore, in animals previously rewarded with food when pressing a lever SD induced lever-pressing with onset latencies corresponding to those for elicited eating.

The high reliability with which consumatory behaviour is elicited by this method led us to attempt to classically condition SD-induced behaviour to a complex CS, consisting of a testing chamber, light, tone and injection procedure. 0.5–2.0 μl KCl solution was injected via plastic tubing and a microsyringe into adult albino male rats with cannula guides placed into the dorsal hippocampus, caudate nucleus and cortex. The animals were at all times kept in their transparent moveable home boxes, where they had *ad libitum* access to food and water.

The procedure was as follows: (a) *Six baseline trials*: The rats were sham injected and placed (while remaining in their home boxes) into the conditioning chamber with light and tone on for 15 min. Onset latencies and duration of eating and drinking were recorded during these 15 min, as well as during the preceding and subsequent 15 min. Each animal was given two trials per day and always tested at the same time each day. (b) *Four conditioning trials*: The procedure was exactly as during baseline, except that the rats were injected with KCl solution that induced a spreading depression. (c) *Extinction trials*: Same procedure as in the baseline. A control group of 6 rats in whom SD did *not* elicit any eating or drinking (all with cortical cannulae) was run under exactly the same conditions.

Conditioning of elicited eating was successful from a total of 21 brain sites (9 cortical, 7 hippocampal, 5 caudate cannulae) in 19 of 22 animals tested. Fig. 2 shows the averaged results of 2 groups of rats. The top group consisted of 6 rats in whom extinction occurred rapidly and trials were terminated early (criterion of 4 trials without eating). The bottom group of 14 rats were given at least 15 extinction trials. The

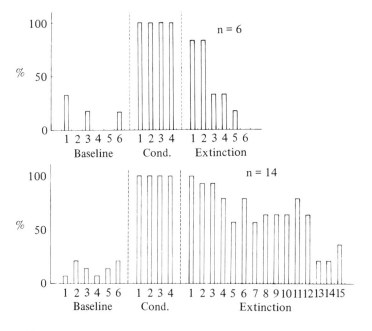

Fig. 2. Probability of eating during 15 min long baseline, conditioning and extinction trials for two groups of rats (see text)

ordinate expresses the percentage of trials during which eating occurred. The mean duration of eating during conditioning for all animals was about 3 min, and during the first 3 extinction trials was about 2 min. The control animals ate only slightly more during extinction trials than during baseline. Conditioned eating failed to undergo gradual extinction in only one animal given cortical SD.

These results suggest that spreading depression-induced eating and perhaps drinking (in one rat) may be conditioned. Conditioned SD-elicited eating differs from conditioned NaCl- and procaine-induced drinking in that it undergoes fairly rapid extinction as does conditioned angiotensin-induced drinking (SELIGMAN et al. 1971).

The course of extinction and the failure of the control animals (who also received SD) to show conditioned eating makes it unlikely that the conditioned eating occurred in response to some possible aversive effects of spreading depression *per se* (e. g. conditioned arousal-induced eating, or escape from a conditioned aversive effect, as in SELIGMAN et al.'s 1971 study). Also, the conditioned eating probably cannot be attributed to repeated experience with spreading depression alone, nor to habituation to the experimental situation. It is still possible, however, that the SD had qualitatively different effects in the experimental and control groups. Measures of steady potential shifts during SD in the cortex did not reveal any differences between SD-induced eaters and non-eaters. However, we did not test for possible differences in the spreading of SD into the amygdala or striatum to account for failure to eat under cortical SD, although this hypothesis, if confirmed, could also lead to some insight into the mechanism and focus of cortical SD-induced consumatory behaviour.

Hypothalamic Stimulation as a CS for Consumatory Behaviour

Electrical stimulation of the lateral hypothalamus of rats can induce eating, drinking and other behaviour. Three points of interest for the present study, based largely on Elliot VALENSTEIN's work, are: (a) Animals which initially exhibit a particular elicited behaviour such as eating, will eventually switch to drinking when food is withheld, and vice versa. (b) Elicited behaviour sometimes develops gradually after many trials, i. e. becomes more reliable with experience. (c) Anatomical specificity for electrically elicited behaviour seems doubtful (see VALENSTEIN, COX, and KAKOLEWSKI, 1970, for a review of these points). Although it is clear from this work that experience plays a role in both the stability and plasticity of hypothalamically elicited behaviour, the dynamics of the learning processes involved have not been analysed. Operant conditioning could be involved because, (a) electrical stimulation, which is usually also rewarding since animals will self-stimulate for it, reinforces the feeding response, leading to further feeding. (b) The consumatory response, e. g. eating, reinforces preconsumatory behaviour (such as approaching food), which increases the probability of further feeding. (c) The consumatory behaviour attenuates aversive effects of the stimulation (e.g. excessive arousal).

In the present study we tested the hypothesis that classical conditioning plays a role in the stability and plasticity of a particular elicited behaviour. We took animals in which hypothalamic stimulation did *not* elicit either feeding or drinking, paired the stimulation with eating induced by food-deprivation, then tested the effects of the brain stimulation on feeding when the rats were satiated. The question was whether hypothalamic stimulation could serve as a conditioned stimulus able to elicit eating.

Adult male rats were implanted with bipolar 0.2 mm diameter stainless-steel electrodes aimed at lateral hypothalamus. Electrical stimulation consisted of 40–50 Hz, 0.08–0.1 msec duration monophasic pulses at amplitudes between 100–200 μA. Water was available in the testing chamber from a spout through the wall, and rat chow was available either as cubes scattered over the floor or as powder in a container.

The procedure was as follows: (a) *Baseline*: Each animal received 48 trials consisting of hypothalamic stimulation for periods of 1 min at 4 min intervals and spaced over 4 days. The animals were satiated and the current was adjusted until it was just sufficient to induce orienting and non-excited locomotion. (The animals were previously tested for elicited eating and drinking using a wider range of current levels). (b) *Conditioning*: The animals were deprived of food for 6 days and the baseline procedure was repeated, except that they had access to the powdered food only during the 1 min stimulation periods. The powder was presented 10 sec after onset of the stimulation. (c) *Extinction*: The rats were allowed two days of *ad libitum* feeding in their home cages, and then were tested for elicited eating exactly as during the baseline conditions (Current levels were kept constant during all phases of the experiment.)

After the experiments the animals were tested for self-stimulation at the current levels used previously, except that the train-duration was reduced to 0.2–0.5 sec.

Six rats showed evidence of classical conditioning in that the hypothalamic stimulation induced significantly more eating during extinction trials than during baseline (Fig. 3). In 5 animals the conditioned eating gradually underwent extinction. Three rats were reconditioned with the same results. In one animal the conditioned eating did not undergo extinction after 120 trials given over a period of 10 days. It should be emphasized that they only ate the powdered food, although cubes were readily available, suggesting that this preference was part of the conditioned response.

Fig. 3 presents the averaged results for the 5 rats, including reconditioning trials in 3 rats. The top graph shows the percentage of rats which

exhibited eating during each testing trial, with trials pooled in blocks of three. The bottom graph shows the mean duration of eating and drinking which occurred during baseline and extinction trials.

One animal in which the stimulation interfered with eating failed to show evidence of conditioning. Only one animal (the one whose conditioned eating failed to undergo extinction) resorted to electrical self-stimulation.

These data suggest that hypothalamic stimulation can serve as a CS for eating after being paired with deprivation-induced eating.

VALENSTEIN et al. (1970) showed that elicited eating can develop gradually with repeated trials. The rapid extinction of the conditioned eating rules out the possibility that it was established merely as a result of experience with the stimulation. Since the stimulation was not rewarding for 5 of the 6 animals it is unlikely that eating was reinforced by the stimulation during the conditioning trials. This is made even less likely by the fact that the onset of the stimulation preceded the availability of food by 10 sec. during conditioning.

In summary, we have shown that hypothalamic stimulation, which had not previously elicited eating or drinking, did so after the stimulation had been paired with feeding induced by food-deprivation. Hence, we have evidence that classical conditioning may in part account for the acquired stability with repeated trials, as well as the plasticity (the switching to another consumatory response) of hypothalamic stimulus-bound behaviour.

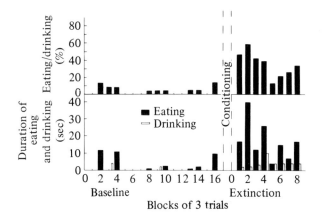

Fig. 3. Top: Percentage incidence of eating during blocks of 3 trials before and after conditioning. Bottom: Mean duration of eating and drinking during baseline and extinction trials

Notes

This work was supported by the Swiss National Science Foundation Grants No. 3.693.71 and 3.8790.72 and the Hartman-Mueller Foundation for Medical Research.

My thanks to Kurt Ornstein and Bert Siegfried who collaborated in the work reported herein and to Claudia Müller for her able assistance.

References

Alvarez-Buylla, R., Carrasco-Zanini, J. A.: Conditioned reflex which reproduces the hypoglycemic effect of insulin. Acta physiol. latinoam. 10, 153–158 (1960).

Anderson, E. E.: The externalization of drive: III. Maze learning by non-rewarded and by satiated rats. J. genet. Psychol. 59, 397–426 (1941).

Andersson, B., Larsson, S.: An attempt to condition hypothalamic polydipsia. Acta physiol. Scand. 36, 377–382 (1956).

Balagura, S.: Conditioned glycemic responses in the control of food intake. J. comp. physiol. Psychol. 65, 30–32 (1968).

Booth, D. A.: Conditioned satiety in the rat. J. comp. physiol. Psychol. 81, 457–471 (1972).

Bures, J.: Reversible decortication and behavior. In: The Central Nervous System and Behavior (ed. M. A. B. Brazier), pp. 207–248. New York: J. Macy Jr. Foundation 1959.

Calvin, J. S., Bicknell, E. A., Sperling, D. S.: Establishment of a conditioned drive based on the hunger drive. J. comp. physiol. Psychol. 46, 173–175 (1953).

Cott, A., Wayner, M. J., Millner, J.: Conditioned drinking: a specific or nonspecific response? Physiol. Behav. 9, 219–227 (1972).

Cravens, R. W., Renner, K. E.: Conditioned appetitive drive states: empirical evidence and theoretical status. Psychol. Bull. 73, 212–220 (1970).

— Conditioned hunger. J. exp. Psychol. 81, 312–316 (1969).

Dollard, J., Miller, N. E.: Personality and Psychotherapy. New York: McGraw-Hill 1950.

Fifkova, E., Syka, J.: Relationship between cortical and striatal spreading depression in rat. Expl. Neurol. 9, 355–366 (1964).

Huston, J. P.: Relationship between motivating and rewarding stimulation of the lateral hypothalamus. Physiol. Behav. 6, 711–716 (1971).

— Yawning and penile erection in rats induced by cortical spreading depression. Nature 232, 274–275 (1971).

Huston, J. P., Brozek, G.: Arousal of consumatory behavior in rabbits by single waves of cortical spreading depression. Physiol. Behav. 7, 595–600 (1971).

— Attempt to classically condition eating and drinking elicited by hypothalamic stimulation in rats. Physiol. Behav. 8, 973–975 (1972).

Huston, J. P., Bures, J.: Drinking and eating elicited by cortical spreading depression. Science 169, 702–704 (1970).

— Effects of cortical spreading depression on behavior elicited by hypothalamic stimulation in rats. Physiol. Behav. 10, 775–780 (1973).

Le Magnen, J.: Regulation of food intake: physiologic-biochemical aspects (peripheral regulatory factors). In: Adv. psychosom. Med. 7, 73–90. Basel: Karger 1972.

Lichko, A. E.: Conditioned reflex hypoglycaemia in man. J. high. nerv. Activ. I. P. Pavlov 9, 823–829 (1959).

Miller, N. E.: Commentary. In: Brain stimulation and motivation: Research and Commentary (ed. E. S. Valenstein), pp. 53–68. Glenview, Illinois: Scott, Foresman and Co. 1973.

— Studies of fear as an acquirable drive: I. Fear as motivation and fear-reduction as reinforcement in the learning of new responses. J. exp. Psychol. 38, 89–101 (1948).

Mineka, S., Seligman, M. E. P., Hetrick, M., Zuelzer, K.: Poisoning and conditioned drinking J. comp. physiol. Psychol. 79, 377–384 (1972).

Mowrer, O. H.: Learning Theory and Behavior. New York: Wiley 1960.

Myers, A. K., Miller, N. E.: Failure to find a learned drive based on hunger: evidence for learning motivated by "exploration". J. comp. physiol. Psychol. 47, 428–436 (1954).

Novin, D., Miller, N. E.: Failure to condition thirst induced by feeding dry food to hungry rats. J. comp. physiol. Psychol. 55, 373–374 (1962).

Segura, E.: Insulin-like conditioned hypoglycemic response in dogs. Acta physiol. latinoam. 12, 342–345 (1962).

Seligman, M. E. P., Bravman, S., Radford, R.: Drinking: discriminative conditioning in the rat. Psychon. Sci. 20, 63–64 (1970).

Seligman, M. E. P., Ives, C., Ames, H., Mineka, S.: Failure to extinguish conditioned drinking: avoidance, preparedness or functional autonomy. J. comp. physiol. Psychol. 71, 411–419 (1970).

Seligman, M. E. P., Mineka, S., Fillit, H.: Conditioned drinking produced by procaine, NaCl, and angiotensin. J. comp. physiol. Psychol. 77, 110–121 (1971).

Siegel, P. S., MacDonnell, M. F.: A repetition of the Calvin-Bicknell-Sperling study of conditioned drive. J. comp. physiol. Psychol. 47, 250–252 (1954).

Siegel, S.: Conditioning of insulin-induced glycemia. J. comp. physiol. Psychol. 78, 233–241 (1972).

Siegel, S., Nettleton, H.: Conditioning of insulin-induced hyperphagia. J. comp. physiol. Psychol. 72, 390–393 (1970).

STILLE, G., SAYERS, A.: Effect of striatal spreading depression on the pharmacogenic catatonia. Int. J. Neuropharm. **8**, 181–189 (1969).

VALENSTEIN, E. S., COX, V. C., KAKOLEWSKI, J. W.: Reexamination of the role of the hypothalamus in motivation. Psychol. Rev. **77**, 16–31 (1970).

WAYNER, M. J., COTT, A.: Conditioned drinking and the effects of saccharin on its recovery after lateral hypothalamic lesions. Physiol. Behav. **7**, 201–206 (1971).

WIKE, E. L., COUR, C., MELLGREN, R. L.: Establishment of a learned drive with hunger. Psychol. Rep. **20**, 143–145 (1967).

WOODS, S. C., SHOGREN, R. E.: Glycemic responses following conditioning with different doses of insulin in rats. J. comp. physiol. Psychol. **81**, 220–225 (1972).

WRIGHT, J. H.: Test for a learned drive based on the hunger drive. J. expl. Psychol. **70**, 580–584 (1965).

ZAKHAROV, S. V.: The problem of conditioned reflex insulin hypoglycaemia. J. high. nerv. Activ. I. P. Pavlov **10**, 280–284 (1960).

The Chemical and Behavioural Specificity of Cholinergic Stimulation of the Tractus Diagonalis

G. K. Terpstra and J. L. Slangen

Introduction

Drinking of water as a result of chemical stimulation of different parts of the limbic system in satiated rats is a well known phenomenon (Grossman, 1960, 1962; Fisher and Coury, 1962). Experiments on the nature of the transmission system involved revealed that the drinking response could be elicited by central administration of cholinomimetics, angiotensin (Epstein, Fitzsimons, and Rolls, 1970) or β-adrenergic substances (Leibowitz, 1971). The drinking in response to cholinomimetics is attributable to activation of cholinoceptive neurones in the limbic system. It has been shown that local application of carbachol in the tractus diagonalis elicits drinking behaviour. The effect of carbachol in this area can be blocked in a dose dependent way by atropine and methylatropine injected into the tractus diagonalis itself (Terpstra and Slangen, 1972a). In the following experiments we have investigated the pharmacological properties of the neurones involved in order to determine to what extent the "drinking"-system located in the tractus diagonalis is specifically sensitive to cholinergic agents.

Since local administration of cholinomimetic drugs in the limbic system can have effects on temperature regulation, and on aggressive and sexual behaviour, and since administration of adrenergic drugs can induce changes in drinking behaviour, temperature regulation and food intake we have also investigated the specificity of the effect of cholinergic stimulation of the tractus diagonalis. Therefore we performed experiments in which we looked for the effects of cholinergic stimulation in the tractus diagonalis on food intake and temperature regulation that might be related to the effects of cholinergic stimulation on water intake.

Methods

Male albino rats of an inbred Wistar strain, weighing about 300 g were used. Cannulae were implanted stereotaxically into the tractus diagonalis as described earlier (Terpstra and Slangen, 1972 a). After operation the animals were housed individually in wire cages with tap water and food (Muracon I pellets) freely available. The room temperature was $22 \pm 2\,^\circ$ C and the lighting was on from 5 a. m. until 7 p. m.

Testing procedure was essentially the same as described earlier (Terpstra and Slangen, 1972 b). At the start of each test a sham injection was given; i. e. the cannula was opened and the stylus taken out of the cannula, cleaned and replaced. After half an hour in which it was possible to check the animal's water intake as a result of the handling and the mock injection, the cannula was opened again and the animal was injected with 1 μl. of the solution containing the drug or, in the case of a control test, with 0.9% NaCl. After closing the cannula the water intake in the next hour was measured on the calibrated drinking tube to the nearest 0.1 ml. Each drug was tested at least three times.

Between two tests there was an interval of at least 48-hours. Saline injections were given at random between drug tests. When the influence of atropine, hexamethonium and decamethonium on carbachol-induced drinking was being tested, these drugs were administered half an hour before the carbachol injection instead of the sham injection. In order to reduce the interaction between food and water intake, food was not available during the drinking tests and water was not available during the eating tests.

Drugs

The drugs administered were: carbachol (carbamylcholine-chloride); pilocarpine nitrate; pilocarpine hydrochloride; nicotine sulphate; hexamethonium chloride; decamethonium bromide; atropine sulphate; noradrenaline bitartrate; isoprenaline sulphate; serotonin creatinine sulphate; histamine acid sulphate; val⁵-angiotensin II-asp-amide (Hypertensin).

For injection the drugs were dissolved in saline except where other solvents are mentioned.

Histology

After completion of the experiments each rat was perfused, under deep pentobarbital anaesthesia, with saline and buffered 10 % formalin (pH 7.0). The brains were removed and stored in 10% formalin solutions. Frozen sections 100 μ thick were cut and stained with Oil red (Sudan III) and Harris' haematoxylin. The stimulation sites were determined microscopically.

Statistics

For statistical evaluation of the results t-tests for differences between the means of two samples with an F-test for equality of variances were used. In case of an inequality of the variances degrees of freedom were adjusted according to Welch (Jonge, 1964).

Experiment I

The Effect of Cholinergic Drugs

In earlier experiments the standard dose of carbachol for the elicitation of the drinking response was defined as 7.2 n-mole (1.3 μg) (Terpstra and Slangen, 1972 a). The central effects of carbachol can be differentiated into muscarinic and nicotinic effects, firstly, by comparing these effects with those of intracerebrally administered pilocarpine and nicotine. Secondly, we can study the effects of atropine (anti-muscarinic), and of hexamethonium and decamethonium (both anti-nicotinic agents; the former a ganglionic blocker and the latter a muscular relaxant) on carbachol-induced drinking. Pilocarpine was injected in 12 rats in doses ranging from 1 to 2048 n-mole, the high doses being included in view of the fact that only after peripheral administration of high doses the effects of pilocarpine are comparable to those of carbachol (Eaton, 1968). The doses used for nicotine were 1, 4, 8 and 16 n-mole (n = 9), for atropine 0.1, 0.45, 1.3 and 4.5 n-mole (n = 7) and for hexamethonium (n = 8) and decamethonium (n = 9) 1, 4, 8 and 16 n-mole.

Results

The effects of pilocarpine and nicotine are compared with those produced by the standard dose of carbachol and are expressed as percentages of water intake after carbachol. Water intakes in the preliminary 1 hour tests after 7.2 n-mole of carbachol were 12.0 ± 1.4 ml. for the pilocarpine group and 15.2 ± 1.5 ml. for the nicotine group. Figs. 1 and 2 show the water intakes in 1 hr after pilocarpine and nicotine respectively. A maximal water intake in the

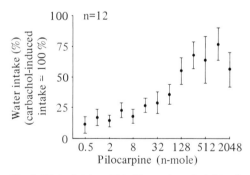

Fig. 1. Water intake within 1 hour after administration of different doses of pilocarpine into the tractus diagonalis of undeprived rats. Water intake is expressed as percentage of the 1 hour intake after administration of 7.2 n-moles of carbachol. Percentages are given as means ± S.E. of mean

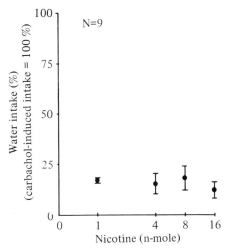

Fig. 2. Water intake within 1 hour after administration of different doses of nicotine into the tractus diagonalis. For further explanation see Fig. 1

pilocarpine group was found after administration of 1024 n-mole. After nicotine the water intake was not significantly different at any dosage from the control water intake after saline administration (14 % of water intake after carbachol.)

In the subsequent series of tests in which atropine was administered one rat stopped drinking to carbachol stimulation and its results are therefore omitted. A second rat lost its cannula and its results are only partially included

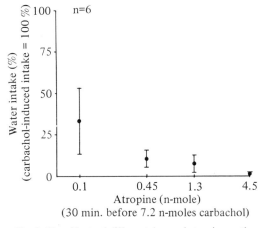

Fig. 3. The effects of different doses of atropine on the water intake within 1 hour following carbachol stimulation. Both drugs were injected into the tractus diagonalis. For further explanation see Fig. 1

in Fig. 3. The inhibiting effect of atropine on the water intake after 7.2 n-mole carbachol appeared to be about equal for doses of 4.5, 1.3 and 0.45 n-mole atropine. The mean carbachol-induced water intake after pretreatment with 0.1 n-mole of atropine appeared to be considerably less than water intake after carbachol alone (11.3 ± 2.5 ml.) but the difference was not statistically significant ($p < 0.1$). The water intake after different doses of hexamethonium and 7.2 n-mole of carbachol did not differ significantly from the water intake after sham injection followed by carbachol injection (13.0 ± 1.7 ml.) (Fig. 4). In these tests one rat lost its cannula and its results are only partly included in Fig. 4.

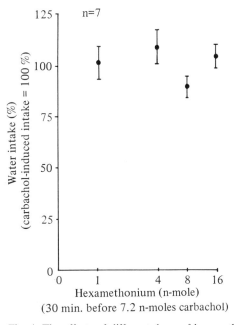

Fig. 4. The effects of different doses of hexamethonium on the water intake in 1 hour following carbachol stimulation. Cf. Fig. 3

In the tests in which decamethonium was administered faulty cannula placements were found in two rats and a third rat lost its cannula during the experiment. The results from the first two rats are not included, and those from the third rat are partly included in Fig. 5. Decamethonium inhibited water intake after carbachol significantly in doses of 1 n-mole ($p < 0.02$) and 8 n-mole (p < 0.01), but not in doses of 4 and 16 n-mole (Fig. 5). It was observed, however, that water intake in the 30 min period between injection of decamethonium and of carbachol was significantly higher than the water intake in the period between the sham injection and injection of carbachol. The increased water intake after decamethonium may have resulted in reduced water intake after carbachol, since QUARTERMAIN and MILLER (1966) have shown that previous water loading lowers the water intake after carbachol stimulation. When the combined water intake after decamethonium and carbachol was compared with the combined water intake after sham injection and carbachol administration no significant differences could be demonstrated at any dose. Rather than having a blocking effect on drinking after carbachol decamethonium seems to have a stimulating effect by itself.

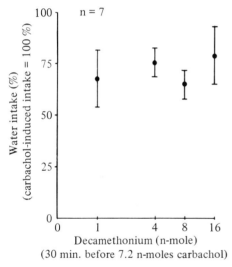

Fig. 5. The effects of different doses of decamethonium on the water intake in 1 hour following carbachol stimulation. Cf. Fig. 3

In order to test whether the effect of decamethonium on water intake is mediated by activation of a cholinergic system one group of rats was tested with 7.3 n-mole of carbachol or with 8 n-mole of decamethonium after administration of 1.3 n-mole atropine or 0.9 % saline in the tractus diagonalis. Water intake after administration of carbachol or decamethonium was

inhibited completely by atropine (Table 1). Therefore it is likely that decamethonium acts through muscarinic receptors.

Table 1. Water intake in 1 hour after administration of carbachol or decamethonium into the tractus diagonalis after a preceding injection of atropine. N = 6

	(Mean ± S.E. of mean)
7.2 n-mole carbachol 30 min after sham injection	16 ± 1.9 ml.
7.2 n-mole carbachol 30 min after 1.3 n-mole atropine	0
8 n-mole decamethonium 30 min after 1.3 n-mole atropine	0
7.2 n-mole carbachol 30 min after sham injection	13 ± 1.5 ml.

Experiment II

The Effect of Non-Cholinergic Drugs

In this series of tests we investigated the effects on water intake of central administration of noradrenaline 10, 20 and 40 n-mole (n = 7), isoprenaline 15, 30 and 60 n-mole (n = 8), serotonin from 2.5 to 39.5 n-mole (n = 7), histamine from 0.8 to 52.5 n-mole (n = 10) and angiotensin from 0.06 to 15.5 n-mole (n = 8).

Results

The effects on the water intake of administration of noradrenaline and isoprenaline in the tractus diagonalis are compared with the effects of 7.2 n-mole of carbachol (10.8 ± 1.0 ml. and 12.7 ± 2.7 ml. respectively) and expressed as percentage of water intake after carbachol (Fig. 6). Maximum water intakes after administration of noradrenaline and isoprenaline (respectively 6 % and 25 %) were not significantly different from water intakes after sham injection.

One cannula placement was incorrect in the group of rats in which histamine was tested. The

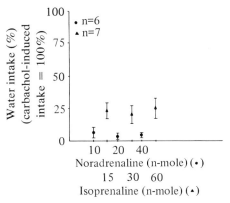

Fig. 6. Water intake in 1 hour after administration of different doses of noradrenaline and isoprenaline into the tractus diagonalis. Cf. Fig. 1

results of the tests in which histamine and serotonin were investigated are given in Figs. 7 and 8. After administration of serotonin as well as histamine no reproducible drinking behaviour was demonstrated. The maximum water intake after serotonin was 21 % and after histamine 36 % of carbachol drinking, but in spite of the wide range of doses no dose-response relationship could be demonstrated. Water intakes in the carbachol tests for the serotonin group amounted to 11.2 ± 2.3 ml. and for the histamine group to 10.1 ± 1.7 ml.

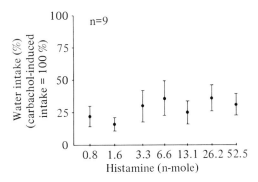

Fig. 7. Water intake within 1 hour after administration of different doses of histamine into the tractus diagonalis. Cf. Fig. 1

The effects of different doses of angiotensin dissolved in saline are given in Fig. 9. Some drinking could be observed after 2.58 n-mole.

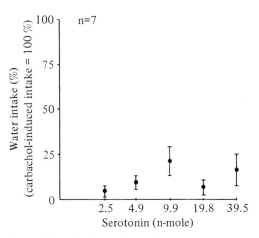

Fig. 8. Water intake in 1 hour after administration of different doses of serotonin into the tractus diagonalis. Cf. Fig. 1

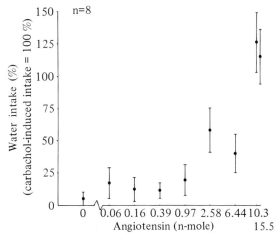

Fig. 9. Water intake in 1 hour after administration of different doses of angiotensin into the tractus diagonalis. Cf. Fig. 1

The drinking response was maximal at a dose of 10.3 n-mole of angiotensin. ANDERSSON, ERIKSSON, and OLTNER (1970) suppose that the effects of angiotensin on drinking are caused by an increase in permeability of the neurones for Na ions. This hypothesis was tested by giving different doses of angiotensin dissolved in different concentrations of NaCl to the same rats as were used in the last experiment. Fig. 10 shows that at no dosage of angiotensin was the water intake dependent on the concentration of NaCl.

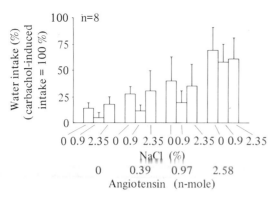

Fig. 10. Water intake in 1 hour after administration of different doses of angiotensin dissolved in NaCl solutions of different concentration. Cf. Fig. 1

Experiment III

The Specificity of Cholinergic Stimulation

As described earlier, cholinergic stimulation of limbic system structures can induce eating behaviour and effects on temperature regulation. It is not known how far these effects and drinking behaviour are interrelated. β-sympathomimetics also influence food intake and temperature. Therefore involvement of the tractus diagonalis in the central control of eating behaviour and temperature regulation was examined by administration of noradrenaline in doses known to influence body temperature and to stimulate food intake when injected into the hypothalamus. The effect of carbachol on food intake and temperature regulation with and without concomitant drinking behaviour was also tested.

A. The Effect of Noradrenaline and Carbachol on Body Temperature. At the start of the experiment the rats were put in restraint cages. Half an hour later the animals received a sham injection. One hour after the start of the experiment they were injected with noradrenaline or carbachol and the water intake in the next hour was measured to the nearest 0.1 ml. The temperature was continuously followed to the nearest 0.1 °C by means of a rectal thermocouple connected with a tele-thermometer (Yellow Spring Instruments).

Noradrenaline was administered in doses of 0.8, 1.5, 3.1, 6.2, 15.4 or 30.8 n-mole. The same rats (n = 6) were used in the carbachol

experiment and were given the standard dose of 7.2 n-mole carbachol. In three animals the effect of carbachol on temperature was investigated in the absence of water, in three others in the presence of water. Later the treatments were reversed for both groups of animals. When water was available it was presented to the animal after the sham injection at 30 min. Before and after the tests in which the effect of carbachol on temperature was being investigated carbachol was administered without measuring temperature.

Results

In two rats the cannulae were wrongly implanted. Results from these animals were not used in Fig. 11 and 12. As Fig. 11 shows, noradrenaline in doses known to reduce the body temperature by 2 ° C when administered into the hypothalamus (FELDBERG and MYERS, 1963), did not influence body temperature when injected into the tractus diagonalis.

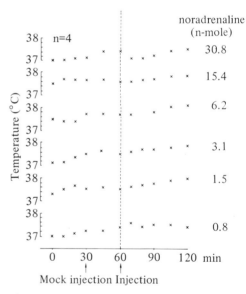

Fig. 11. Rectal temperature changes in 1 hour preceding and 1 hour following the administration of different doses of noradrenaline into the tractus diagonalis. Values are means of four observations

The small temperature changes after carbachol stimulation did not differ from the changes in body temperature before carbachol administration (see Fig. 12). This was also the case in the experiment in which water was available. Drinking a large amount of relatively cold water did not influence body temperature.

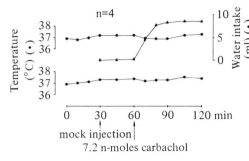

Fig. 12. Rectal temperature changes in 1 hour preceding and 1 hour following the administration of 7.2 n-mole of carbachol into the tractus diagonalis. In the lower part of the Figure rectal temperature changes are given when water was not available and in the upper part temperature changes and cumulative water intake are represented for when water was available to the animal

Conversely, actually measuring the body temperature had no statistically significant effect on the amount of water which an animal drank in response to carbachol stimulation. When temperature was measured during drinking the mean response to carbachol was 8.8 ml. of water. Before and after this series of tests the responses to carbachol were 12.2 ml. and 11.2 ml. respectively.

B. The Effect of Noradrenaline and Carbachol on Food Intake. In the following experiment in which the effects of noradrenaline and carbachol on food intake were tested the methods were essentially the same as described in the methods section. Half an hour after the sham injection of 7.2 n-mole of carbachol, 20 n-mole of noradrenaline or isotonic NaCl was injected into the tractus diagonalis of 6 rats. This dose of noradrenaline is known to induce eating reliably when administered in the hypothalamic region (SLANGEN and MILLER, 1969). Food intake in the next hour was measured by comparing the weight of the food left, including the spillage, with the weight of the food that was offered at the start of the test (about 10 g).

Results

Injection of carbachol or noradrenaline into the tractus diagonalis resulted in intakes of food of 0.6 ± 0.3 g and 0.7 ± 0.2 g respectively, values not significantly different from the intakes in control NaCl tests (0.4 ± 0.3 g and 0.4 ± 0.2 g respectively).

Discussion

From the results of experiment I it appears that cholinergic stimulation of the tractus diagonalis does not necessarily induce drinking behaviour. Stimulation by carbachol or pilocarpine enhances water intake, stimulation by nicotine does not. The assumption that the effects of carbachol and pilocarpine are mediated through muscarinic receptors is supported also by the following results.

Carbachol-induced drinking is inhibited by previous administration of the muscarinic inhibiting drug atropine, but the anti-nicotinic drug hexamethonium has no effect. Additional evidence for the involvement of muscarinic receptors is provided by the results with decamethonium. This drug influences nicotinic receptors in skeletal muscle. However, the block produced by decamethonium bromide seems to be the result of an abnormally prolonged transmitter-like action in which initial excitation is rapidly succeeded by inexcitability (BURNS and PATON, 1951).

The acetylcholine-like action of decamethonium may be responsible for drinking produced by this drug in the diagonal band. The reduced water intake in response to carbachol after pretreatment with decamethonium can be explained by assuming a prolonged depolarization of part of the cholinoceptive cell population in the diagonal band caused by decamethonium. But it can also be explained by assuming that homeostatic mechanisms prevent an overloading of the animal with water. The water intake caused by decamethonium then functions in the same way as a preload of water given before the carbachol treatment which of course reduces the effect of carbachol on drinking (QUARTERMAIN and MILLER, 1966). As Fig. 7 shows the previous administration of the muscarinic blocker atropine prevents the effect of decamethonium on water intake completely. This indicates that decamethonium acts on muscarinic receptors.

Stimulation of several limbic structures with non-cholinergic drugs can induce drinking behaviour (EPSTEIN, FITZSIMONS, and ROLLS, 1970; EATON, 1968; GOLDMAN, LEHR, and FRIEDMAN, 1971). The results from experiment II, however, show convincingly that the tractus diagonalis is insensitive to a rather wide range of doses of sympathomimetics, serotonin and histamine. Only very high doses of angiotensin into the tractus diagonalis enhance water intake. ANDERSSON, ERIKSSON, and OLTNER (1970) claim that the effect of angiotensin on water intake is mediated by osmotic stimulation resulting from an increase in the permeability to Na^+ ions of the tissue between the site of injection and the cells playing a role in drinking behaviour. Administration of angiotensin, dissolved in NaCl-solutions of different concentrations, did not support this hypothesis: water intakes after administration of a low dose of angiotensin in different NaCl-solutions did not differ. Since administration of even a 2.35 % NaCl-solution + angiotensin did not induce drinking, we suppose that ANDERSSON's hypothesis does not hold for the tractus diagonalis.

We may conclude that the structures in the tractus diagonalis that mediate changes in drinking behaviour are specifically sensitive to muscarinic drugs.

The results of experiment III indicate that injection of noradrenaline or carbachol into the tractus diagonalis does not stimulate food intake. Therefore, drinking behaviour seems to be a direct effect of cholinergic stimulation and not secondary to increased food intake. It also appeared from experiment III that neither noradrenaline nor carbachol influenced body temperature. Therefore, the enhanced water intake seen after cholinergic stimulation of the tractus diagonalis cannot be due to stimulation of a system playing a role in the regulation of the body temperature.

It should be emphasized, however, that our results do not necessarily imply any involvement of the tractus diagonalis in drinking behaviour elicited by stimuli that differ from the stimuli that are concomitant with central application of carbachol. We have presented data elsewhere suggesting that the tractus diagonalis may only be involved to a minor extent in deprivation-induced drinking and probably not at all in drinking induced by hyperosmolarity (TERPSTRA and SLANGEN, 1972 b).

Summary

The specificity of cholinergic stimulation of the tractus diagonalis, known to induce drinking behaviour, was investigated by comparing the effects of cholinergic (muscarinic and nicotinic), anticholinergic and non-cholinergic stimulation of the tractus diagonalis. Carbachol, pilocarpine, decamethonium and angiotensin II induced drinking behaviour. The effect of decamethonium could possibly be ascribed to its mechanism of action; the effect of angiotensin II, however, is not readily explained, at least not in the doses used (0.06–15.5 n-mole). Nicotine, noradrenaline, isoprenaline, serotonin and histamine had no effects on water intake. Atropine and decamethonium had an inhibitory effect on carbachol-induced drinking; hexamethonium had no effect.

It is concluded that the tractus diagonalis contains structures specifically sensitive to muscarinic stimulation. The drinking behaviour induced by muscarinic stimulation seems to be a specific effect: no relationship could be demonstrated between drinking behaviour elicited by chemical stimulation and eating behaviour or temperature regulation.

Acknowledgement. The research work discussed in this article was supported by the Netherlands Organization for the Advancement of Pure Research (Z. W. O.).

References

ANDERSSON, B., ERIKSSON, L., OLTNER, R.: Further evidence for angiotensin-sodium interaction in central control of fluid balance. Life Sci. Oxford **9**, 1091–1096 (1970).

Burns, B. D., Paton, W. D. M.: Depolarization of motor end plate by decamethonium and acetylcholine. J. Physiol. Lond. **115**, 41–73 (1951).

Eaton, L. G.: The Merck Index; an Encyclopedia of Chemicals and Drugs, 8th edition, p. 833. Rahway, New Jersey: Merck and Co. Inc. 1968.

Epstein, A. N., Fitzsimons, J. T., Rolls, B. J.: Drinking induced by injection of angiotensin into the brain of the rat. J. Physiol. Lond. **210**, 457–474 (1970).

Feldberg, W., Myers, R. D.: A new concept of temperature regulation by amines in the hypothalamus. Nature **200**, 1325 (1963).

Fisher, A. E., Coury, J. N.: Cholinergic tracing of a central neural circuit underlying the thirst drive. Science **138**, 691–693 (1962).

Fitzsimons, J. T., Setler, P. E.: Catecholaminergic mechanisms in angiotensin-induced drinking. J. Physiol. Lond. **218**, 43P–45P (1971).

Goldman, H. W., Lehr, D., Friedman, E.: Antagonistic effects of alpha- and beta-adrenergically coded hypothalamic neurones on the consummatory behaviour in the rat. Nature **231**, 453–455 (1971).

Grossman, S. P.: Eating or drinking elicited by direct adrenergic or cholinergic stimulation of the hypothalamus. Science **132**, 301–302 (1960).

— Direct adrenergic and cholinergic stimulation of hypothalamic mechanism. Am. J. Physiol. **202**, 872–882 (1962).

Jonge, H. de: Inleiding tot de medische statistiek. Verh. Nederl. Inst. Prev. Geneesk., Leiden **2**, 486–487 (1964).

Koelle, G. B.: Neuromuscular blocking agents. In: The Pharmacological Basis of Therapeutics, 4th edition (Eds. L. S. Goodman, A. Gilman), pp. 601–619. London, Toronto: The Macmillan Comp. 1970.

Leibowitz, S. F.: Hypothalamic alpha- and beta-adrenergic systems regulate both thirst and hunger in the rat. Proc. nat. Acad. Sci., Wash. **68**, 332–334 (1971).

Quartermain, D., Miller, N. E.: Sensory feedback in time response of drinking elicited by carbachol in preoptic area of rat. J. comp. physiol. Psychol. **62**, 350–353 (1966).

Slangen, J. L., Miller, N. E.: Pharmacological tests for the function of hypothalamic norepinephrine in eating behaviour. Physiol. Behav. **4**, 543–552 (1969).

Terpstra, G. K., Slangen, J. L.: Central blockade of (methyl)-atropine on carbachol drinking: a dose-response study. Physiol. Behav. **8**, 715–719 (1972a).

— The role of the tractus diagonalis in drinking behaviour induced by central chemical stimulation, water deprivation and salt injection. Neuropharmacol. **11**, 807–817 (1972b).

Increased Drinking in Rats after Isoniazid Withdrawal

S. ALDER and G. ZBINDEN

In animal toxicity studies it is standard practice to monitor food and water consumption. Changes in these parameters are not only sensitive indicators of general toxicity but may also uncover interesting pharmacological qualities of the test drugs. For example, in chronic toxicity studies on chlordiazepoxide an appetite stimulating effect was discovered which proved to be characteristic of a particular type of antianxiety agents (ZBINDEN and RANDALL, 1961). Chlordiazepoxide also stimulated drinking, an effect known to occur with compounds of various pharmacological classes, e. g. levorphanol, hypnotic barbiturates (SCHMIDT, 1964), antithyroid drugs (FREGLY and TAYLOR, 1964), atropine (SOULAIRAC, 1969), isoprenaline (LEHR, MALLOW, and KRUKOWSKI, 1967) and serotonin (GOLDMAN, KRUKOWSKI, and LEHR, 1968). In this paper increased water consumption by rats treated with isoniazid (INH) is reported. It was accidentally observed during a subacute toxicity study and differed from the effect of the above named drugs in that drinking was not stimulated until 24 hours after withdrawal.

Materials and Methods

CFN Gif rats (Tierzuchtinstitut der Universität Zürich) weighing 38 to 53 g were housed singly in Macrolone cages and received Nafag 850 rat pellets ad libitum. INH (purum, Fluka AG, Buchs, SG, Switzerland) was dissolved in water and administered five times weekly by stomach tube. An equal number of control rats received corresponding volumes of water. Treatments were given between 8.30 and 9.00 a. m. Two bottles, one containing distilled water, the other 0.06 % NaCl solution were offered simultaneously. Their position was changed daily. Fluid consumption was measured between 9 and 10 a. m. The treatment-free period was on Saturdays and Sundays, with the exception of one experiment in which it was on Wednesdays and Thursdays.

Since the supplier discontinued breeding of the CFN rats all further experiments were conducted with Siv 50 rats. Groups of female animals were treated with INH or water five times weekly by stomach tube as described. Only one drinking bottle containing distilled water was offered. After typical drinking behaviour was established rats received subcutaneous injections of 0.5, 1.0 or 2.0 mg/kg of propranolol (Inderal, ICI) or 1.0 or 2.0 mg/kg of azapetine phosphate (Ilidar, Roche, courtesy Dr. Chr. POLZER, F. Hoffmann-La Roche Inc. Basel). Each rat received 3 injections given at 4 p. m. on Fridays and at 10 a. m. on Saturdays and Sundays. Water intake was measured as described.

The effect of INH and INH withdrawal on water and electrolyte excretion was evaluated as follows. 12 female rats (Siv 50) weighing 143–172 g received by stomach tube 200 mg/kg INH 5 times weekly for 2 weeks. Before treatment, after 4 and 9 doses and on the 3rd and the 11th day after the last dose, all rats were given 5 ml. of tap water by stomach tube and were placed in metabolism cages for 24 hr. Total urine, sodium, potassium, chloride and calcium excretion were determined. Two groups of 6 female rats weighing 134–152 g received 5 daily oral doses of 400 mg/kg INH or equal volumes of water. Six and 3 days before the beginning of the treatment, after the 2nd and the 5th dose and 3 and 7 days after the last dose the diuretic response to a water load was measured according to the procedure of HAM and LANDIS (1942.). Rats were fasted for 12 hours and received a priming dose corresponding to 2.5% of body weight of 0.2% NaCl solution per stomach tube. Two hours later the animals were given the hydrating dose of the same NaCl solution equivalent to 5 % of the original body weight. They were placed individually in metabolism cages, and cumulative urine excretion was measured every 15 min for 3 hr.

Effect of INH Treatment and Withdrawal on Fluid Intake

On treatment days total fluid consumption was depressed in animals receiving 600 mg/kg INH (not shown in Fig. 1). It did not differ from that of the controls at INH doses of 25 to 400 mg/kg (Fig. 1). All rats drank more of the 0.06 % saline than of distilled water. Saline intake varied from 70 to 80 % of the total fluid consumption. On treatment-free days, starting 24 hr after the last INH dose, animals increased fluid intake

markedly. This increase was statistically significant at doses of 200 mg/kg and 400 mg/kg. It was also present but not statistically significant in the groups receiving 50 and 100 mg/kg, and was not seen in those treated with 25 mg/kg and in all control groups. Doses of 600 mg/kg were toxic and depressed food and fluid intake markedly; drinking was increased on weekends, but variations between animals were so marked that statistical significance was not reached. The effect on fluid intake was demonstrated with rats of both sexes, and regardless whether the treatment-free period was scheduled on weekends or an working days (Table 1). Preference for saline remained unchanged during INH treatment and after INH withdrawal. Increased drinking on treatment-free days was also seen in rats which had access to distilled water only. Figure 1 demonstrates a typical experiment showing total fluid consumption of rats treated with 400 mg/kg INH or equal volumes of water. Increase in drinking had already occurred after the first week of INH treatment but became more pronounced as the experiment progressed.

Rats receiving three injections of the β-sympathetic blocking drug propranolol and the α-blocker azapetine phosphate at the end of each 5 day INH treatment period, showed the same increased fluid intake as INH treated rats which were given saline injections instead of sympathetic blocking agents.

Table 1. Effect of INH withdrawal on drinking of rats

INH mg/kg 5 times weekly	No. of rats per group	Sex	Strain	Fluid offered 0.06% NaCl	Water	Treatm.-free days	Duration of Treatm. (weeks)	Increased Drinking on Treatment-free days (p[a])
25	10	F	CFN	+	+	Sat. Sun	4	no ($p > 0.1$)
50	10	F	CFN	+	+	Sat. Sun.	4	no ($0.1 > p > 0.05$)
100	10	F	CFN	+	+	Sat. Sun.	4	no ($0.1 > p > 0.05$)
200	8	F	CFN	+	+	Sat. Sun.	8	yes ($p < 0.001$)
200	10	F	CFN	+	+	Wed. Thurs.	6	yes ($p < 0.001$)
200	10	M	CFN	+	+	Sat. Sun.	8	yes ($p < 0.001$)
200	10	F	SIV	−	+	Sat. Sun.	2	yes ($p < 0.001$)
400	8	F	CFN	+	+	Sat. Sun.	5	yes ($p < 0.001$)
600	8	F	CFN	+	+	Sat. Sun.	4	yes?[b]

[a] Mean daily consumption of fluid on all treatment days was compared with that during all treatment-free periods using Student's t test.
[b] Toxic; marked depression of drinking during treatment periods.

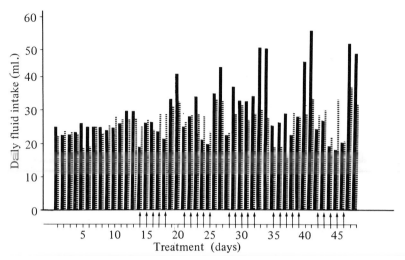

Fig. 1. Fluid intake of rats treated with 400 mg/kg INH intragastrically. Black columns: INH intragastric. Striated columns: intragastric water (controls)

24 hr urine excretion was measured once before, twice during and twice after a 2 week treatment with 200 mg/kg INH. Three days after cessation of therapy 10 out of 12 rats excreted slightly more urine than at any time before or

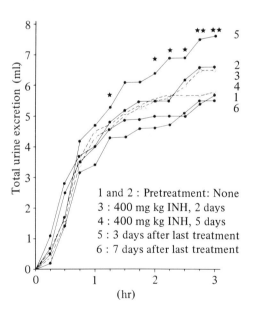

Fig. 2. Urine excretion after hydrating dose of 0.2% NaCl solution (Method of Ham and Landis, 1942) mean of 6 rats. * Statistically significant ($p < 0.05$) compared to both pretreatment curves. ** Statistically significant ($p < 0.01$) compared to both pretreatment curves. (WILCOXON's signed rank test)

during INH treatment. One week later urine volume decreased again in 7 of the 12 animals. There was no significant change in the 24 hr excretion of Na and Cl. In 11 rats 24 hr K excretion was higher on the 3rd day after INH withdrawal than at any time before. After 1 week it had decreased to control levels in 10 rats. There was also a slight increase in Ca excretion on the third day after INH withdrawal in 8 of the 12 rats of the group. On the 11th post-treatment day it was lower than on the 3rd in 11 animals.

Water excretion during a 3 hr period following a hydrating dose of 0.2 % NaCl solution is shown in Figure 2. Urine flow measured twice before and twice during INH treatment did not differ significantly. On the 3rd day after the last INH dose, however, rats excreted significantly more water than before and during INH treatment. 7 days after the last INH treatment rats handled the hydrating dose of NaCl solution normally.

Discussion

Apart from its well recognized effects on peripheral nerves (BIEHL and NIMITZ, 1954) INH also affects the central nervous system: at appropriate doses the drug causes convulsions and lowers the threshold for other convulsant agents (DIENEMANN and SIMON, 1953). These effects are thought to be related to a chemical interaction with pyridoxal phosphate (HOLTZ and PALM, 1964). Recently experimental evidence for an analgesic action and an effect on thirst were reported (ALDER and ZBINDEN, 1973). The change in drinking behaviour was peculiar in that it only developed a day or two after the administration of the drug had been discontinued. Preliminary observations (ALDER, unpublished) indicated that at least 5 daily doses of 200 mg/kg INH were necessary to elicit the drinking response after withdrawal. Lower doses or fewer administrations were not sufficient to induce a significant change in water intake.

Most drugs known to increase drinking act only while they are administered. An exception is amphetamine which increased fluid intake of rats not only during administration but also after withdrawal. In this case, however, the drinking response was only seen when 1 % NaCl was offered, but not when the animals were given water (SOULAIRAC 1969). It appears, therefore, that the increase in drinking after INH withdrawal constitutes an unique effect. It is difficult to speculate about a possible mechanism of action. An effect on the central sympathetic nervous system, such as was demonstrated for the drinking response of rats after isoprenaline (LEHR et al. 1967) and serotonin (GOLDMAN et al. 1968) is not probable since treatment with the α-blocker azapetine phosphate and the β-blocking agent propranolol failed to influence the increase in drinking.

A first indication that increased fluid intake might be associated with diuresis was obtained in an experiment in which rats were given 5 ml. of water and were then placed in metabolism cages for 24 hr without access to food and water. On the third day after INH withdrawal most animals excreted more urine than before or during treatment. Total Na and Cl excretion, however, did not change. K and Ca excretion was increased in most animals on the third day after INH withdrawal. There is no simple explanation for the increase in K and Ca excretion. Water diuresis, however, might be related to a disturbance in neurosecretion or release of vasopressin (vpr). To test this possibility further the

assay procedure of HAM and LANDIS (1942) was used. With this method in which urine excretion is measured after a hydrating dose of 0.2 % NaCl solution, as little as 0.5 mu. of pitressin can be measured in rats. On the third day after INH withdrawal the rats excreted significantly more urine than before and during treatment and 7 days after discontinuation of INH administration. This finding suggests that a concomitant enhancement of drinking and of water diuresis occurs in rats which were previously subjected to intensive treatment with INH. Since urine excretion was increased in rats which did not have free access to water, it is probable that tubular water reabsorption was impaired perhaps through a disturbance of the vpr mechanism. Increased drinking could then be a consequence of an excessive water loss.

From the toxicological point of view it should be noted that the INH doses which caused the change in drinking behaviour were within or close to the toxic range. The animals, particularly those given 400 or 600 mg/kg, were clearly irritated and often went into convulsions when handled. It is not unexpected, therefore, that discontinuation of a chemical which affects many biochemical and physiological processes in the brain (HOLTZ and PALM, 1964) was followed by a disturbance of the water balance. This transient alteration of a physiological regulation could thus be regarded as one of a variety of withdrawal symptoms which occur commonly after prolonged administration of excessive amounts of drugs which act on the central nervous system.

Acknowledgements
We thank Miss G. ODERMATT, Mr. C. HAEBERLIN and Mr. H. NEF for technical assistance.

References

ALDER, S., ZBINDEN, G.: Use of pharmacological screening tests in subacute neurotoxicity studies of isoniazid, pyridoxine HCl and hexachlorophene. Agents and Actions **3/4**, 233–243 (1973).
BIEHL, I. P., NIMITZ, H. J.: Studies on the use of a high dose of isoniazid. Am. Rev. Tuberc. **70**, 430–441 (1954).

DIENEMANN, G., SIMON, K.: Mitteilung eines Todesfalles nach kombinierter Verabreichung von Irgapyrin und Neoteben (INH). SIMON, K.: Tierexperimentelle Untersuchungen in der vorstehenden Arbeit. Münch. med. Wschr. **95**, 221–222 (1953).

FREGLY, M. J., TAYLOR, R. E. Jr.: Effect of hypothyroidism on water and sodium exchange in rats. In: "Thirst" Proceedings of 1st International Symposium on Thirst in the Regulation of Body Water (ed. M. J. WAYNER), pp. 139–175. Oxford: Pergamon Press 1964.

GUILLEMIN, W., KRUKOWSKI, M., LEHR, D.: Prevention of serotonin (5-HT) induced water conservation by beta-adrenergic blockade. Fed. Proc. **27**, 559 (1968).

HAM, G. C., LANDIS, E. M.: A comparison of pituitrin with the antidiuretic substance found in human urine and placenta, J. Clin. Invest. **21**, 455–470 (1942).

HOLTZ, P., PALM, D.: Pharmacological aspects of vitamin B6. Pharm. Rev. **16**, 113–178 (1964).

LEHR, D., MALLOW, J., KRUKOWSKI, M.: Copious drinking and simultaneous inhibition of urine flow elicited by beta-adrenergic stimulation and contrary effect of alpha-adrenergic stimulation. J. Pharmac. Exp. Ther. **158**, 150–163 (1967).

SCHMIDT, H. Jr.: Water intake as an index of drug action. In: "Thirst", Proceedings of the 1st International Symposium on Thirst in the Regulation of Body Water (ed. M. J. WAYNER), pp. 185–209. Oxford: Pergamon Press 1964.

SOULAIRAC, A.: The adrenergic and cholinergic control of food and water intake. Ann. N. Y. Acad. Sci. **157**, 934–961 (1969).

ZBINDEN, G., RANDALL, L. O.: Pharmacology of benzodiazepines: Laboratory and Clinical correlations. Adv. Pharmacol. **5**, 213–291 (1967).

Summary of Discussions

STRICKER to HUSTON: There is increased dopamine turnover in the nigrostriatal bundle following spreading cortical depression. Perhaps this is somehow involved in ingestive behaviour. It is also relevant that TEITELBAUM and CYTAWA found that spreading cortical depression reinstates aphagia and adipsia in rats recovered from lateral hypothalamic damage. Presumably catecholamine synthesis could not keep pace with the increased turnover leading therefore to decreased synaptic activity. — HUSTON: The possible involvement of striatal dopamine in the caudate and cortical spreading depression-induced behaviour is a highly speculative, but reasonable hypothesis, open to test. — LE MAGNEN: Have you tried spreading depression in the amygdala? — HUSTON: We have not induced spreading depression in the amygdala. It is very possible, however, that the amygdala is involved in the spreading-depression-induced consumatory behaviour. A wave of spreading depression induced in the cortex of rats, in most instances, enters the amygdala on its way to the striatum, and vice versa. — LE MAGNEN: Your results of spreading depression in the hippocampus are interesting since hippocampal lesioning has rarely been shown to modify ingestive behaviour.

EPSTEIN: There are 2 methods in general use for injection of chemicals into the brain in the study of drinking. In one, the animal is removed from its cage and restrained while an injection is made. It is then returned, sometimes to a test chamber, and is allowed to behave. In the other, the animal is handled for insertion of a loaded injector. It is returned to its home-cage, given time to settle down, and then injected from a remote syringe. When high doses are used and large phenomena elicited, very little is lost by using the first technique. But, when threshold studies are attempted and when latencies are in question, handling the animal immediately before injection and testing outside ist home-cage should be avoided. — CHARLEBOIS: The Barbary dove (*Streptopelia risoria*) drank more to intracranial angiotensin II and the latency of onset was shorter when the injections were made into a bird that was resting instead of being engaged in some other activity. — SLANGEN: We give a mock injection about $1/2$ hr before the real injection. We compare the behaviour produced by the drug with what happens after the mock injection as well as saline. — SIMPSON: If a filled injector is placed in the guide cannula and the animal then allowed a period to settle down drug may diffuse into the brain before the injection is made. — FITZSIMONS: Allowing the animal to settle down in its testing cage gives it a chance to complete its arousal drinking before the dipsogen is injected. — LEENEN: Simply handling the animals stresses them. Renin levels may be 5–10 times normal. — WEIJNEN: Behaviour may become manifest only at night if the dipsogenic stimulation is weak. — STRICKER: After subcutaneous formalin or PG, drinking of 3% NaCl may only occur 6–10 hr after injection, though 0.9% NaCl is taken within 30–60 min. This is apparently not a circadian effect. — FITZSIMONS: FLUX and myself have found increased intake of 2.7% NaCl within 1–2 hr of subcutaneous formalin. Delayed intakes may be attributable to pain or incapacitation generally.

Section 9
Conclusions

Summary and Comment

J. T. FITZSIMONS

It is appropriate since the meeting on which this book is based took place in Switzerland to call to mind the names and work of three pioneers in our field, two of whom were Swiss by birth and the third Swiss by adoption since he spent the last 20 years of his life in Geneva. It is also useful for our purposes to remember these men because they represent three classical themes in the physiology of thirst which are evident to the present day. ALBRECHT VON HALLER was born in Berne in 1708 and studied medicine under BOERHAAVE and ALBINUS in Tübingen and Leyden. He travelled widely throughout Europe and in 1736 was invited by GEORGE II, Elector of Hanover, to the Chair of Anatomy, Surgery and Botany in the newly founded University of Göttingen. He remained there until 1753 when he retired to Berne. The "Elementa Physiologiae", an extensive and copiously documented compendium of all that was known in physiology at the time, was published between 1757 and 1765. In it there is a chapter entitled "Fames et Sitis" which gives a vivid account of a *dry-mouth* theory of thirst.

MORITZ SCHIFF, born in Frankfurt-am-Main in 1823, studied under MAGENDIE and LONGET in Paris, went to Florence in 1863 and then to Geneva in 1876 where he remained until his death in 1896. SCHIFF is firmly in the tradition of the Paris school as exemplified by MAGENDIE and LONGET, and by BERNARD under whose influence SCHIFF came. He taught that thirst is a *general sensation* arising from a lack of water in the tissues and he was obviously unimpressed by any contribution that a dry mouth might make to

the sensation. His own work and that of his teachers led him to conclude that the passage of water through the oropharyngeal region is neither necessary nor sufficient to relieve thirst.

WALTER RUDOLPH HESS's distinguished experiments on the behaviour resulting from electrical stimulation of the diencephalon in the conscious animal represent the third classical theme in the physiology of thirst. HESS was born in Frauenfeld in 1881 and died at the age of 92 only this year. He spent his professional life in Zurich and received the Nobel Prize in Physiology and Medicine in 1949. It is a pleasure to record the fact that Dr. M. BRÜGGER, one of HESS's pupils, lives in Lugano and attended our meeting. It was she, who in 1943 published the classical paper from HESS's laboratory on electrically induced ingestive behaviour. HESS's work later influenced ANDERSSON, in his study of electrically induced drinking in the goat. HESS and his colleagues favoured the concept of a *localised thirst centre* somewhere in the brain, suggested first by NOTHNAGEL in 1881, and extended by PAGET, BAILEY, and BREMER in the intervening years.

Let me now give a personal summary of what I have learned at this symposium.

The papers of WEIJNEN, NICOLAÏDIS and ROWLAND, and KISSILEFF remind us of the importance of oropharyngeal stimuli in the control of water intake. WEIJNEN found that warm water is less satiating than cold, and that the thirsty rat will lick a metal spout to obtain a small electrical shock. NICOLAÏDIS and ROWLAND showed that the rat can learn to obtain

189

sufficient water to maintain itself by self-injecting water through an intracardiac cannula and indeed it can regulate its intake to some extent because a higher ambient temperature or salt in the diet leads to increased self-injection. On the other hand there was no self-injection response to such unnatural thirst stimuli as systemic hypertonic NaCl, haemorrhage, hyperoncotic colloid, or to central angiotensin or carbachol. Oral intake may have an important fail-safe role as also shown by the asymptotic volume of 10 ml./24 hr drunk when large amounts of water are infused intragastrically or intravenously. There is a basic need to drink water and this need is not met if water bypasses the oropharynx. KISSILEFF and myself have been in disagreement for a number of years on whether there is a non-homeostatic determinant of water intake. The question now seems to be resolved with NICOLAÏDIS and ROWLAND's demonstration that there is an oral need to drink not related to a homeostatic or systemic need. KISSILEFF reported here that there also seems to be a non-homeostatic determinant of saline intake in the adrenalectomized rat for he found that intragastric infusion of 3 % NaCl in amounts that the rat would drink spontaneously failed to stop the animal from taking some 3 % NaCl by mouth. The actual act of drinking, whether it be of water or saline, is important to the animal regardless of whether there is an internal need for fluid or not.

KOZLOWSKI suggested that the circulating blood volume is controlled by thirst and the hypothalamo-hypophysial antidiuretic system. Hypovolaemia causes reduced filling of the left atrium and fewer inhibitory impulses to these systems which therefore become sensitised to osmotic stimuli. Increased vasopressin (vpr.) causes decreased urine flow and a redistribution of blood towards the central part of the circulation. Eventually there is enhanced drinking owing to the increased osmotic reactivity of the thirst centre produced by vpr. and to the diminished input of nervous impulses from the left atrium. The failure of right vagosympathectomy to influence responses to hypovolaemia is puzzling and the finding that vpr. influences water intake in the dog is in contrast to the absence of any effect in the rat. These differences between mammals are of course extremely interesting and important.

MORTON described a sensitive radioimmunoassay for vasopressin and he reported its use in a case of diabetes insipidus which progressed to loss of thirst and severe dehydration owing to destructive invasion of the hypothalamic thirst neurones. On one occasion the plasma vpr. was found to be 4.5 pg/ml. (Normal 4.0–8.0 pg/ml.; dehydrated 6.0–13.5 pg/ml.) and the plasma angiotensin II 510 pg/ml. (Normal 5.0–35.0 pg/ml.) which may have accounted for the oliguria. The extent of the response of the renin-angiotensin system to severe dehydration is noteworthy.

HAACK found that rats with hereditary diabetes insipidus suffer from mild starvation possibly related to the consequences of dehydration such as hyperosmolality, increased activity of the renin-angiotensin system and distension of the stomach. All the changes except the increased osmolality were reversed by treatment with vasopressin which may mean that increased activity of the renin-angiotensin system is responsible for increased thirst in untreated diabetes insipidus especially as there is evidence that there is no cellular dehydration in the disease. This is certainly an interesting new explanation of polydipsia in diabetes insipidus.

KAUFMAN reported that the common iguana has an efficient albeit sluggish osmometric thirst mechanism. After injection of hypertonic solutions of substances excluded from the cells the amounts of water drunk were precisely the amounts needed to dilute the solute to isotonicity though the animals sometimes did not drink for up to 4 hr after injection. The iguana drank more water than the intact rat and about the same quantity of water as the nephrectomized rat to a given osmotic load. In view of the fact that the iguana became practically anuric after a hypertonic osmotic load this result is reasonable and is a striking vindication of the use of nephrectomized rats in the study of osmometric thirst. It suggests that comparative studies may provide valuable insights into mammalian thirst mechanisms.

STRICKER on the basis of experiments with intraventricular 6-hydroxydopamine confirmed UNGERSTEDT's suggestion that the adipsia and aphagia after lateral hypothalamic lesioning are attributable, in part, to transection of the ascending dopamine-containing neurones of the nigrostriatal bundle. He suggested that residual deficits of regulation may reflect the fact that the recovered systems can no longer respond to abrupt and large ingestive stimuli though they may respond appropriately under *ad libitum* conditions when the development of nutritional needs is more gradual. He also found, in confirmation of work by FITZSIMONS and SETLER, that angiotensin-induced drinking was abolished by 6-hydroxydopamine. This made him question the involvement of intracranial angiotensin in polyethylene glycol- and isoprenaline-induced drinking since neither of these were affected by 6-hydroxydopamine.

The role of catecholaminergic mechanisms in eating and drinking was further considered by SETLER who pointed out that the inhibitory role in drinking originally postulated for catecholaminergic mechanisms is an artifact and that the true physiological role of catecholamines is to facilitate eating and drinking. A different catecholamine is involved in each behaviour. Noradrenaline causes eating by activating "command" synapses. The thirst-inducing catecholamine, which may be dopamine, acts less directly, and it might work in conjunction with angiotensin or with cholinergic neurones.

SZCZEPANSKA-SADOWSKA reported that in the dog isoprenaline injected subcutaneously was an even more potent stimulus to drinking than in the rat. She found that, unlike in the rat, the response could still be obtained after nephrectomy. This was disputed by ROLLS who also found that the angiotensin receptor blocker, saralasin acetate, would prevent isoprenaline-induced drinking. SZCZEPANSKA-SADOWSKA and FITZSIMONS believe that drinking in response to isoprenaline is brought about both by hormonal and by non-hormonal mechanisms, the latter being unaffected by nephrectomy, whereas ROLLS and RAMSAY suggest that the response is mediated exclusively by the renin-angiotensin system as many believe to be the case in the rat. SZCZEPANSKA-SADOWSKA and FITZSIMONS found that the dog drinks in response to intravenous renin but that intravenous angiotensin, unless there is an accompanying

osmotic stimulus, is ineffective. They found that, in the dog, components of the renin-angiotensin system generally caused less drinking when given intravenously than intracranially, whereas the reverse was true for isoprenaline.

COOLING reported that the cat drinks in response to intracranial isoprenaline but these responses were not compared with possible responses produced by peripheral administration of the drug.

LEHR questioned the contribution of the renin-angiotensin system to β-adrenergic drinking in the rat. The angiotensin converting enzyme antagonist SQ 20881 enhanced β-adrenergic-induced drinking when it was given systemically but had no effect when given into the cerebral ventricles though intraventricular SQ 20881 would block drinking evoked by peripheral renin.

LEENEN also questioned an exclusive role for the renin-angiotensin system in drinking following a number of different thirst stimuli. No simple quantitative or temporal relationships were found between plasma renin and water intake after these stimuli. There was no drinking after methoxamine despite an increase in plasma renin. After certain doses of histamine and isoprenaline that produced similar intakes of water, drinking occured more rapidly after histamine though the renin level was lower. Renin levels were high after polyethylene glycol, histamine and isoprenaline but other studies have shown that only drinking in response to isoprenaline is completely abolished by nephrectomy; histamine-induced drinking is less affected and polyethylene glycol-induced drinking not at all. If the increase in circulating plasma renin is causally related to water intake, other factors must potentiate or decrease its dipsogenic action.

MEYER on the other hand was firmly of the opinion that drinking to some hypotensive drugs results from activation of the renin-angiotensin system, either reflexly or by direct stimulation of β-receptors. In such cases plasma renin levels correlated well with increased drinking and both responses were prevented by the β-adrenergic antagonist L-propranolol. Increased drinking and plasma renin from reflex activation of the sympathetic system by the α-antagonist phentolamine was prevented by ganglionic block, but ganglionic block did not interfere with the responses to direct receptor stimulation by β-adrenergic agonists such as isoprenaline.

The mechanisms of β-adrenergic drinking continue to excite interest. The experiments reported here indicate that it is by no means established that the response is mediated exclusively by the renin-angiotensin system. Indeed much evidence suggests that it is not, nor do we know whether there are central β-adrenergic thirst neurones as originally suggested by LEHR and his colleagues and by LEIBOWITZ.

EPSTEIN has in a characteristically elegant study shown that by testing animals in their home cages it is possible to make rats drink by infusing physiological amounts of angiotensin I or II. Furthermore intravenous angiotensin-induced drinking can be prevented by prior administration of systemic saralasin acetate, a receptor blocker for angiotensin.

FITZSIMONS pointed out that production of renin and angiotensin is phylogenetically older than synthesis and secretion of aldosterone. However, even in species, in which aldosterone is absent, renal renin levels are still inversely proportional to sodium balance. The physiological significance of the cerebral renin-angiotensin system, particularly in relation to the dipsogenic actions of components of the renin-angiotensin system injected into the brain, is uncertain as is the relationship between renal renin and cerebral renin. The cerebral system, however, explains why renin and peptide precursors of angiotensin II are effective dipsogens, and in experiments carried out with EPSTEIN and JOHNSON using antiangiotensin II serum and peptide antagonists of the system it was found that drinking induced by these substances was mediated by generation of angiotensin II.

BURCKHARDT found that partially purified rat renin is 10 times more potent than hog renin as an intracranial dipsogen though they liberate the same amounts of angiotensin I from plasma angiotensinogen. Intrahypothalamic converting enzyme inhibitor SQ 20881 caused a dose-dependent inhibition of renin-induced drinking and, as expected, had no action on drinking induced by intrahypothalamic angiotensin II. Unexpectedly, and in contrast to the findings of

FITZSIMONS et al., SQ 20881 did not abolish drinking to angiotensin I. BURCKHARDT et al. concluded that SQ 20,881 inhibits the cerebral renin-angiotensin reaction and that either cerebral converting enzyme is unaffected by SQ 20,881, or angiotensin I may be dipsogenic without conversion to angiotensin II.

JOHNSON discussed how circulating angiotensin might reach the brain. On the basis of tracer analysis of the cerebrospinal fluid and autoradiography after intravenous infusion of labelled angiotensin he considers that angiotensin reaches the brain by the cerebral ventricular route. Angiotensin is particularly effective as a dipsogen when administered by this route.

SIMPSON presented evidence which is compatible with this idea. He found that the subfornical organ, a midline neurosecretory structure in the ependyma of the third ventricle, is particularly sensitive to the dipsogenic action of angiotensin and its destruction resulted in a reduction in water intake in response to intravenous angiotensin II. In view of the vascularity of the subfornical organ SIMPSON favours a vascular route of access for circulating angiotensin, but the ventricular route as proposed by JOHNSON is equally compatible with the evidence. The way in which the subfornical organ influences other neural systems involved in drinking is unexplored. The neural connections are unknown and there is also the possibility that some neurosecretory process may in some way be involved.

MOGENSON investigated the neural connections of another angiotensin sensitive region in the brain. He found that injection of angiotensin II into the preoptic region caused drinking and also increased nervous discharge in the lateral hypothalamus and in the ventral tegmental area and reticular formation of the midbrain. Lesions in the lateral hypothalamus and midbrain areas attenuated drinking elicited by preoptic angiotensin. Clearly, wherever the site of maximum sensitivity to angiotensin the effects of stimulation are widespread in the central nervous system.

COOLING reported the most complete investigation to date of angiotensin-induced drinking in a species other than the rat. The cat drinks to intraventricular angiotensin II (1–4000 ng) and the peak response of about 180 ml. water was reached with 100 ng. Angiotensin I was equally effective. Hog renin (0.1–0.25 Goldblatt u.) caused more prolonged drinking but the onset was delayed compared with angiotensin. Saralasin acetate (5 μg) attenuated drinking in response angiotensin I or II (1 μg) and also to renin. The effects of cholinergic and adrenergic blocking agents on angiotensin-induced drinking suggest that the response may be mediated by β-adrenergic neurones. Since drinking could be elicited by doses of angiotensin II that were effective intraventricularly but ineffective given intravenously, though larger doses caused some drinking, it is likely that angiotensin normally acts via receptors in the brain. COOLING and DAY's findings in the cat are very similar to those in the rat except that in the latter dopamine may be the catecholamine involved.

ROLLS and SZCZEPANSKA-SADOWSKA each reported preliminary studies on drinking in response to components of the renin-angiotensin system. Both groups found that the dog drinks to large intraventricular doses of angiotensin and it has been previously reported by the Cambridge-Warsaw group that intraventricular angiotensin lowers the thirst threshold to an osmotic stimulus. Results on the cat and dog reported here reinforce the impression that angiotensin-sensitive cerebral drinking mechanisms are present in most or all mammals.

FISHER found that intracranial angiotensin caused the rat to increase its intake of saline as well as of water and quite often the two fluids were taken in such proportions that an isotonic mixture suitable for repairing an extracellular deficit entered the body. Intracranial carbachol, or cellular dehydration produced by subcutaneous hypertonic saline, on the other hand, led to an equally appropriate preference for water. The sodium intake generated by angiotensin was larger when there was pre-existing hypovolaemia or sodium deficiency. FISHER concluded that angiotensin may play a dual central role by facilitating neurones for thirst as well as neurones monitoring sodium levels and intake. A central effect of angiotensin on sodium intake is an attractive idea because extracellular thirst stimuli, all of which lead to increased activity of the renin-angiotensin system, are invariably followed by increased sodium appetite as well as thirst. Unfortunately the evidence for a direct central action of angiotensin on sodium appetite is at present disputed (see discussion of FISHER's paper, this volume).

MÖHRING found that rats with "two kidney-Goldblatt" hypertension showed an increase in water intake within a week of clamping. In the rats that later developed benign chronic hypertension, water intake and urine volume were positively correlated with blood pressure. Drinking occurred despite the positive water balance and could be related to the increased angiotensin levels. When benign hypertensive rats were offered saline they also increased their salt intake though they were in positive sodium balance. Increased aldosterone could have been responsible both for the increased salt appetite and the sodium retention. In those animals, in which the systolic pressure rapidly rose above 180 mm Hg, sodium and potassium loss occurred and the condition worsened to a state of malignant hypertension with progressive nephrosclerosis of the unclamped kidney. The plasma and blood volumes fell, and plasma sodium was reduced as the animals went into negative sodium balance. Plasma urea and osmolality rose and the angiotensin II and aldosterone levels further increased. With the onset of malignant hypertension water intake increased still further, but even more striking was the big increase in saline intake. This syndrome of "compulsive saline drinking in malignant hypertension" resulted in an improvement in the general condition of the animals. The saline restored the extracellular and intravascular volume thereby reducing the activation of the renin-angiotensin system. The excessive water intake in malignant hypertension may have been caused by the negative water balance and elevated angiotensin II levels. The increased sodium appetite was probably attributable to negative sodium balance and increased aldosterone.

ROLLS reported increased drinking of water in dogs made hypertensive by constriction of one renal artery and removal of the opposite kidney.

WEISINGER said that he was able to condition thirst and salt appetite by pairing the odour of menthol with injection of formalin. He also reported that aldosterone-induced sodium appetite is the result of some learning process. Under natural conditions it is of course extremely unlikely that a rat would experience high aldosterone levels without at the same time having a low body sodium.

HUSTON described how eating and drinking elicited by spreading cortical, striatal or hippocampal depression could be conditioned. He also described how electrical stimulation of the hypothalamus which had not elicited eating or drinking, came to do so after the stimulation was paired with eating induced by food deprivation.

SLANGEN's presentation on cholinergic mechanisms of drinking was salutary. It was the only paper devoted to cholinergic stimulation of the brain in the symposium and this indicates a tremendous shift in interest away from this potent dipsogen in the last few years in spite of its unexplained role in drinking.

ALDER described a new drinking phenomenon in the rat, isonazid withdrawal drinking. Unlike the results described previously where the dipsogenic activity of a drug manifests itself during administration of that drug, isoniazid only elicits enhanced drinking after treatment has ceased. The mechanism of this drinking is as yet unexplained.

It is evident that the 3 classical theories of the subject continue to pervade our thinking. The dry-mouth theory has been displaced from its exclusive and isolated dominance where CANNON had placed it, but oropharyngeal and gastric factors in drinking are extremely important and a number of papers here give witness to this. The general-need-general-sensation theme has developed into a preoccupation with the various stimuli that give rise to thirst and the peripheral mechanisms activated, studies of which are well represented here. These studies have led to an endocrinology of thirst with emphasis on the renin-angiotensin system. The neurology of thirst, also well represented here, has flourished enormously since NOTHNAGEL and HESS. Perhaps the most fruitful approach of recent years has been the analysis of the neuropharmacology of ingestive behaviour by methods which involve chemical stimulation, block or lesioning of brain structures, but the more traditional techniques of electrical lesioning and stimulation continue to occupy our attention and are still fruitful.

Outlook

A. N. Epstein

In concluding this book and a rich and provocative symposium, I want to share with you my excitement and optimism about our field. James Fitzsimons has given you a sensitive and detailed critique of the papers you have heard. I will give you a sermon, hoping to inspire you for the work that remains.

First, I remind you of the happy fact that we have not yet answered our basic question — happy, indeed, when you consider the alternative. If we knew the nature of thirst this would have been a eulogy for an exhausted subject. Instead, it was a programme for a life's work. We still do not know why animals like ourselves drink. Our problem remains and can be stated simply — what is the physiology of spontaneous drinking behaviour? How can we account for its occurence in brief bouts of spontaneous ingestion that nicely repair the accumulated losses of an active life?

We have not answered our basic question because we do not have all the fundamental facts we need. I suspect that we do not yet have a full account of even the old problem of water loss. Most mammals groom themselves with saliva and lose it continually by evaporation, but we have not yet included this item in our thinking about water budgets. We have a growing list of the stimuli of thirst. But is it complete? And how should the stimuli be weighted with respect to each other to predict spontaneous drinking behaviour? We surely do not yet know how they interact within the animal and particularly within the brain to produce thirst. Where in the brain are the signals received and how are they

registered? Where are they integrated to produce episodic behaviour from what appear to be continuous stimulations? And how is the calculation made that relates intake proportionally to losses? And we know precious little about the hedonic aspect of thirst. After all, thirsty animals do not simply drink water. They drink it avidly and their avidity grows with increasing deprivation as surely and as quantitatively as intake itself. In addition, thirsty animals seek water, often taking risks to reach it. Can we avoid the conviction that they do so in anticipation of the pleasure of its ingestion? And thirst is a distinct feeling. Thirsty animals know when they are thirsty and do not confuse thirst with other motives. The *feeling* of thirst is its most immediate and compelling characteristic. In the experiential sense, the feeling *is* thirst. That is what Cannon and other peripheralists were trying to understand. Now that we have moved our work into the brain we must not leave the hedonic problem behind. Although we do not quite know what to do about it as scientists we must continue to include the phenomenon of feeling in our thinking or risk an incomplete understanding of our problem. Again, all that I have just said is good news. A catalogue of our ignorance in a vigorous science is really a shopping-list of opportunities for important discoveries. They lie ahead of us and we can look forward to the excitement of learning the rest of our unfinished story.

And there is no lack of options for our future work. This symposium has been extraordinary in revealing the complexity of our science. Our physiology is now marvelously complex and includes an endocrinology and an elaborate pharmacology. We find ourselves seeking ways to combine nonhomeostatic controls of thirst such as oropharyngeal sensations and conditioning with the stimuli of depletions. We are looking into the brain in new ways and considering how to relate what we find with conventional neurophysiology. We are beginning to confront the biological aspects of our problem. If we are impressed with the diversity of the reptiles in the phenomena of drinking and the mechanisms of thirst, what can we expect of the birds, and, of course, the bees? The insects alone are the most numerous and diverse of all animals and except for the blow-fly that literally drinks to fill itself up, we know nothing about the mechanisms of their drinking behaviour. Other biological aspects of thirst have not been discussed here and will further complicate our work. Thirst has an ontogeny and it occurs in an ecological context that includes competition with other animals and the constraints of the environment.

We are literally surrounded by new problems, new undertakings and new tools for our work. An unsympathetic critic listening to us the last two days might conclude that we are baffled by this complexity and unsure of our future. But he would be wrong. The complexity of our field is encouraging. We created it by giving up old simplifications. We encouraged it by inventing new ideas and by bringing new techniques into our work. And we are going to progress through the complexity with careful experimentation and new insights.

We can be optimistic that the work of our field will be pursued vigorously. We will be testing the quality of our own ideas. The fate of our intellectual children is at stake. I know that we have the ego to foster them and to enjoy their maturity, and I believe we have the goodwill to abandon them when we find that they are not telling us the truth. We will not be delayed by unproductive controversy.

We can be optimistic about our field because some among us have had the good sense and courage to take what we know into the clinic and we are promised the satisfaction of a contribution to human welfare.

Lastly, we can be optimistic because our problem continues to attract young men and women of great charm, great talent and high purpose and our future is therefore assured.

Author Index

198

Subject Index

205

Menthol
odour of as conditioned stimulus   148–152
Merio merio Shawii   53
Mesangial cells of renal glomerulus   114
Metering of fluid intake,
oropharyngeal and gastric   3, 9, 14–21
Methoxamine (α-adrenoceptor agonist)   85, 191
Methylatropine,
intracranial   173
Midbrain, effect of lesions of on angiotensin-induced drinking   129–131, 136, 192
Mineralocorticoids and sodium appetite   4, 5, 144, 145, 151–154, 161, 163–164, 193
MJ 999 see under Sotalol
"Modality specific" hypothesis   16, 17, 20
Monkey   97, 109
Motivation, for drinking   1
Muscarinic receptors,
in forebrain
see Carbachol, as an intracranial dipsogen

N
Nasal salt glands   48
Nasopharyngeal sensations in control of drinking   20
Nephrectomy,
abolition by of isoprenaline-induced drinking in the rat   69, 79–80, 89, 108, 191
attenuation by of drinking in response to caval ligation   79–80, 108, 114
effects of on isoprenaline-induced drinking in the dog disputed   72, 75, 77, 94, 191
failure of to affect drinking in response to hyperoncotic colloid   79–80, 108, 114–115
in the analysis of osmometric thirst   50–53, 190
Neurone discharge, effect of angiotensin on   127–129, 137, 192
Nicotine   174–175, 179–180
Nigrostriatal system and ingestive behaviour   55–60, 63, 94, 190–191
Non-homoeostatic drinking and salt intake
see Secondary or non-regulatory drinking, Non-regulatory salt intake
Non-regulatory salt intake   22–24
Noradrenaline
and sodium appetite   5
inhibition of drinking by injection in the preoptic area   62, 67
in telencephalon and in whole brain   50, 65
lack of effect on feeding and temperature when injected into the tractus diagonalis   178–180
Nucleus accumbens   141
Nucleus reuniens thalami   117

O
One kidney-Goldblatt hypertension in dogs   75–77
Oral intake
of saline, need for   23, 190

of water, need for   16–20, 24, 190
privileged role of   16, 20, 189–190
Oropharyngeal factors
in control of drinking   3, 9, 14–21
Osmometric thirst,
see Cellular dehydration as a stimulus to drinking
Osmoreceptors   2, 24, 25, 34, 52, 108, 135, 190
Oxytocin   37

P
P 113
see Saralasin acetate
Pargyline (MAO inhibitor)   56
"Peak need" hypothesis   16, 17, 24
PEG
see Polyethylene glycol
Pempidine (ganglionic blocker)   90
Pepstatin (renin-angiotensinogen inhibitor)   100, 135
Phenoxybenzamine (α-adrenoceptor blocker)   133–134
Phentolamine (α-adrenoceptor blocker)   63, 90–92, 101, 133–134, 137, 191–192
Phylogeny of water intake   1, 47–53, 97, 190, 192
Pilocarpine as an intracranial dipsogen   174–175, 179–180
Pitressin
see Vasopressin
Pituitary gland
Uptake of angiotensin II   114
Plasma angiotensin I
see Angiotensin I or II, plasma concentrations
Plasma renin activity
see Renin, plasma levels and drinking
Polyethylene glycol
as a stimulus to drinking   3, 4, 16, 26, 58, 60, 67, 79–80, 86–88, 114, 141, 143, 188, 190, 191
and sodium appetite   4, 143, 164
see also under:
Hypovolaemia
Nephrectomy
Practolol (β-adrenoceptor blocker)   133–134
Precision,
of regulation of drinking   22, 50–53
of regulation of salt intake   22–24, 163
Preoptic area,
site of osmoreceptors   108
sensitivity to dipsogenic effect of angiotensin   117, 118, 124–125
sensitivity to dipsogenic effect of renin   103–107
Primary or regulatory drinking, definition of   2
Procaine
as a dipsogen   166
Prolactin, effect on water drive in newts   1
Propranolol (β-adrenoceptor blocker)   69, 89, 101, 133–134, 183–185, 191
Pseudoconditioned sodium appetite   148, 150–151
Pseudoconditioned thirst   148, 150–151
Pseudoconditioning   150

Psychopharmacologia

Editorial Board: H. Barry III (Managing Editor), D. Bovet, J.O. Cole (Managing Editor), J. Delay, J. Elkes, M. Hamilton (Managing Editor), H. Isbell, E. Jacobsen (Managing Editor), M.E. Jarvik, S.S. Kety, C. Kornetsky, R.W. Russell (Managing Editor), M. Shepherd, H. Steinberg, E. Strömgren, A. Wikler

"Psychopharmacologia" is intended to provide a medium for the rapid publication of scientific contributions concerned with the analysis and synthesis of the effects of drugs on behavior, in the broadest sense of the term. Such contributions may be of a clinical nature, or they may deal with specialized investigations in the fields of experimental psychology, neurophysiology, neurochemistry, general pharmacology, and cognate disciplines.

Approx. 6 volumes a year. About 97 % of the articles are in English; the others, in German or French, are preceded by an English summary.

Journal of Comparative Physiology

Founded in 1924 as „Zeitschrift für vergleichende Physiologie" by K. von Frisch and A. Kühn. Editorial Board: H. Autrum, K. von Frisch, G.A. Horridge, D. Kennedy, A.W. Martin, C.L. Prosser, H.H. Weber

The increasing emphasis on the comparative aspects in many branches of biology plus the impetus derived from new findings at the cellular and subcellular level have enhanced the status of comparative physiology. Research results in molecular biology often have implications for comparative physiology studies dealing with more complex organisms and even for exploring ecological problems such as temperature control or the physiological control of behavior. As its broad coverage embraces new areas of investigation and the still important classical ones, this journal mirrors the growing diversification of comparative physiology.

Approx. 6 volumes a year. About 80 % of the articles are in English; the others, in German or French, are preceded by an English summary.

Springer-Verlag
Berlin Heidelberg New York